The Yearbook of PSYCHOANALYSIS and PSYCHOTHERAPY

Volume 2/1987

Editorial Board

THE YEARBOOK OF Psychoanalysis and Psychotherapy

Volume 2

1987

Edited by ROBERT LANGS, M.D.
and the Editorial Board

GARDNER PRESS, INC.
New York & London

Gardner Press, Inc.
19 Union Square West
New York, New York 10003

ALL FOREIGN ORDERS EXCEPT CANADA AND SOUTH AMERICA TO:

Afterhurst Limited
Chancery House
319 City Road
London, N1, England

LC 86-641022

ISBN 0-89876-141-7

ISSN 8756-4998

Designed by Raymond Solomon

Printed in the United States of America

Contents

Editorial Board
Editorial Statement
Contributors

PART I: THE CLINICAL SITUATION

1 A New Model of the Mind
ROBERT LANGS, M.D. 3

2 Unconscious Perception—Day Residue and Dreaming
THEO. L. DORPAT, M.D. 34

3 Discussion: Toward an Understanding of Freud's Overlooking Unconscious Perception
WILLIAM B. GOODHEART, M.D. 48

4 Process Notes as Derivative Communication About the Supervisory Field
STEVEN KORN, PH.D., and ROBERT P. CARMIGNANI, PH.D. 68

5 Discussion: The Well-Tempered Supervisor
JAMES RANEY, M.D. 85

6 Inpatient Group Psychotherapy—Where Treatment Philosophies Converge
HOWARD D. KIBEL, M.D. 94

7 Discussion: Transference Issues in Hospital Groups
LEONARD HORWITZ, PH.D. 117

8 Concomitant Individual and Milieu Psychotherapy and the Borderline Patient: Uses and Misuses
STEVEN H. COOPER, Ph.D. 123

9 Discussion: Milieu Treatment in the Psychotherapy of the Borderline Patient: Abandonment and Containment
GERALD ADLER, M.D. 146

10 The Making of a Communicative Psychoanalytic Psychotherapist
PHYLLIS TERRY FRIEDMAN, Ph.D. 158

11 Discussion: The Development of a Professional Identity as a Psychotherapist
HELAINE RUBINSTEIN, Ph.D. 186

12 The Analyst's Uses and Misuses of Clinical Theory: Interpretation
STANLEY J. COEN, M.D. 200

13 Discussion: The Relationship Between the Method of Data Gathering, the Nature of Transference, and the Interpretive Process: Reflections on Psychoanalytic Clinical Theory
ANNA ORNSTEIN, M.D. 225

PART II: CLINICAL TOPICS

14 Overloving/Underloving
SOPHIE FREUD, A.C.S.W., Ph.D. 243

15 Discussion: "Overloving"—A Misnomer
HAROLD F. SEARLES, M.D. 259

16 The Meaning of Pain: A Developmental Pathway
JANIS KROHN, M.S.W. 271

17 Discussion: Pain: Psychoanalytic Perspectives
B. M. BIVEN, Ph.D. 290

18 Melanie Klein: Achievements and Problems (Reflections on Klein's Conception of Object Relationship)
RUTH RIESENBERG MALCOLM 306

19 Discussion on Melanie Klein
T. ESKELINEN DE FOLCH 322

20 The True and the False
Essay on the Logical Structure of Psychoanalytic Interpretation
ENZO CODIGNOLA, M.D.
Introduction by Paolo Migone, M.D. 326

21 The Psychology of Treason and Self-Pathology
HUMBERTO NAGERA, M.D. 380

PART III: CLINICAL RESEARCH

22 Suitability for Psychoanalysis
JUDY L. KANTROWITZ, Ph.D. 403

23 Discussion: The Assessment of Analyzability and of Analytic Outcomes
ROBERT S. WALLERSTEIN, M.D. 416

Name Index 427

Subject Index 431

Statement by the Editor-in-Chief

The Yearbook of Psychoanalysis and Psychotherapy is dedicated to the clinical practice of psychoanalytically oriented treatment modalities. It will publish clinically based papers that make original contributions of importance to practicing psychotherapists and those engaged in research into the psychotherapeutic process. A discussion format will be used as a means of encouraging debate and clarification and to stress controversial issues and clinical problems. Unsolicited contributions to the *Yearbook* are most welcome. We are pleased to have been chosen as the official journal of the Society for Psychoanalytic Psychotherapy, and we will do our utmost to maintain the highest standards of scholarship, originality, and clinical relevance.

—ROBERT LANGS, M.D
for the Editorial Board

Contributors

Gerald Adler, M.D.
Director, Medical Student Education/Psychiatry, Massachusetts General Hospital, Boston; Lecturer in Psychiatry, Harvard Medical School, Cambridge, Mass.; Training and Supervising Analyst, Boston Psychoanalytic Society and Institute.

Barrie M. Biven, Ph.D.
Faculty, Michigan Psychoanalytic Institute; Consultant, Detroit Psychiatric Institute; Consultant, Institute of Mental Health, Monterrey, Mexico.

Robert P. Carmignani, Ph.D.
Attending Psychologist, McAuley Neuropsychiatric Institute, Saint Mary's Hospital, San Francisco,, Calif. Also in private practice in San Francisco.

Stanley J. Coen, M.D.
Faculty, Columbia University Center for Psychoanalytic Training and Research; Associate Clinical Professor of Psychiatry, College of Physicians Surgeons, Columbia University, New York, N.Y.

Steven H. Cooper, Ph.D.
Instructor in Psychiatry, The Cambridge Hospital, Harvard Medical School, Cambridge, Mass.; Advanced Candidate, Boston Psychoanalytic Society and Institute; Faculty Member, Extension Division, Boston Psychoanalytic Society and Institute.

T. Eslelinen De Folch
Resides in Barcelona, Spain.

Theo. L. Dorpat, M.D.
Clinical Professor of Psychiatry, School of Medicine, University of Washington, Seattle; Director and Training and Supervising Analyst, Seattle Institute for Psychoanalysis.

Sophie Freud, A.C.S.W., Ph.D.
Professor of Social Work, Simmons College School of Social Work, Boston, Mass.

Phyllis Terry Friedman, Ph.D.
In private practice in St. Louis, Mo.

William B. Goodheart, M.D.
Assistant Clinical Professor of Psychiatry, School of Medicine, University of California Medical Center, San Francisco.

Leonard Horwitz, Ph.D.
Training and Supervising Analyst, Topeka Institute for Psychoanalysis, The Menninger Foundation, Topeka, Kans.

Judy L. Kantrowitz, Ph.D.
Adjunct Clinical Associate Professor, Boston University; Instructor, Harvard Medical School; Falculty Member, Boston Psychoanalytic Institute.

Howard D. Kibel, M.D.
Coordinator of Group Psychotherapy at the New York Hospital-Cornell Medical Center, Westchester Division, White Plains, N.Y.; Associate Professor of Clinical Psychiatry, Cornell Medical Center.

Steven Korn, Ph.D.
Psychologist in private practice in San Francisco, Calif.

Janis Krohn, M.S.W.
Trained with the Department of Psychiatry, University of Michigan, Ann Arbor; Associate, Arbor Clinic, Ann Arbor; in private practice in Ann Arbor.

Robert Langs, M.D.
Program Director, Lenox Hill Hospital Psychotherapy Program, New York, N.Y.; founder of the Society for Psychoanalytic Psychotherapy; practicing psychotherapist and psychoanalyst. Dr. Langs is Editor-In-Chief of *The Yearbook of Psychoanalysis and Psychotherapy*.

Ruth Riesenberg Malcolm
Member of the British Psycho-Analytical Society. Holds a degree in social sciences from the University of Chile.

Paolo Migone, M.D.

Fellow of the American Academy of Psychoanalysis. Trained at New York Medical College. Currently practices in Parma, Italy.

Humberto Nagera, M.D.

Professor, Department of Psychiatry, University of Southern Florida, Tampa; Training Analyst, Michigan Psychoanalytic Institute.

Anna Ornstein, M.D.

Professor of Child Psychiatry, University of Cincinnati, College of Medicine, Cincinnati, Ohio.

James Raney, M.D.

Core Faculty, Seattle Institute for Psychoanalysis; Clinical Associate Professor, University of Washington School of Medicine; in private practice in psychoanalysis in Seattle, Wash.

Helaine Rubinstein, Ph.D.

Executive Director, Youth Development Program, Oakland, Calif.; Clinical Faculty, San Francisco State University.

Harold F. Searles, M.D.

Former President of the Washington Psychoanalytic Society, Washington, D.C.

Robert S. Wallerstein, M.D.

Professor of Psychiatry, University of California, San Francisco; President, International Psycho-Analytical Association; Former President, American Psychoanalytic Association.

I

The Clinical Situation

1

ROBERT LANGS, M.D.

A New Model of the Mind

A NEW MODEL OF THE MIND IS OFFERED. STRESS IS PLACED ON THE PROCESSING OF EMOTIONALLY CHARGED MESSAGES. THE MODEL INVOLVES A SERIES OF UNCONSCIOUS STRUCTURES AND PROCESSES PRIOR TO CONSCIOUS REGISTRATION. TWO BASIC SYSTEMS ARE PROPOSED—ONE CONSCIOUS WITH ITS OWN UNCONSCIOUS SYSTEMS, AND THE OTHER DEEPLY UNCONSCIOUS. CLINICAL AND HISTORICAL EVIDENCE FOR THE MODEL IS BRIEFLY NOTED. THE CLINICAL IMPLICATIONS OF THE MODEL ARE DISCUSSED. IN ADDITION, THERE IS A PRESENTATION OF WAYS IN WHICH PSYCHOANALYTIC THEORY, SUCH AS FREUD'S CONCEPTUALIZATION OF PRIMARY AND SECONDARY PROCESS THINKING, ARE IN NEED OF REVISION.

Freud's (1895, 1900) first models of the mind were topographic in nature. Topography later became one of the metapsychological viewpoints, though it was subsequently replaced largely by the structural point of view (Rapaport & Gill, 1959). With this shift stress was placed on Freud's (1923) second, structural theory, which centered on the configurations of the id, ego, and superego. Freud's first theory, the topographical viewpoint of *The Interpretation of Dreams*, in which accessibility of psychic contents to consciousness was the main criterion, was virtually discarded—much of it due to the work of Gill (1963) and Arlow and Brenner (1964). The remaining metapsychological viewpoints (Rapaport & Gill, 1959), those of structure, genetics, dynamics, economics, and adaptation, have continued to elicit some interest, but they have also been subjected to considerable criticism (see, for example, Klein, 1976, among others).

The demise of the topographical approach was signaled by Freud himself (1923), when he specifically acknowledged that defensive and other ego functions that should, in the logic of the topographic theory, belong to the system CS or PCS (i.e., should be within awareness) were actually outside of awareness and clearly belonged to the system UCS. In essence Freud recognized the existence of powerful unconscious defenses and, as a result, could no longer maintain a conflict theory based on an intrapsychic struggle between the system CS/PCS and the system UCS. Clinical consideration of intrapsychic conflict and its role in both psychopathology and the therapeutic interaction was far better served by Freud's structural hypothesis, in which the mind was divided into id, ego, and superego.

Another critical inadequacy in Freud's (1900) topographic model was his location of consciousness at both ends of the information-processing model he proposed—at the point of sensory reception as well as at the responsive motoric act. As a result he was forced to consider the existence of censorship and preconscious processing at both ends of the model, which was based on a simple reflex arc conception. There was, however, virtually no evidence for two types of preconscious systems and two types of preconscious censorship or defense. Freud also had no clinical or research evidence to suggest the possibility that unconscious registration precedes conscious registration in all instances of information processing.

Although the topographical viewpoint is no longer part of current psychoanalytic metapsychology, the topographic distinctions between UCS, PCS, and CS continue to be an important reference point for psychoanalysts. The presence or absence of consciousness in connection with a particular thought or feeling remains one of the guiding considerations of psychoanalytic thinking.

The Interpretation of Dreams (Freud, 1900) is, in one important sense, a study of how we process emotionally laden (charged) information. It is also an attempt to understand psychopathology in light of a basic information-processing model. On the other hand, the structural model—a division of the mind into id, ego, and superego—is basically designed to conceptualize the role of intrapsychic conflict in the development of psychopathology, and is far less a vehicle for understanding the vicissitudes of messages and information. During an era in which psychoanalysis has concentrated its investigations on issues of intrapsychic conflict, ego functioning, object relations, and self psychology, the structural model has served us well.

The communicative approach to psychoanalysis (Langs, 1982, 1985a, 1985b, 1985c) has taken as its point of departure Freud's original concern with information processing. This approach views communication as a fundamental dimension of the therapeutic experience, and of psychopathology as well, and focuses particularly on the spiraling conscious, and especially unconscious, communicative interaction between patient and analyst. With that base established, consideration is afforded to the remaining metapsychological viewpoints and, in particular, to six additional dimensions of the therapeutic interaction: ground rules or frame, mode of relatedness, mode of cure, dynamics and genetics (including issues of death anxiety and intimacy), identity and narcissism, and sanity and madness. It is postulated that all dimensions are interrelated, but each has separate vicissitudes that must be taken into account.

After 15 years of clinical research, an effort has been made to develop a model of the mind that both accounts for the processing of messages and information and also permits the delineation of dynamic, genetic, and other influences on these processes. (For prior and rather different attempts to create information-processing models and to reconsider primary and secondary process thinking, see Basch, 1975, 1976a, 1976b, 1981; Fast, 1985; Holt, 1967; Noy, 1969; Peterfreund, 1971; and Pribrim and Gill, 1979.) The model to be described is unique in that it postulates the processing of three levels of information in some, though by no means all, messages: manifest contents, implications (which can be read out directly from the surface of the message), and encoded meaning (which is always the product of transformation—i.e., displacement and possibly symbolization or disguise). The model is designed to account for the interpersonal and intrapsychic influence of messages on the receiver, and to describe in detail the internal unconscious and conscious sequences to which each of the levels of information is subjected. Furthermore, as indicated, the model is so constructed as to permit the delineation of dynamic, genetic, and other influences on these processes.

The model to be offered has been derived entirely from clinical psychoanalytic and psychotherapeutic work. Each of its elements has been tested clinically, though revisions may, of course, be made in the future on the basis of new clinical findings and understanding. As is true of any metapsychological viewpoint or model of the mind, this particular creation has been developed as a way of better understanding both psychopathology and the nature of the therapeutic interaction—its curative and other effects.

This is an initial presentation. It is confined to the most fundamental aspects of the model. Brief excerpts of clinical evidence are cited wherever possible, and there are brief allusions to supporting experimental and neurophysiological evidence. However, the main goal is to introduce a line of thought that is believed to be uniquely explanatory and heuristically valuable.

THE THERAPEUTIC INTERACTION

Elsewhere (see especially Langs, 1985b), I have offered an extensive clinical study of the therapeutic interaction. Here a brief presentation of the interpersonal and gross aspects of this interaction will prepare us for a more detailed study of the intrapsychic processing of emotionally charged information.

Figure 1 diagrams the essential elements of a single sequence within a therapeutic interaction.[1] This particular model proposes that the patient and analyst are engaged in a spiraling and reciprocal therapeutic interaction in which stimuli are both evoked in and passively experienced by each participant in relationship to the other. For didactic purposes the diagram presents a sequence that begins with the stimulus of an intervention from a therapist and details the patient's conscious and unconscious responses.[2]

It is proposed that, with few exceptions, therapists intervene with comments that have both manifest meaning and a wide range of *implications*. Implications can be read out from the surface meanings of a message, but not all implications are conscious. The therapist is aware of some of an intervention's implications, but not of others; and this is also true of the patient. Therapist and patient may be considerably similar or different in terms of which implications are conscious or unconscious for each.

When a patient is unconscious of an implication that provokes anxiety, he or she will not experience this meaning directly. The free associations that occur in response (either immediately or after a delay) to an anxiety-provoking unconscious implication will generally contain *encoded meaning*. That is, the patient's communication will convey disguised responses to the unconscious implications that have generated the anxiety. Following Freud (1900, 1908, 1915), we may define a message with an *encoded* meaning as an allusion or *derivative*. The encoding process (Freud, 1900) takes place by means of displacement (speaking about one scene or person, but unconsciously meaning another) and quite often symbolization (or broadly, a measure of disguise in which the surface or disguised image is substantially different from the latent or raw image and yet shares some *theme* with the latent content).

[1]The diagram is discussed in detail in Langs, 1985b.

[2]The focus in the present discussion is on the verbal and semantic attributes of the therapist's interventions and the patient's responses. Additional nuances, such as affect, tone, and nonverbal aspects, will be afforded less consideration here as a way of simplifying the model to be presented.

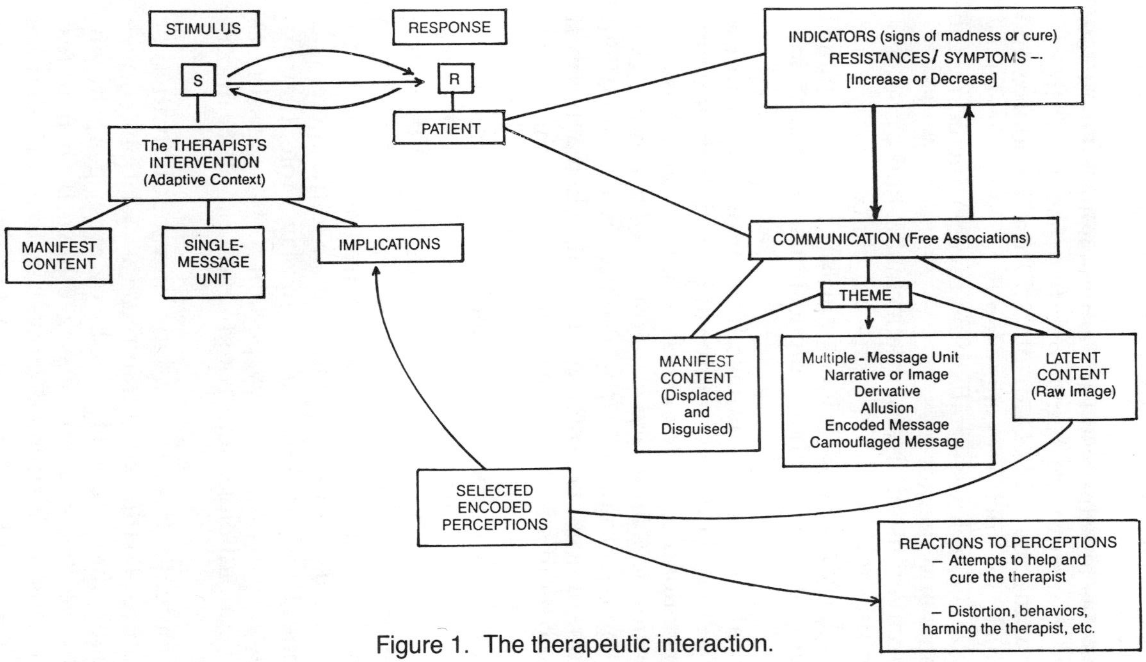

Figure 1. The therapeutic interaction.

The Therapeutic Interaction is circular. If we begin with an intervention of the therapist, we see it is a single-message communication. It has surface meaning and *implications* (it is not usually an encoded message).

The patient responds on two important levels, First, through vicissitudes of madness—intensification or diminution of symptoms and resistances. Second, with communications, mainly free associations. When there are narratives and images, they are usually multiple-message expressions (derivative in nature). They have both manifest and latent (encoded) meaning; the two levels are linked through shared themes.

The latent meaning of the patient's associations is constituted as *selected* (according to the patient's own madness and other interapsychic factors) *unconscious perceptions* of the *implications* of the therapist's interventions. Secondary reactions then follow.

Although all messages have both manifest content and implications (again, meanings that can be extracted directly from the surface communication), not all messages have encoded meaning. In other words, there are both derivative and nonderivative messages (see Figure 2).

Derivative messages are the result of camouflaging a latent raw image or meaning—transforming it into one that has a less threatening manifest meaning and is both displaced from its source and disguised. The vehicle for such messages tends to be a form of extended storytelling that employs narrative and images, including the recounting of dreams and memories.

Evaluations, speculations, analyses, intellectualizations, and generalizations—communications of that type—are almost always *nonderivative* in nature. They are constituted as messages with manifest content and meaning, and a variety of implications, both conscious and unconscious.

To the extent that a therapist confines himself or herself to the material from the patient, both interpretive and noninterpretive interventions tend to be nonderivative expressions. In general it is only when a therapist introduces an image or narrative of his or her own that he or she is communicating in disguised form to the patient unconscious reactions of his or her own. As a result, when a therapist deals only with the patient's material, in most situations the patient is not responding to encoded messages conveyed by the therapist, but rather to his or her own experience of the manifest content and implications, conscious and unconscious, of the therapist's communicative efforts. Figure 1 traces the gross processing of the information contained in such messages.

As indicated in the diagram, the patient's free associations are constituted as an immediate and delayed response to the therapist's interventions. Although outside influences also play a role, they appear to be secondary, especially as they pertain to the vicissitudes of the patient's psychopathology and communication of its unconscious meanings.

As noted, the patient's free associations may be derivative or nonderivative in nature. To the extent that these associations convey narratives and images, they are likely to convey messages with encoded meaning. As we know, such messages have both manifest and latent contents. It is to be stressed, however, that the stimulus and organizer of these latent contents are that of the therapist's intervention, and that manifest contents are a vehicle for displaced and disguised responses to these interventions. That is, the manifest content of the patient's associations contains in encoded fashion raw

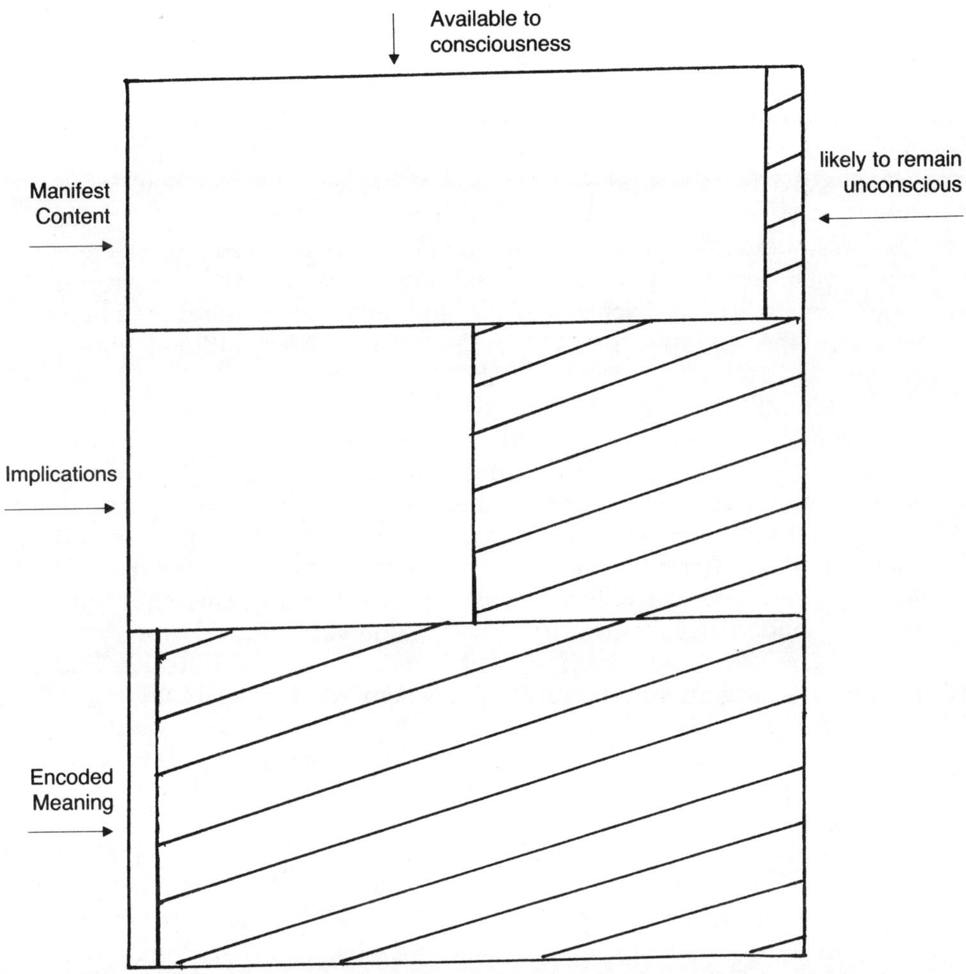

Figure 2. The structure of a derivative message.

images that pertain to the interventions of the therapist.

Clinical study can show, with surprising consistency, that when a patient's initial response to a therapist's intervention takes an encoded form, it is almost invariably constituted as selected unconscious perceptions of that intervention's *implications*, which the patient, because of anxiety, must defend against and not allow direct entry into consciousness. In psychotherapy the main factor in the patient's unconscious *selection* of implications to represent in transformed or disguised fashion is the perceived meanings *pertinent to the patient's own psychopathology*. It is, indeed, the patient's pathology that creates the lens through which he or she unconsciously observes, analyzes, and responds to the anxiety-provoking implications of the therapist's efforts.

Once these implications have registered unconsciously, the patient will react in a variety of ways. Most central among these responses are the vicissitudes of the patient's resistances and symptoms, which may increase or decrease depending on the nature of the therapist's endeavors. Other reactions to these unconscious perceptions include the evocation of memories, responsive distortions (transference in the strictest sense of the term), and attempts to help or harm the therapist in light of his or her interventional efforts (Figure 1).

A brief clinical excerpt is illustrative. A male therapist inadvertently extended a woman patient's session by some ten minutes. In the following hour, the patient mentioned having arrived at home later than usual and wondering if the therapist had allowed her more time. She said the possibility made her feel flattered, because it would mean that the therapist found her interesting. She then went on to mention having been with her brother recently, and said that their meeting had reawakened a memory she had not recalled for many years. When they were both in their teens, she and this brother had been talking together in the furnished basement of their home, when, quite suddenly, he had locked the basement door and kept her from leaving. He had then made sexual advances toward her. It was only when the patient threatened to scream for help that her brother had allowed her to escape.

In associating to the incident, the patient mentioned that her brother was now a physician. She also suggested that the brother must have been in distress at the time, because she later learned that his girlfriend had just broken up with him. Nonetheless, the patient concluded, he should have known better than to express his frustrated social and sexual needs with his sister.

In this instance the therapist's intervention was behavioral—an inadvertent extension of the patient's hour by some ten minutes. The manifest message is apparent: The therapist kept the patient beyond the end of her session. Among the implications of this intervention, some of which would be conscious for the patient and/or therapist, and others unconscious, there is the patient's stated impression that the therapist found her interesting. There is also an evident loss of contact with reality, an expressed need to hold on to the patient, and possible needs to entrap her and block her exit. Both seductive and hostile meanings are possible, as well. To the extent that the therapist was enacting a message to this patient that had been displaced from some other patient or from some individual in his own private life (note the displaced speculations conveyed by the patient in her thoughts about her brother's needs), this particular intervention might also contain some displaced and disguised (encoded) meaning.

In the excerpt the patient clearly alludes to the intervention in question, and she states her conscious sense of its implication—that the therapist found her interesting. She then presents a narrative/memory, whose manifest content involves herself and her brother. In light of the therapist's intervention, it can be proposed that the recollection is derivative in nature, and that it contains in latent form valid raw perceptions of the unconscious implications of the therapist's intervention—disturbing perceptions that have been transformed into the disguised manifest message. These perceptions can be identified through themes shared by the manifest and latent contents. It is to be noted as well (and this appears to be true in principle) that an encoded narrative will, as a rule, pertain manifestly to some scene or context *other* than the therapeutic interaction (context II), whereas the latent and disguised context is *always* that of the therapeutic experience (the raw images and perceptions that require encoding; context I).

Although the patient consciously experienced the therapist's intervention as flattering and pleasing, she unconsciously selected for derivative representation her encoded perception of its entrapping and seductive qualities. These are validly perceived unconscious meanings of the intervention (whose veracity would require an analysis of the therapist's own free associations). Among this patient's symptoms, frigidity was quite prominent. Earlier experiences of seduction and entrapment with the patient's father as well as her brother were a factor in her psychopathology, as were unconscious masochistic wishes and rape fantasies. These elements proved to be a critical factor in the patient's unconscious selection of unconscious implications for encoded representation.

Toward the end of the hour, the patient said that she was again experiencing sexual frigidity in intercourse with her husband. It would appear, then, that among her reactions to her valid selected encoded perceptions of the implications of the therapist's intervention, an exacerbation of her symptoms was rather prominent. In addition the therapist's intervention had been a significant stimulus in evoking the memory of her brother as seductive and entrapping, though the patient's recent meeting with her brother played a secondary role. Another reaction to these selected perceptions was an attempt, on an encoded and unconscious level, to alert the therapist to the possibility that he was acting out something with his patient that stemmed from social and sexual frustrations in his daily life. It is this type of unconscious interpretation on the part of the patient that is characterized as an attempt to help or cure the therapist (Little, 1951).

In the model presented here, the stimulus message is an intervention by the therapist. In this particular instance, the message was not verbal in nature, but was constituted, rather, as a form of action. Nonetheless the message had a manifest content, a wide range of implications, and a possible encoded meaning.

We have seen in a gross way that the patient's free associations in the session following the intervention in some way involved the processing of each of the three levels of information conveyed by the therapist's message. The manifest content was alluded to in the patient's conjecture that the session had been extended. As for conscious implications, the patient expressed her feeling that an extension of her hour would mean that the therapist found her interesting. She also expressed a number of unconscious implications of this intervention as seductive and entrapping by communicating them in derivative form. In addition the patient's associations reflect that she had unconsciously worked over a possible encoded meaning of the therapist's intervention (that the acting out was displaced from another individual).

The description of the transactions presented to this point leaves much to be explained and clarified. The topographic model of the way in which charged information is processed intrapsychically is inherently interpersonal or interactional, in that the sequence of events conceived begins with an outside message; the model is also essentially intrapsychic, in that it describes the internal processing of such a message. An additional and related model could be constructed for the processing of internal messages, somatic and fantasied; however, the following model is designed in terms of the first paradigm.

THE TOPOGRAPHIC MODEL

The topographic model will be presented in keeping with the sequential processing of a message and its information. Once the essentials of the model have been given, two specific vicissitudes will be offered.

The Structure of a Message

As has been shown (Figure 2), a verbal or behavioral message (an action, a visual image, etc.) is a layered communication with manifest content (which is almost always immediately available to awareness), implications (of which some are conscious and others unconscious), and encoded meaning, when present (most of which is entirely beyond the awareness of the sender, and often of the receiver, as well). To clarify further the distinctions involved, we may look briefly at the patient's associations to the incident with her brother. The manifest message of those associations is plainly that her brother had locked her in the basement of their home and made sexual advances to her, and so forth. These surface meanings are self-evident, directly described and stated, and involve manifest or immediate meanings that are in all likelihood conscious for both the patient (the message sender) and the therapist (the message receiver).

As for the implications, it could be proposed that the incident was one of (that is, it spoke for) incestuous seduction, entrapment, loss of control by the brother, a hostile act on his part, and such. Each of these meanings can be extracted and inferred from the manifest content. There is no displacement that must be undone in order to derive them, and there is little suggestion of disguise. In contrast the decoding of an encoded message always involves undoing displacement, and usually requires the undoing of disguise by identifying themes shared in common by both manifest and latent situations.

There are two types of encoded meaning that the narrative of this patient may be conveying. For this reason there are two possible ways to decode her material. In the first the therapist would postulate unconscious fantasy formations as an intrapsychic issue within the patient. In the second the stimulus of the therapist's intervention would be seen as the day residue, or trigger, for the encoded message. In the latter case, the decoding would be carried out in light of the implications of the therapist's intervention and, therefore, with full consideration of the conscious and unconscious aspects of the ongoing therapeutic interaction. Although a measure of unconscious truth is revealed by decoding based on either premise, clinical experience has shown that only the second type of decoding will lead to encoded or unconscious validation from the patient. That is, following such decoding, the patient's response will introduce fresh cognitive material that uniquely extends the therapist's interpretation (cognitive validation) and will contain associations to positively and constructively functioning individuals (interpersonal validation; Langs, 1982, 1985a).

The first type of decoding disregards the ongoing therapeutic interaction; it would presume only that the patient's memory of her brother is a screen for primal-scene experiences, or perhaps a disguised version of a seduction by her father. The second type of decoding would not discount that possibility, but would first establish a central focus for screen memories of that sort. Thus the patient's allusion to the therapist's extension of her hour would be taken as a reference to the stimulus for her reactions, both conscious and unconscious. Such decoding would identify the implications of that stimulus intervention, and recognize their disguised portrayal in the recollection of the brother. This central focus serves to organize the patient's reactions. Now, should further associations permit, additional connections to primal-scene experiences and seductions by the father could be identified and decoded. Even these encoded recollections, however, would be seen to involve pertinent encoded perceptions of the therapist in light of his anxiety-provoking intervention. The additional material from the patient would then be examined for memories—genetic connections, distortions, and other types of responses. It is this latter type of decoding alone that provides access to the deep unconscious system we will soon consider.

Receiving the Message

Figure 3 shows the systems pertinent to the intrapsychic reception and processing of an external message. We shall consider these processes as *mental* phenomena (and not allude for the moment to possible brain correlates).

Whatever the sensory receptor site (SR), the raw message (the auditory or visual elements in their raw form) is received by the respective sensory organ, conveyed through sensory tracks to receptor sites, and quickly forwarded to the appropriate processing or synthesizing centers (SC), where the message is organized into meaningful form. In a sequence of processes, which are remarkably rapid, this information is then sent to the postulated *message analyzing center* (MAC). Whereas Freud's initial topography was not intended to correspond to neurophysiological correlates (for Freud [1915] the issue was not one of location, but one of energics), the present model is designed with neurophysiological verification in mind. However, it must be stressed again that the model has been created on the basis of clinical data; thus agreement with neurophysiological findings would constitute a measure of validation of the model itself. Never-

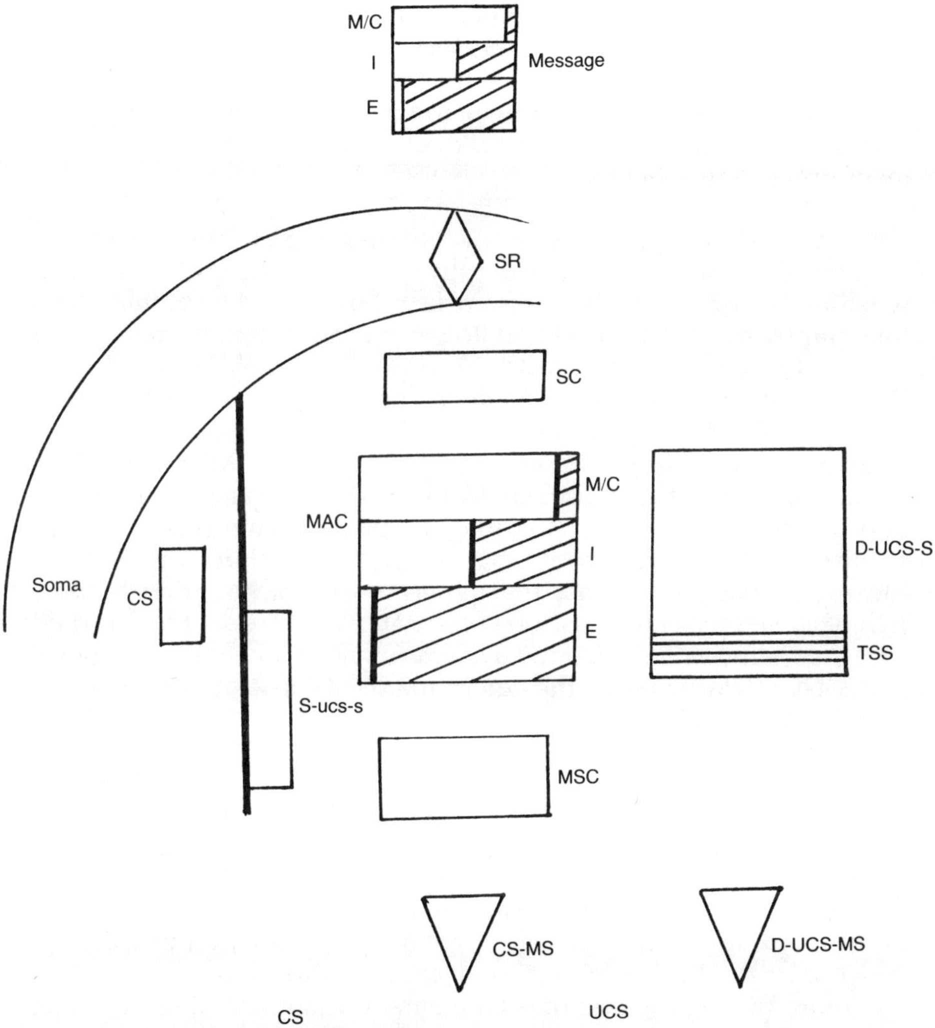

Figure 3. The components of the system for processing emotionally charged information (see text).

theless, to avoid confusion I will, as noted, speak only of *mental* processes—postulated centers and processes of mentation.

Figure 3 shows a message analyzing center, and two rather distinctive unconscious *schemata*—the superficial unconscious system (S–UCS–S) and the deep unconscious system (D–UCS–S). These systems are the means by which we process information, and they determine the nature of conscious and unconscious experience. Each is under the influence of a respective *metaschema* (CS–MS and D–UCS–MS) that critically determines the type of information processed in each center, the premises and rules that guide the way the information is handled, and the types of messages that leave the main processing schema.

As shown later these two sets of schemata operate rather independently. There appears to be a silent measure of influence on the superficial unconscious/CS system by the deep unconscious system; whether the reverse holds true is unclear, but highly likely. In Freud's topography there is a postulated flow from the system he designated as UCS to PCS, and then to CS. The present model proposes that the two systems—conscious and deep unconscious—are, in the main, separately functioning systems.

Figure 3 also shows the *message sending center* (MSC), which is another significant unconscious factor in the messages that emerge into awareness from the two unconscious systems (prior to consciousness, all of the processing takes place without awareness). Meanings that then attract the hypercathexis of attention become part of a fleeting set of conscious schemata; most are sent or returned to the superficial unconscious system for memory storage. The CS and S–UCS–S systems are the determinants of conscious understanding and conscious experience.

Not included in this basic diagram are secondary influencing centers, which shape the functioning of each schema. These involve two distinctive sets of instinctual drives, defenses, memories, identity, and other unconscious components of great importance in determining the fate of information within those parts of the mind that operate outside of awareness. Each of these elements has an influence on the central unconscious ego function of information processing, which is at the heart of the present topographic model.

Before tracing the fate of each element of an incoming message, we may identify some of the characteristics of the unconscious centers that process the information. It can be seen, for example, that the message analyzing center actually has three subdivisions—one for manifest content, one for implications, and one for encoded meanings. Each of these subcenters has its own defensive alignment and anxiety gradient, which guides the analysis of the particular level of meaning with which it deals. On the basis of this analysis, some meanings are forwarded directly to the message sending center, and from there to the conscious system, and on to conscious registration. Other meanings, which are relegated to unconscious processing in the deep unconscious system, will be processed entirely outside of awareness. The information that emerges from this latter, rather inaccessible, unconscious system is always encoded by the transformation subsystem (TSS) before leaving for the message sending center, which then passes on the *encoded* messages to the superficial unconscious subsystem and from there into consciousness. A direct route from the message sending center to conscious awareness probably also exists. The CS system also has a scanning capacity so that it also seeks out selectively information available to awareness.

In substance, then, all incoming messages and meanings are subjected to complex selection and processing procedures before entering awareness. It is the message analyzing center, with its anxiety gradients and defenses and intelligence (all under influence of the many other components of the deep UCS, and CS?, systems), within which, entirely outside of awareness, the decision is made as to whether information will be processed unconsciously or consciously (preconsciously). The anxiety gradient is different for each level of information. In particular, virtually everything contained in the manifest message is sent on to the message sending center for direct communication. In contrast virtually everything analyzed on the encoded level of meaning is relegated to the deep unconscious system, and for this reason can only enter consciousness in transformed (encoded) form.

We may identify other aspects of the deep unconscious system. This system processes information entirely outside of awareness. It is these schemata that account for an unnoticed form of unconscious learning and unconscious experience. The schemata themselves are under the influence of a wide range of dynamic and genetic factors. In addition the motivations, premises, and mode of processing are determined by an entirely separate unconscious system, identified in Figure 3 as the D–UCS–MS—the deep unconscious metaschema.

In a similar fashion, the superficial unconscious and the conscious schemata, which together account for conscious experience, understanding, and information processing, are under the sway of their own metaschema (CS–MS). As suggested, the two metaschemata identified here are quite different in their attributes and often are directly at odds.

To summarize, the model proposes that all information is received unconsciously in a synthesizing center and forwarded to a message analyzing center that also operates outside of awareness. It is in this center that information is sorted out on three levels, and the decision made at each level as to whether the information will be processed entirely outside of awareness or permitted direct access to consciousness. This is a matter of absolute choice, in that only *one* center processes a given segment of meaning—CS or deep UCS. This is necessary because the two schemata maintain distinctly contradictory values and process information toward rather different aims.

In addition a message sending center is postulated, one that facilitates the expression of direct or transformed messages and meanings. The CS system creates hypercathexes of attention that reach out and selectively meet forthcoming messages. Each processing system is under the control of an entirely unconscious metaschema that regulates its operation. Those pertaining to the message analyzing center and message sending center are omitted from the figures for the purpose of simplification.

Of importance to this model, then, is the hypothesis of unconscious registration of *all* incoming sensory registrations—meanings and implications. Postulated, too, is the existence of two distinctive types of schemata for the processing of this information and for the nature of inner experience: one that operates entirely outside of awareness (the deep unconscious system), and one for which accessibility to awareness is easily achieved (the superficial unconscious/conscious system). Finally it is proposed that there are two relatively deeper or less accessible metaschemata that regulate the processing that takes place in the deep (repressed or denied) UCS and CS systems. The clinical data on which these propositions are based and the relevance of these systems to clinical observations will become clearer once we trace the fate of the different levels of meaning in a message and understand the clinical basis on which these propositions are founded.

The Processing of Manifest Content and Meaning

Figure 4 diagrams the processing of manifest content. It can be seen that the part of the message analyzing center that operates on surface information has a very high anxiety gradient. Clearly this gradient is under the influence of the patient's adaptive resources, recent and past traumas, general psychopathology, and such. Nonetheless, despite these influences, it is only in the presence of a high level of sensitivity that a manifest message is misperceived, blocked, or falsely transmitted. With few exceptions, manifest images and meanings are immediately forwarded to that part of the message sending center that transmits direct meaning without significant alteration, though with a measure of personal coloring. From there the information is forwarded either to the superficial unconscious system, where it is potentially available to conscious experience, or directly to the site of conscious mentation. As Freud (1900) postulated, this site of conscious experience, the locus of the hypercathexis of attention, is itself actively seeking the transmitted message and meets it halfway.

Clinical evidence suggests that the conscious system processes information organized as thoughts and words, rather than visual images. The latter processing is characteristic of the deep unconscious system, and is far more efficient and informed. This distinction has

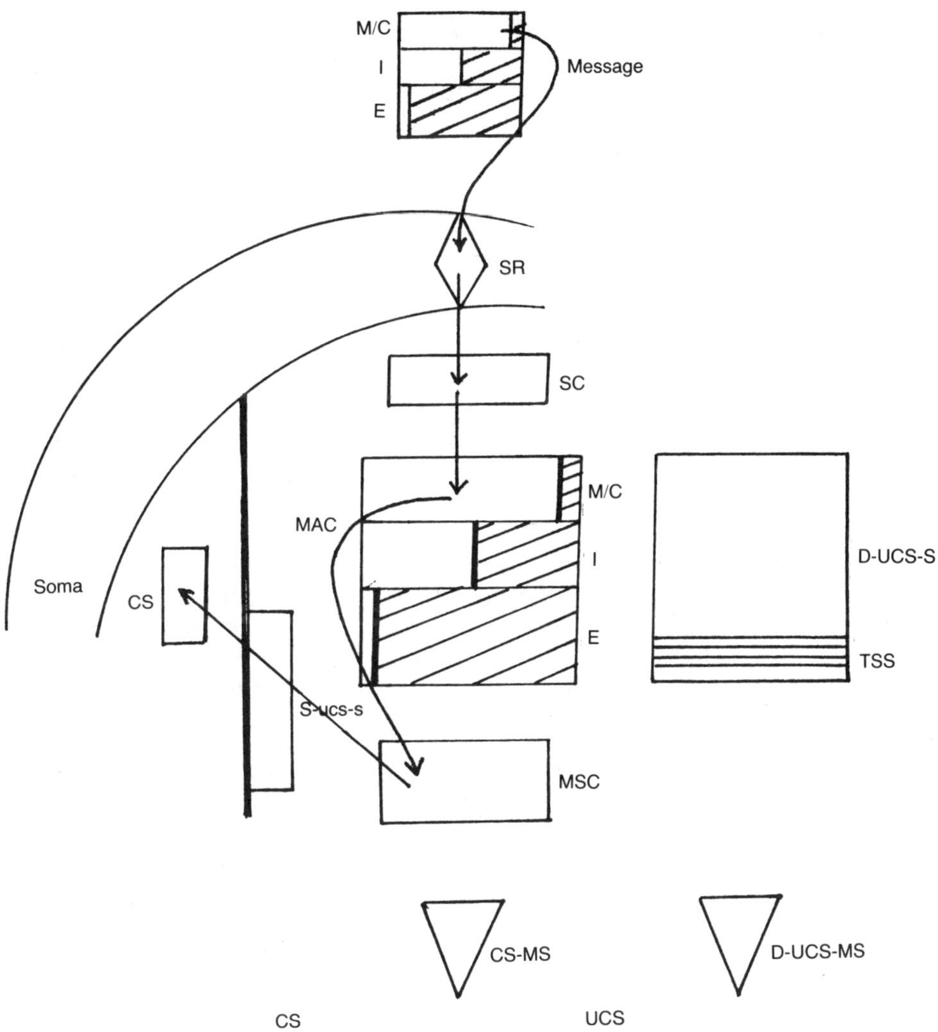

Figure 4. The processing of manifest (direct) meaning (see text).

relevance to the stress on two forms of unconscious registration—verbal and visual—discussed in a recent paper by Bucci (1985).

The diagram suggests a number of loci for defensive operations. They may occur at the perceptual site, though this is rare. Beyond that, defensive operations may take place in the synthesizing center, the message analyzing center, the message sending center, the deep UCS center, the superficial unconscious center, and at the level of conscious experience. The development of evidence for different gradations and locations of defensive operation, and the clinical implications of these distinctions, await further study.

To illustrate briefly, a patient in analysis, a young woman, had entered the analyst's office through one of two doors. The analyst closed the door behind her as she entered, and the patient looked back and made a remark about it. Nevertheless, on leaving the session in a somewhat upset state, she attempted to leave by the wrong door. In this instance direct and manifest information was misremembered, and in some sense misperceived.

The same patient, weeks later, during an analytic session, was describing a dialogue with a friend. When the friend told the patient that she had good news, that she was going to have a *baby*, the patient responded: "You did what with *Bobby*?" Not surprisingly this patient had an unconscious wish to be impregnated and was filled with envy and rage with regard to her friend's news. These and other unconscious factors led to a misperception of the manifest information.

We may postulate that at the level of the message analyzing center, the message was misread and passed on incorrectly to the message sending center. The original message—a charged or raw image—was undoubtedly sent to the deep UCS processing system. It seems likely that this system also provided the substitute word or image; it is usually an evident product of wish fulfillment.

The Processing of "Unconscious" Implications and Encoded Meaning

Those raw images (cf. Freud's [1900] latent dream thoughts) that are deemed by the message analyzing center to be anxiety provoking to a point beyond the tolerance of the CS system are immediately relegated to unconscious processing. This includes both those implications of a message that are perceived as constituting danger situations and threat (Freud, 1923) and most of the encoded level of meaning. As a rule those raw images that are encoded by a message sender are threatening not only to the sender, but to the receiver as well. There is, in general, a universal dread of derivative meaning.

For purposes of discourse, we will label those implications of a received message that are anxiety provoking and relegated to processing by the deep UCS schema "unconscious implications." Figure 5 diagrams the processing of encoded meaning, which is comparable to that of unconscious implications. Though the two pathways are similar, encoded meanings tend to evoke considerably more anxiety than do unconscious implications. In addition clinical studies have revealed that encoded expressions tend to evoke more primitive lev-

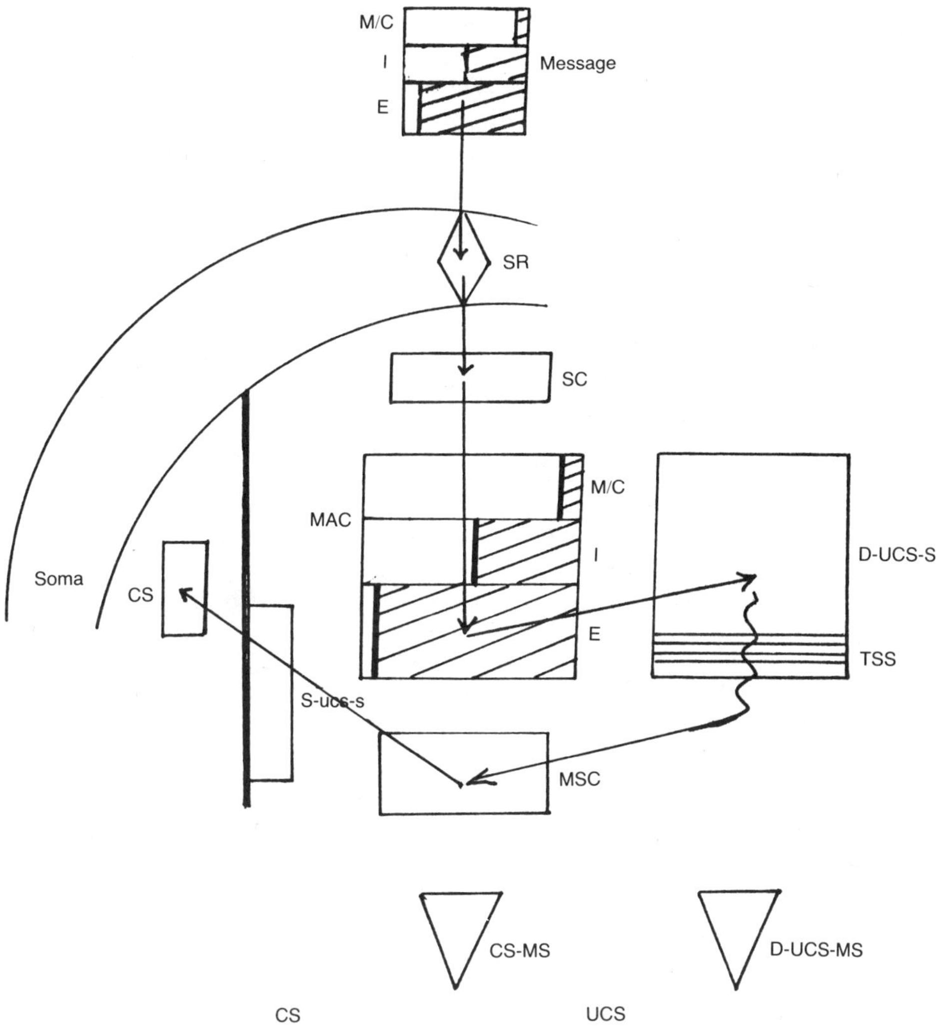

Figure 5. The processing of encoded (indirect) meaning (see text).

els of UCS schemata processing and more disturbing reactions than those evoked by implications. The former generate far more disturbing transformed images than the latter.

As implied by Figure 5, implications are received and recognized by a special part of the message analyzing center. Those implications that do not evoke a particular level of anxiety are processed in keeping with manifest meaning, and are readily accessible to conscious experience (Figure 4). On the other hand, those implications that convey threat (itself a decision under extensive genetic and dynamic influence) are barred direct access to the message sending center and consciousness. Instead they are sent to the schemata for processing information entirely outside of awareness. As discussed in the following, these schemata have a distinctive set of premises and work over the information received in a fashion quite different from that of the CS schemata, which handle information acceptable to consciousness.

There are strong clinical reasons to believe that deep UCS schemata operate with a unique set of *premises*—for example, part equals whole, what happened before will occur again, a possession is the possessor, symbols are real. However, once these premises have been established and accepted, the unconscious system handles information in highly intelligent, *logical, reality-attuned* fashion (see below for discussion of supportive findings and refinements in Freud's [1900] theory of primary process functioning). This processing, which appears to involve visual images, occurs entirely outside of awareness and is safeguarded by a defensive gradient or barrier that imposes itself at the exit point from the processing schema. This barrier is constituted by the mechanisms of transformation described by Freud (1900) in *The Interpretation of Dreams*: displacement, symbolization (disguise), consensation, secondary revision, and concerns for representability. The barrier is essential because of the especially high level of anxiety connected with the information that is processed in this schema system.

In this light dreams and narratives are understood as reflections of underlying processes, as output products, and *not* as processing mechanisms per se. Furthermore, the existence of this information in a transformed state containing meanings beyond awareness creates a situation in which there is powerful unconscious influence without conscious cognition for utilization of the information for conscious adaptation—*influence without choice*. The result of this kind of processing, then, is an encoded message embodied in the conscious image chosen for such a purpose (the utilization of the conscious vehicle is not shown in detail in Figure 5).

As we would expect, there are striking individual differences with respect to every step of the processing of communicated information. The many factors that influence this processing will have rather different, though related, effects on each of the schema systems identified in Figure 3. Thus the selection of information for conscious or unconscious processing varies among patients (and therapists, as well), as does the nature of the processing that takes place in both the deep UCS and CS schema formations. Then, too, the shaping of messages sent is distinctive among patients, as is the nature of the two metaschemata that govern the two main areas where we process information—CS and deep UCS.

Initial clinical evidence suggests that the metaschemata—the structures that determine the motivational factors, premises, and rules of processing for each system—tend to be most powerful and most remote from manifest or derivative expression; in some sense they are most deeply embedded in the unconscious part of the mind. They also tend to reflect relatively universal needs, and therefore to be rather consistent across patients and therapists far more than the processing schema systems.

One clear clinical finding is that patients tend to fall along a continuum, with a strong tendency toward the expression of transformed messages at one end, and a powerful need to avoid transformed messages (the expression of derivative material) at the other. It has been possible to this point to identify two major factors in this aspect of communicative style. The first is the extent of the underlying psychopathology in the patient, in that patients with severe borderline and schizophrenic syndromes tend to be fearful of transformed images because they tend to be especially primitive and to evoke powerful anxieties and dread. (It should be noted that the transformations under discussion here are quite different from the thought disorder characteristic of the schizophrenic patient, a disturbance that is, in all likelihood, located in the conscious part of the message sending center, and in the deep UCS and CS schemata.) The second factor is that of premature or overintense exposure to death anxiety issues, such as early object loss, abandonment, and major illness or injury (for a related discussion, see Langs, 1984–1985). Patients traumatized in this way will show an extraordinary dread of unconscious meaning and a reluctance to express transformed images.

It can be shown that there is also a general and universal dread of derivative communications, and a still greater fear of their decoded realization; that is, the undoing of the transformations so that the underlying raw image, perception, or fantasy is revealed. In this context it is well to stress that it is the major function of the deep UCS system to process information when conscious realization would evoke a significant level of anxiety and dread. It is this quota of unconscious anxiety that seems to explain the human need to maintain such information in unconscious form and to render it into awareness only in transformed messages, even though an enormous unconscious resource is sacrificed—a point recognized with surprise by Neisser (1967) in his discussion of the subliminal processing of cognitive information.

NONCLINICAL EVIDENCE FOR THE MODEL

The present model is supported by 15 years of clinical research during which the vicissitudes of manifest contents, implications, and encoded representations were carefully investigated. There is, however, additional support for the model, which can be cited only briefly here.

The first involves the history of psychoanalysis and its techniques. Here we find support for the proposition that the primary motivational force in the metaschema that governs conscious experience is that of survival through defense (see below). This hypothesis finds support through the documentation of the many self-serving and defensive aspects of psychoanalytic thinking. Of note here is the failure to recognize the primacy of unconscious perception over unconscious fantasy (Langs, 1984–1985) and the misuse and misapplication of the concept of transference (Szasz, 1963; Langs, 1980).

A review of psychoanalytic vignettes (Langs, 1981) reveals a strong tendency toward conceptualization by an analyst on the manifest content and implication levels, and an equally powerful avoidance of efforts at decoding (see, too, Langs, 1984–1985). This avoidance of decoded meaning speaks for its fearsome qualities and for the need for a special means with which to process the information so contained.

Support for the model also comes from a wide range of research studies undertaken from both the psychoanalytic and cognitive points of view. The vast literature on unconscious perception, unconscious cognition, and preconscious processing (see, for example, Dixon, 1981, and Goleman, 1985) amply supports the concept of unconscious processing prior to conscious experience for all incoming information, and the existence of a highly selective filtering and analyzing system that operates unconsciously prior to conscious experience.

Finally, recent neurophysiological studies (see in particular Reiser, 1984, and Winson, 1985) point strongly to the existence of a message analyzing center located on the medial side of the temporal lobe, as well as the presence of unconscious processing structures located in the hippocampus, limbic system, and neocortex. In addition, there is strong evidence for a message sending center that also operates on an unconscious level and is probably located in the frontal cortex. Cooper (1985) has written of the growing influence of neurophysiological studies on psychoanalytic thinking. The present model may serve as a conception based on psychoanalytic evidence that can further neurophysiological research.

SOME IMPLICATIONS OF THE MODEL

If we concentrate on the two basic systems for processing information, deep UCS and CS, the model supports the concept that each system is designed for the separate processing of rather different types of information. In brief the deep UCS system is designed to process emotionally charged information and, in particular, the threatening aspects of instinctual drive expressions and communications conveyed in symbolic (encoded) form. Such messages are encoded to ensure relatively safe interpersonal interactions (e.g., the use of an encoded expression of a murderous impulse as compared with an actual attempt at murder). For purposes of survival, we need a system that will carry out such work without immediate access to consciousness and action.

In contrast, the CS system is designed to process information of immediate import involving measures to ensure direct survival. Such matters as self-protection, arranging for nurturance and shelter, meaningful interaction, and meeting other needs through which we continue to exist and thrive are the province of this particular system. So, too, is the need to rationalize unconsciously motivated, irrational thoughts and behaviors. And when all is secure, the system will also process information related to procreative needs, sexual satisfactions, narcissistic assurances, and the like.

The premises of each system are also quite different. The CS system accepts information at face value, views each manifest meaning on its own terms, maintains immediate contact with reality, and makes use of logical operations. Most important is the acceptance of information as such, in direct and nondisplaced fashion. Most of these properties were characterized by Freud (1900) as secondary process thinking and may now be viewed as a survival-attuned way of communicating, experiencing, and processing information.

It is in the realm of deep unconscious processing that the model and its clinical foundations offer propositions that are especially different from those of Freud (1900) with regard to what he termed primary process thinking. It can be shown that Freud failed to distinguish between the mode of processing and the outcome of this processing, despite the fact that he understood the difference between the latent dream thought and the dream work—that is, a raw image and the means by which it is transformed into a manifest dream content.

In essence it can be shown clinically that the deep UCS system operates on the basis of a distinct set of premises, many of which were identified by Freud (1900, 1915). This includes types of primitive thinking and information processing in which parts equal whole, possessions equal the individual, and symbols are understood in terms of their underlying meanings and experienced as real. However, once a thought, idea, or communication has been established on the basis of these premises, it is processed in a manner surprisingly similar to that used by the CS system. Thus the processing maintains a significant contact with reality, makes use of logical thinking, works over thoughts and images on their own terms, and will not tolerate its own type of contradiction. Furthermore, deep UCS schemata have a significantly greater access to instinctual drive representations, to emotionally relevant memory formations, and to understanding. Indeed the unconscious intelligence (UQ) of every individual far exceeds in certain respects his or her conscious intelligence (IQ), a reflection of a vast amount of learning that takes place entirely outside of awareness throughout the development of the individual.

The finding that deep UCS schemata will not tolerate certain kinds of contradictions is reflected in the first associations of a woman patient seen in consultation with a male therapist with whom she had had significant social contact. The patient began her hour by complaining about a tendency on her part to get into difficulty with the men for whom she worked. Despite every attempt to be otherwise, she said, she seemed to come across as seductive and sexual. Because of this her present boss had made sexual advances toward her, which she had refused with a stern statement: "You can be either my boss or my lover, but it is impossible for you to be both of them."

Here we have a narrative that reflects the outcome of this patient's unconscious perceptions and unconscious processing. The deep UCS system adopts the premise that the therapist who attempts to engage in both a social and a professional relationship is behaving seductively and inappropriately. This patient had no conscious awareness of such impressions; thus it can be argued that her CS schema did not appreciate these implications, although her deep UCS schema both experienced and understood their presence. We are indeed far more perceptive and knowledgeable on the unconscious level than on the conscious level.

In addition, the illustration clearly shows that the patient experienced an unconscious contradiction in the absence of one that was conscious. That is, on the conscious level, she sought consultation with the therapist despite their prior social contact. In terms of the CS schema, there was no contradiction between these two roles, merely a shift from one to the other.

In contrast, in terms of the deep UCS schema, as communicated by the patient's derivative message about her boss, the two roles are contradictory. A choice must be made; to decode the patient's transformed image, the therapist can be either a therapist or a social acquaintance (lover). According to the rules of the deep UCS schema, he cannot be both. Indeed, since he is already a social acquaintance, the encoded images suggest that in terms of the patient's deep UCS schema, it will be impossible for him to function effectively as a psychotherapist—despite the patient's conscious belief that this could occur.

This discussion also indicates the extent to which the premises and intelligence of the CS schema operate on the basis of different givens. Although it is not possible to discuss them in detail, some of the more important differences involve the great concern of the deep UCS schema regarding ground rules and frame, with a relative disregard of such issues in the CS schema; the consistent search for an ideal set of ground rules—for a secure frame (Langs, 1985b)—by the guiding aspects of the deep UCS schema, in contrast to the intense search for deviation in the guiding aspects of CS schema; the avoidance and even falsification of unconscious meaning by the CS schema, in contrast to the consistent search for unconscious truths in the deep UCS schema; the preference for pathological modes of relatedness in the CS schema, in contrast to the search for a healthy symbiosis or commensal relationship by the dee UCS schema; a preference for action-discharge modes of cure by the CS schema, in contrast to the preference of the deep UCS system for truth and insight; a penchant for madness in others in the CS system, where the deep

UCS system prefers attributes of sanity; and an overriding concern about the therapist's interventions in the deep UCS system, whereas this is intermittent and inconsistent in the CS system. Contrary to Freud's (1900, 1915) contention, the CS system tends toward action and immediate discharge, while the deep UCS speaks for delay (CS system actions are typically designed to support denial and manic defenses).

In addition, the CS system makes far greater use of pathological denial than the deep UCS system, and it also avoids direct realization of issues related to death anxiety—a source of anxiety that is central to unconscious processing.

The enormously intelligent processing of which the deep UCS system is capable speaks to representations in the form of images (see Bucci, 1985, for a discussion of the representations of information through thought and image). Blakeslee (1983) convincingly argues for the superiority of visual processing, a characteristic of the usual functioning of the right brain. This same factor helps to account for the unique value of visual models of the mind, and for the predominance of visual material (dreams and stories) in the output from the deep UCS system. The critical factor in this output, as noted, is that it is under an obligation to take place in transformed rather than direct form. In contrast, the output of the CS system is direct and involves words and thoughts—probably a left brain function.

It is in this regard that Freud's basic postulates of the mechanisms of transformation apply solely to the deep UCS system. Dreams and narratives are, then, transformed reports of deep unconscious processing, whenever they involve derivative attributes. It appears that they are not themselves processing operations, but the result of prior internal transactions triggered or activated by interpersonal and intrapsychic messages and meanings.

As for the guiding metaschemata, present evidence suggests that the CS schema system is driven by a need to survive through the use of intrapsychic and interactional defenses that protect the individual regardless of consequences. Need systems are also of importance, especially those related to the satisfaction of hunger and physical care, with sexual needs playing a notable but secondary role. Aggressive needs are reflected in nurturing and protective acquisitions and in reactions to obstacles to the quest for direct survival.

Communicatively the metaschema influences both the CS and superficial unconscious schemata by dictating that anxiety-evoking contents should be barred from their realm. It is this powerful defensive need that helps to account for the rapid decay of interpretations that make accessible to consciousness communicated deep unconscious (transformed) meanings. Interpretations are essentially matters of decoding unconscious meaning in light of triggers or message stimuli. The problem in this instance does not appear to be a matter of incompatibility between CS and deep UCS schemata (a common explanation in the literature), given that conscious learning involves the creation of new schema elements. Instead it appears that the anxiety issue and the dictates of the metaschema account for this decay.

The driving force that guides unconscious processing, and the main proposition of the deep UCS metaschema, is that of a search for truth and knowledge regardless of its quota of actual or potential anxiety. Such a force speaks for the likelihood of an epistemological need that operates as a fundamental unconscious need system. Yet we can bear emotionally charged truths only when they are not directly accessible to awareness, when we are unaware of their presence. Survival, too, is served by having a system designed to process incoming encoded meaning and to comprehend the unconscious messages of others—especially when emotional threat is involved.

A secondary influence of the CS metaschema on the deep UCS system is seen in the requirement that all messages leaving the deep UCS system do so in transformed fashion. Furthermore, the metaschemata appear to be difficult to influence clinically, a factor that may account for many of the limitations in the outcome of insight therapy in general, and psychoanalysis in particular. In addition, the deep UCS schema can be influenced only *by invitation*—by entry through the vehicle of an expressed derivative or transformed image. This principle was actually stated in 1915 by Freud, who, at the time, was skeptical with regard to the extent to which a psychoanalyst could influence the UCS system. Quite clearly he saw that such influence could only be effected through a proper analysis of the patient's derivative material.

Finally, we may note that virtually all interventions currently made by therapists (other than those who work interactionally and communicatively by alluding to prevailing prior interventions, encoded perceptions, and reactions to those perceptions) are based on manifest contents and implications (Langs, 1981). As such these efforts touch on issues within the CS system, including its superficial unconscious component, without allusion to expressions from the deep UCS. Such interventions often evoke direct and conscious support from the patient, though largely for defensive and other pathological reasons. Derivative validation never follows interventions of this type.

In contrast, interactional interpretations that allude to derivative meaning in light of the therapist's interventions involve insights into processes in operation in the deep UCS system. The CS system accepts such insights, conveys derivative validation from the deep UCS system, and then struggles against the understanding because of the enormous anxieties involved. Such are the initial insights into intervening that stem from the present model.

CONCLUDING COMMENTS

On the basis of clinical studies that have distinguished three levels of information in messages, a topographic model of conscious and unconscious information processing has been proposed. It is suggested that the model calls for revisions in our conception of primary process thinking (the unconscious processing of information) and less so with regard to secondary process thinking (conscious and preconscious information processing). In addition, the model demonstrates the presence of three distinctive unconscious systems: the first for receiving and analyzing messages, and sending them as well; the second for processing information, either unconsciously or preconsciously; and the third, metaschemata to guide the operation of the processing systems. Furthermore, the entrance into, the processing within, and the exit from each of these systems are points of distinctive adaptation or possible defense.

Because of space considerations, it has not been possible to amass the clinical data on which the model was constructed, nor has it been possible to do anything but to suggest some of the fresh clinical insights produced by the model. Also, there has been no effort to utilize the model in an endeavor to understand the influence of valid interpretations and erroneous interventions, or more broadly, to define the modes of cure in a psychoanalytic therapy. Many other areas pertinent to the model have also been omitted.

Of particular importance is the need to identify the dysfunctions of each of the information-processing systems postulated here. In general, it would appear that significant dysfunctions of these systems are characteristic of schizophrenia, and that lesser dysfunctions appear in nonschizophrenic patients. Though important, it has also not been possible to indicate the influence of dynamic constellations on each of these subsystems. Further, for purposes of simplification both feedback and feed-forward loops have been omitted.

The present model involves the processing of information toward either direct or indirect (transformed) conscious realization. It also touches on incoming information that is processed silently and never permitted access to consciousness in any cognitive form—though this information may influence behaviors and symptoms. It is necessary now to study the specific basis on which incoming information is processed toward direct or indirect communication through thoughts, words, and images, as compared with processing toward symptomatic expressions. In this regard, future models will take into account the interaction between this particular information-processing system and two additional unconscious constellations: one system embodying *pathogenic* meanings, introjects, and needs, while the other embodies a comparable set of *curative* contents and processes. It is the interplay between the information-processing system and these two unconscious dynamic constellations that accounts for both symptom alleviation and symptomatic regression.

In general, dysfunctions in the information-processing system appear to account less for symptomatic expressions than do the deep constellations with which they interact—areas in which structural conflicts and disorders of the self are prominent. Still, some aspects of pathology may be accounted for in significant fashion by information-processing disturbances. For example, the deep unconscious system, which tends to function at a high level of efficiency, nonetheless reveals particular forms of dysfunction under selected conditions. In the presence of significant levels of death anxiety, for instance, the system tends to blunt morbid, anxiety-provoking, and depressing unconscious perceptions, and to create transformed images that are intensely overidealized—a type of deep unconscious system denial. In addition, the system is prone to high levels of exaggeration and some measure of distortion under secure frame conditions, especially when the patient is overly sensitive to secure frame meaning.

In concluding, the model has been presented as a way of visualizing processes and structures of importance to both psychopathology and emotional health. It appears to produce fresh insights, as well as new questions, for psychotherapists and psychoanalysts. At the very least, the model seems effective in stimulating fresh thinking with regard to the psychotherapeutic process and promises to challenge us further as we continue to explore its ramifications.

REFERENCES

Arlow, J. & Brenner, C. (1964). *Psychoanalytic Concepts and the Structural Theory*. New York: International Universities Press.

Basch, M. (1975). Perception, consciousness, and Freud's "Project." *Ann. of Psychoanal.*, 3:3–19.

——— (1976a). Psychoanalysis and communication science. *Ann. of Psychoanal.*, 4:385–421.

——— (1976b). Theory formation in Chapter VII: A critique. *J. Amer. Psychoanal. Ass.*, 24:61–100.

——— (1981). Psychoanalytic interpretation and cognitive transformation. *Int. J. Psychoanal.*, 62:151–175.

Blakeslee, T. (1983). *The Right Brain*. New York: Berkley Books.

Bucci, W. (1985). Dual coding: A cognitive model for psychoanalytic research. *J. Amer. Psychoanal. Ass.*, 33:571–607.

Cooper, A. (1985). Will neurobiology influence psychoanalysis? *Amer. J. Psychiat.*, 142:1395–1402.

Dixon, N. (1981). *Preconscious Processing*. New York: Wiley.

Fast, I. (1985). *Event Theory: A Piaget-Freud Integration*. Hillsdale, N.J.: Erlbaum Associates.

Freud, S. (1895). Project for a scientific psychology. *Standard Edition*, 1.

——— (1900). The interpretation of dreams. *Standard Edition*, 4, 5.

——— (1908). Hysterical phantasies and their relationship to bisexuality. *Standard Edition*, 9.

——— (1915). The unconscious. *Standard Edition*, 14.

——— (1923). The ego and the id. *Standard Edition*, 19.

Gill, M. (1963). *Topography and Systems in Psychoanalytic Theory*. Psychological Issues. Monograph 10. New York: International Universities Press.

Goleman, D. (1985). *Vital Lies, Simple Truths*. New York: Simon & Schuster.

Holt, R. (1967). The development of the primary process: a structural view. In R. Holt (Ed.), *Motives and Thought*. *Psychological Issues*, Vol. 5, New York: International Universities Press.

Klein, G. (1976). *Psychoanalytic Theory*. New York: International Universities Press.

Langs, R. (1980). *Interactions: The Realm of Transference and Countertransference*. New York: Jason Aronson.

——— (1981). Modes of "cure" in psychoanalysis and psychoanalytic psychotherapy. *Int. J. Psychoanal.*, 62:199–214.

——— (1982). *Psychotherapy: A Basic Text*. New York: Jason Aronson.

——— (1984–1985). Making interpretations and securing the frame: Sources of danger for psychotherapists. *Int. J. Psychoanal. Psychother.*, 10:3–23.

——— (1985a). *Workbooks for Psychotherapists, Volume I: Understanding Unconscious Communication*. Emerson, N.J.: Newconcept.

——— (1985b). *Workbooks for Psychotherapists, Volume II: Listening and Formulating*. Emerson, N.J.: Newconcept.

——— (1985c). *Workbooks for Psychotherapists, Volume III: Intervening and Validating*. Emerson, N.J.: Newconcept.

——— (1985d). The communicative approach and the future of psychoanalysis. *Contemp. Psychoanal.*, 21:403–424.

Little, M. (1951). Countertransference and the patient's response to it. *Int. J. Psychoanal.*, 32:32–40.

Neisser, U. (1967). *Cognitive Psychology*. New York: Appleton-Century-Crofts.

Noy, P. (1969). A revision of the psychoanalytic theory of the primary process. *Int. J. Psychoanal.*, 50:155–178.

Peterfreund, E. (1971). *Information, Systems, and Psychoanalysis*. Psychological Issues. Monograph 25/26. New York: International Universities Press.

Pribrim, K. & Gill, M. (1976). *Freud's "Project" Reassessed*. New York: Basic Books.

Rapaport, D., & Gill, M. (1959). The points of view and assumptions of metapsychology. *Int. J. Psychoanal.*, 40:153–162.

Reiser, M. (1984). *Mind, Brain, Body*. New York: Basic Books.

Szasz, T. (1963). The concept of transference. *Int. J. Psychoanal.*, 44:432–443.

Winson, J. (1985). *Brain and Psyche*. Garden City, N.Y.: Anchor/Doubleday.

2 THEO. L. DORPAT, M.D.

Unconscious Perception—Day Residue and Dreaming

THE AIM OF THIS PAPER IS TO PRESENT SOME CLINICAL FINDINGS AND CONCLUSIONS ABOUT THE SIGNIFICANCE OF DERIVATIVES OF UNCONSCIOUS PERCEPTIONS IN DREAM FORMATION. FOUR CLINICAL VIGNETTES IN WHICH DERIVATIVES OF UNCONSCIOUS PERCEPTIONS OF THE THERAPIST APPEAR IN DREAMS ARE DISCUSSED. A BRIEF SECTION SUMMARIZES THE CONCLUSIONS OF EXPERIMENTAL INVESTIGATIONS ON SUBLIMINAL PERCEPTIONS AND DREAMS. AFTER REVIEWING FREUD'S CONCEPT OF THE DAY RESIDUE AND ITS RELATIONS TO DREAM FORMATION, I SHALL ARGUE FOR A REVISED THEORY ON THE IMPORTANCE OF RECENT EVENTS IN DREAM FORMATION. A MAJOR POINT MADE IS THAT UNCONSCIOUS PERCEPTIONS FROM WAKING LIFE ARE DYNAMICALLY IMPORTANT IN THE FORMATION OF THE DREAM'S LATENT CONTENT.

REVIEW OF LITERATURE

The discovery by Searles (1965, 1979) and Langs (1980, 1981, 1982a, 1982b) of unconscious perceptions in the clinical situation has important implications for the theory of the therapeutic process and analytic technique.

Langs (1982b) holds that the key to neurosis lies with disruptive unconscious fantasies and perceptions. The perceptions are expressed unconsciously and communicated, in turn, in encoded form outside of the awareness of the receiver. Unconscious fantasies and unconscious perceptions are especially central to the understanding of seemingly irrational and unrealistic symptoms.

In Langs' clinical examples, derivatives of unconscious fantasy, memory, and perception are fused. From their inner worlds of unconscious memory and fantasy, patients add elements derived from unconscious perceptions. The role played by valid unconscious perceptions of other individuals, according to Langs (1982b), has been neglected in the etiology of emotional disturbances.

A clinical vignette of Langs (1982b, pp. 198–215) demonstrates the role of unconscious perceptions in dream formation. He wrote about a patient who reported a frightening dream in which a man was chasing her. The man cornered her in a motel room and wanted to rape her. The patient felt furious. Langs traces the entrapment element of the dream back to the therapist's extension of the patient's previous hour by ten minutes. The dream of being chased and cornered was a valid, unconscious perception of one implication of the therapist's frame error. He had indeed attempted to entrap the patient, even if momentarily and unconsciously. The patient's dream of being chased and cornered also symbolized the patient's own involvement in self-punitive rape fantasies, which she tended to act out unconsciously in her everyday life.

Basch (1974) reported an analytic patient's dream that contained derivatives of an unconscious perception from the previous day. He described the patient as a graduate student whose sexual frigidity and fear of marriage were the characterological outcome of a hysterical conflict. Though the patient's analytic hours demonstrated her genuine involvement with the analyst, consciously she experienced the relationship only in displaced form. She was convinced that one of her professors was the hidden object of her erotic dreams and fantasies.

One day the patient and the analyst found themselves entering an otherwise empty elevator, and after greeting each other, they descended a few floors in uninterrupted privacy. They were then joined by a man who knew the analyst and spoke to him. The elevator soon reached street level and the three individuals each went his or her separate way. The next day the patient reported a dream, which (according to Basch) expressed in thinly disguised form her anger at the interruption of their privacy on the previous day and her jealousy of the other passenger. Though Basch's (1974) article does not describe the manifest content of the dream or the patient's associations to the dream, he generously provided the writer with such an account (Basch, 1984).

In the dream the patient is leaving Dr. Basch's office and Dr. Basch follows her. Though she calls him "Dr. Basch," he is really, according to the patient, a 23-year-old man in a white coat. The young man catches up with her, turns her by the shoulder, and, laughing gaily, kisses her. She and the young man are laughing and going down on an escalator. The young man (who also represents the analyst) pushes her from behind, saying, "Come on." Then the patient and the young man are in a doctors' staff dining room, and behind them is an older man who doesn't want to be seen by them. There is a feeling in the dream that the analyst is very young and she wonders if he knows his field.

Her associations to the dream were as follows: The young man was someone who had a crush on her when they were children. The episode in the dining room gave her the same feeling she had had when on a ship and a young man had courted her. While they were dancing, she had stumbled, and saw her father looking at her in disgust. Then, associating to the escalator, she recalled that she and the analyst were in the elevator together on the previous day. She was surprised to have found herself in that situation, and she had wondered whether or not she should talk with him. She questioned aloud whether the analyst was younger than she had previously thought, although, as far as she knew, she had not doubted his skill. She also wondered if the older man in the dream was her father. She found herself feeling angry while associating to the dream, but didn't know why. The patient's later associations led to her rage at being excluded by her parents on various occasions.

Eventually Basch suggested to the patient that her dream may have been a response to the interruption of their elevator ride by a third party. She replied matter of factly, "No, that couldn't have been so. No one else got on the elevator. We were alone."

Basch describes the patient's failure to be consciously aware of the presence of the third party in the elevator as a negative hallucination. She did perceive the interruption by the third party unconsciously, and derivatives of her unconscious perceptions were represented in the dream image of the older man in the dining room. Another derivative of her unconscious perception of the third party was probably encoded in the conscious memory of her father looking at her when she stumbled while dancing.

According to Basch her negative hallucination symptom was related to her disavowal of the analyst's significance to her. As long as she could ward off anxiety through disavowing the meaning of her relationship to the analyst, her insights, though valid, remained intellectual, and the disappearance of many of her symptoms was the effect of an unanalyzed transference cure.

Basch does not mention the possibility that another disturbing stimulus for the dream was the frame disruption of his extra-analytic contact with the patient in the elevator. Derivatives of her unconscious perception of the frame disruption could be the image of the young man who pushed her on the escalator, and the feeling in the dream that the analyst was very young. Her doubts in the dream about the analyst knowing his field could also be a derivative. In her associations to the dream, her memory of stumbling while dancing might derive from her unconscious perception of the analyst's frame error disguised by seeing herself rather than the analyst as the one who stumbles.

TWO FURTHER CLINICAL VIGNETTES

Case 1

A 41-year-old divorced professional woman was given her monthly statement at the beginning of the analytic hour. She looked at the statement and noted a charge for an appointment she had missed. She seemed angry, and began questioning the analyst about the charge. He replied, "Well, let's talk about it," and indicated, with a motion of his index finger in its direction, that she should get on the couch. She reclined on the couch and continued to discuss her feelings about the statement and about being charged for the missed analytic hour. The patient appeared to feel somewhat relieved upon recalling the original contract with the analyst and its provision about paying for missed appointments. Late in the session, she mentioned feeling humiliated by being on the couch rather than facing the analyst while they settled the issue about the payment.

At the next day's session, the patient reported a dream in which she was doing a strip tease in front of the analyst, who became emotionally and physically aroused by her nudity and her erotic dancing. Each time he arose from his chair to move toward her, she put her index finger on his shoulder and pushed him back into his chair. Several times in the dream she told him to "shut up." In the dream she wanted him to beg her for sexual intercourse, which she would then triumphantly refuse. Other associations to the dream concerned her fear that she would be rejected if she told him about her sexual desire for him. While growing up she thought her mother had rejected her when actually, she realized, it was she, the patient, who had rejected her mother.

The patient spoke about her wish in the dream to humiliate the analyst in much the same way that she had felt humiliated about having to get on the couch to discuss the missed analytic session.

The patient's use of her index finger in the dream to control the analyst was a derivative of her unconscious perception of the analyst's directive gesture of the day before. In the dream there was a defensive reversal of roles wherein she became the one who controlled and directed the analyst's behavior rather than the passive victim of his power over her. She had unconsciously perceived and temporarily introjected the analyst's unconscious aggressive and controlling attitude expressed in his gesture indicating that she should get on the couch.

In this instance, as in the other three vignettes presented, a powerful stimulus evoking the patient's unconscious perception was the therapist's commission of some kind of frame error. These disruptive frame infractions evoked intense but mainly unconscious disturbances in the patients, which they defended against by denying both the fact of the frame error and their affective response to it. Their denial prevented them from becoming consciously aware of the frame disruption and their affective reactions. After being unconsciously processed by primary process mechanisms, such as displacement and condensation, these unconscious perceptions were expressed in derivative forms in the patients' dreams.

The analyst's establishment and maintenance of the ground rules and boundaries of the analytic situation are as significant therapeutically as the analyst's interpretations (Dorpat, 1984; Langs, 1982a). Through adherence to these ground rules, the analyst or therapist offers the patient the optimal set of conditions, basic modes of relatedness, and holding-containing environment within which the maximal expression and analysis of the patient's psychopathology are possible.

Clinical investigations by Langs (1980, 1981, 1982a) and others demonstrate the acute unconscious sensitivity of patients to deviations in the ground rules and disruptions of the psychoanalytic frame. These disruptions are among the most powerful adaptation-evoking contents to which patients respond through derivative communication. Derivatives of unconscious perceptions of the analyst's frame infractions often appear in the patient's verbal communications, in symptoms, as well as dreams.

Case 2

One Sunday a middle-aged, recently divorced analysand inadvertently drove past her analyst-candidate's house and saw him working in his yard. During the following Monday morning analytic hour, she reported seeing him on his front lawn, but dismissed the incident with, "Oh well, it doesn't matter." She went on to talk about her teenage son, who, according to her account, attempted to dominate her as his father had done while married to her. The candidate was silent in the Monday hour except for some nonverbal utterances, to be discussed later.

During the next analytic hour on a Tuesday, the patient recounted a dream in which a man was using a garden tool to turn over pieces of turf on a lawn. There was no pattern or system to his performance, and he seemed to be working on the turf in a disorganized manner. He turned over some pieces of lawn and others he did not. While associating to the dream, she recalled seeing the analyst working in his yard during the previous weekend. Later in the hour, the analyst responded to something the patient said with what the patient earlier had described as a "grunt," a short "aah, aah" kind of vocalization.

The patient complained about the analyst's grunts, stating that she no longer liked this type of intervention. At the beginning of the analysis, his "aah, aah" expressions seemed to be reassuring to her, but later he had stopped responding in this way. The patient felt puzzled as to why he had now resumed these supposedly reassuring nonverbal sounds.

About a year previously, the candidate's supervisor (who is also the author of this paper) had actively worked with the candidate on this same type of interaction, and had demonstrated from the patient's derivatives that the candidate's nonverbal interventions were unnecessary, and even antianalytic.

Early in the analysis, the patient had been unconsciously using the candidate's nonverbal interventions as a directive for what she was supposed to talk about. In this way the analyst-candidate and the analysand were enacting the same kind of pathological symbiotic and eroticized relationship the patient had unconsciously enjoyed with her seductive father.

After the candidate recalled that on the previous day (Monday) he had uttered several grunts, he made the following interpretation to the patient. "You were troubled yesterday by my grunts, especially since we had talked about this before and I had stopped doing it. I think my going back to the grunts puzzled you, and you symbolized your puzzlement and consternation in the dream about a man who was turning over the pieces of turf in a disorganized manner."

The patient spoke about feeling troubled after the Monday hour. She said she had struggled, with the analyst's help, to grow away from her disturbing relationship with her father. In her interactions with her father, she explained, he had assumed an apparently benevolent but actually directive and intrusive attitude toward her.

The patient's conscious and preconscious perceptions of the analyst working on his lawn provided images she later used in the formation of her dream's manifest content. These perceptions constituted what Freud called the "day residue." The candidate's relapse into using the antitherapeutic nonverbal communications was correctly, though unconsciously, perceived by the patient and symbolized in her dream by the image of a man turning over pieces of turf in a disorganized manner. Derivatives of her unconscious perceptions of the analyst's frame errors (i.e., his nonneutral grunts) and their meaning as disorganized and disruptive intrusions on her autonomy were represented in the dream. These unconscious perceptions contributed dynamically important elements to the latent content of her dream.

Both transference and nontransference sources were represented in her dream's latent content. A nontransference aspect was the patient's valid, though unconscious, perception of the analyst's seductive use of a nonverbal communication. This intrusive communication evoked transference memories of similar kinds of communications from her father to her. Her unconscious perception was a minitraumatic stimulus because it disrupted the psychoanalytic frame, and because it replicated similar kinds of intrusive and falsely reassuring communications made by her father to her.

"Transference" refers here to the pathological aspect of the patient's relationship to the analyst (or therapist), including distorted and inappropriate responses and perceptions of the analyst. The term "nontransference" is used here to denote the nonconflicted component of the patient's relationship to the analyst, and it is exemplified by the patient's valid and appropriate conscious and unconscious reactions to and perceptions of the analyst (Langs, 1982a). Even the nontransference aspects of unconscious perceptions often have their genetic counterparts. In the case described, the analyst's nonneutral interventions probably evoked unconscious memories of the patient's traumatic interactions with her father.

THE UNCONSCIOUS PERCEPTION OF SOMATIC STIMULI IN DREAMS

Another example of unconscious perception appearing in derivative form in dreams is somatic sources of stimulation occurring during sleep. Exogenous stimuli may be represented in dreams by an immense variety of ideas; dreams contain symbolizations of bodily organs and functions (Freud, 1900).

Somatic stimuli that are symbolized in dreams may include such noises as the sound of an alarm clock, bright lights, digestive disturbances, and the like. These external stimuli are not represented in their true character, but invariably by some other image. The ringing of an alarm clock, for instance, is represented by something else, and the symbol of water in a dream frequently represents a urinary stimulus.

In Freud's view the dream work makes use of somatic sensations to represent the fulfillment of some wish that is normally repressed. Somatic sources of stimulations, according to Freud, play a part in the formation of dreams that is similar to the part played by recent impressions left over from the previous day (i.e., the day residue).

The dream is a reaction to everything that is currently active in the sleeping mind, including childhood fantasies and memories, the day residue, and somatic stimuli (Freud, 1900). What is important for the purposes of this study is the point implicitly made by Freud that somatic stimuli undergo the same kinds of primary process transformations as does the day residue.

The information received from somatic stimuli during dreaming is subject to mechanisms of displacement and condensation, and the derivatives of these transformations appear in dream symbols. Whether occurring during sleeping or during waking life, unconscious perceptions are processed by primary process mechanisms.

An important difference between unconscious perception in sleep and in the waking state is that in the sleeping state intense or traumatic stimuli escape the subject's censorship and awaken the sleeper, whereas in the waking state potentially traumatic stimuli and disturbing perceptions may be successfully defended against and thus not allowed access to consciousness.

EXPERIMENTAL STUDIES

A large number of experimental studies demonstrate that unconscious perception does take place and that derivatives of unconscious perception may appear in the subject's dreams as well as in waking imagery (Fisher, 1954, 1956, 1957; Fisher & Paul, 1959; Poetzl, 1917; Shevrin & Luborsky, 1958; Silverman, 1976). Fisher and others demonstrate that stimuli exposed tachistoscopically at a speed so great that nothing more than a flicker of light could be consciously perceived nevertheless would register in the brain and affect behavior. When subjects were asked to free-associate or "free-image" (i.e., draw whatever comes to mind) immediately after such subliminal exposures, derivatives or aspects of the stimulus would often appear in their productions.

Silverman and his associates (1967) discovered that if the subliminal stimulus has "psychodynamic content" (i.e., content related to unconscious wishes, anxiety, or fantasy), in addition to its content becoming retrievable, the person's level of psychopathology would be affected. The subliminal content would unconsciously stir up motives congruent with the particular stimulus, and symptoms rooted in those emotions would emerge or become intensified. For example, the subliminal message evoking a fantasy of symbiotic gratification, "Mommy and I are one," led to reduced thought disorder and more adaptive ego functioning in a group of schizophrenic patients.

In a pioneer laboratory investigation of dream imagery, Poetzl (1917) discovered that his subjects dreamed about the originally unreported parts of a previously exposed picture. He flashed slides of everyday scenes at 1/100 second and asked subjects to describe and draw what they saw. Then he told them to record any dreams they had that night. On the following day, when he asked the subjects to describe and draw their dreams, he found that their dream imagery borrowed extensively from the unreported portions of the picture. Other investigations have confirmed Poetzl's findings (Fisher, 1954, 1956, 1957; Shevrin & Lubovsky, 1958; Silverman, 1976).

Both Poetzl and Freud were aware of the parallel between Freud's theories of dreams and Poetzl's findings. The "indifferent" perceptions that Freud identified as day residue represented in the manifest content of dreams, Poetzl equated with the unreported parts of the picture that were later dreamed about.

According to Fisher (1954), findings from experiments on subliminal perception necessitate a very great expansion of the role of the day residue in the process of dream formation. Fisher and Paul (1959) argue persuasively that the first phase of the "Poetzl phenomenon" (i.e., sensory registration outside of awareness) cannot be considered preconscious in the psychoanalytic meaning of the term. By definition "preconscious" refers to contents not in consciousness, but that may, with varying degrees of difficulty, merge into it. Subliminal perception and the first phase of the "Poetzl phenomenon" involve unconscious, not preconscious, perception.

DISCUSSION

The foregoing clinical and experimental findings argue for a revised theory about the importance and function of recent events in dream formations. Freud's theory on this topic is incomplete. A major omission in Freud's (1900) writings on the day residue was his failure to account for the contribution made by derivatives of unconscious perception to the latent content of dreams.

In what follows Freud's (1900) views on the day residue are summarized, and some modifications and additions to the theory about the role of recent events on dream formation are offered. According to Freud (1900), dreams are triggered by events that happen shortly before the dream, and he called these events the "day residue" and the "preconscious residue." Dreams pick up the "indifferent refuse" left over from the previous one or two days, and these trivial and indifferent impressions provide some of their manifest content (Freud, 1900, p. 589). What is "subsidiary" and "unnoticed" in the previous day may appear in the manifest content.

Freud described a number of different thought impulses carried over from the previous few days that persist in sleep. These include "unsolved problems," "tormenting worries," "overwhelming impressions," "indifferent" daytime impressions, and whatever has been "suppressed" during the daytime.

Freud believed that preconscious residues from the previous day play the same part in dream formation as that played by the material from somatic sensations that becomes active during sleep (Freud, 1900, p. 554). He did not attach much dynamic importance to the day residue, and he believed that it was the "innocent" and "unimportant" actions and perceptions of the previous day that are repeated in dreams (Freud, 1900, p. 21). That is, what is "indifferent," and consequently unnoticed, appears in dreams. The fact that the content of dreams includes remnants of trivial experiences he explained as a manifestation of dream distortion by displacement. Dream distortion was conceptualized as a product of the censorship (Freud, 1900, p. 177). He asserted that the neutral or indifferent character of the preconscious residue permitted it to serve as a "cover" for unconscious infantile wishes that would not otherwise escape dream censorship. The true meaning of dreams, he held, resides in their latent content, and this is comprised of repressed infantile wishes and conflicts.

According to Freud the preconscious residues must connect with infantile wishes from the *UCS*. The "motive force" dreams require is provided by infantile unconscious wishes (Freud, 1900, p. 561). There occurs a transference (by displacement) of psychical intensity from these unconscious wishes onto the preconscious residues, and the latter provides part of the manifest content. Preconscious experiences left over from waking life are relegated to a secondary position with respect to dream formation (Freud, 1900, p. 554).

Freud (1900) admitted that there is a whole class of dreams the "instigation" of which arises principally from residues of daytime life, although "the *motive force* which the dream required had to be provided by a wish" (pp. 560–561). Not until much later, in *Beyond the Pleasure Principle*, did Freud (1920) modify his theory about unconscious wishes being the only type of motive force in dream formation. There he noted that dreams that take place in the traumatic neuroses and dreams that bring to memory the psychical traumas of childhood are exceptions to the rule that dreams are wish fulfillments. In dreams associated with trauma, the repetition compulsion, rather than wishes, provides the dynamic impetus. In Freud's (1920) view, the repetition compulsion is a motive force that is "more primitive, more elementary, more instinctual than the pleasure principle which it overrides" (p. 23).

Though Freud's comments about the repetition compulsion, trauma, and dream formation indicated the necessity for major changes in the theory of dream formation, few analysts since Freud's time have assimilated insights about the relationship between the repetition compulsion and dreaming into their concepts of dreaming. In her book *Dream Analysis*, Sharpe (1937) follows the earlier views of Freud (1900). Few since Freud have considered this topic, and there appears to be a general unawareness of the importance of derivatives of reality experiences in dream formation, and a concomitant excessive, and almost exclusive, emphasis on the role of unconscious infantile wishes and fantasies.

An exception to the neglect of reality experiences in dream construction is a paper by Langs (1971) entitled "Day Residues, Recall Residues and Dreams: Reality and Psyche." In his discussion of several clinical vignettes, Langs observed links between the day residues and *both* the manifest and latent dream content. According to him interventions and experiences within the psychoanalytic situation are among the more crucial sources of reality elements that contribute to day residues. His hypothesis that day residues derive from actual experiences that are a significant part of an ongoing interaction between the individual's psyche and reality is one of the few in the psychoanalytic literature stressing the role of reality experience in dream formation. Reality experiences interacting with unconscious fantasy create a totality out of which neuroses and dreams develop.

Freud's theory on the role of recent events in dream formation was mistaken or incomplete on several counts. First, he was unaware of the existence of unconscious perception. He mistakenly believed, as did many others of his time, that perception is a sensory given and immediately known to the subject—for example, Pcpt = Cs (Freud, 1900). He held that sensory stimuli, in contrast to drive derivatives from the *UCS*, have direct access to consciousness. Several analysts, including Basch (1981), Fisher (1957), and Stewart (1970), have discussed Freud's error in equating perception and consciousness and the implications of this error for Freud's metapsychological theories.

Many investigations in cognitive psychology and perception demonstrate that perception is a multistage process and that it can be arrested at any one of several sequential stages before the precept becomes conscious. This total process, from the time of sensory end-organ stimulation until there is a conscious perception of the stimulating object, takes place in a very short time, and the perceiver becomes conscious of only the end products of this complex and unconscious process (Erdelyi, 1974).

Fisher's (1957) experiments indicate that not only drive derivatives, but also incoming sensory input, have registration and undergo transformations in the unconscious and preconscious before attaining consciousness (see also Stewart, 1970). Both drive derivatives and sensory input in this process come into contact with memory traces that give the percept meaning and the drive a psychical representation.

A second and major error made by Freud in his theory about the place of recent events was his consistent tendency to minimize their dynamic importance and to overlook their role in the formation of the dream's *latent* content. He did recognize the significance of preconscious residues in dream formation, but he assigned them the relatively unimportant and subsidiary function of contributing to the dream's *manifest* content. He believed that recent events making up the day residue were of a trivial and indifferent kind and that their function in dream formation was simply one of providing images for the manifest content. The major thesis advanced here is that unconscious perceptions of recent events are dynamically important in dream formation, and that they, in addition to derivatives of unconscious memory and fantasy, contribute to the unconscious meanings (i.e., latent content) of dreams.

Freud's theory of the day residue (or preconscious residue) explains how unimportant perceptual images carried over from the preceding day provide for the dream's manifest content. However, his explanation of the role of recent events of dream formation is not adequate or comprehensive because it does not include the significance of unconscious perceptions in the formation of the dream's latent content and in contributing to (along with unconscious fantasies and traumatic memories) the motive force for dreaming.

SUMMARY

Four clinical vignettes were used to illustrate and discuss the dynamic importance of unconscious perceptions of recent events in the formation of the latent content of dreams. A summary of clinical and experimental evidence demonstrates how unconscious perceptions formed the previous day may be carried over and provide dynamic and powerful sources for the unconscious meanings of dreams. Freud's theory about the day residue is incomplete because it covers only the role of the preconscious residue in the formation of the dream's manifest content. He was unaware of the existence of unconscious perception and its significance in the formation of the dream's latent content.

REFERENCES

Basch, M. F. (1974). Interference with perceptual transformation in the service of defense. *Annual of Psychoanalysis*, Vol. II. New York: International Universities Press.

——— (1981). Psychoanalytic interpretation and cognitive transformation. *Int. J. Psychoanal.*, 62:151–175.

——— (1984). Personal communication.

Dorpat, T. L. (1984). Technical errors in supervised analyses. In *Listening and Interpreting—The Challenge of the Work of Robert Langs*, ed. J. Raney, New York: Jason Aronson, pp. 195–213.

Erdelyi, M. H. (1974). A new look at the new look: Perceptual defense and vigilance. *Psychlog. Rev.*, 81:1–25.

Fisher, C. (1954). Dreams and perception: The role of preconscious and primary modes of perception in dream formation. *J. Amer. Psychoanal. Assn.*, 2:285–445.

——— (1956). Dreams, images, and perception: A study of unconscious–preconscious relationships. *J. Amer. Psychoanal. Assn.*, 4:5–48.

——— (1957). A study of the preliminary stages of the construction of dreams and images. *J. Amer. Psychoanal. Assn.*, 5:5–60.

——— & Paul, I. H. (1959). The effect of subliminal visual stimulation on images and dreams: A validation study. *J. Amer. Psychoanal. Assn.*, 7:35-83.

Freud, S. (1900). The interpretation of dreams. *Standard Edition* 5.

——— (1920). Beyond the pleasure principle. *Standard Edition* 18:3–64.

Langs, R. J. (1971). Day residues, recall residues, and dreams: Reality and the psyche. *J. Amer. Psychoanal. Assn.*, 19:499–523.

——— (1980). *Interactions: The Realm of Transference and Countertransference*. New York: Jason Aronson.

——— (1981). *Resistances and Interventions: The Nature of Therapeutic Work*. New York: Jason Aronson.

——— (1982a). *Psychotherapy: A Basic Text*. New York: Jason Aronson.

——— (1982b). *The Psychotherapeutic Conspiracy*. New York: Jason Aronson.

Poetzl, O. (1917). Experimentall erregte traumbilder in ihren Beziehungen zum indirekten gehen. *Ztschr. f. d. ges. Neurol. und Psychiat.*, 37:278–349.

Searles, H. (1965). *Collected Papers on Schizophrenia and Related Subjects*. New York: International Universities Press.

——— (1979). *Countertransference and Related Subjects*. New York: International Universities Press.

Sharpe, E. F. (1937). *Dream Analysis*. London: Hogarth Press.

Shevrin, H., & Luborsky, L. (1958). The measurement of preconscious perception in dreams and images: An investigation of the Poetzl phenomenon. *J. Abnorm. Soc. Behav.*, 56:285–294.

Silverman, L. H. (1976). Psychoanalytic theory: "The reports of my death are greatly exaggerated." *Amer. Psychol.*, 31:621–637.

Stewart, W. A. (1970). The split in the ego and the mechanism of disavowal. *Psychoanal. Q.*, 39:1–16.

3 WILLIAM B. GOODHEART, M.D.

DISCUSSION:

Towards an Understanding of Freud's Overlooking Unconscious Perception

AT THE TIME FREUD (1900) WAS LAYING DOWN HIS BASIC FORMULATIONS IN THE INTERPRETATION OF DREAMS, ESPECIALLY IN CHAPTER IV ("DISTORTION IN DREAMS"), HE UNCONSCIOUSLY WAS COMPELLED TO WALL OFF FROM HIS AWARENESS A CERTAIN SIGNIFICANT AND UNPLEASANT FRAGMENT OF HIS IMMEDIATE PROFESSIONAL AND PERSONAL REALITY AND HIS REACTIONS TO IT. HOWEVER, HE POSSESSED A FULL, UNCONSCIOUS PERCEPTION OF THAT REALITY AND UNCONSCIOUS PERCEPTIONS OF HIS ACT OF WALLING IT OFF AND OF THE FULL IMPLICATIONS OF THAT ACT. THESE UNCONSCIOUS PERCEPTIONS ARE REVEALED IN HIS DREAM "MY UNCLE WITH THE YELLOW BEARD," IN HIS ASSOCIATIONS TO THAT DREAM, AND IN THE IMAGES AND METAPHORS THAT CAME TO HIS MIND AS HE WROTE CHAPTER IV AND CONSTRUCTED HIS ORIGINAL MODEL OF THE INTRAPSYCHIC REALM.

CONSEQUENTLY THE CONCEPTUAL SYSTEM OR MODEL OF THE PSYCHE THAT FREUD ACHIEVED AT THAT TIME WAS BUILT UPON IMAGES USED AS METAPHORS THAT WERE ACTUALLY PORTRAYING REPRESSED BUT CRITICAL UNCONSCIOUS PERCEPTIONS. AS A RESULT OF BOTH HIS UNCONSCIOUS NEED TO EXCLUDE THIS REALITY AND HIS USE OF THESE PARTICULAR IMAGES AS METAPHORS TO CONCEPTUALIZE INTRAPSYCHIC ACTIVITY, FREUD WALLED OFF, AS WELL, THE INCLUSION OF UNCONSCIOUS PERCEPTION FROM HIS PSYCHOANALYTIC THEORY. HE THEREFORE MISSED THE ROLE OF CRUCIAL, ONGOING, INTERACTIONAL EXPERIENCE AS A SIGNIFICANT, UNCONSCIOUS, PSYCHICAL SOURCE OF STIMULATION THAT GIVES RISE TO DREAMS, ASSOCIATIONS, AND SYMPTOMS (WORKING IN CONJUNCTION WITH INTRAPSYCHIC WISHES).

THE DATA

In Chapter IV of *The Interpretation of Dreams*, Freud sets out to demonstrate how "the meaning of *every* dream is the fulfillment of a wish." He presents an extensive interpretation of a dream of his own as proof of this thesis. As a preamble to the dream, he notes that in the spring of 1897, he had been recommended to the Medical

Faculty Board by two professors for appointment to the highly prestigious position of assistant professor, or "professor extraordinarius," at the University of Vienna (Freud, 1900, pp. 136–137; Shengold, 1979, pp. 29–30). Freud professed to be honored, but emphasized that he consciously avoided attaching "any expectations to the event." He said further that he was completely resigned to the fact that he and several of his colleagues who had also been recommended, all of whom were gifted and of outstanding ability, would not be approved by the Minister of Education because they were Jewish. A strong anti-Semitic feeling was pervasive in academic circles that blocked such appointments. Freud stated that "there was no question of pronouncing the grapes sweet or sour; they hung far too high over my head" (p. 137).

One of his colleagues, "my friend R.," who also had been recommended but not appointed, and who also was Jewish, visited Freud one evening. He related that on that day he had gone directly to the Ministry of Education and had "driven the exalted official into a corner and asked straight out whether the delay in his appointment was not in fact due to denominational considerations." The official replied with an evasive, affirmative acknowledgment. R. states: "At least I know where I am now" (p. 137). Freud reflects: "It was not news to me, though it was bound to strengthen my feelings of resignation."

That night, following this intimate and emotionally moving experience with R., Freud had a dream. Unfortunately, Freud tells us only the first part of the dream, because he felt the second half "has no connection with the purpose for which I am describing the dream."

The dream was recorded as follows (p. 137):

> I. . . . My friend R. was my uncle—I had a great feeling of affection for him.
> II. I saw before me his face, somewhat changed. It was as though it had been drawn out lengthways. A yellow beard that surrounded it stood out especially clearly.

Freud's first association was to his Uncle Josef.

> In his eagerness to make money, he allowed himself to be involved in a transaction of a kind that is severely punished by the law, and he was in fact punished for it. My father, whose hair turned grey from grief in a few days, used always to say that Uncle Josef was not a bad man but only a simpleton; those were his words. (p. 138)

The face with "the elongated features and yellow beard" reminded Freud of his friend R., whose dark beard was also turning from its original black through "an unpleasing change of color," yellow, then to grey. He noted that this described his own beard, R.'s, and Uncle Josef's as well. He likewise recognized that his uncle's and R.'s faces were "like one of Galton's composite photographs," in which "in order to bring out family likenesses, Galton used to photograph several faces on the same plate" (pp. 138–139). He notes that his uncle was a "criminal" and that his friend R. "bore an unblemished character" (p. 139).

He then recalls meeting N. a few days earlier, another friend who had received a recommendation to a professorship, but who also was Jewish and had not been appointed. This friend jokingly stated that he was not appointed because "there was something definitely against *me*" (p. 139). N. described how he had recently extricated himself from a legal proceeding brought against him by a woman that was nothing more than "a disgraceful attempt at blackmail, and I had the greatest difficulty in saving the prosecutrix from being punished" (p. 139). He bantered that the Ministry could use this as an excuse not to appoint him and thus cover up the real reason, the anti-Semitism. But they could not do this with Freud, N. said, for he had an "unblemished character."

THE DATA: ORGANIZED AS WISH FULFILLMENT

Freud here developed a reading of the dream into an interpretation.

> My Uncle Josef represented my two colleagues who had not been appointed to professorships—the one as a simpleton and the other as a criminal. I now saw too why they were represented in this light. If the appointment of my friends R. and N. had been postponed for "denominational" reasons, which did not apply to me, my hopes would remain untouched. This was the procedure adopted by my dream; it made one of them, R., into a simpleton and the other, N., into a criminal, whereas *I* was neither the one nor the other; thus we no longer had anything in common. I could rejoice at my appointment to a professorship, and I could avoid drawing the distressing conclusion that R.'s report of what the high official had said to him must apply equally to me. (pp. 139–140)

Freud's perspective here is that he strongly desired to be appointed professor and would "rejoice" at the opportunity, which was obstructed by the Minister and the Ministry of Education solely on the basis of anti-Semitism. This became clear in the meeting with R. He was sorely distressed at this (and not quite as "resigned" as he had initially stated he was). He postulated that in reaction to this realization of the true state of things there was activated or arose in him an unconscious wish that constructed a desired, fantasied reality in which the actual situation would be replaced with one in which he could be appointed. This wish-fulfilling, fantasied reality was one in which anti-Semitism was not an issue; it was one in which N. was rejected solely because he was a criminal, and R. because he was a simpleton like Uncle Josef. And it was a reality in which Freud would be thoroughly eligible and immediately appointed, as he was neither a criminal nor a simpleton.

He continues:

> I was still uneasy over the light-heartedness with which I had degraded two of my respected colleagues in order to keep open my own path to a professorship. My dissatisfaction with my conduct, however, had diminished since I had come to realize the worth that was to be attached to expression in dreams. . . . what my dreams had expressed was only *my wish that it might be so*. The assertion in which my wish was realized . . . made cleverer use of the actual facts in its construction, like a well-designed slander of the kind that makes people feel that "there's something in it." (p. 140)

Let us step away from the interpretation itself, and carefully track how Freud approaches and uses the images presented to him in his dream and associations. A flood of rich imagery and narrative emerges as he free-associates around the dream. Freud extracts from it the themes of simpleton and criminal, and of degrading his friends with these charges for his own needs. He sees the wish as cleverly using this rich panoply of imagery and narrative to create "the assertion" or fantasied reality in which the wish can be realized and, at the same time, to disguise the actual wish. The imagery of dream and association is approached by Freud's method with a certain probing attitude: What is the underlying wish this image and narrative are concealing? How is it distorting reality or creating a false reality to suit its needs?

The interpreting attitude then reaches into the imagery and narratives, and searches out their distortions, their falsely constructed, wish-fulfilling, fantasied realities and their well-disguised slanders that make up and express the latent wish. Once these have been extracted and grasped, the kernel of the images and dream is felt to be discovered, and the empty husks of the images are allowed to fall away. He emphasizes that what the images ultimately express is "*only* my wish that it might be so." The images then are to be explored and harvested *exclusively* for this wish and its fantasy. The worth of the images rests only in the wish they are carrying and disguising. The actual meeting with R. likewise falls away as having been no more than an event that posed the harsh reality of the anti-Semitic obstruction to Freud's hopes, and which thus, like a day residue, triggered the latent slumbering wish into activating the dream and then fell away into secondary importance.

Next in the text, Freud's further associations bring up how "ungenuine and exaggerated" seemed the feeling of affection he had experienced for his uncle in the dream. Then an image crossed his mind: "If my little daughter did not want an apple that was offered to her, she asserted that the apple tasted sour without having tasted it" (p. 141). This portrays for him the sort of resistance and withdrawal he experienced when he first approached this dream, sensing that the interpretation would hold something he struggled against knowing. He follows with a discussion of the process of unconscious "distortion" and "dissimulation." He reasons that he put up a defense against the slander against R. contained in the dream wish by experiencing consciously a feeling of affection for him.

ORGANIZING MATERIAL—UNCONSCIOUS PERCEPTION VERSUS WISH FULFILLMENT

The approach to the images from the standpoint of the attitude that recognizes the presence and influence of unconscious perception differs from the approach utilized by Freud. The approach through unconscious perception assumes that in the significant interaction with R., to which the dream is clearly related, there will have been factors present that were completely unconscious to both parties but were of considerable significance and were carefully recorded and perceived unconsciously by each. Freud (1900) spoke of the remarkably perceptive powers of the unconscious.

> No one who occupies himself with dreams can, I believe, fail to discover that it is a very common event for a dream to give

> evidence of knowledge and memories which the waking subject is unaware of possessing. (p. 14)

Freud was referring to the emergence of such perceptions in the manifest content of dreams. We are discussing the unconscious perceptions as being an integral part of the latent content of the dream, and as disguised as are wishes and impulses, and, indeed, disguised by the same processes of displacement, condensation, symbolization, and secondary elaboration.

Still the approach to the image is somewhat different from Freud's, as the images are felt to be *portraying* in this disguised way certain critical and *valid* perceptions of an interactional reality that are totally unconscious or, one could say, in the darkest, impenetrable shadows of the interaction. Images do not only disguise; they also illuminate these darkest areas of an interaction and reveal its contents. In approaching the images with a different intent and goal than did Freud, the interpreter holds onto the image longer, and allows it to reach a complete existence and full statement in its own right, to amplify itself and to tell its full story without constricting it, considering it solely as fantasy and distorting reality, or putting wish fulfillment expectations upon it. Allowing it to illuminate an interaction is a different process than reaching into it, probing it, and extracting from it, while assuming all along it is basically fantasy and is *distorting* reality rather than *illuminating* reality in some valid way (Langs, 1982, p. 72; 1978a, 1978b).

The image of a "simpleton," for example, can be held for awhile, and allowed its fuller expansion into "the man is a simpleton because he lets the desire for money involve him in an illegal transaction." And the image of "criminal" expands into "having false and trumped-up charges placed on someone in a scandalous and evern blackmailing manner." So heightened and amplified, these images are held up to the specific event or context that activated the dream and its associations with the assumption and expectation it might illuminate previously unanticipated, unconscious aspects of the event.

This event is the meeting with R. and Freud, which centered around their discussion of their now overtly clear rejection by the Ministry because they were Jewish. The full images, carrying hidden, unconscious perceptions of this meeting and its implications, portray the following: "This whole refusal-of-appointment business is a network of trumped-up charges, of false and illicit legal proceedings; it is scandalous and close to blackmail, clearly criminal, and itself illegal; and for us to go along with it is akin to our being simpletons."

In this approach the images are seen to be illuminating the darkest corners of the interaction and its implications. These are rich and complex aspects that are otherwise not allowable to full awareness, and a good part of which would remain unconscious and unspeakable. Likewise, any wish that is immersed in the images will be discovered to be a response to these aspects of the interaction, to their unconscious perception and their introjection.

THE DATA AS ORGANIZED AROUND UNCONSCIOUS PERCEPTION

The reader is asked to reflect on the following array of images and trains of thought that Freud brings forward in response to his visit with R., but from another perspective. That perspective involves recognizing within them unconscious perceptions and commentaries that portray the full significance and wide implications of Freud's experience with R., of their facing the Minister's blatant anti-Semitism, of their mutual, subsequent attitude, and of the conclusions they reached during their discussion that evening.

Composite photographs of family members on the same plate, family likenesses.
Aging, yellow beards in common.
Uncle Josef, Freud, R., N., Freud's father—Jewishness.
Out of eagerness to make money, allowing oneself to become involved in illegal and shameful transactions and being punished for it.
Hair turning grey from grief over this illegality and punishment.
Not doing it out of badness, but from being naive, simple, a simpleton.
False, legal proceedings brought against someone.
A disgraceful attempt at blackmail.
Protecting the very blackmailer from being punished, the one who pressed the false charges.
Covering up anti-Semitism.
Criminality.
Well-designed slander.
Distortion of reality.
Dissimulation.
Ungenuine and exaggerated affection.

Avoiding an offered apple by claiming it is bitter without having tasted it.

Using the visit with R. as the central organizing source of psychic stimulation and as the main organizer of this material, we can begin to see reflected in this imagery and narrative Freud's unconscious perceptions, introjections, and commentaries arising from his and R.'s specific interaction that evening. Unconsciously Freud is essentially stating:

> You, R., have brought into the open the anti-Semitic obstruction to the positions to which we are certainly intellectually and creatively worthy for appointment, and we are submitting to this obstruction. I am here portraying this commonality we have—our Jewishness, being on the same plate, of the same configuration—you, me, my father, Uncle Josef, our family likenesses, our beards. We are perpetrating a crime in our submission, resignation, and implied acceptance of this obstruction, and we are being punished as if we were criminal. There is something illegal and criminal, as well, in our tolerating this. We are aging and grief ridden from this. We are being simpletons, as well, you and I, in tolerating with our submission and resignation these false and malicious public proceedings against us, and in so doing we protect the very ones who perpetrate this. There is a blackmail of some sort going on. Possibly it is out of our "eagerness to make money," our (not unrealistic) fear that all income would be cut off if we did other than submit, that we allow this crime to continue. Yet we slander ourselves by in any way sanctioning this; and to sanction it, we are distorting reality. We are dissimulating. We are involved in ungenuine and exaggerated affection. We are avoiding biting into this apple of reality by our submission and resignation.

Freud emphasizes the distortion of the images of R. and N. by his dream wish, but he does not consciously recognize that such a wish would overlook, bypass, allow to slumber, deny, and even require acceptance and submission to the blatant perniciousness of the anti-Semitic reality that was slandering himself as well as N. and R. Yet, unconsciously, he fully perceives this.

This approach, then, adds to Freud's interpretation that the most monstrous slander of all in this material is the way that R., N., and Freud were being treated by the Ministry, that it was blatantly criminal, and that one would be a simpleton not to recognize the inhuman violence within and behind it. To see any other problem or actuality than this as paramount would be a distortion and dissimulation imposed upon this reality. Again, unconsciously, Freud is aware of this.

This formulation emerges solely out of a standpoint that acknowledges that dreams and associations are equally responses to and portray valid unconscious perceptions of the full implications of the most critical, hidden issues that are going on, or have gone on, in a significant interaction with another. These perceptions are unconscious, compared with the conscious dimensions of awareness of the interactional event, because, as Freud says later in this same chapter:

> The interpretation of these dreams has brought us up each time against topics about which people are loth to speak or to think. The distressing feeling aroused by these dreams is no doubt identical with the repugnance which tends (usually with success) to restrain us from discussing or mentioning such topics. . . . (p. 159)

To call R. a simpleton or N. a criminal is minor compared with the repugnant truths lying in Freud's commentary on R., himself, and the Ministry of Education, as revealed in the above formulation of this material.

This formulation organizes all of the material presented in a comprehensive manner, and this suggests validity. But the final proof must come from seeing whether subsequent associations fit, or even extend and amplify, such an initial formulation. Thus we have learned to listen in order to test formulations in the analytic hour, and so we might listen to Freud's further working over of this material.

Freud immediately goes on to reflect:

> I will try to seek a social parallel to this internal event in the mind. Where can we find a similar distortion of a psychical act in social life? Only where two persons are concerned, one of whom possesses a certain degree of power which the second is obliged to take into account. In such a case, the second person will distort his psychical acts or, as we might put it, will dissimulate. The politeness which I practice every day is to a large extent dissimulation of this kind. (pp. 141–142)

This image and train of thought are a startling confirmation and more concise expression of the previous formulation, both extending and amplifying it. Freud has postulated that the problem lurking behind the dream as a symptom lies in the wish, an intrapsychic and internal event. But now he counterpoises or rectifies that assumption by producing an image and narrative of an *external, interpersonal,* and *interactional* event that harbors the problem. His "social parallel" is the precise calling forth of the fragment of interactional reality he was avoiding consciously, but which, as we have seen, he was fully aware of unconsciously. He can accept it, not as a disguised and displaced, valid, unconscious perception, but as an image he builds into an "as if," that is, into a metaphor. By the metaphor he simultaneously divorces himself from both the fragment of reality and his unconscious perception of that reality. Only then can he discuss explicitly this interactional event consisting of "dissimulation" and "distortion of psychical acts" in deference "to one in power." The irony here is fierce, for as he is developing this metaphor, he is acting out unconsciously the very sequence of events he is describing. Likewise, he is portraying himself at that moment in his act of formulating and building the rudiments of his intrapsychic model. And he is portraying the full reality of the actual situation described by R. in his relationship to the Minister, and of R.'s and Freud's mutual resignation to the one in power, which they shared during their conversation.

The social parallel was turned by Freud into a metaphor that became his first basic model of the intrapsychic realm. The irony mounts, for what was a clear representational image of his unconscious perception of the darkest and most avoided aspects of his and R.'s behavior became the basic configuration of his formulation of a model of the psyche that excluded entirely the possibility of valid, unconscious perception being a major source of intrapsychic activity and stimulation. With this act of formulating, Freud completely buried for himself any awareness and embracing of this fragment of interactional reality of his unconscious perception of it, and of his full range of reactions to it. He also buried any possibility of including unconscious perception in his model of psychical dynamics.

In the next sentence, Freud uses a quotation from Goethe's *Faust,* which is described in the footnotes as a favorite of his, and with which he desires to indicate the need for distortion by the wish.

> Das Beste, was du wissen Kannst,
> Darfst du den Buben doch nicht sagen. [The finest of what you know cannot be told to those lads.]
> (Part I, Scene 4, lines 1840–1842)

This choice by Freud introduces further important perceptions with respect to his meeting with R. and to his ongoing actions of formulating in Chapter IV. This passage is an extremely significant one in *Faust*. It is Mephistopheles' crowning argument to Faust to convince him to renounce his last connections to a scholarly and academic life and to his students, or "lads." Mephistopheles goes on to say (line 1846): "Komm, gib mir deine Rock und Muetze." ["Come, give me your cap and gown."] It is a moment of renunciation for Faust of a scholarly career that had been founded on detached, intellectual reflection and longing, in order to plunge into the more vital, unknown world of instinct and impulses. Similarly, this was a critical moment for Freud and R.; the dominating unconscious perception within Freud's dream, his associations, and the theme of this quotation is a renunciation, the pursuit of an entirely different path and the giving up of the conventional "cap and gown." For Freud and R., this was accepting abusive social and professional repression by anti-Semitic forces. It was allowing himself and R. to be treated as if they were immoral or of lesser value, and thus to be delimited and excluded. It was allowing themselves to be publicly censured and censored. To continue in any relationship with these forces other than that of open confrontation and direct interaction over the issue required dissimulation and distortion.

Clearly such an action would have invited an almost impossible struggle against powerful, pervasive, and deeply ingrained attitudes and prejudiced social actions. Yet these could have been met with dignity only by outrage, dissent, and a disposition to revolution.

Like Faust, Freud and R. renounced their right to the cap and gown, and Freud plunged in his own reflective way into the world of the instinctual life. But there is a difference between Faust's and Freud's renunciations. Faust's leap was to free himself from detached reflection and arid, overintellectualized scholarship. He had tried, in vain, mystical and similar approaches to relieve his sense of emptyness and aridity, and now chose unrestrained submission to his impulses and instincts in the sensual world. He chose action. "In the beginning was the deed." Freud's choice was to resign from direct action, from grappling outwardly with this fragment of reality that was directly oppressing his life's momentum. Instead he began to analyze dreams and to conceptualize an intrapsychic realm filled with wishes, impulses, and repressions in raging conflict with one another, and finding equilibrium only in mutually resigning compromises. In contrast to Faust, Freud turned to reflection, intellectual activity, and concept building, only to create a new form of effective action—psychoanalytic treatment.

THE AVOIDANCE OF UNCONSCIOUS PERCEPTION

Next in this chapter, Freud introduces the concept of "censorship." This, he states, is the intrapsychic force analogous to the social-political force of censorship of which "the political writer who has disagreeable truths to tell those in authority" must be "beware."

> A writer must be beware of the censorship, and on its account he must soften and distort the expression of his opinion. According to the strength and sensitiveness of the censorship he finds himself compelled either merely to refrain from certain forms of attack, or he must conceal his objectionable pronouncement beneath some apparently innocent disguise: for instance, *he may describe a dispute between two mandarins in the Middle Kingdom, when the people he really has in mind are officials in his own country*. The stricter the censorship, the more far-reaching will be the disguise. (p. 142, author's italics)

Freud begins here to elaborate a construct of the mind that contains a dispute between the two psychic agencies of wish and censorship in the "middle kingdom" of the unconscious life. Again this construct is built of an image that came to him as the precisely accurate portrayal of his unconscious perception of the critical implications of his behavior as he was forming his model of internal events. He poignantly, and in barely disguised fashion, portrays in this image, made into a metaphor, that *he* is being "beware" and is compelled to conceal any "objectionable pronouncements" he may have. *He* is refraining from "certain forms of attack" by means of an "innocent disguise." The disguise lies in his describing a dispute between two agencies in a psychical middle kingdom, when the agencies he really has in mind are officials in his own country! And again, he is taking an image that portrays an unconscious perception of himself, his acts and their implications, and building it into a metaphor that will become, together with the previously discussed metaphor, the fundamental cornerstone of his model of the intrapsychic realm. And this model will exclude, necessarily, out of his unconscious need for concealment, unconscious perception as being of major significance.

Consciously Freud is experiencing himself as an exploring scientist discovering the modes of functioning and the structure of the unconscious psyche. Unconsciously he sees himself as a "political writer" who is displacing the external, social, repressive forces, the censuring and the censorship, and his submission and compromise into this middle kingdom of conflicting, psychic agencies, forces, currents, or systems. His "objectionable pronouncements" and potential "forms of attack" have been translated into forbidden wishes and equated with censorious instincts that are seen as wild, infantile, and uncivilized, and that need taming, containment, and censorship.

His very act of creating a model of the human mind is at the same time displacing him away from any possible active and direct assertion, "forms of attack," or objectionable pronouncements," and removing any such specific urges or wishes from his consciousness. It is replacing them with a conceptual model that buries them in a postulated pot pourri of universal seething, undifferentiated, infantile, and instinctual forbidden desires and wishes that emphasize sexuality over aggression. This act is removing, finally, from his conscious perception and focus the most repugnant aspects of this fragment of reality to which he is capitulating, and, at the same time, his potential, directly aggressive responses to that reality.

Freud, then, has interposed a new imaginatively constructed and more manageable intrapsychic reality to replace an actual unmanageable fragment of his own reality. His constructed model, therefore, could not have included unconscious perception; this would have led him, unavoidably, straight into a conscious recognition of exactly this forbidden fragment and these unresolvable, forbbidden, personal, submissive, and aggressive tendencies associated with it that it had been constructed to wall off and bury. His creation was not only a discovery, but also a self-protective invention. The primary intrapsychic reality, the "first system," that underlies all of the unconscious psyche's functioning came to contain only intrinsic, internal, infantile, and forbidden wishes and fantasies toward others rather than also to include unconscious perceptions.

Consequently the entire thrust of Freud's therapeutic exploratory and interpretative efforts was to probe for unconscious forbidden wishes and their fantasies within himself or his patients rather than unconscious perceptions of unconscious realities occurring in one's interactions with significant others (especially those that might be perpetrating mutual unconscious violence and misuse), and that would serve as a primary stimulus as well to the formation of dreams, associations and symptoms.

Dorpat states in Chapter 2:

> Freud was unaware of the existence of unconscious perception. He mistakenly believed . . . that perception is a sensory given only and immediately known to the subject. . . . He held that sensory stimuli, in contrast to drive derivatives from the *unconscious*, have direct access to consciousness.

This, of course, does not leave room for the intermingling of unconscious perceptions and their introjects as stimuli and activators to dreams, along with wishes, fantasies, and drives. Likewise, according to Freud, drives and their derivatives are what are disguised by the primary processes, but not derivatives of unconscious perception. As Dorpat points out, the primary processes are seen as working over loathsome, forbidden, conflict-laden drives, impulses, wishes, and memory-fantasy constellations, but not loathsome, forbidden, conflict-laden, immediate, unconscious perceptions and introjects from current critical interactions with significant others.

FREUD'S UNCONSCIOUS AMBIVALENCE TOWARD HIS OWN AGGRESSION

Freud goes on in the text:

> Let us imagine a society in which a struggle is in process between a ruler who is jealous of his power and an alert public opinion. The people are in revolt against an unpopular official and demand his dismissal. But the autocrat, to show that he need take no heed of the popular wish, chooses that moment for bestowing a high distinction upon the official, though there is no other reason for doing so. (pp. 144–145)

Here are images of active revolt, a demand for the dismissal of, and a direct attack upon, an unpopular autocratic official. There is no dissimulation of taking the struggle to a disguised middle kingdom. This is not writing politically, indirectly, about the problem; this is taking on the problem directly and aggressively.

Freud is continuing to work over the undesirable, unconscious aspects and implications of his meeting with R. Are resignation and submission the only route available? Does such public repression, "jealousy of power," directed against a Jew need to stand untouched? Is dissimulation the only choice? Again, Freud's image of the political writer who is compelled "to refrain from certain forms of attack" comes to mind. What forms of attack? Are there any forms of attack available? Here we have images of *action* rather than *resignation*: images of attack, of public uprising against "those in authority," against a ruler "jealous of his power," against the "autocrat."

There is a dimension of healthy unconscious functioning that does not accept the status quo of a violatory, but generally sanctioned, set of interactional conditions, no matter how benign they might appear, consciously, to the social system. An individual in such a system will be consciously agreeing, but will possess an uncanny, unconsciously perceptive ability to ferret out precisely where those unrecognized forces are impinging on his or her integrity and legitimate boundaries in a violent and destructive manner (Langs, 1979, p. 464; 1978c, pp. 141–154; 1982, pp. 171–173, 261, 322; Searles, 1979, pp. 380–459).

For example, Langs and others (Langs, 1982, p. 426; Cheifetz, 1984) have shown this quite clearly with patients who are in a clinic situation in which the patient and the therapist innocently have assumed that certain adjuncts to the treatment will have no harmful impingements. These adjuncts include such things as involvement of third parties (secretaries, supervisors, ancillary personnel, evaluators, psychological testers), record keeping, audio and even audiovisual recording, public waiting rooms, and fee manipulation, often by a third party. Though the entire system—patients and therapists included—consciously perceives no harm in these ancillary involvements, patients unconsciously introject them and respond to them with portrayals in dreams and associations as violations of the integrity of the patients and the therapy situation. Likewise, patients in response to such introjects produce images that portray actions, which, if taken, would correct the situation. Langs has referred to this dimension of the healthy unconscious working over of such unperceived personal violations as "models of rectification" (Langs, 1982, pp. 46, 171–173, 322).

One wonders how close these urges toward direct assertive action came to consciousness in Freud and his friend that evening in Vienna. Did they discuss any alternative ways of taking action? Did they in any way express their frustration, disapproval, feelings of revolt, and other aggressive fantasies and urges against such autocratic injustice? In any case we know that such embryonic urges toward rectification existed in Freud and his friend, and were portrayed in his associations.

Yet the subsequent image in Freud's analogy portrays, instead of taking action, a bestowing of "high distinction" upon the unpopular official in an effort to ignore and unrail the "discontent and active stirrings." Here is a further, poignant, unconscious perception of how R. and Freud were resolving their dilemma, their urge to action. They continued to express esteem for the Minister of Education, an act that took no heed of, and, indeed, covered over, their more aggressive attitude toward him. In fact, in his description of R.'s confrontation with this official, Freud, and possibly R., described him as an "exalted official." Here is more of the dissimulation of the politeness and flagrant exaltation and excessive affection that conceals and overrides stirrings toward aggressive uprising.

Later, in Chapter V (pp. 191–193), Freud returns to this dream to acknowledge that he was not satisfied with his interpretation of it, and that he was avoiding recognizing the extent of his ambition and its frustration that gave rise to such a dream. In his associations he recalled the aura around his birth that implied a "great man" had been brought into the world. He spoke of his "thirst for grandeur" as a youngster. He reports that from the age of 11 or 12, he had the fantasy that he would "grow up to be a Cabinet Minister." This remained a childhood fantasy for a considerable time, especially since "there had even been some Jews among them" (Ministers). Freud then recognized that in this dream and its associations, he had actually identified himself with the Minister of Education and was "mishandling my two learned and eminent colleagues because they were Jews. . . . I was behaving as though I were the Minister, I had put myself in the Minister's place, turning the tables on His Excellency with a vengeance! He had refused to appoint me professor extraordinarius and I had retaliated in the dream by stepping into his shoes!" (p. 193).

Freud here is moving closer to recognizing his unconscious compliance and the violent betrayal and abnegation of his dignity and that of his friend that arises from it. He is also commenting more directly on the inhumanity and vengeance that the anti-Semitism and the minister represented to him. But he never approached it consciously with the full outrage it deserved, and which only his unconscious life was able to perceive and give voice to in disguised form.

Immediately following in Chapter V, for example, Freud goes on to refer to another dream that brings up his identification with the persevering, aggressive, heroic, single-minded, Semitic Hannibal. Hannibal's father had made him swear to take vengeance on the Romans, who represented, in Freud's boyhood fantasies, the Catholic Church and the embodiment of the anti-Semitic attitude. He contrasts the relationship between Hannibal and his father with an episode involving Freud and his own father, who described the passive acceptance of humiliation at the hands of a Christian. Freud relates:

> He [Freud's father] told me a story to who me how much better things were now than they had been in his days. "When I was a young man," he said, "I went for a walk one Saturday in the streets of your birthplace; I was well dressed, and had a new

> fur cap on my head. A Christian came up to me and with a single blow knocked off my cap into the mud and shouted: 'Jew! get off the pavement!' " "And what did you do?" I asked. "I went into the roadway and picked up my cap," was his quiet reply. I contrasted this situation with another which fitted my feeling better: the scene in which Hannibal's father, Hamilcar Barca, made his boy swear before the household altar to take vengeance on the Romans. Ever since that time Hannibal had had a place in my phantasies. (p. 197)

DELIMITING OF THE INTERACTIONAL CONTEXT OR DAY RESIDUE

Freud thus did not focus significantly on the nature of the precipitating contexts or the reality to which he was adapting. According to Dorpat, he consciously saw himself as having aggressive attitudes toward his friends. His lack of focus on interactional contexts rendered the Ministry's anti-Semitism and denominational rejection of him and his friends relatively "innocent" and "unimportant"—the terms that Freud went on to apply to day residue or events in current reality that are found in dreams, but carry for him only secondary importance as stimuli. To what was a major iniquity in his own reality, he imparted a subsidiary and minimal status and turned the search for iniquity upon himself, upon his and his patients' intrapsychic lives, especially upon the wellspring of infantile impulses and wishes.

As we have seen, this bent of his thought processes arose out of the nearly intolerable conflict-laden situation or context in which he was immersed. In the midst of this context, out of his dream, the associations to it, and the images portraying unconscious perceptions of himself and R., he created the metaphors and theoretical constructs that became Chapter IV of *The Interpretation of Dreams*.

This chapter laid a fundamental orientation that established what Dorpat describes as:

> . . . his consistent tendency to minimize their [recent events'] dynamic importance and to overlook their role in the formation of the dream's *latent* content . . . but he assigned them the relatively unimportant and subsidiary function of contributing to the dream's *manifest* content. He believed that recent events making up the day residue were of a trivial and indifferent kind.

Working around this limitation, Freud gave the Western world the foundations it needed for achieving an understanding of the primary processes, of the nature of intrapsychic conflict, of the interpretation of dreams and psychological symptoms. He gave us the analytic situation and the use of neutrality and free association. And he created the conceptual and observational tools that began to illuminate the roots of psychic conflict and of anti-Semitism. But this limitation and bent compelled him to be partially blind to the full implications and major significance of the ongoing, unconscious, interactional reality between patient and therapist, and to the fact that the patient's flow of unconscious perception, introjection, and continuous monitoring of that reality, which includes the analyst's behaviors, serves as a psychical source of stimulation that gives rise, as well, to dreams, associational images, and symptoms.

AFTERWORD

Freud proved to be a scientist, researcher, and clinician of monumental stature who grappled successfully with disorder and established a system of order and understanding in its place. Einstein (1918) characterizes such scientists and creators by the following:

> One of the strongest motives that lead men to art and science is flight from everyday life with its painful harshness and wretched dreariness, and from the fetters of one's own shifting desires. A person with a finer sensibility is driven to escape from personal existence and to the world of objective observing and understanding. . . . With this negative motive there goes a positive one. Man seeks to form for himself, in whatever manner is suitable for him, a simplified and lucid image of the world, and so to overcome the world of experience by striving to replace it to some exteent by this image. (pp. 107–110)

We have seen the specific steps by which Freud achieved his simplified and lucid image of the internal world upon which the science and practice of psychoanalysis were founded.

Karl Marx (quoted in Gould, 1980) noted that Darwin's theory of natural selection has close similarities to the constellation of economic and social forces present in Darwin's socioeconomic world. Marx stated:

> It is remarkable how Darwin recognizes among beasts and plants his English society with its division of labor, competition, opening up of new markets, "invention," and the Malthusian "struggle for existence. . . ." (p. 68)

In commenting on this passage, Gould notes:

> Creativity demands breadth . . . analogy is a profound source of insight—great thinkers cannot be divorced from their social background. But the source of an idea is one thing; its truth or fruitfulness is another. The psychology and utility of discovery are very different subjects indeed. Darwin may have cribbed the idea of natural selection from economics, but it may still be right. (p. 68)

Likewise, Freud may have compressed into a simplified and lucid intrapsychic model the irrational divisions of his social context, but when great minds so act, they forge fruitful schemata that carry us into new arenas of questioning and present us with new vistas on our way toward understanding. We have traced the "psychology of discovery" leading to Freud's model of the mind, but its origins did exert a certain limiting and skewing influence on its immense "utility of discovery." Likewise, even by forming an exclusively intrapsychic model of conflict, Freud, through reflection and withdrawal from direct action, actually took a major aggressive step toward an understanding and possible resolution of the social forces that give rise to such irrational conflict as anti-Semitism. He created an analytic situation, a virtual laboratory in which the sources, emergence, and manifestations of such irrationalities, such symptoms, in the individual could be contained, made visible, monitored, interpreted, and resolved.

This was the only way he could act; its obverse side is now clear. Freud unconsciously perceived and protested this obverse side, the steps of flight, evasiveness, and dissimulation it required. Yet, too, he was certain that ultimately his efforts would begin to have a direct effect on such unresolved and pernicious social divisions, oppressions, and shared neuroses (Freud, 1910).

> The community cannot respond with sympathy to a relentless exposure of its injurious effects and deficiencies. . . . Powerful though the feelings and the self-interest of men may be, yet intellect is a power, too. It has not, perhaps, the power that makes itself felt immediately but one that is all the more certain in the end. The most mordant verities are heard at last, after the

interests they injure and the emotions they rouse have exhausted their frenzy. It has always been so, and the unwelcome truths which we psychoanalysts have to tell the world will undergo the same fate. Only it will not come very quickly; we must be able to wait. (pp. 291–292)

REFERENCES

Cheifetz, L. G. (1984). Framework violations in psychotherapy with clinic patients. In *Listening and interpreting*, ed. James Raney. New York: Jason Aronson, pp. 215–253.

Einstein, A. (1918). Prinzipien der Forshung, Rede Zur 60. Geburtstag von Max Planck. In *Mein Weltbild*. Ullstein Verlag, 1977, pp. 107–110. Translated *Ideas and Opinions*. New York: Crown, 1954, pp. 224–227.

Freud, S. (1900). The interpretation of dreams. *Standard Edition*, 4, 5:136–137.

——— (1910). The future prospects of psychoanalytic theory. *Collected Papers*, 2:292–292.

Gould, S. J. (1980). *The Panda's Thumb*. New York: Norton, p. 68.

Langs, R. (1982). *Psychotherapy: A Basic Text*. New York: Jason Aronson.

——— (1978a). *The Listening Process*. New York: Jason Aronson.

——— (1978b). Dreams in the bipersonal field. In *Techniques in Transition*. New York: Jason Aronson, pp. 539–586.

——— (1978c). The patient's unconscious perception of the therapist's errors. In *Techniques in Transition*. New York: Jason Aronson, pp. 141–154.

——— (1979). *The Therapeutic Environment*. New York: Jason Aronson.

Searles, H. (1979). The patient as therapist to his analyst. In *Countertransference and Related Subjects, Selected Papers*, pp. 380–459.

Shengold, L. (1979). Freud and the idea of a university. In *Freud and His Self-analysis*, edited by Mark Kanzer and Jules Glenn. New York: Jason Aronson, pp. 21–37, 29–30.

4

STEVEN KORN, Ph.D., and ROBERT P. CARMIGNANI, Ph.D.

Process Notes as Derivative Communication About the Supervisory Field

THIS PRESENTATION IS FOUNDED ON LANGS' VIEW OF THE PATIENT AS UNCONSCIOUS SUPERVISOR TO THE THERAPIST. THE SUPERVISOR THEN USES THE UNCONSCIOUS PERCEPTIONS OF THE PATIENT TO DETERMINE THE EFFECTIVENESS OF BOTH THE SUPERVISOR'S AND THE SUPERVISEE'S INTERVENTIONS. THIS PAPER EXPANDS THE USE OF UNCONSCIOUS PERCEPTION BY VIEWING THE SUPERVISORY RELATIONSHIP AS A BIPERSONAL FIELD IN WHICH THE SUPERVISEE COMMUNICATES UNCONSCIOUS PERCEPTIONS OF THE SUPERVISOR THROUGH DERIVATIVE COMMUNICATION. THE PROCESS NOTES ARE SEEN AS ONE OF THE MAJOR VEHICLES OF SUCH DERIVATIVE COMMUNICATION. EMPHASIS IS PLACED ON THE FACT THAT THE THERAPEUTIC AND SUPERVISORY BIPERSONAL FIELDS INTERSECT. THE NOTES ARE SEEN AS A COMPLEX, LAYERED MESSAGE TO THE SUPERVISOR IN WHICH THE FUNCTIONING OF ALL THREE PARTIES—SUPERVISOR, SUPERVISEE, AND PATIENT—CAN BE ASSESSED BY DECODING THE PREVAILING SUPERVISORY AND THERAPEUTIC ADAPTIVE CONTEXTS.

Robert Langs (1977, 1982) has made a substantial contribution to the fields of psychoanalysis and psychotherapy in describing the therapeutic relationship as a bipersonal field that is dynamic and interactional. In this bipersonal field, a play space is created in which the patient uses unconscious perception as expressed in highly selected (i.e., in terms of the patient's own history and conflicts) derivative communication to describe the nature of the relationship with the therapist. Derivative communication implies that underlying the manifest communication is an encoded message. By means of both a listening and a validation process, the therapist can interpret these encoded messages, and can allow them to guide the therapy. Langs calls this technique "communicative therapy."

Langs (1979) has described the therapeutic and supervisory bispersonal fields as sharing components of the framework and ground rules. Each requires a fixed location, and set fees, hours, and length of session; and each requires total confidentiality and relative autonomy of supervisor or therapist. They differ in that the therapeutic bipersonal field requires the rule of abstinence and the free association of the patient. The supervisory bipersonal field allows some informal exchange between supervisor and supervisee appropriate to colleagues, and in place of free association the supervisee presents process notes. The process notes represent a strictly sequential, direct presentation of the behavior and communications of the patient and therapist in the therapy session. The goal of therapy as defined by Langs (1979) is to use the dynamic, interactional components of the bipersonal therapeutic field for the insightful cure of the patient's symptoms or characterological disturbances. The goal of supervision is the analysis and understanding of the therapeutic interaction, and through this experience to broaden the supervisee's theoretical and technical education.

Langs (1979), in his book *The Supervisory Experience*, describes the supervisor's role as active and dynamic. He believes that the supervisor has the responsibility to intervene upon observing a significant disturbance in the therapeutic or supervisory bipersonal fields. He sees the patient as the unconscious supervisor to the therapist. Through the process notes, the supervisor can gauge the effectiveness of both the supervision and the work of the supervisee by the unconscious perceptions of the patient.

At times the supervisee fears these encoded perceptions, does not recognize them, or shifts away from them. Such unconscious communications point to the patient's primitive mental world, and the supervisee may dread their contents.

Langs believes that the supervisor should be able to manage the supervisee's and patient's communications and projective identifications by metabolizing, understanding, and returning them to the supervisee and patient detoxified. By so doing the supervisor is providing the supervisee with a management introject and a useful insight.

One of the major teaching aids used to demonstrate such management is what Langs calls the anticipatory interpretation. Such interpretations use the unconscious perceptions of the patient to describe the current therapeutic situation to the supervisee and its meaning in current and future sessions. Any disturbance in the therapeutic bipersonal field in terms of management of the frame or erroneous interventions will activate the patient to comment through derivative communications. Such difficulties or correct work are the adaptive contexts of the session, and they help organize the decoding of the derivative communication. By demonstrating this process to the supervisee, and seeking validation for such an understanding in the future behavior and communications of the patient, the supervisor is demonstrating to the supervisee how to listen and interpret. This is done in a style that can eventually provide the patient access to the disturbing aspects of both his or her own inner world and relationship with the supervisee. In this play space, the symptoms and characterological disturbances are modified by the supervisee's understanding, containing, and managing the patient's expanding, and at times frightening, selected unconscious perceptions of both the patient and the supervisee.

Emphasis is placed on the process notes because they record the derivative communication of the patient. It is through these encoded messages of the patient that the supervisor has a method of validating the work with the supervisee. The process notes bring an order and methodology to the supervision.

SUPERVISION AS A BIPERSONAL FIELD

The purpose of this paper is to take a fresh look at the nature and function of the process notes, given Langs' expanded view of the importance of unconscious communication and perception. In the work of Langs, much of the attention has been focused upon the interaction of the supervisee and the patient.

He has also emphasized the importance of unconscious communication in the supervisory bipersonal field. Langs examines the patient's material for clues to the disruptive or distorting influence of the supervisor. In *The Supervisory Experience*, he has said:

> We must establish the truth about the therapist before we can know the truth about the patient; similarly we must establish

> the truth about the supervisor before we can know the truth about the supervisee and his patient. (p. 198)

Now we wish to turn to the supervisory field itself and view its bipersonal dynamics in more detail. If the supervisory field is, in fact, a bipersonal field, then it will have interactional dynamics and unconscious process similar to, as well as different from, those of the therapeutic bipersonal field. Because the supervisory field does not allow for the free associations of the supervisee and is not designed for the supervisee's therapy, the play space is more restricted. The supervisee is limited to presenting the process notes and any extraneous comments to the supervisor. At the same time, the supervisee is highly activated to adapt to both the supervisor and patient, and to do so will attempt to use both conscious and unconscious communication. The supervisee's unconscious perceptions are sensitive to the behaviors and comments of both the patient and supervisor.

On a manifest level, the supervisee is concerned with the treatment of the patient. Such treatment is a direct responsibility, and any efforts there are also a measure of the supervisee's development as a therapist. On another level, however, partly manifest and often quite latent, one of the supervisee's prime concerns is the skill and professional functioning of the supervisor. The supervisee consciously and unconsciously monitors the supervisor's expertise. Is the supervisor making a meaningful contribution to the supervisee's treatment of the patient? Is the supervisor effectively containing, understanding, metabolizing, and interpreting the material being presented? Is the supervisor introducing extraneous comments or otherwise interfering inappropriately (i.e., in terms of supervisor "countertransference")? The supervisee unconsciously makes the same assessment of the supervisor as the patient makes of the therapist, but does not have the same means of communicating these perceptions to the supervisor.

PROCESS NOTES AS A REFLECTION OF UNCONSCIOUS PERCEPTION

The supervisory bipersonal field is rich with unconscious meaning expressed by both supervisor and supervisee. It is the hypothesis of this paper that the supervisee will turn to the process notes as a vehicle for communicating unconscious perceptions of the supervisor's conscious and unconscious communications. As in the therapeutic field, the supervisory bipersonal field also provides a play space in which both supervisor and supervisee use selective unconscious perception. These serve to express, via derivative communication, distortions of the nature of the relationship between patient and therapist and between therapist and supervisor. In the therapeutic bipersonal field, the free associations of the patient become the medium of such derivative communication. In the supervisory bipersonal field, the selected and shaped process notes become the instrument of such communication in addition to their manifest purpose of recording the events of the therapy session.

The supervisee's assessment of the supervisor leads to a variety of consequences, and some of these are depicted in the process notes. If the supervisee determines that the supervisor's expertise is sound, the supervisee will present the material that reflects some combination of the supervisee's own countertransference difficulties and a more or less accurate portrayal of the patient. The less conflicted the supervisee, the more accurately the process notes will depict the behaviors and communications of the patient.

In addition, if the supervisor's expertise is deficient because of poor recommendations regarding frame management or interventions that are not validated by the patient, then the supervisee will unconsciously shape the process notes accordingly. Information about the patient will be reduced and derivative communication related to the supervisor's performance increased. This shift reflects efforts to adapt to and rectify poor supervisory work to the benefit of both supervisee and patient. Such efforts may be conscious and manifest, but often are unconscious and latent—not detected by supervisee or supervisor.

In the supervisory play space, the supervisee has unconsciously developed several methods of communicating with the supervisor. When needed, the supervisee can unconsciously select for reporting those passages that best describe his or her unconscious perceptions of the supervisor's efforts, especially their errant aspects. The supervisee may shape the passage and use language that also helps to convey unconscious meaning. He or she may also make extraneous comments or tell extraneous stories to the supervisor that are, in fact, derivative communications about the nature of the supervisory field. Further, the supervisee may intervene with the patient in part to convey unconscious perceptions of the supervisor, which are then developed further in the patient's material. The supervisee may actually make an interpretation to the patient that is, in fact, intended for the supervisor. The patient may unconsciously perceive disturbances in the supervisee that imply the existence of problems in a supervisor, and may comment accordingly, thus alerting either or both parties to the disturbance.

In the dynamic bipersonal field of supervision, the process notes can be viewed as communication defined by two poles of a continuum. At one end of the continuum are perceptions of the supervisor's expertise. At the other end of the continuum are perceptions of the behavior and communications of the patient. The supervisee is positioned between these two poles with his or her unconscious perceptions and technical skill and countertransference difficulties. The supervisee is divided between the supervisory field and the therapeutic field. As Langs (1979) has pointed out, these two bipersonal fields, the supervisory and the therapeutic, intersect. Information communicated in the process notes therefore will be viewed as multilayerd and multidimensional (i.e., it touches on both fields).

Because these two fields intersect, there are supervisory as well as therapeutic adaptive contexts. The more the process notes point to the behavior of either the patient or therapist, the more the supervisor can function in an explanatory, interpretative mode. However, when the process notes point more directly to the behavior and personality of the supervisor, then self-analysis and management of the supervisory frame become necessary. From the supervisee's conscious and unconscious communications concerning the supervisor's performance, the supervisor can establish a strategy of rectification for his or her supervision. By means of self-analysis, countertransference issues may be isolated that are disturbing the supervisor's interactions with the supervisee or assessment of the patient. Hypotheses about the dynamics of either the supervisee or patient can be reformulated, and breaks in the supervisory frame that are disruptive to the supervisee can be rectified.

A failure to respond in such a fashion leads to disruptions in the supervisory alliance. Under such circumstances the supervisee may continue to maintain the manifest alliance by providing the supervisor with process note material that depicts some elements of the patient's functioning, but the communicative network will become progressively more restricted as the supervisee loses trust in the supervisor's capacity to receive and metabolize derivative information. Such loss of trust in the supervisor ultimately can result in a misalliance. The supervisee then experiences a negative management introject. Under the influence of such a negative introject, the supervisee will have progressively more difficulty in managing the patient's symptoms and derivative communication.

CASE ILLUSTRATION: DEAD BATTERY (DEPRESSION)

The supervisor arrived late for the group supervision meeting. He apologized, and explained that his car battery had gone dead. He had tried unsuccessfully to phone one of the supervisees for a ride to the meeting, and had finally called the AAA to "jump" his battery.

The usual procedure of the meetings was for one of the supervised therapists to present a case, but nobody had one prepared. Finally, one of the supervisees broke the silence, explaining that although he had not prepared a case, a vignette had come unexpectedly to mind.

The vignette was of a recent therapy session in which the patient entered the office and, instead of walking directly to the couch, first plugged a battery charger into the wall socket. The patient explained that he wanted to recharge his battery during the hour, and then took his place on the couch. During the hour the patient talked about his conflicted thoughts about doing his personal taxes on the office computer. He felt guilty about using office equipment to do personal work during office hours, but often did company work on the train to the office.

The supervisee did not know why that vignette had just occurred to him, but said that he was puzzled by the session.

Discussion

The supervisee who presented this vignette was the one whom the supervisor had tried to phone when he was unable to start his car. The supervisor's dead battery story, told shortly before the vignette came to mind, can be seen as a current adaptive context that evoked the vignette. The vignette emerged spontaneously, the way an association comes to mind during a therapy session. The therapist was unaware of any derivative meaning to the vignette.

Just as an alert psychotherapist considers his or her own statements during the session as providing adaptive contexts for the patient's subsequent associations, it is helpful for a supervisor to consider the effects that his or her statements have in shaping the supervisee's subsequent "associations" during the supervisory session.

We can see that the patient's associations about his use of the office computer was a derivative comment about his similar use of the therapist's office and the therapeutic hour to recharge his battery. Repeated by the therapist, these comments take on a derivative meaning about the current supervisory hour, and the supervisor's request for the supervisee's help when his battery went dead.

In discussing this derivative, the supervisor and the group realized that the dead battery represented the supervisor's (as well as the patient's) depression, which had been discussed at the previous meeting. The supervisor's story of the phone call was, in itself, a derivative that communicated the supervisor's frustrated attempts to get the supervisees' help with his depression (dead battery). In addition, the material about the patient's conflict over doing his personal finances at work may be a derivative communication to the supervisor about his using supervisory hours to discuss his financial problems, which he had brought up in talking about his depression.

This vignette illustrates a supervisory adaptive context that arose during the meeting, and that, in the same meeting, stimulated the unconscious selection of therapy material as a derivative reference to that new supervisory adaptive context. Taken as a whole, the supervisory meeting with the supervisor's and supervisees' comments reveal a complex unconscious discussion about the supervision.

CASE ILLUSTRATION: PUBLIC SPEAKING

Supervision

The supervisor of our supervision group announced a meeting, which interested psychotherapists were invited to attend. He planned to start a local professional society. The supervisor made all the arrangements for the meeting, and set the agenda. He chaired the meeting, and conducted the election of society officers and board members—choosing the nominees, including himself as president. He then presented a paper he had written, one that seemed too sophisticated for its audience.

A psychotherapist who attended that meeting became interested in supervision, and decided to join both the local society and our supervision group—one of the groups affiliated with the society.

At the first meeting the new member attended, he volunteered to present a case once he had attended a few meetings and had become more comfortable with presenting it. At the close of that first meeting, the supervisor announced that he was increasing the fee for supervision. He explained that these supervisory hours were a burden in his overcrowded schedule, and that even the increased fee he was asking was too low to warrant such a hardship.

Supervisory Adaptive Contexts

We predicted that the new supervisee's initial case presentation, delivered in the highly charged context of entering supervision, would contain an especially dynamic selected derivative communication about supervision. This encoded communication would reflect the therapist's own feelings about returning to a student role and presenting to a group that had been meeting for a year. It would, in addition, contain unconscious perceptions of the supervisor's teaching abilities. These perceptions would reflect the positive aspects of the supervisor's presentation at the meeting, and a negative image of his powerful ways in controlling the meeting.

We expected the process notes to organize around specific adaptive contexts—the supervisor's dominating presence, his handling of the fee for supervision, and his discussion of his financial problems.

Process Notes

The therapist chose for his initial case presentation an adolescent male patient who had been referred by the court after his arrest for exhibiting himself in public. The patient—a compulsive exhibitionist—had just returned to therapy after a one-year interruption, with renewed worries over his impulses to expose himself, and his attendant fears of being caught. The therapist presented three consecutive sessions, numbers 3–5.

SESSION 3

Larry started the hour by giving Dr. A. a check signed by Larry's mother. He clarified his inability to pay for the sessions himself, although Dr. A. wanted him to do so. He was worried that Dr. A. might not accept the check.

Larry asked about the book on Dr. A.'s desk. He also asked about Dr. A.'s car and about his family. He wondered what had happened to the family picture that Dr. A had previously kept on his desk.

Larry wondered if the sessions would be different if he paid for them himself. He was curious about what was in the books in the office; he'd like to look at them to get an understanding of what he was saying to Dr. A.

He laughed—he was looking at Dr. A.'s watering can. He couldn't imagine Dr. A. walking around the office watering his plants from the can.

He thought about bringing his father into therapy. He felt the same way with his father as with Dr. A. He thought more about Dr. A. than about his own thoughts; he was more concerned with what Dr. A. thought than with what he thought himself.

Dr. A. ended the session by saying that much of what Larry talked about had to do with his questions and thoughts about Dr. A.

SESSION 4

Larry felt better about coming in. He'd received Dr. A.'s bill in the mail, and felt encouraged that Dr. A. was interested enough to send a bill. It was exciting—the therapist seemed more involved than in the past.

He had only $100 for Christmas, and didn't think that he'd be able to pay for his own therapy until after Christmas.

Dr. A. commented that Larry was excited and comforted in seeing his bill, and saw Dr. A. as being more interested in him—and that Larry also recognized the importance of paying for his own therapy. They needed to discuss the arrangements for therapy, and set a fee, with Larry responsible for all sessions.

Larry said that he was forecasting what Dr. A. was going to say, and that he didn't need a reduced fee. But a reduced fee would be easier for him to pay. If Dr. A. did reduce the fee, he'd wonder about it. Why did he reduce the fee? Why hadn't he reduced it before? How did he set the fee? He wondered why Dr. A. didn't buy himself a more comfortable chair.

Dr. A. asked Larry to pay on a monthly basis, rather than weekly, and to pay at the beginning of each month, keeping track of his own sessions.

Larry said that he had finals the following week, and might have one at the time of his session. He'd stop by the office and let Dr. A. know, so they could find another time.

Dr. A. said that he wouldn't change the time.

Larry said that, in other words, he was responsible for the hour. Dr. A. was really putting it to him. He'd be there.

SESSION 5

Larry had two checks for Dr. A., but didn't know what to do with them. His mother said to take the check back to Dr. A., and "not let him bullshit you." She seemed more upset since he'd come back to therapy. Larry thought that he wasn't doing any better, and was upsetting his parents. He still owed them money. He didn't know how he'd pay Dr. A. He just felt like sleeping, and not look for a job or do his homework.

Dr. A. said that Larry was having difficulty in accepting responsibility for paying for his therapy, as well as for other areas of life. Much of Larry's concern related to establishing a workable arrangement for therapy, and his difficulties in structuring his life and carrying out responsibilities. The therapy seemed to be precipitating Larry's concern about the difficulties in his life.

Larry complained that Dr. A. just seemed to repeat Larry's words without adding any understanding. He didn't know whether Dr. A. understood what Larry was trying to tell him. He wished that Dr. A. would say something that would make a difference—something that would help him to understand himself better and to get up and go. He wondered what Dr. A. thought of him when he was criticizing Dr. A., as when he questioned whether this was worth the money, or if the therapist was a quack or really good or just average. He wished there were some way to find out. If he found out that Dr. A. was really good, it would help to motivate him and get him started on working things out. He wondered what it would take.

Dr. A. commented that Larry was expressing a wish for Dr. A. to relieve his burden of responsibility through insightful and motivating comments. Larry was finding that Dr. A.'s remarks repeated what Larry said, without further insight or understanding, and lacked usefulness in helping him to deal with his responsibilities for the therapy and finding work. His statements didn't provide Larry with "get up and go."

Larry said that he wasn't talking about girls very much in therapy, as he used to do.

Dr. A. ended the session by saying that they would not be meeting the following week because of vacation.

Commentary

This new supervisee, through his selection of an initial case presentation, provided an especially vivid encoded perception of the supervision and the supervisor. In choosing for his presentation a patient who was a compulsive exhibitionist, he unconsciously selected a case that communicated his perception of the supervisor's exhibitionistic qualities.

Taken on a derivative level, these process notes present a complex picture of supervision. The therapist presented a case that reflected—through the patient's manifest remarks about the therapist—a commentary about the supervisor.

Dr. A. came to supervision for help, and found that the supervisor was having difficulty. The supervisor's difficulties dominated the field, eclipsing those of the supervisee; and the supervisee found himself more involved with the supervisor's thoughts than with his own. The supervisor was not hearing the derivative meaning in the process notes. He made manifest interpretations that focused on the mistakes of the supervisee.

This experience stimulated the supervisee to wonder whether the supervisor was really any good or just a quack. Just as the patient, entering an expensive and disruptive therapy, wonders whether it is worth the expense, the therapist is stirred to work over the great expense—emotionally and professionally—of this supervision. He wishes that the supervisor could address these issues, which might motivate him to continue.

The overwhelming concern for the therapist seems to be whether the supervisor can understand the material being presented, and use it to rectify the supervisory framework. The patient's comments reflect the therapist's questions about the supervisor: Is there a reality to his presenting himself as having a great deal to offer in supervision, or is it an exhibitionistic and grandiose display, such as walking around the office with a large watering can?

The patient's comments about the therapist's awkwardness in handling the fee provide an unconscious commentary on the supervisor's handling of a fee for supervision.

The process notes furnish images of rectification for the supervision. The therapist's removal of his family picture reflects the supervisor's limiting his inappropriate dominant presence. Finally, the exhibitionistic young man's return to therapy is a rectifying image for the supervisor to return to therapy for help in controlling his own exhibitionistic impulses.

CASE ILLUSTRATION: SEMMELWEIS

Supervision

At a group supervision meeting, the supervisor was talking about his financial difficulties. He felt that his practice was suffering because of his colleagues' rejection of him and his work, which they could not understand. He went on to tell the story of Ignaz Semmelweis, the doctor who discovered the cure for puerperal ("childbed") fever.

Semmelweis thought that doctors were spreading the disease from infected mothers to healthy mothers, and so ordered his students to wash their hands before examining patients. Semmelweis felt that his work was unappreciated by his contemporaries, and that they were critical of him for his advanced ideas.

After leaving the meeting, the supervisor continued his Semmelweis story to a female supervisee, with the conclusion of Semmelweis' isolation, depression, and eventual suicide. The supervisee felt that this reflected a disturbing derivative meaning about the supervisors' feelings of isolation and depression, and mentioned her concern to him. The supervisor said that there was no meaning to his story, and ended the discussion. She was left to work over her concern for the supervisor's derivative story about suicide, with no opportunity for discussion and conscious resolution.

[Semmelweis, by the way, did not commit suicide. Ironically, his illness and death were caused by an infection on his right hand, apparently the result of an operation he had performed. He died of the disease for which he had found the cure, unable to benefit from his own discovery. At the following meeting, the supervisor corrected his story and supplied the historically accurate ending. Neither the meaning of this addition, nor the incorrect story of Semmelweis' suicide, was discussed consciously as a derivative about the supervisor's unconscious feelings about the results of his own work.]

Supervisory Adaptive Context

We saw this postmeeting discussion, with the story of Semmelweis' depression and suicide, as presenting an adaptive context or evocative stimulus to the supervisees. We predicted that, deprived of an opportunity for a conscious discussion, the supervisee who heard this story—and who was to present a case at the next meeting—would use derivative material embedded in process notes to communicate to the supervisor her concerns. We expected that the case selected for presentation would be one that contained an unconscious reference to this adaptive context.

Process Notes

At the next supervision meeting, the therapist—who had been in supervision for a year and a half—presented a therapy session of a woman who was in the process of breaking off an unsuccessful one-and-a-half-year relationship.

Ms. B. started the hour with a report on her progress in leaving her boyfriend. She discussed her feeling that her leaving would hurt him, and referred to her ambivalence about being independent after the separation.

She mentioned a man who wanted to date her, one whom she had heard was weird, having sent dog shit to a former girl friend. He'd told Ms. B. that he wouldn't do that to her, but she didn't believe him.

She went on to talk about another man, who was on the edge of comitting suicide, or perhaps homicide. As he carried a gun, it could happen. He was angry with his girlfriend. Ms. B.'s friend Judy had told her about this man's behavior. Ms. B. was afraid that he might hurt Judy, but Judy said that he needed a friend, somebody to listen to him without rejecting him. Judy had spent three hours listening to him pour out all his sadness, anger, fears, and torment. He'd said that he was middle-aged and alone and wanted to kill himself. He'd ended with a long, passionate kiss. Ms. B. had told Judy that she was afraid that he might have raped Judy and that she should have resisted. Judy had told Ms. B. that at that moment he'd just needed her to be there for him. He'd let go, said thanks for being a friend, apologized for the kiss, and left. He was going to contact his former therapist and try to work out a way to pay his outstanding bill so that he could return to therapy. Maybe he'd be OK. He'd been abused as a child and his story really touched her deeply.

Dr. C. said that this man's story touched something in Ms. B. and that Ms. B. was questioning whether Dr. C. could be there for her the way her friend Judy had been there for the man in the story. She said that there was some part of this story of separation that Ms. B. wanted to tell, and it was painful and perhaps violent.

The hour was up.

After reading her process notes to the group, Dr. C. said that she had chosen this session to present because she was disturbed about her intervention at the end of the hour. Even while saying it, she had thought that it was an inappropriate intervention, yet she could not resist the impulse to say it. She was presenting the session to the group for help in understanding that session and, in particular, why she had felt compelled to make that intervention to the patient.

Commentary

Dr. C. offered a conscious rationale for presenting that particular hour: she needed help to understand her inappropriate intervention. Her unconscious needs, though, were far different.

Dr. C.'s selection of this patient conveys to the supervisor—through the patient's comments about leaving her boyfriend—the therapist's dissatisfactions with the supervisory relationship, and her wish to leave supervision. Dr. C.'s conflicted feelings about terminating supervision are represented in the patient's discussing her ambivalence over leaving her friend.

The content of the hour presented communicates a perception of the supervisor evoked at the previous meeting by the postmeeting Semmelweis story. The patient's story is about a depressed, suicidal, middle-aged man who feels alone. His outpouring to Judy, and its effects on her, reflect the therapist's feelings about the supervisor's similar unburdening. The process notes present an image of the discussion as inappropriate and one-sided, and as serving the needs of the supervisor at the expense of the supervisee. Judy's story also represents (in the long, passionate kiss) the unconscious eroticized aspect of the supervision, and the supervisee's feeling of being sexually abused. The image of a man who sent dog shit to his girlfriend conveys the aggressive instinct, a comment on the way in which the Semmelweis story was delivered.

Finally, the process notes present a model of rectification for the supervisor: to return to therapy and to straighten out his money problems.

Besides illustrating the derivative meanings in the patient's material, this case demonstrates the therapist's unconscious use of the therapy hour to work over the supervisor's problem and its influence on her interaction with the patient.

The therapist, at the end of the session, felt compelled to make a statement to the patient that was more appropriately aimed at the supervisor. The supervisory adaptive context from the previous meeting was so highly charged for the therapist that when the image of the suicidal man emerged in the patient's material, the therapist lost sight of the patient in favor of her material's associative value in working over the supervision. When read back to the supervisor, the intervention becomes a verbatim (albeit unconscious) interpretation to the supervisor.

CONCLUSIONS

The material presented shows that, when under stress, a supervisee provides a supervisor with encoded material concerning the supervisor's difficulties. The supervisor who can decode the supervisee's derivative communications as expressed in the selected process note material can then reevaluate his or her own work as it is experienced by the supervisee. Blind spots can be resolved and, when needed, the supervisory frame can be restored or properly established. Such an approach allows the supervisor maximum access to unconscious perception in a better understanding of the communicative networks of both the therapeutic and supervisory bipersonal fields.

His or her blind spots may cause the supervisor to offer interventions to the supervisee that focus upon transference and fantasy, whereas the supervisee's derivative communications to the supervisor are based upon nontransference and the realities of the supervisory bipersonal field. Langs (1984) makes a similar observation in describing the distorting elements of a training analysis. This serious rupture in the communicative network between supervisor and supervisee may cause the supervisee to make similar errors in interventions to the patient, thus disrupting the therapeutic communicative network. In this fashion the supervisor's blind spots are transmitted to the patient through the supervisee. The supervisee may then appear to be ineffectual or a slow learner in the work with the patient.

Langs (1979) cautions that the rectification of disruptive inputs by the supervisor must take precedence over teaching. Only through such rectification are the communicative properties of the supervisory bipersonal field restored. Langs says:

> Without rectification . . . the supervisee's anxieties will remain quite intense, his therapeutic work will be essentially countertransferenced based and the supervisory interaction will be infused with disruptive influences. (p. 199)

The process notes offer the supervisor unconscious perceptions of any blind spots and sufficient derivative material to rectify such difficulties. The ongoing monitoring of the process notes allows the supervisor to evaluate his or her inputs for their disruptive potential. By using this awareness to aid in managing the supervisory framework, the supervisor can maintain the focus of supervision upon the supervisee and patient rather than him or herself.

REFERENCES

Langs, R. (1977). *The Therapeutic Interaction. A Syntehsis*. New York: Jason Aronson.

——— (1979). *The Supervisory Experience*. New York: Jason Aronson.

——— (1982). *Psychotherapy: A Basic Text*. New York: Jason Aronson.

——— (1984). The framework of training analyses. *Int. J. Psychoanal. Psychother.*, 10:259–287.

JAMES RANEY, M.D.

Discussion:

The Well-Tempered Supervisor

SEVERAL OF KORN AND CARMIGNANI'S IDEAS ARE DISCUSSED. THEIR CENTRAL IDEA THAT THE MISCONDUCT OF A SUPERVISOR APPEARS IN DERIVATIVES, OR IS SYMBOLIZED IN SELECTED PROCESS NOTES OF THE SUPERVISEE, SEEMS SOUND. PROCESSES IN SUPERVISION SUCH AS THE SUPERVISORY FRAME, PROCESS NOTES AS THE COUNTERPART OF FREE ASSOCIATION, AND THE SUPERVISORY INTROJECT ARE DISCUSSED AND SOME DISAGREEMENTS NOTED. ADDITIONS SUCH AS VALIDATION OF THEIR ASSUMPTIONS AND THE STUDY OF WELL-FUNCTIONING SUPERVISORS ARE SUGGESTED. THE VIEW THAT THIS PRELIMINARY CONTRIBUTION IS POTENTIALLY USEFUL AND SHOULD BE EXTENDED CONCLUDES THIS DISCUSSION.

INTRODUCTION

In their paper on process notes and the supervisory field, Korn and Carmignani reexamine the supervisory process and offer a means by which to determine the hour-by-hour adequacy of supervisory interventions. If they are correct, they have added a useful method to monitor and improve the efficacy of the supervisory behavior and interventions in psychoanalytic supervision. By examining the dynamics of the supervisory process, they disturb a province that is rarely systematically studied, yet is a major part of the development and ongoing career of all therapists (Lewin & Ross, 1960).

Relatively few have written and little is regularly taught about psychoanalytic supervision (Schlesinger, 1981a). A few principles have been outlined in print (Arlow, 1963; Langs, 1979), but otherwise supervisory methodology is learned through example, in a preceptor situation, or through conferences of supervisors (Lewin & Ross, 1960). The result may be that supervisors, especially those outside the inner councils of psychoanalytic institutes, tend to be idiosyncratic about supervision (Schlesinger, 1981a); more so even than they might be as therapists in their work with patients. Articles and studies of the supervisory process may also be rare because supervisors, like therapists, are reluctant to have their personal idiosyncracies exposed. Most authors, brave enough to expose their supervisory work, have reported examples that appear to be their own. Korn and Carmignani may have provided some objectivity, or at least another useful perspective, as they appear to have observed supervisors other than themselves.

In their paper Korn and Carmignani reiterate a perspective that psychotherapy supervision is a bipersonal field that is analogous to that of psychotherapy (see also Searles, 1955; Arlow, 1963; Langs, 1979; Schlesinger, 1981a). They consider the supervisee's commentary in this charged field to be a complex, many-layered communication that is the counterpart of free association in therapy. Their perspective that process notes are selected as an unconsciously directed commentary that can be used by the alert supervisor to monitor the efficacy of his or her functioning should enhance further study of the supervisory process.

DISCUSSION

I have some suggestions to make about the study and several minor disagreements with the authors.

1. I agree that both supervisory and therapy frames require a fixed location, and set fees, hours, and length of session. Total confidentiality and relative autonomy of the supervisor and therapist are mandatory for optimum learning and development of the supervisee (see also Gedo, 1984). I do not entirely agree with some specifics of the authors' view that the supervisory frame and the therapeutic frame share some components and do not share others.

Confidentiality and autonomy of the supervisor seem logical even though nonexistent in most supervisory situations. For example, training institutions and clinics use supervisors with administrative responsibilities that are counter to each of these desirable qualities. Although these and other components of the ideal supervisory situation make common sense, we need more evidence of their value than Korn and Carmignani provide.

The supervisory and therapy situations do not differ *in essence* in the employment of the *rule of abstinence* or in the phenomenon of *free association* as much as the authors suggest. The rule of abstinence is a relative concept, and in therapy means that the therapist does not directly gratify the libidinal wishes of the patient. The therapist instead fulfills the primary function of interpretation (Laplanche & Pontalis, 1973). The rule of abstinence means only that the therapist function in a fashion appropriate to the therapy circumstances. Therapists, for example, do not share personal revelations, social discourse, and the like—and as a general rule, neither should supervisors. Despite the authors' assertion that the supervisory field allows some "informal exchange between supervisor and supervisee appropriate to colleagues," any exchange in supervision should be congruent with the supervisory task. Further clarification of this statement is needed.

The authors suggest that the supervisee unconsciously identifies with the supervisor. Because identification could include identifications with aspects of the supervisor that are more subtle than his or her supervisory interventions—for example, the supervisory process itself or variations from the supervisory rule of abstinence—the definition of *abstinence* (as well as other aspects of the supervisory frame) should be clearer.

I believe that there are more similarities than differences between free association in therapy and the presentation of process notes in supervision, especially if unconscious motives and processes are taken into account. The authors write, "Because the supervisory field does not allow for the free associations of the supervisee and it is not designed for the supervisee's therapy, the play space is more restricted." (I assume the metaphor "play space" connotes the range of expressive license of the supervisee.) The design of the supervision does not restrain the unconscious of the supervisee as much as seems implied. Their first case vignette, in which the supervisee's derivatives were as rich and evocative as any that appear in therapy, contradicts this thesis.

The supervisee comes to supervision with an unconscious motivation for libidinal gratification, a motivation that is similar in patients attending therapy and in other persons anticipating virtually any relationship. The supervisee is, therefore, unconsciously motivated to adapt to the supervisor in accordance with transference and experiential vicissitudes (Langs's "madness") to obtain these gratifications. Therapists may selectively record process notes and make interventions in the therapy, where the material for the process notes is generated, to accomplish this unconscious goal. The ego, in effect, seeks out or creates subject matter to discuss. The possibilities are extensive. Arlow (1963) and others have noted that therapy and supervision have similar dynamics, although Arlow did not recognize the bipersonality of the therapy or supervisory field in 1963. The patient endeavors to adapt to perceived requirements of the therapist by utilizing an idiosyncratic interpretation of the basic rule of free association. This process results in interpretable derivatives. Psychoanalytic supervisees provide derivatives of their unconscious perception and processing in their variations and selected aspects of the process notes.

Derivatives of supervisees differ in that they are technically not interpretable, nor should they be interpreted. While the supervisee's basic rule is to present process notes, such notes are not restricting in an absolute sense. Process notes are selectively recalled, written, and presented with the transferences of the patient, the transferences of the therapist, and the perception of the supervisor "in mind." The "play" of the supervisee is limited only by the supervisee's ingenuity in utilizing the rule. Presented notes are also subject to displacement, symbolization, condensation, and even considerations of representability. The range of subjects is more restricted in one hour of material as opposed to a lifetime of memories, but the therapist/supervisee nevertheless has some ability to manipulate the material, with interventions in the therapy sessions as well as selective recall of the material to suit the unconscious communication to the supervisor. Much of the supervisee's presentation has a type C quality because there is no direct representation of the adaptive context. Therefore, the supervisor's primary responses to derivatives that concern him or her are frame rectifications (Langs, 1982), or responses in spirit (Searles, 1962), rather than direct interpretations. The optimum outcome is increasingly congruent conscious and unconscious communication. This congruence appears as fewer omissions of important sequences and clear material that are increasingly more that of the patient than that of the therapist or supervisor. The manifest presentation is clarified as it is less complicated by the unconscious processes and communication.

A good supervisor attends to the unconscious libidinal wishes implicitly by holding out good regard and positive expectations for the supervisee without compromising the reality of problems with cases. Direct gratification of the wishes is sidestepped. Sublimation in the form of listening and interpretive tools needed to be a more effective professional are provided instead. Supervisory interventions symbolize a backdrop of loving regard and are sublimated gratifications of the instinctual wishes. When a bond of good regard is established, which is the supervision equivalent of the therapeutic alliance, the hard part, the often hurtful narcissistically deflating and sometimes disillusioning work around the cognitive and technical deficiencies of the student, can be more smoothly accomplished. This is further foundation for the perspectives offered in this paper.

Inevitable ruptures of the free flow of associations occur in therapy that are often prompted by transference-based resistances or inteferences of the therapist. These ruptures are intervention points in therapy. A similar dynamic produces ruptures in the understanding of the supervisee, and also provides intervention points for the supervisor.

2. In their description of the dynamics of the supervisory relationship, the authors seem to restrict their view, or confuse my view, by mixing levels of analogies and metaphors. Two metaphors are unnecessary and misleading. These are: "The supervisee is divided between the supervisory field and the therapeutic field" and, referring to Langs (1979), in supervision "These two bipersonal fields [therapy and supervision] intersect." In the therapy situation, references to other people, including spouses, lovers, and parents, are heard as metaphors or derivatives of the bipersonal field. The intersecting metaphor could be applied then to therapy as well, but would have no utility. Supervisory listening to process notes can be better described as having two separate perspectives: first, listening to content for supervisory interventions; and second, listening to metaphor to monitor the well-being of supervisory work.

3. The authors review the important goals of supervision: (a) the broadening of the supervisee's theoretical and technical education through analysis and the understanding of the therapeutic interaction; and (b) a major aspect of the supervisory experience, the introjection by the student of the role model of the supervisor. To provide a sufficient but not exclusive (i.e., not overly conforming) identification (Fleming & Benedek, 1966), it behooves the supervisor to have been well analyzed in order to manage the supervisory situation well, and to have the capacity to project a benevolent and expectant identification "into" the supervisee. The benevolent introjection of a positive supervisor is a major goal of the supervisory experience. The introjection and identification with a well-functioning therapist are a major component of therapy as well. This paper gives examples of supervisors who provide deficient introjects and identification models.

I would like to have seen examples of well-functioning supervisors who, if the authors' thesis is correct, would supply useful and positive introjects to facilitate the consolidation of the supervisee's professional identification. Examination of several supervisory sequences in Wallerstein (1981), however, hint that tracking derivatives of good, or at least less obviously disturbed, supervisors would be a very difficult study, because the derivatives seem to be more obscure. Perhaps this should be a separate study. I found support for the authors' thesis in another example from Schlesinger. In this vignette a supervisor was undecided as to whether he wanted to take on a particular supervisee. One of the initial problems in the case was the supervisee's difficulties in arranging time to begin the analysis with his patient. This enactment may have reflected the supervisee's unconscious awareness of the supervisor's reluctance to see him (Schlesinger, 1981b, p. 287).

4. There is another very important field present in most supervisions. Most supervisees have a current or very recent personal analysis that creates a supervisor–supervisee–analyst configuration that could also bear further examination from Korn and Carmignani's communicative perspective (Searles, 1962; Fleming & Benedek, 1966; Langs, 1979). Langs has suggested a fourth bipersonal field when the supervisor is also in analysis (Langs, 1979). Arlow (1963) and Schlesinger (1981a) add the potential for a fifth in their discussions of the relationships of each participant to the training institution in which the supervision may be taking place.

The supervisor's similarities to the supervisee's personal therapist, especially when both belong to the same training institution, and may even have communication with each other, can create a division or a splitting of the supervisee's transference. The supervisor may inadvertently gratify the wishes that are stimulated or uncovered in the supervisee's personal therapy. Especially when a negative transference is in place with the supervisee's therapist, the supervisor may be the object of a displaced positive or need-gratifying transference. The supervisor may reciprocate with a displacement from some difficulty with an analysand of his or her own (Searles, 1962). The potential for splitting the supervisee's transference between the therapist and supervisor (and the reverse) in such a situation is a major justification for the stringency of the supervisory frame. This does not mean a coldness or rigidity. The supervisor is inherently more gratifying, yet must limit gratifications to empathic observations, suggestions, advice, and technical and theoretical comments, and avoid gratifying and seductive personal revelations and discussion. Adherence to strictures of time, fee, frequency, and so on enhances the inherent message that instinctual gratifications will be sublimated to the primary supervisory intervention function.

5. Finally, an enthusiastic but one-sided employment of this communicative perspective in the supervisory field might distract from the fact that some people are ill suited for the defined and demanding role of analytic therapist (Ekstein, 1960; Gedo, 1984). How to distinguish the real problems of unsuitable therapists from deficiencies in supervision is a serious matter for further study. Korn and Carmignani may have provided an important foundation for this critical and difficult task.

THE CASE ILLUSTRATIONS

First Case

The first vignette is a brief and striking example that illustrates the similarity of free association and case reporting. The student's association to a case vignette that was a telling derivative of his unconscious perception and working over of the supervisor's behavior exemplifies the rich "free association" that is possible in supervision, enhanced perhaps by the group setting (Durkin, 1964, pp. 134–135).

Second Case

The next vignette is less clear. In this example three sessions of a therapy were presented to an insensitive, arrogant, and exhibitionistic supervisor. The authors predicted that the student would select process notes that would refer to derivative communication about the therapist's own feelings about returning to a student role and specific adaptive contexts of the supervisor's teaching abilities, positive aspects of his presentation at the meeting, his negative and powerfully controlling ways, his dominating presence, his handling of the fee for supervision, and his discussion of his financial problems.

The only prediction that was supported was that of the appearance of communications relating to money problems. The supervisor's fee change and financial problems may have appeared in the derivatives of the therapist changing his mode of collection and in the patient introducing the possibility of a reduced fee. The latter might also have reflected the therapist's wish for a lesser fee. The therapist's difficulties that dominated the therapy field are too general to qualify as a specific derivative of the supervisor's difficulties. In supervision all therapists present cases in which their difficulties dominate the field.

The authors might have discussed why the other predictions were not realized and why the unpredicted exhibitionistic derivatives appeared. In the scientific method, one makes assumptions, but must entertain the possibility of other assumptions, as well. When the data suggest compelling hypotheses that differ from predictions, further hypotheses and observations must be made.

Third Case

The third example is somewhat vague. The unique element appears to be the personal revelation of the supervisor and his parapraxis about the suicide of Semmelweis. The authors propose that, as in the therapy bipersonal field, variations in the secure supervisory frame (.e.g., the self-revelation in their example) are followed by derivatives that are organized around the perception of the variation. More specific predictions might have been made prior to the supervision seminar that they described. Had they predicted that the process notes of the next meeting would contain images of depression, isolation, denial, arrogance, and similar qualities that burdened the interaction of this supervisor and his students, and then confirmed these predictions, their exposition would have been significantly improved. If the predictions had not been confirmed, the new data and retrospective conjectures could have been converted into new predictions to be studied in subsequent sessions.

CONCLUSIONS

This preliminary study presents an interesting and potentially useful perspective on the supervisory situation. Further tightly designed studies with predictions, validation, and especially instances in which supervisors "rectify" the supervisory frame would be of great interest. For example, with confirmation of predictions in process notes, rectification (removal) of supervisors' disturbing behavior with examination of subsequent derivative communication could follow. If the authors are correct, derivatives should change in concert with the change in the supervisors' behavior. In case presentations that follow the rectification, derivatives would reflect positive images of empathy, trustworthiness, and the like.

The hypotheses of Korn and Carmignani require further elaboration and study before they can be added to supervisory procedure. Their examples are of clear breaches of the supervisory frame. Whether this perspective is useful in more subtle instances of supervisor error or success remains to be demonstrated. Their ideas are worth considering and can be worked over in each reader's supervisory efforts, whether as supervisor or supervisee. Their work deserves to be elaborated upon and expanded.

REFERENCES

Arlow, J. (1963). The supervisory situation. *J. Amer. Psychoanal. Assn.*, 11:576–594.

Durkin, H. E. (1964). *The Group in Depth*. New York: International Universities Press.

Ekstein, R. (1960). Panel: The teaching of psychoanalytic technique, R. Ekstein, reporter. *J. Amer. Psychoanal. Assn.*, 8:167–174.

Fleming, J., & Benedek, T. F. (1966). *Psychoanalytic Supervision*. New York: Grune & Stratton.

Gedo, J. E. (1984). *Psychoanalysis and Its Discontents*. New York: Guilford.

Langs, R. (1979). *The Supervisory Experience*. New York: Jason Aronson.

——— (1982). *Psychotherapy: A Basic Text*. New York: Jason Aronson.

Laplanche, J., & Pontalis, J.-B. (1973). *The Language of Psychoanalysis*. London: Hogarth Press.

Lewin, B. D., & Ross, H. (1960). *Psychoanalytic Education in the United States*. New York: Norton.

Searles, H. (1955). The informational value of the supervisor's emotional experiences. In *Collected Papers on Schizophrenia and Related Subjects*. New York: International Universities Press, pp. 157–176.

——— (1962). Problems of psychoanalytic supervision. *Sci. Psychoanal.*, 5:197–215.

Schlesinger, H. J. (1981a). General principles of psychoanalytic supervision. In *Becoming a Psychoanalyst*, ed. Robert Wallerstein. New York: International Universities Press.

——— (1981b). On being the supervisor studied: Observations and confessions. In *Becoming a Psychoanalyst*, ed. Robert Wallerstein. New York: International Universities Press.

Waelder, R. (1960). Panel: The teaching of psychoanalytic technique, R. Ekstein, reporter. *J. Amer. Psychoanal. Assn.*, 8:167–174.

Wallerstein, R. S., ed. (1981). *Becoming a Psychoanalyst*. New York: International Universities Press.

6

HOWARD D. KIBEL, M.D.

Inpatient Group Psychotherapy— Where Treatment Philosophies Converge

IT IS CONTENDED THAT MULTIPLE COMPREHENSIVE ASSUMPTIONS UNDERLIE THE USE OF GROUP PSYCHOTHERAPY IN AN INPATIENT SETTING. THE WRITER USES HIS OWN MODEL OF TREATMENT TO DEMONSTRATE HOW SPECIFIC PREMISES AFFECT THE FUNCTION OF THE SMALL THERAPY GROUP AND ITS RELATIONSHIP TO THE TOTAL TREATMENT. GENERAL-SYSTEMS AND OBJECT-RELATIONS THEORIES INFLUENCE THIS APPROACH. BASIC VIEWS ON THE NATURE OF PSYCHOPATHOLOGY ARE EXPLORED; DIFFERENCES IN THIS AREA ACCOUNT FOR MUCH OF THE VARIATION FOUND IN ACTUAL PRACTICE.

The purpose of this paper is to demonstrate the multifarious treatment orientations employed by the inpatient group psychotherapist. Specific, manifold viewpoints guide the behavior of all therapists, even those who profess to be eclectic. This concept is known to apply to outpatient groups.

THE DILEMMA OF THE THERAPIST

Groups are complex entities. To be effective, psychotherapists must give selective attention to the sundry elements of group life. Viewed in one way, the therapist chooses among three classes of configurations that phenomenologically describe the members' emotional attachments within the group. The focus may be on the individual within the group, on subgroups or member dyads, or on the group as a unit (Parloff, 1968). These may be said to describe a *horizontal* continuum, proceeding from a focus on the individual to a view of the group as a dynamic system. In contrast, the group can be viewed as an entity with a depth psychology of its own. Bion (1959) was representative of this view. He postulated the simultaneous existence, within the group, of several primitive and mature levels of functioning. Such a theory of groups can be diagrammed *vertically*.

The foregoing contrast between these so-called horizontal and vertical dimensions of group dynamics dramatizes the dilemma for the therapist. It is impossible to pay attention simultaneously to all facets of group life. Any attempt to do so overloads the therapist with data, resulting in paralysis. Kernberg (1975) put this another way. He visualized the dynamic components of a group as an amalgam of nonconcentric circles. In general-systems terms, the separate systems of the group cannot be reduced to a unified whole. The therapist's interventions at one dynamic level of the group will have uncertain and unpredictable effects on its other systems. For this reason interventions in groups, unlike those in individual psychoanalytic treatment, do not readily yield feedback that confirms their effectiveness. At any point in time, the therapist is often left in a quandary as to whether the interventions have facilitated or impeded the treatment and the group's progress.

Every therapist deals with these complexities of group life by discriminantly focusing on only certain of its elements. Given that selective attention is both required and used, the therapist's interventions are inevitably derived from his or her treatment philosophy. This is not only influenced by the therapist's view of the mutative forces in groups, but ultimately by his or her notion of the very nature of psychopathology, as discussed later.

When conducting an inpatient group, the problems of the therapist are compounded because the dimensions of such groups are more numerous; that is, the context influences the group in a multiplicity of ways (Klein, 1977). The milieu—that is, the organization of the psychiatric unit, its administrative structures, and the nature of the overall treatment program—has a vital impact on the course of therapy in the group. Consequently the therapist's scope of observation must extend beyond the group itself to the entire unit, and even sometimes to institutional influences, in order to appreciate the reciprocal relationship between the group and its environment. From this perspective the small therapy group can be understood as a subgroup of larger systems, which are highly influential.

Within the group itself, validation of one's interventions by either feedback or long-term analysis of process is limited by patient turnover and by a milieu that is in a state of constant flux. These curb the group's development into a stable, cohesive entity. For this reason techniques for inpatient group psychotherapy have emerged generally from clinical intuition rather than from well-tested assumptions.

There are additional complicating factors. Consider the existing diverse opinions about inpatient treatment, apart from their application to the small group. Even with analytically oriented treatments of patients with severe psychopathology, diverse methods are employed, which are based on various nuances of theory. Since these disorders presumably harken to preverbal experiences, dynamic theories of origin rest upon high degrees of inference, and perhaps even hunches or beliefs. Theory that is barely open to verification or refutation is still highly influential on technique (Friedman, 1975).

When inpatient group therapy functions coherently within a psychiatric unit, there exists an implicit harmony between multiple assumptions underlying treatment in the small group and in the system at large. In both instances selective attention is paid to similar aspects of collective life. The goals of each are consonant with one another when their respective views on the nature of psychopathology and the function of inpatient treatment are in accord.

In the remainder of this paper, a model for inpatient group psychotherapy, which was previously presented (Kibel, 1981), will be restated. Its articulation here will illustrate how several underlying assumptions determine its method. Others who work in this field, it is hoped, will examine their own methods in a similar vein. Specific attention will be given to the dynamic exchanges between the small group and its milieu, an analytic view of inpatient treatment, some unique qualities of the small therapy group, and a particular object-relations view of psychopathology. Clinical examples will be used to illustrate these facets of treatment. The illustrations are drawn from sessions conducted on several units of a large psychiatric hospital. Some of these units are short term (i.e., with a length of stay averaging four weeks), but others provide intermediate care (i.e., a length of stay of three to six months). Typically these inpatient groups comprise eight to 12 patients, and meet two or three times per week for 45 to 60-minute sessions. Almost all patients attend group psychotherapy. They are generally assigned to the group according to their membership on a particular treatment team. Usually the groups are conducted by cotherapists, who are also members of the team.

They are often trainees, but may be members of the permanent staff. Some of these groups have silent observers, who are also on that team (Oldham, 1982). In any case the structure of these groups emphasizes the integration of group psychotherapy with the overall treatment in the milieu. Variations in structure, from unit to unit, reflect the unit's history and nuances of its treatment orientation.

THE SMALL THERAPY GROUP AS A SUBGROUP

From a general-systems perspective, an organization such as a hospital is conceived of as an overall system, dynamically and hierarchically integrating its component subsystems, such as the administrative structures of the institution, its clinical and professional divisions, and each treatment unit (Kernberg, 1978). The hierarchy of these systems spans boundaries from the environment, at the periphery, through the entire organization to the individual member. At the interface of systems, transactions, exchanges, and mutual influences occur to the degree that the boundaries of each are permeable. Studies of small therapy groups on psychiatric units indicate that the boundaries between these two are readily permeable. Klein (1977) reviewed a series of experimental studies that provided "evidence that the social system, with its norms, expectations and values plays a particularly important role in determining patient behavior in group meetings and has a significant impact on the therapeutic process" (p. 201). The highly influential social system of the psychiatric unit cannot be ignored. As Astrachan (1970) noted, "Without an appreciation of the impact of the structure of the therapy on patient behavior, the temptation is to perceive the patient's behavior as individually determined, be it conscious or unconscious, and to ignore the manner in which the setting facilitates or inhibits feelings and actions" (p. 114).

A psychiatric unit, as any large group, is subject to regressive forces that find behavioral expression among the patients (Stanton & Schwartz, 1954). Whenever patients congregate, shared tensions will be acted out. These are reflected in the small therapy group. Thus the therapy group can be seen as a biopsy of the milieu within which it resides (Levine, 1980). Conversely, events in the small therapy group symbolically reflect the dynamics of the unit as a whole. Therapeutic use of such interdependence will be discussed later. For now it is sufficient to reflect only on the manner in which a systems perspective influences one's selective attention to the myriad of meanings conveyed in the material of a group session. The following example illustrates this point.

Vignette 1

This is a report of the first 15 minutes of an inpatient group, conducted on a Monday morning. At the outset one of the therapists announced that he would be rotating out of the group the following week. (This was anticipated. The periodic interchange of therapists and observers is one of the unit's traditional practices.) His announcement was ignored. At first the tempo of the session was slow, but it soon gained momentum. A few members sluggishly remarked that on weekends life on the unit was tedious. One member suggested that weekend activities could relieve the monotony. Several offered some practical suggestions, and soon most members were vigorously discussing plans to initiate a weekend activity program. In the midst of this frenzy, worry crept in. Several were concerned that it would be difficult to involve the more passive and withdrawn patients. At first they merely lamented the latter's seclusiveness, but soon the inertia in these patients became a collective obsession. Members offered the notion that passivity could have a negative therapeutic effect. They worried that it could aggravate emotional disorders, implying that the consequences might be dangerous. Nonverbally, the patients moved from active interchange with one another, when planning for activities, to taking fleeting glances at the therapists, when indicating that passivity could be dangerous.

Discussion

This material becomes comprehensible when seen against the backdrop of the unit as a whole. During the preceding weekend, a disturbing incident had occurred. A manic patient had assaulted a passive, withdrawn one. Both were men. The former was a strong, vigorous, and menacing individual, while the latter was confused and had previously verbalized fears of being raped. The manic patient had grabbed the young man in a sexual embrace, jumped on him, and bit him on the shoulder.

Clearly this incident terrified everyone else. By means of the group session, the members were metaphorically communicating their anxieties. They identified with the ostensible victim, in this instance. Their complaints about the weekend emanated from a sense of being unprotected by the staff. As if forced to fend for themselves, the members tried to arrange activities; as an organized group, they could provide mutual protection. Discussing this temporarily provided them with a sense of mastery and a false sense of security, and served to deny their realistic fears. However, once their concern was expressed for those passive patients who would be reluctant to participate, their fears returned. They once again identified with the apparent victim and looked to the therapists for protection.

This instance demonstrates the unique contribution of a general-systems perspective; specifically, how it alters one's view of the material. With only a narrow focus on the group itself, one might easily misinterpret the content as reflecting only the transference[1] that was stimulated by the opening announcement, or as comprising resistance to the exploration of other material. Viewed against the backdrop of the milieu, one can appreciate that these patients were attempting to cope with some realistic stresses of hospital life.

Certainly transference always stimulates process and content, but so do actual events. Realistically, inpatients are highly dependent upon their environment. The other patients, nursing staff, social workers, therapists, and administrators impact in crucial ways on these patients' present well-being and administratively determine their immediate future. For this reason reality has a powerful impact on the process and content of these groups, more so than in outpatient groups. The dynamics traditionally ascribed to small groups, in this situation, are overwhelmed and overshadowed by those of the unit. They still operate to shape the process so that ambient influences and small group dynamics converge in the content of any particular session. The therapist uses the latter to facilitate an understanding of the clinical material, but uses the former to facilitate the patients' understanding of the contextual meaning of their experience in the group, as described later. In this example the rotation

[1]Classically transference has been used to denote an unconscious phenomenon in which feelings, attitudes, and wishes originally linked with important figures in one's early life are projected onto significant others in current life. When working with patients with severe psychopathology, who use splitting rather than repression and who use projection quite freely, it becomes necessary to broaden the use of this term. Here it refers to that facet of any therapeutic relationship into which the patient projects and/or reenacts a significant aspect of his or her internal world of objects. In other words, it refers to the pathologically contaminated part of the relationship. In this paper, unless otherwise indicated, it is used to refer to the relationship of the patient(s) with the group therapist, not to the relationships among the group members.

of the therapist stimulated the patients' fear of abandonment by their protectors. Since he was merely rotating from the group to the observers' circle, to be replaced by one of the current observers (i.e., since he would still be in the group room and his overall influence as a member of the treatment team would remain basically the same), this action was affectively far less immediate than the weekend's events.

A FUNCTIONAL VIEW OF INPATIENT TREATMENT

According to analytic models of hospital treatment, conflicted, primitive, internal object relationships are reenacted within the interpersonal field of the hospital milieu. This affords new opportunities for diagnosis, but more important, primitive object relations can be gradually influenced by confrontation, explanation, and clarification (Kernberg, 1976a). This is easier said than done.

An inpatient atmosphere of neutrality and benign ministration is difficult to achieve. Hospital systems are fraught with tensions (Borriello, 1976), derived in part from organizational stress and in part from the very reenactment of the internal conflicts we aim to treat. Patients use one another and the staff as objects for projective identification. Reactive responses of the recipients cause projective counteridentifications, as Grinberg (1973) termed it, to resonate throughout the unit. The result is a complex of patterns of introjective–projective relatedness (Volkan, 1976). In other words, a matrix of primitive identifications infiltrates and enmeshes the milieu.

Another way to view tensions on the unit relates to the ambiguities inherent in the staff's therapeutic role and in the patient role. If we consider the psychiatric unit to be a large group, we recognize that ambiguity and an impersonal social system are sufficient to induce massive regression. In fact, in anyone—and particularly in those with severe character pathology, such as borderline conditions and psychotic disorders—when ordinary social structure is lost and the usual social roles are abrogated, primitive levels of psychological functioning emerge. For these patients, when multiple objects are simultaneously present in a relatively unstructured setting, the potential for acting out increases geometrically, and can even run amok. Therefore, the challenge for inpatient treatment is to contain acting out within manageable limits and, without regimentation, to explore therapeutically a matrix of primitive identifications. One also must nurture, simultaneously, the neutrality of the hospital atmosphere, that is, the experience of the unit as a whole as sort of a sanctuary. The small therapy group is ideally suited to this endeavor.

The traditional analytic model of hospital treatment uses the interpersonal field of the inpatient milieu as an object of investigation. This same modified here-and-now approach is appropriate for the small therapy group. Thus, stemming from a general-systems perspective, the object of inquiry in the group should be the here-and-now of the milieu or, in short, the hospital experience. For most patients this approach optimally titrates the level of anxiety tolerance in a group. An intragroup transference focus is usually too intense for inpatients (except when treatment is long term, the group is stable, or the pathology is less severe). A genetic focus may further the opening of regressive channels, thereby unraveling rudimentary defenses even more. In contrast, a there-and-now focus, so common in hospital groups (e.g., "what happened out there to cause you to come in here?") is mortifying, narcissistically injurious, or, at best, allows patients defensively to project blame. For most patients the concrete experience of hospital life is affectively immediate, readily available, and cognizable.

An appreciation of the effects of hospital life on one's emotions or behavior is enormously therapeutic. In general it converts the experience of hospitalization from a disturbing, or even frightening, one into a soothing one. For borderline patients clarification of milieu issues can lay fertile ground for interpersonal learning. Each individual can then use the group or individual therapy to examine his or her own participation in the process. For psychotic patients clarification demystifies the experience of their immediate world, with the hospital used as a paradigm of living. Understanding provides a sense of mastery. Clarification helps to create order out of chaotic experiences. In group sessions explanatory interventions should be stated in a manner that conveys to the patients the idea that their symptoms and disordered internal experiences, while unique in their form and intensity, are reactive to the environment, analogous to the response of normal individuals. In short, this method promulgates the notion that what seems incomprehensible and frightening is actually understandable.

While the earlier example demonstrated the necessity to look beyond the small group to understand its contents, the following example demonstrates that the here-and-now of the milieu is affectively meaningful.

Vignette 2

Early in the session, members talked briefly about a hospital talent show that had taken place the previous evening. One man was commended for his performance. Then another member asked the therapists if patients were permitted to read their own charts. One therapist asked the members what they wished to learn from their charts, and an active discussion ensued. Several expressed interest in reading their diagnoses (which are traditionally shared on this unit during individual sessions). One individual wondered if he had a split personality; another feared that an ability to perform on stage was indicative of a split in personality; others described someone with a split personality as one who acts in a manner that is alien to that person.

The focus of the discussion shifted to people who were not labeled mentally ill. This was prompted by a remark that everyone is somewhat neurotic. The patients began to share impressions of family members and other nonpatients, all of whom allegedly possessed neurotic traits. They tended to blame parents for their ills and mocked these others, whom they labeled neurotic. However, the members were drawn back to their concerns about their own behavior. They shared information about their own alterations of mood and certain disturbing behaviors. In general they were mutually reassuring that these seemed rather normal. From here, the patients began to give each other feedback on a variety of behaviors, as if each were advising the other to change. As particular individuals became the focus of discussion, the subject of the talent show reappeared. What now emerged quite clearly was that there had been a rivalry between two women to perform with the man who was commended earlier. Specifically, one of the women had convinced the man to abandon a tentative commitment to perform with the second, in favor of her. This rivalry, a triangulation, stood out as the session ended.

Discussion

This material can be viewed in a variety of ways. The first mention of the talent show could be seen as signaling the presence of concealed rivalries among the group members. The members' examination of each other's behavior, the feedback, and the encouragement to change could be seen as productive efforts by the patients to help each other modify maladaptive behavior. Yet recurring themes that reflected the members' concerns with self-image could be understood as an expression of the transference vis-à-vis the therapists, induced by experiences in the small therapy group.

Against a backdrop of current hospital life, the group material can be interpreted differently. In recent weeks there was a notable disparity in sessions between the more verbal members and the less verbal ones. This was noted spontaneously by the patients, with each subgroup expressing a similar concern, namely, that they had said or might say the wrong thing. At this time the majority of members were either involved in or approaching the discharge-planning phase of hospitalization. Yet all were engaged in some sort of reality-oriented struggle over treatment: some patients were pressing their therapists to hasten discharge, some were resisting referrals to structured environments, such as a halfway house, and some were protesting their status as involuntary patients.

With this information on hand, the session took on additional, broader meaning. The preoccupation with the talent show could be said to reflect the members' concerns about their "performance" in the group, that is, it is as if they were "on stage" and undergoing continuous evaluation by the therapists (and the observers, who are also part of the same treatment team). Many of the interactions that seemed to have been productive of mutual feedback were really part of this collective performance. They constituted resistance in the sense that they obscured the central conflict within the overall system of treatment. The phenomenon of rivalry, in this context, represented a retreat and displacement from their anxieties vis-à-vis the entire treatment team. It was understandable, then, that the patients felt as if they had some sort of split personality; they were in a dilemma, caught between their wish to talk and a defense of silence, between engaging in order to look good to the staff and a recognition that talking would reveal the extent of their pathology. Such patients generally have difficulty in exposing their psychopathology, for both narcissistic and paranoid reasons. It is demoralizing and they anticipate an adverse reaction by the staff; awareness of their own pathology is frightening and they often do not trust the staff, in this case with respect to discharge planning.

The therapists' task here is to recognize and verbalize these patients' narcissistic and paranoid concerns. This should be done by clarification of the members' struggles over their current treatment. Clarification should identify the group conflict between their fears of revelation and their wish for help. The restrictive group solution should be explained according to its relation to conscious defenses, such as the shame associated with self-exposure and the erroneous ideas concerning staff reactions to psychopathology. This approach not only relieves paranoid fears and corrects a defensive stance, but also paves the way for exposure of the patients' struggles with their therapists and for exploration of their very real dependency needs and fears. The aim, in this instance, is to help the patients negotiate appropriately with their therapists. The actual transactions ultimately take place throughout the milieu, for example, within the context of discharge planning. In group sessions, following repeated clarification of central conflicts within the overall treatment, patients reveal much more of themselves. They discuss their concerns more freely and explore a gamut of inner attitudes about the group therapists. Thus the process of investigation of the interpersonal field in the milieu moves freely and salubriously from the small therapy group to the larger system at hand.

In short, as we have indicated, the treatment setting, in a variety of ways, induces regression in patients. In the therapy group, clarification of this experience demystifies it, and thereby facilitates partial reintegration. Inherent properties of both the patients' psychopathology and large group dynamics combine to cause this sequence to be repeated over and over. However, such regressive–reintegrative cycles are therapeutic in themselves, promoting ego mastery and providing new opportunities for the development of adaptive defenses. The small therapy group operates at the reintegrative phase of these cycles.

UNIQUE ASPECTS OF GROUP

The literature on group therapy is replete with descriptions of its special therapeutic qualities. Two that are relevant here are the relationship of the members to the group as an entity and the alterations in transference as compared with individual therapy.

Scheidlinger (1974) has described the patients' relationship to the group as an entity as a primitive identification, akin to early patterns of object attachments. When the group entity is perceived in a positive and benign vein, it functions as a nurturing and need-gratifying object, thereby facilitating safe exposure of conflicted internal relationships. In this instance, "the group leader and the other members become . . . the objects of a gamut of partially ambivalent but largely hostile and fearful attitudes" (p. 425). This dichotomy is available as an avenue for the therapeutic expression of splitting.

Mutual identification with a group imago serves the development of cohesiveness and the therapeutic alliance. The therapist can foster the evolution of a positive group introject by respecting the members, tolerating their incoherence, and being willing to provide the kind of support that encourages both participation and risk-taking, while protecting the group from disruption. Interventions should be generally nonconfrontive, but accentuate the cohering aspects of the group and the universality among its members. Once created, the "good" group image serves as sort of a protective umbrella under which a host of noxious and fearful attitudes can be expressed.

Cohesion is promoted when the therapist focuses attention on the common concerns of the members, be they inside or outside the group. Likewise it is enhanced when major interventions, such as groupwide clarifications, are directed toward the group as a whole. The experience of mutuality among the patients binds together their separate "good" self-images into one supportive unit. Herein lies the rationale for a relatively group-centered technique.

The following example demonstrates the coalescence of group members after grappling with some shared concerns of hospital life. Once cohesion was attained, the patients revealed pertinent and poignant aspects of their experience. The process was facilitated because the group therapist, in this instance, supported the integrity of the group.

Vignette 3

At the beginning of the session, one patient talked about her case conference, which had just ended. (This meeting, a standard evaluation practice of this unit, included an interview with the patient by a visiting consultant. The interview was conducted before the entire staff.) A new member asked the others for an explanation of the purpose and substance of this meeting. Although most had been through this procedure, none could provide one. The few statements that emerged suggested that the patients found the conference stressful.

In the midst of this discussion, a latecomer entered the room. This man sat on the periphery of the group circle, apart from all others. When invited by the group therapists to move closer, he gruffly refused. At first the other group members seemed afraid of him. Consequently the therapists asked them a series of questions, all of which were designed to get them to talk with the latecomer. During this sequence one therapist hinted that recent events might be germane to the immediate situation. With this support from the group leaders, the members revealed a possible precipitating event. On the previous evening, this man had become unreasonably angry at another (nongroup) patient, who appropriately asserted her right to use the public telephone. The man refused to yield usage, and became vituperous, verbally abusive, and intimidating. The group members agreed that this incident frightened everyone. With support from the therapists, the patients gradually engaged the man. Through empathic questions and statements of commonality, the members helped him to say that he was lonely and frightened, and clung to the phone as if it were a lifeline to a salutory world outside. At this point the members could empathize with him. The discussion enabled them to move from a position of intimidation, via expression of sympathy, to bold confrontation, as they connected his menacing behavior of the previous evening to the precipitants for his current hospitalization. Likewise, the man moved from a position of defiance and detachment to one of integration into the group.

A pause followed, after which one of the therapists invited the patients to reopen the first topic of the session. This time the explanation of the case conference was clear and meaningful. When asked what it was like to be interviewed, the members responded expressively. They spoke eloquently about feeling shame, fear, and resentment. Through mutual encouragement these patients explored many facets of the experience. Then one of the therapists drew an analogy between the case conference and that day's group session. In both instances they initially felt frightened and resentful; yet in both they managed to communicate effectively. As if in response to this intervention, one of the patients remarked, "If we can live here with each other's problems, why can't others, our family and friends, live with them?" With a sense of amazement the members concurred. They noted that varieties of pathological comportment, while intolerable to much of society, were endured and negotiated by those in the hospital. During this phase of the session, the patients revealed a gamut of pathological behaviors.

Discussion

Events in the treatment environment, because of their realistic importance and immediacy, not only are a focus of patients' concerns, but also become a fulcrum of group interactions. This serves as a basis for the development of cohesion, and ultimately for the expression of both transference reactions and interpersonal conflicts. Transference, in the foregoing example, was stimulated by attention to the case conference, which generally was pivotal to these patients' experience with the treating staff. However, expression of underlying reactions was muffled, as we later learn, by the patients' ambivalent, but largely hostile and fearful, attitudes toward the staff.

The behavior of the latecomer was salient to the rest. He may have embodied their defiant urges and antagonistic potential. Yet, we can speculate, he simultaneously served as a focus for displacement of awesome transference images. By successfully engaging him, the membership coalesced, and, in a small way, dissipated a paranoid aspect of the transference. The process was facilitated by the therapist's interventions. Simultaneously the therapist demonstrated that he cared and that the latecomer was approachable. Once all this was accomplished, the patients were able to discuss their reactions to the case conference in a more revealing way; they were no longer oppressed by a fantasy of retaliation. Under the protection of a benign group image, they divulged more of the behavioral aspects of their psychopathology. The development of cohesion was pivotal to this process.

A group-centered technique reaps benefits in terms of therapist transference by furthering its dilution. Patients with severe psychopathology can falter in a dyadic psychotherapy relationship, especially when they have to rely on the therapist (and associated staff members) for maintenance of the environment and assistance with decisions that will be crucial to their future (Gootnick, 1971). In a dyadic relationship, the therapist is potentially the recipient of omnipotent and sadistic object projections. In a therapy group, mutuality permits a merging of the members' separate self-images, thereby reducing fearful attitudes toward the therapist. A technique that stresses commonalities fosters the sense of mutuality. Through such a partial, therapeutic merger, the group entity serves, for each member, as a buffer against the awesomeness of transference.

The collective relationship with the group therapist will, by virtue of his or her association with the treatment team, bear heavily on the members' response to their overall treatment. In a general-systems sense, the group therapist serves as sort of a gatekeeper of the boundary between the small group and the treating staff. This boundary must be permeable enough to allow transactions to occur, yet strong enough to maintain the mutual integrity of the staff and patient groups. Information must flow back and forth between these two, while their respective roles remain well defined.

The following example demonstrates the nodal position of the group therapist as an extension of the entire treatment team in the eyes of the patients.

Vignette 4

At the start of this session, the patients joked about their individual psychotherapists by drawing analogies to characters from "Star Trek." The therapists were caricatured as Spock. Patient M. referred to her therapist as "Spockitch." The group members laughed heartily. Another patient playfully challenged M. to "get out of that one." Obviously this joke consisted of a pun that made reference to the crotch. What was known to all, but unsaid, was that the group therapist, a female psychiatric resident, had a name that lent itself to puns of a similar nature.

Following the challenge, several members began to talk rapidly and conversations intruded on one another. Patient G., whose both parents are physicians, began to cry. She attempted to leave the session, but was successfully coaxed into staying by the therapist. The members tried to soothe G., and offered sympathy and support, although the nature of her distress remained unspecified. Next the patients began to identify with her and compared her suffering to memories of their own torment. They alluded to their own neediness, but switched the focus to the alleged impoverishment of the physically handicapped. At one point patient M. described crippled patients "without arms and legs, who were truly needy." From here on the content was fragmented; different members spoke of a loss of a sense of identity, a belief that they were a burden to others, and terror during previous states of anguish. Others exhorted their peers to "pull themselves together."

Discussion

The traditional interpretation of this material, such as with an outpatient group, would consider the initial caricature of the individual psychotherapists as a displacement from the transference within the group. However, additional considerations are required for inpatient treatment, particularly in this case, since this therapist was peripherally involved with this unit. (She did not have administrative responsibility in these patients' treatment, unlike in the other examples used in this paper.) Also, the group met only once each week and its nature was supportive. The individual therapists were definitely more important to these patients, realistically and as transference objects. Therefore, the relationship to the group therapist, in this instance, must be seen as an extension of the more fundamental transference paradigm; that is, through her they were testing reactions that emanated from their individual psychotherapies and permeated other therapeutic encounters.

Given this perspective, the pun on the therapist's name can be seen as a dramatization of comprehensive ambivalence. She served as a focus for complex reactions to treatment, in general. The playful challenge exposed covert hostility toward the group therapist. Despite an evidently positive therapeutic alliance with her, the patients were afraid that she would become angry and retaliate. Patient G., whom we can construe by history was sensitive to enmity toward physicians, was vulnerable to the group's tension and acted out their wish to flee. When the therapist failed to reassure them against their fantasies of retribution, as she might have done through clarification and interpretation of the material, the collective group ego, if you will, deteriorated. An opportunity to work on some of their convoluted treatment reactions was lost. Primitive fantastic group images were condensed into G., at first, and later into M. Gory fantasies revealed that these emerging sadistic images were uncontained. The group had become psychotic-like.

THE NATURE OF PSYCHOPATHOLOGY

Specific techniques of group therapy will be dictated not only by the therapist's perception of the group in relation to the overall treatment system, but also by the therapist's concept of the nature of psychopathology. Each therapist has his or her own particular assumptions about the essential properties of mental disturbances. These form the basis of methodology, explicity or implicity. Articulation of these assumptions (which is not usual) brings coherence to an approach and helps one draw comparisons to others. This notion needs further explication, which will be done from the author's viewpoint and contrasted with others.

Elsewhere (Kibel, 1981) I have articulated an object-relations view of the process of decompensation and reconstitution for patients with both psychotic and borderline ego structures. In brief, decompensation can be conceptualized as a process whereby the central ego core, which is built around positive internalizations, is invaded by its aggressively linked counterpart. Although the degree of disturbance in psychotic and borderline patients differs, their decompensatory processes are comparable. In both instances, in the face of unmetabolized aggression, aggressively linked internal representations are untethered and the ego core or central experience of the self is weakened.

This object-relations view presumes the existence of conflict between opposing aspects of the core of personality. From this perspective a particular view of treatment goals follows. On the one hand, there needs to be what might be called a partial detoxification of aggression in order to diminish its contamination of the so-called "good" ego core by "bad" introjects. On the other hand, simultaneously, there needs to be narcissistic reinforcement of the libidinally linked internal constellation.[2] In the former instance, the self and the external world will be experienced as less frightening, less "bad," and less stressful. In the latter instance, the ego is shored up and unfettered so that latent adaptive functions emerge. According to this view, successful treatment produces a reorganization of internal representations in their relationship to one another, so that equilibrium develops between opposing forces. While this theory is rooted in an assumption of conflict, treatment could be experiential rather than rely upon confrontation, new learning, or the development of insight. In other words, the observing ego need not be the mediator of change. Salutary effects can issue from participation in the group; that is, through the development of cohesion, members identify with a benign group imago, and through the therapist's empathic acceptance of untoward affects (and sometimes also their symptomatic counterparts), these affects are moderated.

Specific techniques develop from one's theoretical assumptions about the nature of psychopathology. This is so because these same assumptions influence the therapist's view of the material presented in session, and, by inference, his or her view of the experience of the patients. For example, when one presumes the existence of a debilitated ego in the face of unneutralized aggression, one views the adoption of a paranoid/schizoid-like position as a defensive necessity. Then two divergent poles of behavior—negativism, argumentativeness, and disruptiveness, on the one hand, and passivity, inertia, and withdrawal, on the other—are seen as derivatives of projective mechanisms that produce equivalent distorted perceptions of authority as depriving, persecutory, or even sadistic. The group therapist must recognize that such patients, under stress, anticipate persecution, and at best, chronically expect to be disappointed. It is the therapist's task to put these attitudes into words and to help the

[2]Detoxification refers here to the development of tolerance for one's own aggression, while narcissistic reinforcement refers to the bolstering of self-esteem and enhancement of a general sense of internal self-worth.

patients express their fears and attendant anger. While this may be stated, at first, vis-à-vis the treating community at large, it ultimately must be connected to their experience with the therapist in the group. This technique, in effect, sanctions the development of a benign group paranoia, in which the group therapist serves as a container (Bion, 1962) for projected aggression. Clarifying that group behavior is reactive to confluent environmental and transference influences serves to demystify (Levenson, 1981) both external and internal experience. This process serves to attenuate (i.e., partially detoxify) the members' experience of their own aggressive drive derivatives.

The view that these patients are intolerant of their own aggression will cause one to provide them with soft words to convey strong affect; for example, anxious or worried instead of afraid, irritated or frustrated instead of angry. The wording of interventions is crucial and can be the difference between a detoxification of aggression and untoward stimulation.

Narcissistic reinforcement, as previously noted, simultaneously must be incorporated into technique. This occurs naturally in the group as members assist each other in a variety of ways. It is a by-product of interventions that are directed toward the group as a whole, for reasons noted earlier regarding the development of a "good" group introject. Viewed in this way, the usual supportive techniques are seen to nurture the group's sanctuaried atmosphere (i.e., the experience of the group as a refuge from chaos, as a sort of haven) so that members, through identification, can complement their self-regard.

As noted, the inpatient group psychotherapist does well to view the small group in context. Not only can it be used to biopsy the climate of the unit (Levine, 1980), but dynamically it functions as an interface between the intrapsychic experience of each member and the conflicts that are generated within the system at large. Granted, such a delineated focus may, at times, obscure recognition of other unconscious processes. However, it serves to integrate the group psychotherapy with the overall treatment and achieve the specific goals noted above.

Not all techniques can be illustrated here, but the following demonstrates the detoxification of aggression through the sanctioning of benign group paranoia and clarification of the external precipitants for the patients' behavior. The emphasis in this example will be on the therapist's clarifying statement; the group content will be abridged.

Vignette 5

This group was minimally cohesive, with several newly admitted members. The early phase of this session centered around a marginally functional borderline patient, who had a history of suicidal gestures and explosive behavior that was usually associated with alcohol abuse. The group members were generally aware of this woman's symptomatology, but not of her history of marital battles during states of intoxication; these had frightened her children. During the previous evening, she had had an argument with a staff member, after he told her that she could no longer use the public telephone that evening because her use had been excessive. This patient opened the session with a complaint that the staff member had prematurely terminated her telephone conversation with her husband. Her complaint generated group support. Then she complained about her husband, and alleged that he failed to discipline the children in her absence. From this point on, the other members began to complain, more or less, about relatives, friends, and employers who were unresponsive to their needs or treated them unfairly. This discussion constituted a major portion of the session. The patients were clearly annoyed, and even implied that those people were responsible for their ills.

The therapist intervened a little more than halfway through the session. He said: "I can see how frustrated you are with a number of people. You feel upset with them for seeming to restrict your lives. This is much like the feelings you shared when you complained about the incident of the telephone. It seems that you're upset, feeling that you are restricted in the hospital in a number of ways. I'm reminded of yesterday's community meeting, when you complained that we, the staff, were too conservative with hospital privileges; and I'm aware that several of you were denied passes for this weekend. Being restricted by us—and this includes me—is undoubtedly frustrating for you, as it would be for anyone." Following this statement, the patients began to share their disappointment with and doubts about the willingness of their individual and group therapists to care. They even wondered aloud if these therapists perversely enjoyed holding positions of power. These sentiments had been suggested by the content of the previous session, but had resisted decoding. Following the therapist's clarification here, the subsequent discussion was more candid and revealing of such consciously withheld attitudes. It was as if the patients now felt that it was safe to talk.

Discussion

This example is deliberately condensed and simplified for illustrative purposes. Interpretation of the group process need not be comprehensive; simple statements that facilitate the uncovering process are preferable. In addition, the style of intervention need not be as supportive as shown here. The higher the functional level of the patients, the longer the stay, and the more stable the group, the more explorative the approach can be. Still, certain technical aspects of therapy are generally illustrated by this vignette. The initial support given to this woman by the group members was defensively necessary. Their early alliance with her developed from a common paranoid position, which is generally associated with a deprecated self-image. Like her, many had previously behaved distastefully, having acted out frankly sadistic components of personality. Premature interpretation of the underlying aggression would have been experienced as a narcissistic blow. It would have, in effect, reedified an already noxious concept of self. Elaboration of various grievances was necessary, both for abreaction and to create a supportive network among the patients. Next, while displacement and projection were used as primary mechanisms for the expression of anger, treatment was served when the restrictive boundary between the therapists and patients (i.e., in the transference) was opened. The therapist's awareness of current milieu issues allowed him to decipher the content as a metaphor, which could link the experience in the milieu with that of the group. Last, as in most instances, interpretation of the group process was simultaneously explorative and supportive; that is, it permitted new material to emerge while elucidating what had transpired.

Most practitioners of inpatient group therapy do not appear to embrace an object-relations point of view.[3] The common approaches in use rely upon education (Maxmen, 1978), confrontation of maladaptive patterns of behavior (Rabiner et al., 1973; Waxer, 1977), or a combination of the two (Yalom, 1983). Differences among methods lie in the manner in which their proponents view the nature of psychopathology. An object-relations model postulates the existence of internal conflict. Educative and confrontational group therapies are based upon a different paradigm, which is usually not elucidated. They rest on the assumption that the patient, on any level, is unaware of the consequences of behavior and is ignorant of its deviancy, or,

[3]This statement is inferential, since most authors, when describing their methods, do not articulate their underlying assumptions.

more specifically, that the ego is deficient to begin with. To compensate for a presumed arrested development, they use guidance, modeling of behavior, and socialization; the treatment is designed to promote some sort of ego growth. It is no accident that the recent literature on the treatment of patients with severe psychopathology has drawn heavily upon the works of Kernberg (1976b) and Kohut (1971). The former presents a conflict theory, and the latter presents one of psychic deficit (Kernberg, 1982). In fact, the variety of inpatient group methods can be broadly dichotomized and classified according to their influence by these two schools of thought.

Kernberg's object-relations theory is based upon a particular notion of conflict, namely, that the individual is unable to manage those impulses that are mutually antagonistic. The ego core is impaired in the presence of unneutralized aggression. Disability results from a failure to manage opposing parts of the personality; it is not merely because the individual's early experience lacked the psychological nutriments for growth. In contrast, Kohut's self psychology proposes that certain preoedipal character pathology reflects an insufficient development of the self—specifically, that a partially underdeveloped ego is wanting of narcissistic supplies. In his system aggression is not a given; it is a disintegration product of fragmentation of a feeble self. Accordingly treatment ought to provide the patient with a second chance, so to speak, to develop personality structures the earlier environment had precluded. Inpatient group psychotherapists who find kinship with one system or the other do so because of their own assumptions as to whether the patient is restricted by internal conflict or is suffering from such a structural deficit. In fact, variations in technique generally reflect such underlying assumptions, for example, whether the task of treatment is to help the patient modulate internal aggression or to undo arrested development.

It is interesting to note that, in the ordinary use of language, aggression is associated with hostility, belligerence, and viciousness, whereas underdevelopment in childhood is associated with innocence. By extrapolation we can construe that contemporary notions on the nature of severe psychopathology reflect basic assumptions on the essence of humankind. This derives from the idea that psychopathology is basically a disorder of normal functioning. Conflict theory is consistent with the traditional notion that human beings need structure in order to contain and control dual forces. A deficit theory (used in the above sense) is consistent with the humanistic notion that structure is constraining, whereas self-actualization can be achieved through nurturance of inner potentials. One of these two positions can usually be found to lie behind any particular approach to inpatient treatment. For example, the method described here aims to produce a palliative juxtaposition of personality components, whereas many common methods use empathic techniques to effect some sort of ego training.

In short, then, technique emanates from explicit or implicit theory, which in turn rests upon particular assumptions about the essence of human nature. These assumptions cannot be tested; they are unverifiable. However, such premises of clinical thinking should be recognized. Failure to do so is risky. Albert Einstein once observed that "everyone sits in the prison of his own ideas." This truth should not dismay us. Rather, it should encourage us to learn about and know well the walls of our prison.

REFERENCES

Astrachan, B. M. (1970). Towards a social systems model of therapeutic groups. *Soc. Psychiat.*, 5:110–119.

Bion, W. R. (1959). *Experiences in Groups*. London: Tavistock Publications.

——— (1962). *Learning from Experience*. New York: Basic Books.

Borriello, J. F. (1976). Group psychotherapy in hospital systems. In *Group Therapy 1976*, ed. L. R. Wolberg & M. L. Aronson. New York: Stratton Intercontinental, pp. 99–108.

Friedman, H. J. (1975). Psychotherapy of borderline patients: The influence of theory on technique. *Amer. J. Psychiat.*, 132:1048–1052.

Gootnick, I. (1971). The psychiatric day center in the treatment of the chronic schizophrenic. *Amer. J. Psychiat.*, 128:485–488.

Grinberg, L. (1973). Projective identification and projective counter-identification in the dynamics of groups. In *Group Therapy 1973: An Overview*, eds. L. R. Wolberg & E. K. Schwartz. New York: Stratton Intercontinental, pp. 145–153.

Kernberg, O. F. (1975). A systems approach to priority setting of interventions in groups. *Int. J. Group Psychother.*, 25:251–275.

——— (1976a). Toward an integrative theory of hospital treatment. In *Object Relations Theory and Clinical Psychoanalysis*. New York: Jason Aronson, pp. 241–275.

——— (1976b). *Object Relations Theory and Clinical Psychoanalysis*. New York: Jason Aronson.

——— (1978). Leadership and organizational functioning: Organizational regression. *Int. J. Group Psychother.*, 28:3–25.

——— (1982). Book review of advances in self psychology, ed. Arnold Goldberg. *Amer. J. Psychiat.*, 139:374–375.

Kibel, H. D. (1981). A conceptual model for short-term inpatient group psychotherapy. *Amer. J. Psychiat.*, 138:74–80.

Klein, R. H. (1977). Inpatient group psychotherapy: Practical considerations and special problems. *Int. J. Group Psychother.*, 27:201–214.

Kohut, H. (1971). *The Analysis of the Self*. New York: International Universities Press.

Levenson, E. A. (1981). The rhetoric of intimacy. *Group*, 5(4):3–11.

Levine, H. B. (1980). Milieu biopsy: The place of the therapy group on the inpatient ward. *Int. J. Group Psychother.*, 30:77–93.

Maxmen, J. S. (1978). An educative model for inpatient group therapy. *Int. J. Group Psychother.*, 28:321–338.

Oldham, J. M. (1982). The use of silent observers as an adjunct to short-term inpatient group psychotherapy. *Int. J. Group Psychother.*, 32:469–480.

Parloff, M. B. (1968). Analytic group psychotherapy. In *Modern Psychoanalysis*, ed. J. Marmor. New York: Basic Books, pp. 492–531.

Rabiner, E. L., Wells, C. F., & Yager, J. (1973). A model for the brief hospital treatment of the disadvantaged psychiatrically ill. *Amer. J. Orthopsychiat.*, 43:774–782.

Scheidlinger, S. (1974). On the concept of the "mother-group." *Int. J. Group Psychother.*, 24:417–428.

Stanton, A. H., & Schwartz, M. S. (1954). *The Mental Hospital*. New York: Basic Books.

Volkan, V. D. (1976). *Primitive Internalized Object Relations*. New York: International Universities Press.

Waxer, P. H. (1977). Short-term group psychotherapy: Some principles and techniques. *Int. J. Group Psychother.*, 27:33–42.

Yalom, I. D. (1983). *Inpatient Group Psychotherapy*. New York: Basic Books.

7

LEONARD HORWITZ, Ph.D.

DISCUSSION: *Transference Issues in Hospital Groups*

H. D. KIBEL'S PAPER IS A FIRST-RATE CONTRIBUTION TO THE LITERATURE ON INPATIENT GROUP THERAPY AND REPRESENTS A SOPHISTICATED INTEGRATION OF THEORETICAL PERSPECTIVES ON GROUP PSYCHOTHERAPY, OBJECT-RELATIONS THEORY, AND GENERAL-SYSTEMS THEORY. DR. KIBEL PRESENTS A MODEL IN WHICH THE PRIMARY FOCUS SHOULD BE ON THE PATIENTS'COMMON REACTIONS TO SIGNIFICANT EXPERIENCES WITHIN THE HOSPITAL UNIT. THIS WRITER BELIEVES THAT THE AUTHOR'S DEEMPHASIS UPON THE USE OF TRANSFERENCE WITHIN THE GROUP IS TOO CONSTRAINING SINCE THERE MAY BE OCCASIONS WHEN THESE REACTIONS ARE MOST RELEVANT AFFECTIVELY. OTHER ISSUES RAISED BY THE PAPER INCLUDE DR. KIBEL'S VIEW OF TRANSFERENCE DILUTION, AS WELL AS HIS BELIEF THAT THE THERAPIST'S INTERVENTIONS WITHIN AN INPATIENT GROUP ARE NOT CAPABLE OF BEING VALIDATED.

Dr. Kibel has raised the level of discourse on the subject of inpatient group psychotherapy by a quantum leap. He has drawn on his expert knowledge of the theory and practice of group psychotherapy and hospital treatment, while also bringing in general-systems theory as well as object-relations theory. All of these factors are integrated in delineating the complex forces impinging upon a small inpatient group. He provides the group therapist with a consistent definition of the primary task and a rationale for understanding and organizing the multiple array of pressures to which the therapist is subjected in this medium. Also, the clinical grounding of the theory that emerges is everywhere apparent. In this paper you see an expert clinician using theory to his advantage instead of imposing a theoretical approach as a constraint upon the clinical phenomena.

Many clinicians who operate in groups, however well trained in individual treatment, frequently tend to subscribe to the naive notion that one can simply "go with the flow" and the patients will somehow benefit. The hazard of adopting such an undisciplined attitude is beautifully illustrated in Dr. Kibel's paper, in which the complex interaction of the hospital milieu with the dynamics of the small group is dramatically portrayed. Therapists in such a setting, who do not have a clear definition of their task, are likely to be buffeted about by the many forces operating on them, with the result that any potential therapeutic benefit will be compromised. This is not to say that there is only one correct rationale for working with inpatient groups, but only that a clear and reasonable model should be adopted. The paper presents an admirable method.

In this critique I shall focus primarily on issues raised by the model of therapy Dr. Kibel has presented. His view is that the hospital patient's psychopathology will be played out primarily in relationships with both staff and other patients in the hospital unit. He sees the therapy group as being on the interface between the patient's intrapsychic difficulties and the hospital environment. He draws the conclusion that the therapist's focus should be on the interrelationships, strains, and conflicts that emerge in the patient's daily life in the hospital unit. The small group provides the opportunity to clarify and interpret for all patients the internal problems they carry within them, which lead them into various interpersonal difficulties. He describes this method as an emphasis upon the "*there-and-now*," since it is a focus that looks outside the small group rather than inside.

Dr. Kibel recognizes that there is a special dynamic within the small group, and, in particular, he is cognizant of the transference to the therapist that will have some impact upon the group's functioning. But he offers two reasons why the therapist should not focus on this particular dynamic. First, he believes that the interactions outside the inpatient group tend to predominate over the transference dynamics in the therapy room. "The dynamics traditionally ascribed to small groups, in this situation, are overwhelmed and overshadowed by those of the unit." Second, he believes that a focus on the intragroup transference is usually too intense for inpatients who would have difficulty in tolerating the anxiety that is thus generated. His reasoning is that a long-term group, particularly one that is stable in membership and where the pathology of the patients is less severe, is the appropriate medium for a here-and-now focus.

While I do not quarrel with the focus he suggests, I am concerned that his formulation may be overly constraining. I believe that useful material that emerges within the therapy room, particularly the transference to the therapist, may sometimes be extremely important to address. Even if it is not a special focus of the treatment, I question whether it should be avoided under all circumstances.

Dr. Kibel's first vignette—which concerns the anxious preoccupation of the group with passive patients on the unit being victimized by the aggressive ones—illustrates my point. The session starts with the announcement by one of the cotherapists that she will be leaving the group the next week. Then, with increasing momentum, discussion ensues about passive patients being exploited and hurt by the more aggressive ones, a concern stimulated by an incident on the hospital unit the night before when an aggressive-manic patient prevented another patient from using the telephone. The author correctly sees an interaction, even a convergence, between the outside hospital event and the inside therapy group event. But his suggestion is that "the therapist uses the latter [inside] to facilitate his understanding of the clinical material, but uses the former [outside] to facilitate the patient's understanding of the contextual meaning of their experience in the group . . ." Thus he recognizes that the therapist terminating his role (actually he was rotating to the observers' circle) "stimulated the patient's fear of abandonment by their protectors." But he regarded this occurrence as "affectively far less immediate than the weekend's events."

I am not as persuaded as Dr. Kibel about the relative weakness of affective impact concerning the rotation of therapists. Even though it is customary for therapists to rotate, and even though the therapist will remain in the role of observer and team member, the impact of losing the therapist in the accustomed role can hardly be overlooked. Therefore, I would regard *both* the inside and the outside events as potentially useful therapeutically in giving the patients an understanding of how their treatment experiences lead to particular anxieties. In fact, the internal events within the group, the patients' transferences toward the departing therapist, potentially provide an excellent opportunity to convey to the patients how they are feeling passively victimized in relation to a perceived separation or abandonment. My main point here is that even though the ideal focus for the group therapy in general may be on events outside the group, the transference within the group may sometimes be quite helpful when clarified and interpreted, and indeed under some circumstances may become a major factor. In terms of helping to strengthen the therapeutic alliance within the group, the work on transference to the therapist can be potentially quite helpful.

Since this paper is so richly elaborated with clinical vignettes, I gradually became convinced that Dr. Kibel uses the therapist transference to a greater extent than he seems to acknowledge. An example is the vignette in which the patients started with hostile puns on the name of one of their individual therapists, with a clearly implied hint of doing the same with the name of their group therapist. Following this hostile bantering, the group session gradually degenerated into a relatively unproductive and disorganized expression of anxiety about physical and mental suffering. The author correctly observes that the group had become fearful lest their covert hostility *toward the group therapist* would cause her to retaliate against them. "When the therapist failed to reassure them against their fantasies of retribution, as she might have done through clarification and interpretation of the material, the collective group ego, if you will, deteriorated."

This vignette and discussion highlight the fact that, under some circumstances, the model proposed in the paper (using transference toward the group therapist for understanding but not for interpretation) cannot hold up in all instances. Certainly when the patients are experiencing strong affective reactions toward the therapist that are conscious or close to consciousness, as they were in this case, it behooves the group therapist to help the patients verbalize and understand their reactions. Otherwise, as occurred here, intense resistances set in and the group therapist as well as the patients become unproductively distant from each other. Furthermore, Dr. Kibel goes to great lengths in this vignette to establish the fact that the basic transference with which the patients were dealing was toward the individual therapist. Even if this observation is correct, as it seems to be, the concomitant transference to the group therapist, in my view, also needs to be worked with as a first step in clarifying the total of their "convoluted treatment reactions."

A related issue has to do with the author's assertion that dilution of the therapist transference is assisted by a group-centered technique. The example he used to illustrate the point was that of a paranoid member who was successfully engaged by the group therapist, and this process helped to reduce some of the fearful aspects of the group's transference. One can equally argue that a group-centered technique may serve to intensify the transference if the group therapist wishes to move in that direction. I have written elsewhere (Horwitz, 1977) that group psychotherapy, particularly the group-centered approach, has the potential for either diluting or intensifying the transference, and which aspect gets emphasized depends largely upon the therapist's decision as to which technique would be most therapeutically useful. For example, insofar as the members are able to experience the communality of their transference perceptions of the therapist, they are able to experience a protection within the group, a "safety in numbers," that will permit them to own their perception and deal with it in a deeper, more intense way. This last observation can be restated in terms of the group therapeutic alliance becoming stronger, and hence the patients commit themselves to dip deeper into anxiety-laden perceptions and distortions of the therapist.

Finally, I would like to deal with the issue of whether or not a group therapist's interventions in an inpatient group may be validated within the group process. According to Dr. Kibel, "Interventions in groups, unlike those in individual psychoanalytic treatment, do not readily yield feedback that confirms their effectiveness." He offers a number of reasons for this uncertain state of affairs. First, a therapist's interventions "at one dynamic level of the group will have uncertain and unpredictable effects on its other systems." Next, because of rapid turnover in the group and the presence of a milieu that is in a constant state of flux, one does not have access to external validation criteria. While the latter point is undoubtedly true, I do not share the same pessimism about obtaining reliable indicators of one's therapeutic methods in an inpatient group. I believe that the main source of data that all therapists use to assess the effectiveness of their work is the observation of relatively short-range effects of therapeutic interventions. In most therapies the therapist attempts to observe whether his or her intervention strategy helps to strengthen or weaken the therapeutic alliance. Concomitantly, does the intervention result in a deepening of associative material, or is there increased resistance, distance, and confusion? These observations are equally accessible to the psychoanalyst with an individual patient, to the group psychotherapist doing a long-term outpatient group, and to the group psychotherapist working with a rapidly changing hospital group. An example of my thesis is contained in the vignette concerning the group's reaction to the therapist working successfully with the paranoid belligerent latecomer to the group. The therapist's efforts were validated by the group's positive response to witnessing the therapist's successful interaction with this patient, and they were able to become more open and communicative about their feelings concerning the anxiety-laden experience of being subjected to a case conference.

In my critique of this article, I have attempted mainly to address the issue of how best to use the transference to the therapist in a rapidly changing inpatient group with multiple influences from the hospital milieu. While I agree with Dr. Kibel's main thesis that the primary task of the group should be devoted to examining conflicts and tensions generated in the hospital environment, I would personally opt for a somewhat greater latitude in interpreting the here-and-now of the therapy group. The rich clinical data presented here lend weight, in my opinion, to the potential value of also addressing the therapist transference, particularly when it threatens to become a resistance. These differences aside, Dr. Kibel has presented a highly sophisticated integration of his wide clinical experience and theoretical perspective that provides the inpatient group therapist with a most useful model.

REFERENCE

Horwitz, L. (1977). Group psychotherapy of the borderline patient. In *Borderline Personality Disorders,* ed. P. Hartocollis. New York: International Universities Press.

8

STEVEN H. COOPER, Ph.D.

Concomitant Individual and Milieu Psychotherapy and the Borderline Patient: Uses and Misuses

THIS PAPER DESCRIBES PARTICULAR ISSUES INVOLVING THE BORDERLINE PATIENT'S LEVEL OF PSYCHOPATHOLOGY AND POTENTIAL FOR THERAPEUTIC IMPASSE THAT REQUIRE OCCASIONAL USE OF MILIEU TREATMENT AS AN ADJUNCT TO INDIVIDUAL PSYCHOTHERAPY. SPECIFICALLY, BORDERLINE PATIENTS' FAILURE TO DEVELOP EVOCATIVE MEMORY, THEIR SPLITTING OF THERAPEUTIC FIGURES, AND THEIR TENDENCY TO EVOKE STRONG COUNTERTRANSFERENCE REACTIONS (BOTH PATHOLOGICAL AND "INEVITABLE") PROVIDE FERTILE GROUND FOR THE USE OF ADJUNCTS TO THE INDIVIDUAL PSYCHOTHERAPY. THE PAPER IDENTIFIES THOSE WAYS IN WHICH ADJUNCTIVE TREATMENT MAY BE USED THERAPEUTICALLY VERSUS THOSE INSTANCES IN WHICH REFERRAL FOR ADJUNCTIVE TREATMENT IS REFLECTIVE OF PATHOLOGICAL COUNTERTRANSFERENCE.

Milieu treatment is often a necessary adjunct to the individual psychotherapy of patients diagnosed as borderline personality disorder. While dimensions of milieu treatment and individual psychotherapy have been described as separate processes in numerous accounts, there has been relatively little discussion of the various therapeutic issues that necessitate the use of these combined procedures in the ongoing treatment of borderline patients. Most descriptions of adjunctive milieu treatment for borderline patients have emphasized its valuable functions as an average expectable environment and transitional object (Adler, 1977; Brown, 1981). Yet these accounts have not specifically addressed issues relating to borderline patients' developmental deficits and frequently encountered forms of therapeutic impasse that require or contraindicate concomitant milieu treatment and individual psychotherapy.

In this paper I will examine those aspects of psychotherapy with borderline patients that necessitate the occasional use of adjunctive milieu treatment. These include borderline patients' needs for transitional objects to militate against painful separation anxiety, their failure to use evocative memory adaptively, and their predilection toward splitting of therapeutic figures. I will also differentiate between pathological versus "inevitable" countertransference responses (Langs, 1981), which motivate the referral of borderline patients for adjunctive milieu treatment in order to identify those circumstances in which adjunctive resources may serve as an aid to ongoing psychotherapy.

Psychiatric day hospital rather than adjunctive inpatient treatment will be the focus because of the former's particular efficacy in treating borderline patients during intermediate levels of regression. For deeply regressed borderline patients in severe crisis or therapeutic impasse, referral to an inpatient setting is often the additional treatment of choice. Many borderline patients can often negotiate difficult periods during psychotherapy if the therapist employs such occasional parameters as extra support and clarification (Kernberg, 1975), confrontation (Adler & Buie, 1972; Buie & Adler, 1982; Corwin, 1972), or the provision of transitional objects (Deutsch, 1965; Adler, 1980; Buie & Adler, 1982). However, for patients who need adjunctive resources beyond the individual psychotherapy but are not so regressed as to necessitate the use of inpatient treatment, day hospital is often the treatment of choice. The term adjunctive milieu is used here to refer to psychoanalytically oriented day hospital programs in which the psychotherapist is independent of the milieu but works in conjunction with the milieu staff.

DEVELOPMENTAL BACKGROUND: BORDERLINE PSYCHOPATHOLOGY AND TRANSITIONAL RELATEDNESS

The contributions of Winnicott (1953) and Tolpin (1971) in examining transitional phenomena and Modell's (1963, 1968) applications of the transitional object mode of relating to the understanding of transference phenomena among borderline patients offer a context for examining these patients' experience of a therapeutic provision such as the adjunctive milieu.

Winnicott's (1953) seminal work introduced the term transitional phenomena to designate an intermediate area of experience between internal and external reality and an intermediate mode of object relating between the capacity to perceive an object and the capacity to retain a constant object. Winnicott described the transitional object as an object that exists in the "real world," which the infant believes owes its existence to the infant's need for the object. Thus the infant endows an object in the surroundings with soothing and tension-relieving properties that can be utilized at times of separation or when the mother is not able to provide soothing.

Winnicott proposed that the fate of the transitional object is not that it is an object to be forgotten, repressed, or mourned, but that it undergoes a kind of diffusion over the whole cultural field and concomitant gradual decathexis. Tolpin (1971) suggested, in contrast to Winnicott, that the soothing and anxiety-regulating functions of the blanket are internalized, thus providing a self-soothing structure. According to Tolpin it is through repeated experiences of losing and recovering the transitional object and its accompanying valence as an auxiliary soother that the child replaces maternal soothing with internalized tension-relieving mental activity.

Modell (1963) posited that the borderline level of structural organization results from a developmental arrest of object relationships at the stage of the transitional object. Thus, in Modell's view, borderline patients have been unable to rely safely on the transitional object as an auxiliary soother in a "sufficient enough" manner to decathect and internalize the object. Modell suggests that borderline patients have unconscious fantasies about the therapist, in which the therapist, like the transitional object during development, is recognized as an object that exists outside the self but owes its existence to processes (usually needs for the object) that arise within the individual. Borderline patients often develop conscious and unconscious fantasies in which the therapist exists only for the individual, and exclusively for the gratification of needs. In these fantasies the therapist is regarded as being able magically to provide a feeling of safety in the world through sustained contact. Just as the infant attained absolute omnipotent control over a "first possession," the "me/not-me" possession or transitional object, the borderline patient clings to the magical belief that he or she can demand the same degree of control with regard to the environment, psychotherapist, or therapeutic community.

Adler and Buie (1979, p. 87) have emphasized the developmental inability of the borderline patient to replace or maintain the affectively charged memory of the soothing properties of the transitional object with evocative memory. They suggest that parental availability and support during the child's use of the transitional object are crucial in the development of evocative memory capacity.

The borderline patient's arrest at the level of transitional relatedness has important implications for understanding patients' reactions to the offering of milieu treatment as an adjunct to individual psychotherapy. Implicit in these developmental formulations is the notion that the success of maternal efforts at supplying a transitional object is unlikely unless it is predicated on a "good enough" adaptation by the mother to the infant's needs—only then can the gratification of needs be conceived by the infant as being under the infant's magical control. Thus the eventual task of disillusionment can occur only with the supplying of sufficient opportunity for illusion (Winnicott, 1953). Traumatic disappointments by the mother in the form of encouraging either premature or belated displacements to another object for soothing eventuate in ongoing, archaic, aggressively determined magical beliefs that objects do, or should, offer protection to the individual in the face of anxiety and separation.

PSYCHOTHERAPEUTIC IMPLICATIONS

Individual psychotherapy concomitant with adjunctive milieu treatment offers a unique therapeutic framework, and is often a major aspect of the patient's conscious and unconscious experience within both the psychotherapy and the milieu. The adaptive context (Langs, 1981)—that is, the specific reality within the psychotherapy that evokes intrapsychic and communicative responses—involves the offering of a third object (milieu) by a primary object (the therapist). The adjunctive milieu is often, manifestly, a provision by the psychotherapist introduced to reduce anxiety connected to feelings of abandonment or rage. During development the transitional object is a useful prototype for understanding the patient's conscious reactions to adjunctive treatment since it is offered by the parent or is independently secured by the infant with the explicit purpose of providing soothing in the face of separation anxiety with regard to parental figures. The unconscious meaning of this therapeutic provision is complex and varied, as discussed later in the paper.

This developmental paradigm for understanding the meaning of adjunctive treatment for many borderline patients is also relevant since numerous clinical and theoretical reports have emphasized these patients' possible developmental arrest at the stage of the transitional object. It is important to note, however, that attempts to understand the adjunctive milieu, introduced as a soothing, holding object, do not always account for the richly varied functions that the transitional object milieu performs for these patients. Some patients, for example, require transitional objects as a defense against separation anxiety concerning their psychotherapist or others. In such instances these patients have failed to develop evocative memory (i.e., the inability to evoke soothing parental images to lessen separation anxiety). The milieu may be used to help deny painful experiences of separation or disappointment. For other borderline patients, often those who have been able to develop a sense of trust in the psychotherapist as a reliable and holding self-object, a transitional object such as the adjunctive milieu may provide an opportunity for gradual practice in the areas of separation and autonomy. Thus the model of the milieu as a transitional object must include a variety of functions performed during psychotherapy with borderline patients.

In examining the different varieties of transference and therapeutic impasse that borderline patients experience toward their psychotherapist and which lead to the need to provide a transitional object milieu, I will be using Langs' (1981) definition of transference as distorted perceptions of the therapist based on pathological unconscious fantasies, memories, and introject.

DEVELOPMENT OF EVOCATIVE MEMORY

Therapeutic impasse with borderline patients is often related to their difficulty in establishing and maintaining a sense of the psychotherapist as a steady, holding self-object. Many borderline patients lack internalized self-soothing capacities, which renders these patients vulnerable to painful experiences of aloneness, panic, and abandonment in their relationships, particularly toward their psychotherapist. In a series of papers, Adler and Buie (Adler, 1980; Adler & Buie, 1979; Buie & Adler, 1982) have elaborated developmental failures and suggested that transitional objects specific to the psychotherapist, such as holiday address or an appointment card, may serve as activators for the patient to remember the soothing properties of the psychotherapist at times of separation.

An adjunctive milieu aids in the development of evocative memory in much the same manner that Buie and Adler have suggested for a variety of objects specific to the therapist. Adjunctive treatment may be provided at times when the patient finds the level of abandonment anxiety unbearable. This is one of several examples of when, in the treatment of borderline patients, there is a need for greater activity from the psychotherapist in order to clarify and contain the patient's level of regression.

A primary function of the adjunctive milieu is to provide an environment in which the patient may experience the mirroring of images of the psychotherapist or other soothing objects even in the absence of such figures. For example, the milieu may affirm the existence of the psychotherapist at times when the patient questions or denies the continued existence or involvement of the therapist in the treatment. Milieu staff, like the psychotherapist, should attempt to understand the patient's experience of aloneness, which is not only a part of disappointments from past relationships, but is often also reactive to a revival of these feelings with the psychotherapist. The psychotherapist's "inevitable countertransference" (Langs, 1981)—that is, expected or nonpathological countertransference—often involves feelings of exhaustion, futility, or rage in response to the patient's angry demands and desperate experience of abandonment. In turn this may exacerbate the patient's conviction that he or she will be deprived of a holding self-object. Thus the adjunctive milieu may aid, indirectly, in the patient's development of holding self-objects by supporting the psychotherapist through discussion and clarification of the patient's experience of the psychotherapeutic relationship as painfully depriving.

Borderline patients who suffer from extreme dependency conflicts and anaclitic depression are often those who most require the use of adjunctive milieu treatment. The acknowledgment and interpretation of the borderline patient's sense of aloneness are often a useful and necessary stage of psychotherapy, albeit fraught with turbulence and resistance to the helper's efforts to provide containment and relief. To minimize the patient's regression to overwhelming feelings of abandonment, the psychotherapist must, in addition to providing adjunctive milieu support, actively interpret aspects of the manifest negative transference that focus on feelings of abandonment and clarify why adjunctive resources are necessary. Sometimes clarifications require that the therapist explicitly communicate his or her limits so that the therapy is tolerable and conducive to discussion of the patient's experience of the therapist as a fallible object with personal needs.

The nature of clarification is often one of differentiating between the patient's unconscious, grandiose expectation that the psychotherapist or patient should not need additional resources such as a milieu versus the patient's feeling of abandonment by the therapist. One borderline patient responded to my suggestion for adjunctive treatment by conceding in a condescending way: "If you feel you need this in order to work with me, I'll go along with it." In this example the patient was partly correct in that I did need this adjunct because I could no longer tolerate her potential for suicide and excessive demands. Yet I wanted to provide her with additional resources to express her panic and rage. Her statement to me involved a nearly complete projection of the need for this treatment onto me, which I gently challenged by stating that it was my sense that we both needed the adjunctive resources. With repeated instances of challenging this projection of need and responsibility onto me, the therapeutic alliance was enhanced; specifically, the need for an adjunctive milieu was increasingly experienced as a shared need that revolved around the considerable difficulty encountered in developing a therapeutic alliance. An intermediate step, however, involved the patient's sense of herself as repellent, poisonous, and worthy of rejection. It was as if the patient moved from complete projection of need to full responsibility for the need (along with severe self-reproach) when I clarified the necessity for milieu treatment. The patient's sense of self-reproach was interpreted and challenged, but as was her initial attribution of blame to me. Not surprisingly, the early stages of her psychotherapy were dominated by alternating feelings of contempt for me and for herself.

The psychotherapist thus may usually acknowledge the patient's disappointment or contempt directed toward the psychotherapist or the self by pointing up the need for adjunctive treatment, while clarifying that he or she is unwilling to tolerate the patient's often complicated reactions, including both relief and disappointment that the therapist is not able to tolerate limitless demands for contact with the patient. The psychotherapist must also work with the milieu staff in allowing for an open acknowledgment and interpretation of the patient's experience, including the patient's disillusionment with the psychotherapist. Concomitantly, the psychotherapist and milieu staff must clarify reasons why adjunctive treatment was sought in the face of the patient's persecutory fantasies about being the "abandoned child" (Adler, 1977) vis-à-vis the psychotherapist as described earlier.

Just as important are those instances in which apparent manifestations of evocative memory failure instead involve partial defenses against conflicts. In these circumstances the use of a therapeutic milieu as an adjunct to individual psychotherapy is sometimes contraindicated. The following segment of a long-term psychotherapy illustrates the often complicated relationship between a patient's reported evocative memory deficits, defenses, and conflicts, and the indications and contraindications for concomitant milieu and individual psychotherapy.

Case Vignette 1

Ms. A., a 30-year-old divorced graduate student, entered twice-weekly psychotherapy after five years of intermittent psychotherapy with several psychotherapists. She wished treatment because of her tendency to seek intimacy with married, unavailable men while deprecating more accessible men who expressed interest in her. She had also suffered from experiences of derealization since adolescence, particularly after sexual intercourse. These episodes of derealization were usually followed, first, by intense rage directed toward the man she was with, and then by abrupt flight and avoidance of these men. In retrospect she would complain of her experience of their invasiveness with some awareness that they had done little to deserve her rage. Finally, she complained of exhausting episodes that involved taking on too much work with the hope of renouncing all needs for intimacy.

Ms. A. was the older of two sisters and grew up in a middle-class family in which the sexuality both of her parents and of their children was emphasized in a variety of ways. Her parents, devoted nudists, were often nude in the house throughout her childhood and adolescence. Ms. A.'s father displayed an ongoing preoccupation with her physical development during adolescence, which he monitored by making frequent, explicit comparisons between Ms. A.'s physical and intellectual attributes and those of her mother. Ms. A. grew up with the strong sense that her father criticized and deprecated his wife through these comparisons. She recalled that her father frequently fondled her arms and legs when she was a child. Ms. A. prohibited such touching when she was approximately 16 years old, at which point she curtailed both being nude with other family members and being alone with her father in any context.

The patient's first two years of psychotherapy were replete with feelings about her experience of me as a failing holding self-object. She interpreted any incidental movements by me during our sessions as indications of my boredom and contempt for her and my wish to see my other patients. Separations between sessions were even more difficult. She would complain of fantasies in which I would enact my dislike for her by plotting to refer her to another psychotherapist. Despite her anger toward me during sessions, she said she felt relieved to be with me in comparison with her between-session fantasies about me as a malevolent and uncaring individual. Additionally, she feared that if she trusted me, I would prove to be a narcissistically vulnerable individual (explicitly likened to her father) who would force her to minister to my sexual needs.

During the first two years of psychotherapy, despite her ongoing rage and disappointment with me and intermittent mild suicidal feelings, she made no requests for adjunctive milieu treatment. In contrast, she had made frequent requests during earlier psychotherapies for adjunctive day hospital treatment, and had twice been involved in concomitant day hospital and individual psychotherapy with a previous psychotherapist.

After two years of psychotherapy, Ms. A. showed some indications of increased tolerance for intense ambivalence conflicts in her psychotherapy. Her anger and sense of disappointment with me became far less pronounced, as did her fantasies about my wish to terminate the psychotherapy. Ms. A. then developed a rather abrupt and intense erotic transference marked by various fantasies about supplanting my wife. Between sessions Ms. A. had masturbatory fantasies involving me holding her, sexual intercourse, and marriage. The patient showed no signs of developing a psychotic transference despite her experience of painful longings for me to display love for her overtly.

During the next year, Ms. A. began complaining that our two hours of psychotherapy a week were not enough. She felt that during the time between our meetings it was difficult to remember the trust she had developed in me. These separations between psychotherapy hours were characterized by oscillations between pleasurable fantasies of the two of us together and anger and distrust toward me. Concurrently with her extended fantasies between sessions, she began making occasional requests for milieu day treatment as an adjunct to her individual psychotherapy. She felt preoccupied with me between sessions and wished to speak about this with others, although she did not report feeling suicidal or seem in need of inpatient hospitalization. She hoped that milieu treatment would relieve her of both her extreme anxiety about being alone and her inability to feel certain that I would be present at our next meeting.

I repeatedly told the patient that we needed to explore these feelings further in order to consider the potential value of concomitant milieu treatment. She agreed reluctantly, but then actively participated in this exploration. Although I provided considerable acknowledgment of her discomfort, my unwillingness immediately to agree to her request for milieu treatment made her angry and disappointed in me, as reflected in feelings that I was punishing her because she had allowed herself to trust and acknowledge more dependency needs.

Despite these fears Ms. A. was able to explore the meaning of her complicated fantasies. Her associations to her wishes for closeness and her masturbatory fantasies about me revolved around deep longings for closeness with her father, longings that reminded her of his love and availability for her before he became preoccupied with her sexual development. Ms. A. also had many associations to an exclusive, favored relationship with her father, coupled with feelings of extreme competition and fears of retaliation with regard to her mother. She had always experienced her mother as filled with vengeance and wishes to undermine Ms. A.'s sense of security and power. Ms. A. expressed the hope that I would be able to tolerate her sexual feelings for me without "ruining" our therapeutic relationship by being seduced by or seducing her. At the same time, she spoke often of feeling tortured by the lack of sexual gratification in our therapeutic relationship. Ms. A. attributed her angry feelings during separations to the awareness that I was not actually available to her in the way she wished me to be in her sexual fantasies. She associated to many episodes with men (mostly her father and two uncles) before the age of eight in which she recalled enjoying exhibiting her intellectual, dancing, and acrobatic skills. She wished for exclusive attention at these times, and currently with me. Ms. A. experienced the frame of our psychotherapy, as well as my unwillingness to accede immediately to her request for milieu treatment, as a painful deprivation and punishment for her strong longings and illicit sexual wishes. Finally, in connection with her angry feelings toward me, she described fantasies in which I secretly succumbed to her seduction of me, in turn engendering feelings of disappointment, despair, and rage toward me for having such overriding needs.

Over a period of time that extended from the end of the third year to the middle of the fourth year of psychotherapy, Ms. A. began to describe ambivalence about her wish to be involved in concomitant adjunctive milieu treatment. At times she strongly resented her pain and her preoccupation with me between sessions. Gradually she reported feeling more hopeful and encouraged by her increasing ability to tolerate these strong feelings, as well as by her awareness of her ability actively to explore the meaning of these recollections and fantasies. For example, Ms. A. eventually began to express the wish that her mother had protected her from her father's intrusive demands. Ms. A.'s erotic transference subsided by the beginning of her fifth year of treatment, at which point she became strikingly less defensively self-sufficient and more active in dating, and in the following year she became involved with the man to whom she is currently married.

This highly condensed segment of the psychotherapy illustrates a number of complicated choices that confront the psychotherapist working with borderline individuals who have a broad range of strengths and weaknesses. Ms. A.'s ability to weather her considerable rage and abandonment anxiety during the early stages of psychotherapy (partly through intermittent defensive self-sufficiency) allowed her eventually to explore the depth of her distrust of men as well as her early longings for an exclusive relationship with her father. In some sense Ms. A.'s trust in me allowed her more openly to express her wish for an adjunctive therapeutic milieu. If so, why not employ the milieu to assist the patient's ability to maintain a continued sense of the psychotherapist as a holding self-object in conjunction with the active exploratory work of psychotherapy, as has been suggested by Adler and Buie in a long series of papers (e.g., Adler & Buie, 1979)?

I believe that Ms. A. displayed capacities to do the exploratory work of psychotherapy without the aid of adjunctive treatment, and that, in fact, such an adjunct might have slowed down or impeded our work. It is important for the psychotherapist to assess at what point in the treatment process the patient or therapist believes that an adjunct would be useful. Ms. A. requested adjunctive treatment at a point when she trusted me enough to suspend more entirely her defensive self-sufficiency, which allowed her to verbalize her feelings of aloneness and inability to remember me during painful separations. In the early stages of treatment, as well as at the time she made these requests, Ms. A.'s level of anxiety and self-destructiveness never reached the point of instilling "inevitable countertransference" (Langs, 1981) reactions of extreme exasperation, concern, and guilt. Often severe evocative memory problems are manifested by patients with striking difficulty in verbalizing their inability to recall their psychotherapist. To the extent that Ms. A. not only expressed her anxiety during our sessions, but, even more important, continued exploring various forms of her ambivalent wishes and conflictual fantasies, the therapeutic milieu as an adjunct to individual therapy was not necessary. The defensive component of her request for concomitant treatment was that, to the extent that her self-sufficiency began melting and her longings continued to increase, she wished to diffuse the transference through a change in the framework of our psychotherapy. While there is often a partly defensive component in patients' inability to retain a soothing image of their psychotherapist, the crucial decision for the psychotherapist with regard to providing a transitional object milieu is to what extent the patient appears able to tolerate this anxiety.

After I insisted that we first examine Ms. A.'s request for adjunctive treatment, much of the patient's associative content (e.g., elaborations of the meaning of her fantasies) consisted of wishes for and dread of special, exclusive contact with me and her father. These associations far outweighed her feelings and thoughts about her inability to remember me at all. The patient's requests seemed to be partially motivated by some difficulty with remembering me between sessions, but, even more salient, by a wish to remember me in the way she most wanted. Ms. A. wished that I were a benevolently loving father with whom she could safely express the full weight of her own sexual fantasies and needs without fearing intrusion. She also wished me to be a strong, idealized mother who could give to her without competing to save herself from her husband's deprecating remarks.

Psychotherapy with Ms. A. was only "interrupted" by a rupture in the patient's experience of me as a holding self-object during the early stages of treatment (broadly, the initial two years of psychotherapy), when her extreme self-sufficiency functioned, essentially, as a therapeutic milieu might have for a patient with more overt dependency needs or anaclitic depression. In the segment of psychotherapy described here, Ms. A. tolerated strong affects and used the therapeutic relationship to explore her requests and fantasies despite considerable anger and frustration about the failure of her requests to be met.

Thus, in making a decision about the appropriateness of adjunctive milieu treatment, the psychotherapist must assess the level of the patient's self-destructive behavior and desperation. Often milieu treatment is useful when a patient's suffering reaches such great proportions that the psychotherapist's inevitable countertransference reactions of exasperation, futility, rage, and guilt necessitate the use of adjunctive treatment, in order to mitigate both the patient's pain and the psychotherapist's tolerance for that pain. The case of Ms. A. highlights a crucial decision point for therapists whose patients have been able to develop enough trust in their psychotherapist to accept a transitional object. Specifically, the psychotherapist in such cases must assess the extent to which the patient requires such a parameter to maintain and continue the exploratory work of psychotherapy.

FORMS OF SPLITTING AND CONCOMITANT ADJUNCTIVE AND INDIVIDUAL PSYCHOTHERAPY

Borderline patients demonstrate a variety of forms of splitting (Kernberg, 1975; Stolorow & Lachmann, 1980) that may be resolved through the use of concomitant milieu and individual psychotherapy. They often demonstrate splitting by a repeated pattern of seeking other psychotherapists at times when they experience empathic failures within their ongoing psychotherapy. At such times the patient's already precarious ability to experience ambivalence toward the psychotherapist may be threatened by strong feelings of disappointment and rage. The patient is motivated to seek alternative help by the need actively to separate positive feelings of love, admiration, and sometimes idealization toward the psychotherapist from disillusionment and rage. Therapeutic impasse may result when the patient expresses these ambivalence conflicts through compromise formations that revolve around repetitive helper-seeking rather than coming to therapy appointments to verbalize these conflicts.

One solution to this tendency to form split transferences outside the psychotherapy is to create a therapeutic situation that includes an opportunity for expression of ambivalent feelings through concomitant individual and adjunctive milieu treatment. Through such a procedure, resolution of the therapeutic impasse may be aided by placing the tendency to enact such ambivalence conflicts under the aegis of the psychotherapy. In my experience referral to a milieu within an ongoing psychotherapy often tends initially to exacerbate defensive splitting as manifested by the patient's tendency to view the psychotherapist and milieu in both idealized and deprecated turns. For patients who have developed the capacity to view the psychotherapist, albeit fleetingly, more benevolently, defensive splitting appears in the form of prominent derogation of the milieu—the milieu, here, may be targeted for the feelings of disappointment and reactive anger that have been difficult to express directly to the psychotherapist.

At other times the milieu appears to represent parts of the self that the patient views as defective. One patient told me that the milieu could never be of help because: "They're all stuck in this shit hole, too. We're all pieces of shit; they've all been placed here by their therapists." Thus the milieu may become the repository for the experience of the patient as a rejected, defective individual by virtue of the patient's and psychotherapist's need for adjunctive treatment. This takes another form when the patient deprecates the psychotherapist as unable to "handle" the patient. Despite the tendency for splitting to increase during the early stages of concomitant milieu and individual psychotherapy, this arrangement eventually allows for considerable exploration of intense ambivalence conflicts that cause defensive splitting.

Another form of splitting is demonstrated by patients who experience rapidly fluctuating, oppositely valenced affects and images linked to the psychotherapist, described by Stolorow and Lachmann (1980) as prestages of splitting and by Lichtenberg and Slap (1973) as the splitting of mental contents. Clinically this is seen with borderline patients who have an extremely fluid and fleeting sense of trust in the psychotherapist. I believe that fears of aloneness and the failure to develop evocative memory underlie this form of splitting, since this defense mechanism is invariably heightened at times of separation from the psychotherapist. In fact some borderline patients regress from using the type of splitting manifested by split transferences to this "prestage" splitting at times when separation (e.g., vacations) is imminent. For such patients concomitant milieu treatment is quite useful during early phases of the psychotherapy to remind the patient repeatedly of the image of the psychotherapist during times of separation, and thus aid in the development of evocative memory.

Psychotherapists who use adjunctive milieu treatment as a way to obviate the exploration of negative transference invariably promote splitting of therapeutic figures. This may take the form of the psychotherapist offering the milieu as a seductive way to prevent the patient from expressing anger toward the psychotherapist about inevitable separations or empathic failures. The patient, at such times, often unconsciously, feels that the milieu, rather than the psychotherapist, is the only appropriate target for angry feelings. Thus the use of a concomitant milieu with individual psychotherapy may never substitute for exploration of the patient's negative experiences of the therapeutic relationship.

COUNTERTRANSFERENCE ISSUES

Countertransference reactions, as used here, refer to those conscious and unconscious conflicts of the psychotherapist that obstruct examination of the patient's experience of the therapeutic relationship. Potent countertransference reactions of the psychotherapist sometimes lead to premature referral for adjunctive treatment. Psychotherapists who are frightened of assessing the patient's regressive potential, implicitly or explicitly ask the milieu to make such an evaluation. The patient's conviction that he or she repels or creates anxiety in the psychotherapist is often confirmed at such times.

The following brief clinical vignette illustrates how countertransference reactions quite early in treatment led to the premature referral of a borderline patient to adjunctive milieu treatment during an initial evaluation.

Case Vignette 2

Ms. C., a 28-year-old, unmarried businesswoman, was referred for individual psychotherapy following a brief psychiatric hospitalization. Ms. C. had been hospitalized because she had become mildly suicidal and destructive of property when her lover of six months broke off their relationship.

Ms. C. was the youngest of three children in an upper-middle-class family. She described her mother as an extremely judgmental, verbally acerbic person who criticized her husband and explicitly invited her three children to join with her in such criticism. Ms. C. sought as much closeness with her mother as possible, feeling ever frustrated in her wish that mother would support and love her. The patient experienced her mother's love as highly contingent upon successful performance at home and school. Unconsciously she believed and wished that renunciation of her sexual feelings, particularly during adolescence, would extract her mother's love. Ms. C.'s father was a highly intelligent but depleted individual who attempted to diffuse his wife's attacks through self-deprecation and self-destructive business dealings. Ms. C. grew up with a deep sense of inferiority, and identified with her father as a "loser." She believed that only through joyless hard work and the avoidance of men would she be lovable to her mother. Ms. C. felt labeled as the "bad child" (her term) during childhood in that she was more prone to being demanding and to sadness, anger, and irritability than her siblings.

She was frequently likened to her maternal grandmother as being "highly emotional."

Although she had had no contact with boys during adolescence and only a few brief relationships with men since her early 20s, Ms. C. became seriously involved with a man at the age of 27. After six months she became profoundly ambivalent about this relationship because she partly wanted to agree to his request that she live with him but felt that her mother and closest female friend disapproved of him. Extreme anxiety and doubt over a period of two months yielded to uncontrollable bouts of testing the man to see how much he loved her. She would repeatedly demand, for example, that he stay home from work in order to prove his love for her; otherwise, she said, she would realize that he really did not care for her. When he did reject her shortly after these demands increased, Ms. C. cut her hand upon smashing a glass on the floor, and began a period of uncontrollable intermittent screaming over a weekend. She was hospitalized for approximately two weeks following this incident, and almost immediately regained her sense of control. Upon discharge from the hospital, she was referred to me for psychotherapy.

During the first several evaluation meetings, Ms. C. appeared to be agitated, depressed, and very angry about having been hospitalized. She fluctuated between extreme self-reproach, blaming herself for having driven her friend away, and contempt for the psychiatrist who had decided to hospitalize her when she was sent to an emergency room following her violent episode. She interpreted most of my questions during the evaluation as insults and indictments of her for being a "bad" person, and she told me she was certain that her family would interpret her outburst and hospitalization in this way as well. During moments when she was not vehemently blaming herself or others for events surrounding her hospitalization, Ms. C. reported feelings of emptiness and profound loneliness. She felt lost and uncertain as to whether she could see friends for fear of humiliation about her outburst. She felt bitter about her boyfriend and desperately curious about whether he had met another woman. She reported some thoughts of suicide, but indicated no immediate plans. Whenever she spoke of mildly suicidal thoughts and feelings of worthlessness, Ms. C. would also confess her fear that I would overrespond to these feelings and hospitalize her. Her interpretation of this fantasied scenario was that I would view her as an unwieldy, "bad" person. She said several times, "You'll be like all the others and decide that my behavior is bad and needs to be modified. I drive everyone away with my bad behavior."

Ms. C. actively participated in each of her four evaluation meetings, despite telling me I would be unable to understand her. She angrily agreed to phone me if she noticed any heightening of her suicidal thoughts. Despite her very mild suicidal ideation and no past ideation or attempts, my conscious reactions to her centered on some concern about her feelings of futility and hopelessness, as well as on what seemed to be a strong contempt for me and our future psychotherapy. Upon completing my evaluation, I recommended twice-weekly psychotherapy and concomitant milieu day treatment. I made such a recommendation based on my sense that the patient's level of severe mistrust required an adjunctive milieu that would provide a holding environment during the initial stages of psychotherapy to aid in the development of a therapeutic alliance. It seemed that such a milieu might also provide an alternative way to begin to discuss her hopelessness and humiliation in contrast to the isolation that she sought from friends and family members. I thought that she would experience a milieu as an intermediate form of holding for her feelings of rage and futility without stimulating her sense of being banned and punished, as her inpatient hospitalization had done.

Ms. C. responded to this plan with profound disillusionment with me. She told me that she had secretly hoped that I would be able to work with her without fear or overriding anxiety about her current hopelessness and mildly suicidal feelings. She experienced my recommendation as a confirmation of her "badness," in essence, a prediction that she would continue to explode as she had (for the first time in her life) prior to her hospitalization. She told me that I was more frightened of her than she was of herself.

Initially I viewed Ms. C.'s scornful reaction as a repetition of her view of her father as a bungling, incompetent figure who invited her contempt. However, I was quickly struck by the fact that what she said about my reactions to her made sense. Ms. C.'s regressive and suicidal potential seemed far less severe than that of other borderline patients with whom I had used concomitant individual and milieu treatment. Furthermore, her level of distrust of me, while fairly high, failed to instill the strong, preoccupying concerns that would usually lead me to consider the necessity of a holding environment. Instead, I felt angry, punitive, and vaguely frightened by the level of her potential demands. I realized that I was made most uncomfortable by what I initially perceived to be her potential to become involved in psychotherapy, expressing to me the same needs for an omnipotent mother than she had manifested with her boyfriend. My recommendation for a psychotherapeutic framework consisting of concomitant individual and milieu treatment was aimed less at providing a holding environment for her than at warning her that I unconsciously required a commitment from her to diffuse the level of her oral cravings in whatever transference manifestations might emerge. In essence she refused to make such an agreement for fear that she was once again being told to dilute her emotional reactions (particularly disappointment and anger) in order to avoid rejection.

After examination of this pathological countertransference, I decided to modify this plan with the understanding that we would begin psychotherapy and evaluate in an ongoing way the necessity for any additional treatment. It is important to note, however, that it was useful for Ms. C. to examine in what ways she might have felt it essential to keep secret her hopefulness about each of our abilities to tolerate and understand her strong affects. Parenthetically, Ms. C. productively used twice-weekly psychotherapy, and required only occasional emergency phone calls, without adjunctive milieu treatment, for five years before moving to a new city.

The inevitable countertransference reactions that are a useful guide for the use of concomitant individual and milieu psychotherapy were largely absent in the case of Ms. C. I was not convinced of her severe potential for suicide, self-destruction, or anxiety intolerance. While I was impressed by her level of distrust, I ignored her accompanying ability actively to communicate, and to some extent to be curious about, these feelings. Pathological countertransference reactions, involving the premature use of this arrangement, as in the case of Ms. C, usually have as their objective some form of diffusion of strongly negative and positive transference.

Another common pathological countertransference issue motivating referral for adjunctive treatment involves the psychotherapist's own fear of rejection. For borderline patients who have frequently begun and terminated psychotherapy, referral to the adjunctive milieu may represent the psychotherapist's wish for self-protection against the fear of rejection by the patient by declaring first rights to terminate the relationship. This sometimes results in the patient's use of defensive splitting, in which the milieu is idealized as "the new therapist" (unconsciously recommended by the psychotherapist) while the psychotherapist is deprecated or irrevocably rejected.

It is also important for the psychotherapist to determine to what degree countertransference hate (Winnicott, 1949; Maltsberger & Buie, 1974) or feelings of entrapment and exhaustion contribute to the perception that such a milieu is necessary. In other words, the psychotherapist's perception of the patient's experience of hostility and helplessness directed toward the psychotherapist may be colored by the psychotherapist's projection of his or her own feelings of depression, rage, and helplessness. Nadelson (1976), in discussing psychotherapeutic interactions with borderline patients, referred to "sadomasochistic reciprocity" as that process by which the psychotherapist, having received the patient's projections of fear, helplessness, and self-negation, place these uncomfortable affects back in the patient. The psychotherapist must always be thoughtful about whether the decision to seek adjunctive treatment is a form of projective counteridentification (Nadelson, 1976) in which the psychotherapist unconsciously agrees with the patient's projections that he or she cannot be of help.

The referral for adjunctive treatment cannot obviate the analysis of a variety of types of negative transference within the psychotherapy. Another form of pathological countertransference relates to the psychotherapist's inability to tolerate the borderline patient's negative transference that revolves around a view of the psychotherapist as unable to accept, understand, or promote the patient's wish for separateness and autonomy. Some patients, for example, view their psychotherapist as so fragile and narcissistically vulnerable as to maliciously or unwittingly impede their own interpersonal or professional ambitions. The psychotherapist who is anxious about being viewed as a restrictive or emotionally crippled, individual occasionally will make a referral to a milieu as proof of good wishes for the patient. This may impede the analysis of the negative transference and confirm the patient's worst fears about the psychotherapist as having a restrictive effect on the patient.

Some pathological countertransference reactions obstruct the psychotherapist's capacity to use adjunctive treatment when it is required. Usually these reactions consist of heroic, extremely competitive or grandiose needs to manage a highly suicidal or destructive patient without the help of others.

Finally, some nonpathological countertransference reactions accompany the use of ongoing adjunctive milieu and individual psychotherapy. These reactions are usefully described by Langs (1981) as the "inevitable countertransference," suggesting that they are inescapable reactions that, when examined and integrated by the therapist, provide useful insights about the patient's affective experiences. Psychotherapists who refer patients for adjunctive treatment often have countertransference reactions that include feelings of competition with the day hospital about who is better acquainted with or more helpful to the patient. The psychotherapist may also experience a sense of the psychotherapy as being interrupted, or even invaded, by the patient's milieu treatment. Finally, the psychotherapist, as is frequently true for the patient upon referral for milieu treatment, may have feelings of being exposed and, in some measure, evaluated. The sophisticated milieu is able to help (quietly or explicitly) both the patient and the psychotherapist to cope with these reactions.

NEGATIVE THERAPEUTIC REACTIONS TO ADJUNCTIVE TREATMENT

In some instances referral of the borderline patient to the milieu by the psychotherapist is met with considerable narcissistic injury and rage. Often this reaction is reflective of an already existing problem in the psychotherapy. For example, if the patient senses that the psychotherapist is unconsciously (or consciously) frightened by the intensity of the patient's oral craving, the patient may interpret, correctly, the referral to an adjunctive milieu, when there is no ostensible crisis, as an indication that the psychotherapist wishes to diffuse these cravings, as in the case of Ms. C. However, it is striking that within some psychotherapies that are not contaminated by pathological countertransference, the patient responds to the psychotherapist's suggestions of adjunctive treatment with severe anxiety, rage, or disillusionment with the psychotherapist.

I understand this phenomenon as an inadvertent (and sometimes inevitable) interruption of the patient's wishes and fantasies revolving around the infinite capacity of the psychotherapist to fulfill a variety of needs, such as the satisfaction of oral cravings, or to militate against separation and annihilation anxiety.

The reasons for these reactions are complex and beyond the scope of this paper, but are discussed in greater length by Cooper and Adler (under review). Buie and Adler's (1982) outline of the phases of psychotherapy with borderline patients suggests that the earliest task in the treatment is to help the patient develop a sense of the therapist as a holding self-object, sometimes requiring the therapist to offer transitional objects specific to the therapist. The negative reactions described here point to a problem that Buie and Adler (1982) do not address, namely, those instances when the borderline patient's experience of aloneness, panic, and abandonment are worsened by the psychotherapist's efforts to provide holding and containment for the patient. The patient's conscious perception of a variety of empathic failures by the therapist as a holding self-object may occur while the psychotherapist unconsciously is regarded as a perfectly empathic, idealized self-object. Paradoxically, the therapist's acknowledgment of the patient's needs for additional treatment implicitly, but radically, may negate the unconscious fantasy that the psychotherapist function as a genuine holding self-object.

To lessen the level of the patient's regression to overwhelming feelings of abandonment and annihilation anxiety during these negative reactions, it is necessary that the psychotherapist clarify why he or she believes that adjunctive resources are necessary. These clarifications should be explicit about the psychotherapist's inability or unwillingness to accept particular behaviors or demands by the patient, if this is a major determinant in making the referral for milieu treatment. While these clarifications often do little to mend the ruptured unconscious fantasies, they do help reduce the patient's persecutory fears of the therapist as a malevolent or abandoning figure. These clarifications are usefully made by the milieu and the psychotherapist.

CONCLUSIONS

The psychotherapy of borderline patients is often fraught with various types of impasse, including the patients' intolerance of aloneness, their splitting of therapeutic figures, and their tendency to stimulate strong countertransference reactions. I have discussed how milieu treatment as an adjunct to individual psychotherapy may be used to help mitigate borderline patients' overwhelming experiences of anxiety, as well as to provide an integration of their intensely polarized affective reactions toward the therapist. This procedure should be used primarily when the patient's pain and self-destructive potential are life-threatening, or when they pose a threat to the continuation of analysis of the patient's experience. Another situation in which adjunctive resources are useful is that in which the psychotherapist feels that the patient's needs and demands exceed his or her tolerance capacity. Here the psychotherapist must assess whether the experience of intolerance is an "inevitable" form of countertransference created by the patient's unconscious and conscious conflicts or a form of his or her own pathological countertransference. In the latter case, referral to an adjunctive milieu is doomed to failure since the patient will inevitably interpret it, in one form or another, as the psychotherapist's wish to reject the patient, or at least to diffuse his or her own affective experience of the patient. The value of this therapeutic procedure lies not only in the quality of the therapeutic milieu itself, but with the psychotherapist's ability to understand the impact of this therapeutic framework on the ongoing conscious and unconscious experience of both the patient and the therapist.

REFERENCES

Adler, G. (1973). Hospital treatment of borderline patients. *Amer. J. Psychiat.*, 130:32–36.

——— (1977). Hospital management of borderline patients and its relation to psychotherapy. In *Borderline Personality Disorders: The Concept, the Syndrome, the Patient*, ed. P. Hartocollis. New York: International Universities Press.

——— (1980). Transference, real relationship and alliance. *Int. J. Psychoanal.*, 61:547–558.

——— & Buie, D. (1972). The misuses of confrontation with borderline patients. *Int. J. Psychoanal. Psychother.*, 1(3):109–120.

——— ——— (1979). Aloneness and borderline psychopathology: The possible relevance of child development issues. *Int. J. Psychoanal.*, 60:83–96.

Brown, L. (1981). The therapeutic milieu in the treatment of patients with borderline personality disorders. *Bull. Menninger Clin.*, 45(5):377–394.

Buie, D., & Adler, G. (1982). Definitive treatment of the borderline personality. *Int. J. Psychoanal. Psychother.*, 9:51–89.

Cooper, S. and Adler, G. (under review). Toward an integration of the transitional object and selfobject concepts in the treatment of the borderline patient.

Corwin, H. (1972). The scope of therapeutic confrontation from routine to heroic. *Int. J. Psychoanal. Psychother.*, 1(3):68–89.

Crafoord, C. (1977). Day hospital treatment of borderline patients: The institution as transitional object. In *Borderline Personality Disorders: The Concept, the Syndrome, the Patient*, ed. P. Hartocollis. New York: International Universities Press.

Deutsch, H. (1965). *Neuroses and Character Types*. New York: International Universities Press.

Horton, P. (1981). *Solace: The Missing Dimension in Psychiatry*. Chicago: University of Chicago Press.

Kernberg, O. (1975). *Borderline Conditions and Pathological Narcissism*. New York: Jason Aronson.

Kohut, H. (1971). *The Analysis of the Self*. New York: International Universities Press.

Langs, R. (1981). *Resistances and Interventions*. New York: Jason Aronson.

Lichtenberg, J., & Slap, J. (1973). Notes on the concept of splitting and the defense mechanism of splitting of representations. *J. Amer. Psychoanal. Assn.*, 21:772–787.

Mahler, M. (1968). *On Human Symbiosis and the Vicissitudes of Individuation.* Vol. I. *Infantile Psychosis.* New York: International Universities Press.

Maltsberger, J., & Buie, D. (1974). Countertransference hate in the treatment of suicidal patients. *Arch. Gen. Psychiat.*, 30:625–633.

Modell, A. (1963). Primitive object relationships and the predisposition to schizophrenia. *Int. J. Psychoanal.*, 44:282–292.

——— (1968). *Object Love and Reality.* New York: International Universities Press.

Nadelson, T. (1976). Victim, victimizer: Interaction in the psychotherapy of borderline patients. *Int. J. Psychoanal. Psychother.*, 4:115–129.

Stolorow, R., & Lachmann, F. (1980). *Psychoanalysis of Developmental Arrests.* New York: International Universities Press.

Tolpin, M. (1971). On the beginnings of a cohesive self: An application of the concept of transmuting internalization to the study of the transitional object and signal anxiety. *Psychoanal. Study Child*, 26:316–352.

Winnicott, D. (1949). Hate in the countertransference. *Int. J. Psychoanal.*, 30:69–74.

——— (1953). Transitional objects and transitional phenomena. *Int. J. Psychoanal.*, 34:89–97.

9 GERALD ADLER, M.D.

DISCUSSION: *Milieu Treatment in the Psychotherapy of the Borderline Patient: Abandonment and Containment*

MILIEU TREATMENT CAN BE USEFUL FOR BORDERLINE PATIENTS IN PSYCHOTHERAPY WHEN ALONENESS ISSUES EMERGE SECONDARY TO THEIR INCREASING ANGER IN THE TRANSFERENCE. WHEN THE HOLDING AND CONTAINING SELF-OBJECT FUNCTIONS PROVIDED BY THE THERAPIST FAIL, AND HOLDING INTROJECTS BECOME INCREASINGLY UNSTABLE, THE MILIEU CAN FUNCTION AS BOTH A SELF-OBJECT AND A TRANSITIONAL OBJECT. HOWEVER, BORDERLINE PATIENTS CANNOT UTILIZE TRANSITIONAL OBJECTS EFFECTIVELY UNTIL THEY EXPERIENCE THE THERAPIST OR MILIEU AS ADEQUATE HOLDING AND CONTAINING SELF-OBJECTS. MILIEU SELF-OBJECT FUNCTIONS INCLUDE PROTECTING THE PATIENT; PERFORMING A CAREFUL EVALUATION OF THE PATIENT, FAMILY, AND PSYCHOTHERAPY; AND ASSISTING THE PATIENT AND THERAPIST TO RESOLVE THE INTENSE TRANSFERENCE AND COUNTERTRANSFERENCE ISSUES. THE MILIEU ALSO PERFORMS A SELF-OBJECT FUNCTION FOR THE THERAPIST BY PROVIDING CONSULTATION THAT IS SENSITIVE TO FEELINGS OF COUNTERTRANSFERENCE SHAME AND GUILT.

The successful psychotherapy of borderline patients inevitably includes an exploration of their propensity to feel painfully alone. These aloneness experiences occur as a manifestation of their vulnerable capacity to hold and soothe themselves, as well as an interpersonal style that provokes rejection in people they desperately need. When these aloneness issues emerge in the psychotherapy of borderline patients, the capacities of their therapists are stressed in their attempts to contain their patients' aloneness feelings and the rage that often accompanies them, without retaliating, abandoning, rejecting, or destroying. Dr. Cooper's paper provides an excellent framework in which to formulate and discuss some of these complex and clinically important ideas. We can focus on understanding the needs of these patients that can include a milieu setting and the countertransference responses of therapist and milieu staff that can make successful treatment so difficult.

Since borderline patients usually must face their aloneness feelings, at what point is something required beyond individual psychotherapy when these feelings finally emerge? In order to answer such a question, we must examine the basic capacities and vulnerabilities the patient brings to the treatment situation, and the skills and limitations of the therapist, including the inevitable and pathological countertransference (Langs, 1981). The results of such an understanding can then be applied to treatment decisions for the patients, which can include the use of a milieu.

The borderline patient's lack of a solid capacity for self-holding and self-soothing usually emerges in a dyadic relationship that promises something the patient desperately needs, often related to the holding and soothing capacities he or she sees in the other person that cannot be counted on to be present in the patient him or herself. The patient ultimately fails to get what is needed from the other person for a number of reasons. The intense longings involved have a hungry, devouring, and, therefore, potentially destructive quality. In addition, this hunger includes a wish for a merging closeness. All of these longings threaten the patient's ego boundaries, often leading to a protective retreat in the face of increasingly intense wishes. The "need–fear dilemma" that Burnham and colleagues (1969) describe for schizophrenics is also true for borderline patients. Borderlines fear the disintegration of ego and self whereas schizophrenics experience it. The dilemma for the borderline patient is that this neediness threatens intactness. At the same time, the frightening rage increases, as the important person in the patient's life cannot fulfill his or her intense wishes, and so inevitably disappoints. Thus it is both the fear of intense longings and the inevitable failure of the other person in the dyad to fulfill them that leads to the escalation of rage seen in the borderline patient's regression in psychotherapy.

The burden for the person important in the borderline's life is manifold. The patient, in addition to the manifest longings and anger, may project them onto the other, and provoke that person to act out the projection in relation to the patient, as in projective identification (Ogden, 1979). Thus the patient longs, wishes, demands, projects, and provokes, while the other person is in a painful position of being buffeted by intense feelings in a way that can confuse and infuriate, and elicit a wide range of countertransference responses.

Another aspect of the borderline patient's pathology that makes it difficult for the patient to get what he or she needs is the primitive quality of the guilt. Their voraciousness and rage are seen by such patients as a part of a total badness, deserving of capital punishment. They must punish themselves for their longings and neediness, since these are tied to their oral incorporative urges and rage, both of which feel destructive. As an aspect of their self-punishment, they cannot allow themselves to take what they need from other persons in a manner that would lead to soothing and holding capacities becoming a part of themselves. In addition, the primitive quality of their superegos is manifest by the ease with which they project their guilt onto the others and expect retaliation from those persons for the conviction of their own badness.

Thus borderline patients' inability to use the other persons in a way that fills their own emptiness based upon the need–fear dilemma, and their primitive guilt account for the basic vulnerabilities that they bring to the dyadic relationship, as well as the reasons that the dyadic situation usually does not lead to a growing capacity to heal the emptiness, neediness, and aloneness. This basic incapacity of borderline patients to make use of relationships can be defined as their incapacity to introject aspects of the other persons so that they may ultimately lead to structural change. They therefore come to a new relationship with an inability to count on their own self-holding and self-soothing, which remain a vulnerability usually not repaired in the new dyadic relationship.

The psychotherapeutic relationship offers the borderline patient the opportunity to address this basic incapacity that feels so resistant to change. By their very nature, borderline patients will tend to lose their holding and soothing introjects when their rage emerges in the psychotherapy, usually secondary to the inevitable disappointments in the face of their increasing neediness, and fueled by their guilt and fears of taking what they feel they need. The loss of these holding and soothing introjects compromises their capacity to tolerate separation and leads to their increasing sense of painful aloneness, often accompanied by panic. This relative or profound loss of an evocative memory for the therapist's holding and soothing qualities is often at the core of issues related to the need for more from the therapist, which can include the need for milieu therapy, when holding and soothing introjects are regressively lost.

The assessment of the patient's need for adjunctive treatment includes an evaluation of the basic ego strengths and vulnerabilities brought into treatment. For example, in assessing the patient's strengths, it is important to consider that some borderline patients have an almost unbelievable capacity to continue with their jobs or professions in the midst of an intense borderline regression. Not only does their work keep them busy and help contain their panic by the structure and relationships it offers, but it also supports their extremely shaky self-worth. Any program that removes them from work may lead to a significantly more severe regression and an increase in the suicidal potential that usually accompanies such a regression. In contrast, other borderline patients may quickly lose their internal capacities to cope in the face of the regression following their rage, as well as their ability to make use of dyadic relationships. Borderline patients thus vary in their basic inner resources, their ability to maintain them in the face of stress, the degree to which they lose their holding and soothing introjects, and their ability to use people and other resources in their environment. In addition, real environmental supports can be very different for different patients. Available and caring family members can sometimes determine how the borderline patient can contain a regression that occurs in psychotherapy. The borderline patient who is alone in the world can be in a very different position in needing adjunctive treatment when compared with another borderline who lives within a supportive family structure.

The therapist's understanding, clinical capacities, and countertransference responses are also crucial in evaluating whether the therapy itself can contain the regressed borderline patient. The self-holding and soothing that the borderline patient cannot provide reliably for him or herself must gradually become a part of the psychotherapeutic setting. Although it is not the therapist's role to make up for failures in the patient's past life and experiences, it *is* the therapist's task to understand the patient's vulnerabilities and need to be contained and symbolically held in the midst of increasingly disruptive feelings and needs. The different capacities that therapists possess to respond optimally to their borderline patients, communicating their understanding of a patient's pain while maintaining an optimal distance, play an important role that may determine whether or not a marginally functioning borderline patient in a regression requires adjunctive treatment. Obviously the therapist's capacity to monitor and use countertransference responses creatively is important at such times.

Winnicott's (1965) transitional object concept and Kohut's formulations (1971, 1977) of the self-object and self-object transferences are relevant in discussions of the patient's, therapist's, and milieu's roles in the psychotherapy of the borderline patient. Kohut has defined the self-object transferences as the primary ones present in the treatment of the narcissistic personality disorder. As a manifestation of more profound difficulties, the borderline patient cannot reliably utilize and maintain the therapist as a stable self-object, regardless of the therapist's skills (Adler, 1981). Although the patient may begin by idealizing the therapist and using the therapist's "mirroring" responses to feel understood and momentarily more cohesive, the inevitable borderline issues and difficulties emerge. Disappointments escalate to rage, and therapist responses that previously were part of transiently stable self-object transferences lead to increasing neediness, anger, and rejection of the therapist. "Fragmentation" follows a regressive pathway that ultimately leads to loss of affective evocative memory for the formerly holding and soothing therapist introjects. At such times, when self-object functions that the therapist provided begin to break down, transitional objects become especially important to the regressed borderline patient (Adler & Buie, 1979; Buie & Adler, 1982). Tangible evidence of the therapist's existence and caring becomes extremely helpful in reestablishing the transiently lost evocative memory. This includes, for example, appointment cards for the next session with the therapist, the therapist's last bill, or, when the regression occurs secondary to the therapist's vacation, a postcard from the therapist, a diary that the patient keeps, or regular tape recordings that the patient makes in the therapist's absence as aids in evoking the therapist's felt presence.

There are important distinctions between the self-object functions the therapist or the milieu provides and the transitional objects the therapist or someone else may offer when self-object transferences falter. Dr. Cooper stresses the transitional object functions provided by the therapist and milieu, and the complex interaction around these transitional object functions when the therapist refers a patient for adjunctive treatment. His emphasis on the transitional object functions requires an elaboration of the role of the self-object and the distinctions between transitional object and self-object (Cooper & Adler, submitted for publication).

TRANSITIONAL OBJECTS AND SELF-OBJECTS

For transitional objects to be of use to someone, sufficient internalization of self-object functions provided by important people is crucial. For the child—for example, the 15–24-month-old who is just developing a solid evocative memory capacity—many parental self-object functions are only tenuously internalized. The transitional object is used by the child to evoke the real as well as idealized self-object functions that the parents are and have been providing. We also know that when parental or parent-substitute self-objects fail too extensively, the child loses the capacity to utilize transitional objects. For example, toward the end of his nine-day separation from his mother while in a residential setting with inadequately available staff, 17-month-old John almost completely lost his ability to use his teddy bear to comfort himself (Robertson & Robertson, 1971). Similarly, with adult borderline patients, transitional objects are of use when the patient has had an experience of the therapist providing holding, soothing, and containing functions in the past, and when the present emerging rage in the transference is not too disruptive. The borderline patient experiencing diffuse primitive rage (Adler & Buie, 1979) not only regresses to the panic of losing both evocative and recognition memory for the therapist, but would also be incapable of utilizing any transitional object the therapist offered at that point. Once the acuteness of the regression is addressed in therapy, leading to the return of recognition memory and the transient availability of evocative memory, transitional objects again become functional for the borderline patient. In contrast, transitional objects are usually of use for the person on the continuum from narcissistic personality disorder to neurotic to normal, almost regardless of the current availability of self-objects. Such healthier people have sufficiently internalized holding and soothing introjects so that only the most *profound*, overwhelming stress would shake the capacity to be in touch with these introjects, and thus the ability to use transitional objects.

These distinctions become important in sorting out some of the complex psychoanalytic literature. For example, Modell's (1963) pioneering discussion of transitional object relatedness, in his conceptualization of the borderline patient, emphasized the transitional object concept in a context that did not address the need of borderline patients for the self-object functions provided by the therapist to allow transitional objects to be useful to the patient. Borderline patients cannot utilize the therapist as a transitional object to the degree that Modell describes unless the therapist is experienced by the patients sufficiently as a holding and soothing self-object. The conceptualization of the therapist as a self-object allows us to define the many ways that the patient uses the therapist and the differing ways in which the patient utilizes transitional objects that the self-object therapist offers.

THE MILIEU AS TRANSITIONAL OBJECT OR SELF-OBJECT

The therapist who considers adjunctive treatment for a patient is in a position to define his or her understanding of the reasons for the patient's current regression, the nature of the patient's vulnerabilities, and the real supportive environment available to the patient in daily life. Based upon this assessment, the therapist can ask a milieu to perform both transitional object and self-object functions. When the therapist, in correctly assessing the patient's needs and vulnerabilities, sends the patient for milieu treatment in the midst of a regression with transient loss of evocative memory and holding introjects, the holding and protecting self-object functions of the milieu of a day hospital, for example, help bolster the patient's faltering evocative memory. The staff's self-object function of defining the patient's current overwhelmed state and day-to-day protective and containing needs provides the structure that can reverse the transference regression of mounting need and rage that led to the transient loss of holding and soothing introjects. At that point the patient can utilize the milieu as the transitional object, representing the therapist's caring wish to protect the overwhelmed patient and so help the patient to evoke the affective memory of the therapist. Thus the milieu can function as the transitional object supplied by the therapist when its structure and activity have performed self-object functions that restored the patient to a point where transitional objects were again utilizable. Comparably, as already noted, the regressed borderline outpatient can only utilize, for example, the therapist's appointment card as a transitional object when holding and soothing introjects are not totally lost, and when the therapist's self-object function can readily be reevoked; with further regression, such transitional objects offered by the therapist fail.

CONTAINMENT, TRANSFERENCE, AND COUNTERTRANSFERENCE: MILIEU, PATIENT, AND THERAPIST

The initial function of the milieu is to provide the protection and containment the borderline patient requires, including the rapid assessment and management of suicidal and homicidal dangers. This initial assessment merges with the important function of a detailed evaluation of the patient and family, and a careful exploration of the psychotherapeutic relationship between patient and therapist. It is not uncommon to have a borderline patient admitted to an adjunctive setting who has never had a thorough evaluation, including a thoughtful formulation and treatment plan. Often borderline patients relatively rapidly provoke a therapeutic situation of neediness, action, and disorganization, so that the therapist may inadvertently, or by choice, give up the goal of carrying out the evaluation. In addition, the intense countertransference feelings aroused, often in response to the patient's reliving of childhood hopelessness, helplessness, and rage, may preclude the possibility of such an evaluation being thoughtful.

Since the need for adjunctive treatment usually occurs in the midst of intense transference and countertransference feelings, the assessment of the psychotherapy is particularly important (Adler, 1977). The task usually requires tact and an appreciation of both the patient's and the therapist's vulnerabilities. Insufficient attention is usually given to the therapist's feelings of shame and guilt upon referring a patient for adjunctive treatment. Countertransference feelings of hate, sadism, and rejection toward the patient are usually accompanied by some degree of guilt. In addition, the therapist working with a patient who has repeatedly devalued any attempts to be helpful, and often has left the therapist feeling helpless and hopeless, has had little in the interchange that validates a sense of professional competence and worth. Therapists, even when they do not have serious narcissistic pathology, still require validation that they are competent and have something of worth to offer (Adler, 1984). The experience with the patient who is struggling with the borderline issues that necessitated adjunctive treatment is certainly not providing such validation. Understandably, the therapist will be feeling vulnerable with transient or more sustained feelings of shame, worthlessness, and guilt. The milieu staff's understanding of such therapist vulnerability can allow them to provide self-object functions to both therapist and patient, and carry out a thorough evaluation of the treatment in a setting that respects the vulnerabilities of each.

The milieu's countertransference not infrequently prevents the staff from being optimally helpful to both patient and therapist. The sense of competence that a good adjunctive unit possesses can readily shift to a position of grandiosity and specialness. It may then begin to work under the assumption that every admission of a patient in psychotherapy by definition involves a patient who is in a bad psychotherapeutic relationship. As part of this countertransference constellation, the therapist is not contacted for participation in the evaluation, is not urged to continue to work with the patient while in the adjunctive setting, or is treated in a way that supports feelings of guilt and shame. This variation of the well-known "splitting" phenomenon (Adler, 1973) is particularly destructive to both patient and therapist, as it does not provide the framework for both to clarify and work through the intense transference–countertransference feelings that often have led to the admission. Of course, a careful evaluation in a well-functioning unit can conclude that the therapist and patient are not in a therapeutic relationship that is viable, and recommend that they terminate. Under these circumstances a self-object function of the unit is to allow them to take leave of each other in a way that maximizes the positive gains and takes into account the vulnerabilities of both.

Dr. Cooper's paper beautifully illustrates the importance of the therapist's attempts to examine the inevitable and pathological countertransference responses (Langs, 1981) to the borderline patient in order to determine the need for adjunctive treatment. The clinical examples also define the potential misuses of the milieu. The two patients discussed illustrate the countertransference dilemmas in work with borderline patients and the importance of the therapist having a formulation to help understand the meanings of the transference–countertransference experience. Dr. Cooper's formulation of his first patient clarified her wish to diffuse the intensity of the erotic transference she was experiencing, as well as getting herself punished through her request for adjunctive treatment. He also noted her good capacity to contain aloneness issues at that time and the relative absence of his inevitable countertransference responses. Adjunctive treatment would have allowed her to act out her conflicts rather than examine them in the psychotherapy at a time when she had that capacity.

The second patient helps define the importance of the therapist being willing to acknowledge in an appropriate way elements of the pathological countertransference that led to a wish to provide adjunctive treatment in order to avoid the intensity of the patient's orality and neediness, and ultimately the negative transference. His ability to modify his position in response to the patient's concerns and objections, and to see validity in her perceptions, resulted in two important achievements: (1) it allowed both patient and therapist to work in a manner that was optimal for the patient, and (2) it provided a model for the patient of someone who could own an incorrect decision and modify it. Most borderline patients have had childhood/family experiences in which denial and projection were major ways of dealing with feelings and conflicts. The rigid therapist who does not own his or her limitations and errors is acting in a way that is too close to the patient's pathological childhood scenes. Dr. Cooper's modification of his stance with his patient offered a new kind of experience to the patient and allowed her to see him as separate from her parents and previous therapists, who had also repeated aspects of her early pathological relationships.

The therapist's correct assessment of the need for adjunctive treatment does provide the containment the patient requires, and the adjunctive self-object transferences and transitional objects necessary to continue the work with the patient. As the author notes, the use of adjunctive therapy can also define the limits of the therapist. Although the patient may become angry at such times, he or she can also experience relief that feelings of rage can be contained with the help of the milieu and worked through with the therapist in a more protective setting. When adjunctive treatment is part of a correct assessment of the patient's and therapist's need to work together, the patient's fears of abandonment are also addressed. The patient must perceive the therapist's inevitable intense, and at times pathological, countertransference feelings, and thus be made aware of the possibility of abandonment by the therapist's acting out of the rejection of the patient. Adjunctive treatment that is part of continuing psychotherapy contains the patient and obtains the additional self-object and transitional object help that the patient senses is necessary at that time. It also can provide self-object functions for the therapist: consultation and a safe setting in which to work with the patient and further the exploration of vulnerable areas.

Why do some patients seem to get worse when the therapist attempts to provide the containment and holding the patient needs? A variety of complex reasons can account for this apparent paradox. I only wish to examine two elements here. I have been impressed that some therapists rarely or never have had experiences with borderline patients in which aloneness issues were in the forefront, whereas others have patients in which aloneness and abandonment themes are frequently present. It could be that some therapists work with higher level borderlines where these themes are less in evidence. On the other hand, I believe that some therapists, through their person and style, are able to communicate to their patients that they are there to listen to everything the patient brings; others, in similar nonverbal ways, let their patients know that there are limits to what they can and want to hear. Most patients will comply with the limitations of their therapists and try to make optimal use of what the therapists have to offer. Some patients who need a therapist who works in some other way will leave treatment and keep searching until they find one who offers what they need. Of course, much clinical research is required to determine the strengths and limitations of each psychotherapeutic approach, which patients are benefited by a stance that opens up aloneness issues and which patients are harmed, and which patients should be treated only by the milieu and not by individual psychotherapy at all because they do not have the emotional resources or reality supports to tolerate it.

The other element in patients who seem to become worse in treatment that offers containment and holding can be the result of the therapist's unrecognized pathological countertransference responses, resulting in the patient idealizing the therapist, but being unable to be aware of the negative transference that is split off and denied. The therapist's holding responses may mask a wish to avoid the patient's rage. The patient unconsciously perceives the therapist's difficulties and complies, consistent with the false self themes (Winnicott, 1965) seen in many borderline patients who attempt to survive within the limitations of the therapist's capacity, rather than risk aloneness, abandonment, rage, and dissolution of the self.

REFERENCES

Adler, G. (1973). Hospital treatment of borderline patients. *Amer. J. Psychiat.*, 130:32–36.

——— (1977). Hospital management of borderline patients and its relationship to psychotherapy. In *Borderline Personality Disorders*, ed. P. Harticollis. New York: International Universities Press, pp. 307–323.

——— (1981). The borderline-narcissistic personality continuum. *Amer. J. Psychiat.*, 138:46–50.

——— (1984). Issues in the treatment of the borderline patient. In *Kohut's Legacy: Contributions to Self Psychology*, ed. P. E. Stepansky & A. Goldberg. Hillsdale, NJ: Analytic Press, pp. 117–134.

——— & Buie, D. H. (1979). Aloneness and borderline psychopathology: The possible relevance of child development issues. *Int. J. Psychoanal.*, 60:83–96.

Buie, D. H., & Adler, G. (1982). Definitive treatment of the borderline personality. *Int. J. Psychoanal. Psychother.*, 9:51–87.

Burnham, D. G., Gladstone, A. I., & Gibson, R. W. (1969). *Schizophrenia and the Need–Fear Dilemma*. New York: International Universities Press.

Cooper, S. H., & Adler, G. (Submitted for Publication). Toward an integration of the transitional object and self-object concepts in the treatment of the borderline patient.

Kohut, H. (1971). *The Analysis of the Self*. New York: International Universities Press.

——— (1977). *The Restoration of the Self*. New York: International Universities Press.

Langs, R. (1981). *Resistances and Interventions*. New York: Jason Aronson.

Modell, A. (1963). Primitive object relationships and the predisposition to schizophrenia. *Int. J. Psychoanal.*, 44:282–292.

Ogden, T. H. (1979). On projective identification. *Int. J. Psychoanal.*, 60:357–373.

Robertson, J., & Robertson, J. (1971). Young children in brief separation: A fresh look. *Psychoanal. Study Child*, 26:264–315.

Winnicott, D. W. (1965). *The Maturational Processes and the Facilitating Environment*. New York: International Universities Press.

10 PHYLLIS TERRY FRIEDMAN, Ph.D.

The Making of a Communicative Psychoanalytic Psychotherapist

LEARNING THE COMMUNICATIVE APPROACH TO PSYCHOTHERAPY IS A DIFFICULT TASK. IT REQUIRES AN ALTERATION OF THERAPEUTIC STYLE AND SETTING, AND IS INITIALLY EXPERIENCED AS A GREAT INJURY TO THE THERAPIST'S SELF-ESTEEM. IN MAKING THE TRANSITION TO THE COMMUNICATIVE APPROACH, THE THERAPIST IS IN A PAINFUL BIND: THROUGH SUCCESSFULLY DECIPHERING THE PATIENT'S ENCODED PERCEPTIONS OF HIS OR HER INTERVENTIONS, THE THERAPIST HEARS AN ABUNDANCE OF CRITICISM BUT IS AS YET WITHOUT THE SKILLS TO RECTIFY THE ERRORS. THE THERAPIST MAY RESPOND WITH GUILT AND ACTING OUT FREQUENTLY ENSUES AT THIS JUNCTURE. DESPITE THE DIFFICULTIES IN LEARNING THE COMMUNICATIVE APPROACH, THE TECHNIQUE PROVIDES THE THERAPIST WITH A TREATMENT MODALITY THAT IS THOROUGH, OPTIMISTIC, AND GENUINELY RESPECTFUL OF THE PATIENT. IN ADDITION, AFFORDING THE PATIENT SOUND TREATMENT AND POSITIVE REGARD ULTIMATELY RESULTS IN INCREASED SELF-REGARD FOR THE THERAPIST.

At this writing I have been in supervision with Robert Langs for some four months. In this brief span of time, a number of unanticipated issues have arisen in my struggle to adjust to the communicative approach to psychotherapy. As part of my self-therapy in surviving this radical transition from the usual dynamic approach to this new way of doing therapy, I wish to document the process involved. To that end I have interviewed other therapists new to the communicative approach and will present our collective story in the hope of elucidating the major themes that are integral to this shift, as the transition appears to be not without its painful moments.

WHY DO IT?

I had known for awhile that my own therapeutic technique was inadequate. While many patients showed improvement, therapy with the more difficult ones was stalemated and years would pass without any noticeable change. I frequently found myself struggling with the question of what to do with these patients. Unfortunately my series of supervisors offered only ineffectual solutions. For example, in a case with an acting-out, delusional adolescent, my supervisor, in an attempt to mollify my feelings of failure, explained that there simply were no answers to her situation. With regard to several ambulatory chronic schizophrenic patients I was treating, another supervisor advised me to use "supportive" therapy (i.e., empathic listening and discussion of daily activities) because cure, or even significant psychological integration, was not possible. A third supervisor proposed behavior therapy techniques with the implicit assumption that there are no other psychological issues beyond reduction of manifest symptoms. In the end, however, all of this well-intentioned "help" only left me feeling more discouraged and despairing; it dampened my natural optimism about the efficacy of psychotherapy and thus rendered me all the more impotent as a therapist.

In addition to these unhappy supervisory experiences, I was aware that I lacked a coherent system of treatment: a little Carl Rogers, a little Gestalt therapy, some psychosynthesis, a press to uncover the genetics of symptoms, a dab of feminist counseling, and more recently, a healthy sprinkling of family systems theory. The technique on which I focused was more likely related to the book I was reading that week, or the orientation of my supervisor that year. (I had already ended a Carl Jung phase so he was no longer included in the composite.) My determination of the success of my therapeutic endeavors was based on both a shift in attitude and an observable behavioral change on the part of the patient. To achieve this end, abreaction was the key: if a patient could reach through to his or her tears, I thought, then he or she must be healing. In retrospect I wonder who often the patient was instead reacting mainly to my harsh, haphazard technique rather than his or her own painful memories and unfulfilled fantasies.

I gleaned this particular theory of cure from my last supervisor. He was a bright young psychologist who had been well trained in psychoanalytic therapy. However, his own aberrant practices with clients should have warned me about the validity of his technique.

He was consistently late for sessions, sometimes as much as two hours; he spoke undisguisedly about patients and the content of their sessions; and he was seductive with patients to the extent that he would give them rides in his car. On one occasion he received a pornographic letter from a female client (who suffered symptoms of a constricted throat) and he happily shared it with me. He held it as a sign of the wonderful "simpatico" that had developed between them, and when I flinched, he accused me of being sexually repressed.

All of this is to say that although my own therapy technique may have been ineffectual, chaotic, and at times hurtful, a plethora of deviant role models from all theoretical persuasions was available to me. And from what I have since read and observed, it appears that abuses and misalliances are unfortunately more often the rule than the exception. In my case, however, it was the awareness of my confused, unsuccessful technique and a desire to be a more effective therapist that brought me to Langs.

Other therapists echoed my concern about ineffectual technique when asked why they were drawn to the communicative approach. One clinical psychologist explained: "I just was not feeling good about my work and I was honestly ready to give up clinical practice. I wanted growth but I was stagnating and I really did not have any sense of effectiveness. I am talking about my more difficult patients. I had a supervisor who really believed it was all in the transference. But he did not have it systematized. I wish that he could have explained his system to me. But he could not. I was very frustrated."

Other clinicians explained that they were attracted to communicative psychotherapy because it provided a system of greater depth and thoroughness for comprehending patients' communications. The following vignette from a training analyst speaks to the pressing need for penetrating the latent content of therapy sessions. The analyst had been treating the patient for five years, during which time he had presented the case for weekly supervision and periodic case conferences. It was agreed by the supervisory staff that this patient was ideal for analysis. Eventually, because of the success of his treatment, the patient was terminated. Several months later the patient committed suicide unexpectedly. His therapist, the training analyst, was convinced that crucial communications in the therapy had been entirely overlooked, thus resulting in tragedy.

For another group of therapists, interest in the communicative approach was spurred by their own experience of abusive psychotherapy. One male therapist recalled his treatment in a residential setting where the patients lived with the therapists who were supposed to "reparent" them. No boundaries whatsoever were observed here. There was neither privacy nor confidentiality, and sessions were typically scheduled in a haphazard manner, with the therapist habitually arriving late. He remembered imploring his therapist to arrive on time. However, any mention of issues pertaining to the adaptive context (e.g., privacy, confidentiality, regular sessions) was promptly ignored. Treatment was a failure, and he reflected, "I didn't know what was wrong exactly. I just knew that I never could talk about anything that really mattered to me." Years later, when reading about communicative psychotherapy, he found an explanation for the lack of depth in his own therapy and understood that his yearning for structure was in fact a sane request of a "mad" therapist.

In summation then, it appears that the decision to become a communicative psychotherapist arises out of the experience of the superficiality, ineffectiveness, and failure of other treatment modalities. New communicative therapists typically are not neophytes who are being introduced to psychotherapy for the first time, but rather are experienced practitioners who are reexamining their clinical practices and asking for a model of treatment that is more systematic, thorough, and better adept at deciphering the deepest layers of patients' communications. For many of us, the communicative approach is the phoenix arising out of the ashes of past therapy failures.

WHAT DO YOU MEAN, NO CONFRONTATION?

In my first supervisory sessions with Langs, he pointed out that my style of incessant questioning (who, what, why, then, where, how) was overactive and intrusive, thereby interfering with the patient's ability to produce derivatives, that is, to encode unconscious material. I needed to give them room, he explained, by becoming silent so that the unconscious content could flow forth. Though I had read that the communicative approach precluded this question-and-answer interview-style technique, I did not understand the rationale, or the critical need for silence. Among my noncommunicative colleagues, it was agreed that such silences on the part of the therapist were unnecessary, and actually lessened the vitality of the therapeutic interaction. I seem to have maintained the fiction that learning the communicative approach meant fixing the frame (preferably as quickly as possible) and then interpreting the dynamics of the material the patient presented (i.e., the manifest content) as usual, without any particular attention paid to the style in which this was done.

In retrospect I am surprised that although I had previously acquainted myself with Langs through his books and lectures, I had missed entirely his observations that improper technique made the production of derivatives and interpretation of breaks in the frame difficult or impossible. This focus on precision of technique was the first rude awakening I experienced (many more were to follow) and a minor blow to my self-esteem. Other therapists I interviewed who were trained in more traditional analytic techniques had less difficulty with this aspect of the transition, as they were accustomed to sitting in relative silence.

Langs further explained that my technique of direct confrontation (in retrospect I see that I was virtually combative) had the effect of wounding the patient without adding any understanding of his or her difficulties. I was stunned, since confrontation accounted for a good two-thirds of what I did. Upon examination I could understand from the derivative material that what I called healthy confrontation in fact came across to my patients as cruel and provoking, and they responded in kind. This reaction was most clearly seen in the feedback I received from a young man with a borderline character structure. (I have the impression that, among all the personality disorders, the borderline patient is the most sensitive and most reactive to frame deviations. If one wishes to determine the flaws even in the most ostensibly tight frame, a borderline patient will instantly, if not dramatically, ferret out one's failings by typically responding to deviations with action or verbal abuse.) The patient was a seriously disturbed young man who had been in treatment with me for five years. He was functionally impaired by symptoms of anxiety and depression, as well as obsessional thoughts and compulsive, ritualized behaviors.

To illustrate my pre-Langs therapeutic style as background for all the changes I have had to undergo, I submit the following summation of two of our therapy sessions:

> The patient, an attractive man in his early 20s, entered the office and angrily asked me if I would be in for our next session, as it was a minor holiday. I said yes, and he replied that he would not be coming. I asked why, and he said because it was a holiday for him. "I don't understand," I said, "Why does that mean you're not coming?" He then explained that I did not come on holidays so why should he? I confronted him, telling him that his not coming was an expression of anger at me and a desire

> to retaliate. He agreed and told me how his parents said he was wasting his money by coming to therapy.
>
> At the following session, I informed him that I was obliged to change my office hours and that I would need to reschedule him. He burst out that I always said no, that I always changed things on him, and that I could not be trusted. I pointed out that he seemed angry. He responded with a verbal bombast at my inadequacies. I confronted him again, pointing out that he was personalizing his necessary change. He agreed and sarcastically replied, "So what?"

From this vignette numerous difficulties are apparent that were attributable to the use of flawed technique. The style of quick response and questioning focused therapy on the surface of the material and deprived the patient of the space he needed for the production of spontaneous images, memories, and vignettes, that is, the derivative expression of unconscious material. The use of confrontation only caused him to feel blamed and punished, and did nothing to further his understanding of the genesis of his feelings and behavior. The injury caused him is evident in his response, which was equally cruel and chastising. Each time I pointed to his failings, he would point to mine, directly telling me that I was inadequate and worthless. The result was that we remained embroiled in endless verbal sparring without resolution. The material did not deepen and there was no insight. Instead we were trapped in a sadomasochistic misalliance with the designated therapist playing an active role in repeating the earlier destructive relationship the patient had had with his parents. When I attempted to salvage my actions by pointing out the patient's aggressive and insulting behavior toward me, Langs would not let me ignore my own part. "You were getting your licks in, too," he said, "implying that he was so stupid as to think you shouldn't have a holiday." It was clear that this new technique meant that no longer could I entirely blame the victim when therapy failed.

In addition to hearing on a derivative level about injury resulting from interventional errors, I further discovered that the treatment conditions that deviated from an ideal frame were also experienced by the patient as injurious. The following vignette illustrates this point:

> The patient was a young, divorced woman whom I had been treating for severe depression. Because of her complaints about financial problems, I had offered her a reduced fee. My usual fee was $50 and she was to pay $30.

> She began this session by asking what her new fee would be. She then spoke about lower back pain and her anger toward her ex-husband. Halfway through the session, she passionately recounted an incident that recently occurred: She had hired a gardener to clean her yard and prune her trees. When she inquired how much he would charge, he explained that normally it would cost $100, but he would do it for her for $75. "So he came over one day and when he left—what a mess! Dirt everywhere! I couldn't believe it! He didn't clean up at all! I tell you it was awful!"
>
> The next day when the gardener returned to collect his pay, the patient berated him for leaving such a mess. He apologized and she asked him about trimming another tree. He told her that normally he charged $50 "but for you, $35." He complained about her abusive language and then added, "I know what you need. You need a kiss." The patient was infuriated and commented, "Like just because I was a woman he thought he could take advantage of me."

If one understands this story as a comment on the conditions of treatment, it is evident that the offering of a reduced fee had a deleterious effect. The patient seemed to be saying that by reducing her fee I, like the gardener, was making a terrible mess out of things. "Bargain" prices resulted in bad service. Moreover, there was an element of seduction in the reduced fee. (It is noteworthy that in the second part of her story the gardener's initial price and the reduced amount are nearly identical to my regular and reduced fees.) Just as with the gardener, a reduced rate meant that she was now beholden to me and that I was in a position to exploit her. For this patient the exploitive element was sexual: If the gardener could insist on a kiss to reward his "favor," what might her therapist demand? Clearly, despite my good intentions, this deviation from the sound ground rules of treatment was hurtful.

There was no denying it. My deviations and my hostile and aggressive technique were recorded through material that I had carefully typed out myself. I had a fleeting urge to be more discreet with what I "remembered" of the next sessions, but quickly saw the futility in that. It was another bruise to my self-esteem, though. Were it simply that Langs had judged the treatment conditions or my therapy style abusive, I am certain I could have dismissed it. But deciphering the patient's encoded perceptions made it indisputably evident that it was the patient who found me abusive. I could not dismiss this fact and it was hurtful.

The experience of acknowledging one's destructive behavior in therapy is indeed a narcissistic wound and frequently engenders defensive maneuvers on the part of the therapist (see Raney, 1984). The defenses typically mobilized at this point are denial, disavowal, and projection of blame. One therapist attempted to deny his errors by deleting material for supervision that he thought might show him in a negative light. The only problem with that method, he explained, was that in presenting his "good" interventions, his flaws came to light anyway, only with added injury because he had presumed that he had done exemplary work. Other therapists attempted to deny outright that the derivative material contained encoded perceptions of them. They also resorted to blaming the problems of therapy on the patient's resistances, lack of motivation, hostility, or primitive character structure. At times Langs was blamed for adhering so rigidly to the concept of the frame and the patient's derivatives. This was probably so because he was the bearer of bad tidings (i.e., the patient's encoded perceptions of the therapist) and therefore aroused the impulse to "kill the messenger," just as the ancient Greeks did.

For most therapists, however, these flimsy defenses inevitably broke down and psychological symptoms were experienced. Depression seemed to be the most commonplace. This included self-doubt, tremendous feelings of inadequacy, and self-deprecating thoughts that became ruminative and obsessional. One therapist seriously wondered whether he possessed the intellectual capacity to learn the approach. Another was convinced that he could not continue practicing the communicative approach without massive doses of personal psychotherapy. And a third therapist did return to therapy when her self-worth took a dramatic plunge.

It seems, then, that the general reaction to the initial learning of the communicative approach is the experience of a great hurt to one's self-esteem and the feeling of being wounded, as it became evident from the patients' material—mainly, though not always, on the derivative level—that we, as therapists and espoused helpers, were actually causing them injury. The wound was compounded because we are all trained and experienced therapists with pride in our expertise. Langs (1982a) did not exaggerate when he said, "The blow to one's self-esteem in recognizing that he or she has been hurtful to a patient is enormous. It asks a great deal of a therapist to be honest in the appraisal and appreciation of his or her own therapeutic work and to tolerate the personal mortification that is an inevitable part of the learning experience" (pp. 19–20). Taking the communicative approach seriously meant having to start all over from scratch after years of working in the field.

One therapist summed up the situation in his reaction: "This has been difficult work. It means, in essence, taking everything I have known to do, everything I have perfected in the sphere where I feel most confident, and tossing it aside, or at least having to make major renovations. It is as though I have built a house that I believed to be a beautiful, sturdy house, and yet when I look at the foundation with Langs, I see that there are all sorts of flaws and termites, and that the foundation is not at all substantial. So on one hand I am excited because I will possibly be able to build a substantial foundation for my therapy work, but on the other hand it is a blow to have to admit that the foundation is faulty."

Despite my own injured sense of esteem, I was curious to hear how my other patients might be perceiving me unconsciously. Being unaccustomed to silence, it was an effort for me to remain quiet. Nonetheless I disciplined myself and was then privy to my patients' encoded perceptions. One patient spoke about being at a party where there was an obnoxious, competitive man who wouldn't let anybody else get a word in. As a result the patient withdrew into the background. Maybe 50 percent of what the man had to say was actually important, my patient continued, but he was so obnoxious with the other half, that who wanted to listen at all? Other patients produced similar descriptions: One talked about a boss who stood over her and criticized her every move so that she made more mistakes than ever. Another discussed his helpless parents for whom he had to shovel the walkway. A nurse described how shabbily the doctors treated the technicians where she worked. Yet another patient spoke about his aggressive wife who liked to display her power in front of her family.

In interpreting these descriptions as unconscious perceptions of the therapist, they suggest tremendous negativity about my style of treatment. Though I will not go into the details of these cases, in each situation I had behaved in such a way as to warrant the criticism and the encoded perceptions where an accurate portrayal of my actions. (At times like these, I wish my defense of pathological denial were more intact.) Clearly my patients were telling me that I was the obnoxious, intrusive, competitive person at the party (I had argued with the patient over one of my interpretations the week before); I was the critical boss (using manifest material, I had pointed out the patient's numerous deficits in the previous session); I was the aggressive, powerhungry wife (again, I had argued with the patient about an interpretation he would not accept); and I was the helpless parent whom my patient had to take care of (I, too, had treated my patient shabbily). Interestingly enough, as I became more silent, the images of aggressive, intrusive, critical people diminished. For now, however, I had learned just enough to hear from my patients many—perhaps most or all—of the mistakes I was making.

THE BIND

Other therapists provided similar examples of how their patients, through derivative communications, expressed accurate, albeit negative, perceptions regarding the conditions of treatment and the nature of their interventions. However, it appeared that this newly acquired ability to discern derivatives created many problems for the vulnerable therapist. Specifically it meant hearing an abundance of negative perceptions about oneself without as yet having acquired the skills with which to rectify and properly interpret the patient's unconscious perceptions of errors. Initially the problem was that the more adept one became at translating derivatives into perceptions of the therapist, the more criticism one heard.

One male therapist provided the following case example, which illustrates the negative perceptions he now understood to refer to himself.

> The previous week the patient had called and asked to reschedule therapy because of a business conflict. The therapist was unable to reschedule him and so the session was canceled until his regularly scheduled time the following week. The therapist did not charge for missed sessions. On the phone he had accusingly questioned the patient's motives for asking to change the time of therapy.
>
> The patient began the next session by talking about an old girlfriend whom he had suddenly begun thinking about, and how he was overwhelmed with anger toward her. Some of her mail had been mistakenly sent to him. He had had an argument with his friend about who was the best skier. The patient was a genuinely good skiier and felt confident about his ability. He would argue fiercely with anyone who suggested it was not so. There were few things he felt confident about, but since he truly was a fine skiier, he resented anyone implying otherwise. He knew that he had a tendency to put himself down and to belittle his positive attributes. He was feeling good about being alone. As he looked at other people's relationships, he could see that none of them were good. He talked about the previous therapy session at which he had discussed how he felt criticized by his boss. If he was prepared for criticism, he was okay; otherwise he took it to heart.

In this vignette the patient is telling the therapist, via derivatives, that he was angry with him. The therapist had sent him the wrong message and their relationship was poor. The therapist discounted the patient's strengths, abilities, and those aspects of his personality that were genuinely good; he was overly critical, like the patient's boss, and he, the patient, took that criticism to heart. Relating these images to the therapist's behavior on the phone, it appears that the therapist's accusatory way of handling the matter left the patient feeling criticized and devalued. Unfortunately the therapist could only vaguely connect the encoded images to the therapy situation, and although the patient responded by acknowledging the specific adaptive context (the therapist's suspicious interrogation on the phone), derivative validation was not achieved.

However, once the therapists are able to understand that the negative imagery pertains to themselves, the problem can be quickly recast as one of how to rectify the situation. Thus new therapists are caught in a particular dilemma because in this interim phase they are left in the mortifying position of being able to hear that they have injured their patients, but are helpless to alter the situation. Versatility in identifying the adaptive context, understanding the more subtle aspects of derivative communications, and making effective interpretations, all of which are the necessary accompaniments to actual rectification of errors and the frame, is still to be learned. Communicative interpretations are particularly difficult to organize because they require the sophisticated ability to link unconscious communication to both the reality stimulus (adaptive context) and the patient's symptoms and resistances (indicators). In the meantime the therapist can only bear witness to how he or she has injured the patient.

"The better I got at comprehending derivatives, the worse I felt," explained one therapist. "It was awful to hear that I had hurt my patients when I was sincerely trying to help them. At times I wanted to burst in with apologies: 'I'm sorry, I'm sorry, I'm sorry, I didn't know.' And then sometimes I wanted to tune out entirely."

"The unfortunate part about all of this for me," explained another therapist when we discussed this dilemma, "was that I had no idea what to do with the material. I would understand all the critical things people were saying about me, but I had difficulty finding an adaptive context to which to relate them. So I felt stuck. Like here I am, having to listen to all this negative stuff about me, wishing that maybe I never could understand what it was anyway, but not knowing what to do with it."

My own experience was similar. It was extremely painful to listen to a barrage of negatives about myself (and in silence no less!), while I was still too unskilled to know how to rectify and understand the situation. (Langs was adamant that I could not follow my preferred method of dispensing with the problem by walking into therapy sessions and announcing all the frame rectifications that would be in place from then on.) I, too, was caught in the bind.

Fortunately, despite my lack of sophistication with the technique, I was able from time to time to rectify frame deviations and provide interpretations that were partially validated. On these occasions I was struck by the depth and power of the communicative approach. To my surprise issues I had previously ignored as inconsequential were now shown to have a profound impact on the patient. And when I held the frame or could effectively relate the derivative material to the adaptive context and indicators, the system worked as predicted: I heard narratives about positive objects and events, the derivative validation of my intervention. For example, when, as the result of interpretive work, one female patient agreed to pay for her own therapy instead of using insurance, I heard a story about a beautiful and expensive present she intended to buy for her husband. With another patient I held the frame by refusing to speak with his mother when she walked into my office unannounced and demanded to see me. When I informed the patient of his mother's visit, he said, "I don't know what to say about that right now. Mostly this week has been pretty good. I spent a lot of money. That always makes me feel really good. I got a lot of new clothes. And then Easter was pretty nice. I went to see my friend and was at her house all day. So that was all pretty nice." In this way both patients provided positive imagery that suggested an unconscious appreciation of my intervention.

The following clinical example from another new communicative therapist will provide a more detailed description of partial validation that may be achieved early in the learning process.

> The patient was a young, married woman who complained about feelings of depression and the chronic lack of nurturing in her life. In the previous session, the therapist's office was in disarray because he was in the process of moving to a new suite. This session was the first one in the new office and things were still somewhat disorganized.
>
> The patient began the session with a passing comment about how the office was much more organized this week. She then spoke about her husband, who was home sick with the flu. She described him as critical, demanding, and childlike when he was sick. He insisted that she stay home with him. When she was

> sick, however, the reverse was true. He did not bother to take care of her. She had volunteered him to take pictures at a friend's wedding, but even though he was an experienced photographer, he couldn't get the lens on the camera and he acted infantile. Everything went wrong at the wedding—the pictures didn't turn out and there wasn't enough seating for all the people.
>
> The therapist intervened. He pointed out that after mentioning the chaos in the office, the patient had described several situations where there was chaos and where she was not accorded the care and nurturing she needed: there were not enough chairs at the wedding, the pictures were bungled, and her husband did not take care of her properly when she was sick. It seemed, suggested the therapist, that through these images she was commenting on the effect of his disorganization in relocating offices. By creating such chaos in moving, he had bungled the situation and was behaving a lot like the uncaring husband she described. As a result she felt nonnurtured in therapy as well as at home.
>
> The patient agreed and began crying. She remembered that the music box her mother had given her had suddenly began playing the night before. She took this as a sign from her mother (who lived overseas) that she, the mother, was caring for her and trying to help her. After a period of silence, the patient again described people who were critical of her.

In this vignette the therapist received some derivative validation despite his neglect of certain relevant aspects of the original descriptions. (He ignored her derivative portrayal of him as sick, infantile, and exploitive, for example.) He did partially touch on the central issue of the session, however, as confirmed by the patient's derivative communication about her nurturing mother. Unconsciously she recognized his intervention as caring and as an attempt to help, although her further negative comments suggested that missing elements in his intervention remained to be addressed and rectified.

The achievement of partial validation by the new communicative therapist is a salient feature of the learning process as it brings the theory of the communicative approach to life. The positive unconscious response of the patient to interpretations demonstrates in vivo the validity of the approach to the therapist, that is, that attendance to derivative communications and the frame of therapy in fact holds tremendous significance for the patient. In the previous vignette, for example, the therapist might easily have taken the patient's comment about his topsy-turvy office at face value, thus dismissing it as no more than polite conversation, or perhaps regarding it as insignificant in comparison with the genetic and dynamic issues yet to be explored.

However, with the partial validation of his intervention, the therapist could see how his poor management of the frame affected the patient. Through derivatives she affirmed that his handling of the office move effectively recreated an experience of deprivation for her, thus lending credence to a prime tenet of communicative therapy that frame deviations are experienced by patients as hurtful.

Additionally, partial validation means that despite the clumsiness, crudeness, or incompleteness of the new therapist's interpretations, he or she still may intervene effectively at times. This periodic success with the approach provides the therapist a glimpse into the power and potential of the technique, thereby offering a vigorous incentive for overcoming the tribulations involved in apprenticeship.

GUILT

As therapists continued developing an awareness of their own hurtful practices and the need for rectification of errors, guilt was a common reaction. Compromised frames, patients accepted from improper referral sources, and corrupt or even unethical practices quickly came to light through the patients' derivative communications, and guilt feelings would frequently ensue. Sometimes therapists would deal with this by confession of their "sins" or errors to the patient or supervisor in expectation of punishment; at other times they might overemphasize their participation in deviations or hurtful interventions. One therapist provided an example of his confession to a patient:

> The patient and therapist were discussing the problem of a fee, which the therapist felt was too high because of the patient's modest income. At present the patient was paying half his usual amount, though the therapist still feared that this caused a financial hardship. The patient had just produced a lengthy derivative about an auto mechanic who offered a cheaper rate and then did not fix the car properly. The patient had paid a lot of money—$275—and still the workmanship was shoddy. In response the therapist said: "You talk about having to pay out all this money for a bad job. It seems that perhaps you see me as ripping you off financially." The patient responded by assuring him of his fairness and that he was a good therapist. He even produced examples of other doctors in the community who spoke highly of the therapist.

With this intervention the therapist missed the essence of the patient's communication (that the deviation lay in the reduction of his usual fee) and instead focused the therapy on his concern about a supposed overcharge. His guilt seems evident. This had the effect of drawing the patient's attention away from his own concerns so that he could comfort—or punish—the therapist. Obviously, though confession is reputedly good for the soul, it is inappropriate and ineffectual when used in therapy by the therapist.

Another therapist, equally culpable about an inappropriate referral he had accepted, sought to terminate the patient. The therapist was treating a woman and her best friend simultaneously and both patients were producing derivatives about betrayal, breeches of confidentiality, and untenable triangles.

> In this session the original patient was talking about her job. She and another woman were sharing a job that was really designed for only one person. As a result they competed fiercely over territory. She kept telling her boss about the problem but he never did anything about it. He promised her support, but the very next day [the therapist was scheduled to see the patient's friend the next day], she saw him talking privately with the other woman. When the two went out to lunch together, the patient was convinced of their collusion and felt betrayed. It was an impossible situation and she was miserable. She never got enough attention from her mother except when she was sick. She made a vague reference to her friend. "I'm not getting anywhere in the therapy," she complained to the therapist.
>
> The therapist then made the interpretation that her work situation was analogous to the therapy situation in which he was also seeing her friend. The result was that she felt miserable and betrayed, and therapy did not progress. She seemed to be saying that the conditions of therapy were impossible. As a solution the therapist suggested termination. The patient was shocked and felt hurt and rejected.

Here we have a combination of guilt and solution by acting out. The therapist introduced the rectification of the problem rather than waiting to hear a representation from the patient. The solution was beyond the patient's conscious awareness or unconscious communications, and as a result she felt hurt. On the therapist's part, he wished to undo his mistake and attempted an instant solution to avoid prolonging his guilt feelings. His goal was appropriate. Unfortunately abandoning the principles of the communicative approach to carry out that goal generated further injury to the patient.

In conclusion, it appears that feelings of guilt are a typical reaction to learning the communicative approach. Guilt is an indication that the therapist is genuinely concerned about providing good treatment, and that he or she has truly heard the patient's complaints about unsound practices. Guilt, however, is often an unbearable feeling so that the therapist may resort to confession or acting out in an attempt to be rid of it. The two previous vignettes illustrate how, when the therapist becomes caught up in guilt, therapy is obstructed. As Searles (1979) has pointed out, our immersion in guilt tends to blind us to the patient such that "in our guilt, we become overactive and intrusive, and interfere with the analytic-growth process" (p. 31). Nonetheless, it may be that guilt, at least at this stage of learning, is an inevitable part of practicing psychotherapy. Searles agrees, and concludes:

> One needs to come to reject, for example, the goal of enduring freedom from envy or guilt, or whatnot, on the part of either patient or analyst. One does not become free from feelings in the course of maturation or in the course of becoming well during psychoanalysis; one becomes, instead, increasingly free to experience feelings of all sorts. (p. 35).

NO EXIT: YOU CAN'T GO HOME AGAIN

The initial bind in learning the communicative approach to psychotherapy was that, typically, the therapist was skilled enough to comprehend many of the derivatives, but not yet able to work effectively in that treatment modality. This dilemma intensified because it also left the therapist devoid of his or her usual techniques in working with the patient. One therapist wrote in her journal: "These last two weeks in supervision have been very difficult for me in continuing my therapy work. I find that in many sessions I have no idea what to say or do, which has not been the case in the past years, as I have known exactly what I am attempting to do. But now all my points of reference have been scrambled, turned inside out and upside down, and so at times I am left having no idea how to help the client, and unfortunately they leave reflecting my confusion."

Typically at this point therapists would revert to their former style when they could not sensibly organize the patient's material according to the principles of the communicative approach. "I wanted to go back to what was at least familiar, where I did know what I was doing, because I felt so helpless," explained one therapist. "I know in a number of sessions I would do this, I would retreat to the safety of analyzing the material solely in terms of the patient's dynamics and pathology, and abandon any effort to analyze how I was contributing to the problem."

"I remember one time," continued the therapist, "when a patient kept asking me questions and then attacking me verbally for my silence. I did not know what to do since he was not producing derivatives and I felt utterly exasperated. So halfway into the session I gave up and decided to analyze his behavior. I said 'When you do this [i.e., ask questions and then attack me verbally] then you don't say what is on your mind. It seems that you want to avoid doing that and the way you avoid is to try and get me involved in answering your questions.' I knew this response was in contradiction to the practice of communicative therapy, but it was certainly a relief to be back on familiar turf again."

In an effort to deal with the feelings of helplessness created by the difficulties in learning the communicative approach, I, too, would revert to my former style. Feeling lost, I attempted some compromise or blending of my old "eclectic" technique with this new approach. I would listen in silence for a while with an ear for the derivative communications. Then when I felt lost, not knowing what to make out of the derivatives, or what to do even when I could decipher them, I would return to my typical interview style. With a sigh of relief, I would take up an issue and actively deal with the manifest content. But my blending only seemed to confuse my already confused patients. They would discuss an issue and then wait for me to respond as usual. When I became silent, they were confused, frequently angry, and complained about having to carry on a one-sided conversation. At other times I would answer direct questions and involve myself in a "rational" discussion of some therapeutic issue, thus giving mixed messages.

Langs agreed that my partial application of the technique only served to confuse my patients, because, on the one hand, I would ask them to free-associate and then await derivative expressions, and, on the other hand, would contradict myself by focusing on the surface of the material. As an example, in the middle of a session with a female patient who had to be rescheduled because of an alteration in my office hours, I opened my appointment book when she asked about a new therapy time. In contrast, at the beginning of the hour I had responded to her query about rescheduling by assuring her we would deal with that concern, but "first let's see what comes to mind." After the new schedule was set, the patient asked more questions and I answered some but remained silent in the face of others. Thus, in an attempt to integrate techniques, I presented the patient with competing messages: direct questions would be both answered and not answered; manifest content would be dealt with and ignored; and she should both free-associate as I asked and take action as I did. The patient, distraught by my impossible signals, became angry with my silence, refused to communicate using derivatives, and, encouraged by my example of taking action with the rescheduling, attempted to take action herself: Did I have change for the money she owed me? Integration of my old therapy style and this new one was obviously a failure.

It began to dawn on me that this was an all-or-nothing approach. Halfway measures were ineffectual at best, and chaotic and contradictory at worst, often leading to regression or premature termination. This presented me with a frightening proposition: If the communicative approach could not be applied incrementally and I was not as yet able to apply it effectively, what was I to do? I had hoped to introduce the approach to only a few patients at a time, beginning with the more pressing cases. Once I learned, however, how to decipher derivatives, it became impossible to cast patients' vignettes as solely manifest content that had no relation to me. The following case will serve to illustrate how the derivative material from my patients made it impossible for me to return to my original style of therapy.

> This case involved a young, married woman whom I had been treating in a behavioral manner. This week, however, I decided to listen to her derivatives. In the previous session, I had given her the task of paying day-to-day attention to her feelings, as she tended to ignore them. This led to the subsequent difficulty of determining how she really felt about her husband. (This exercise, I believe, was derived from some combination of Gestalt and behavior therapy.)
>
> In her next therapy hour, the patient reported some positive effects from the exercise. She said that she found she was not fearful of negative emotions and that they quickly receded, unlike when she had attempted to deny them, and they would linger. In addition, she found that she did not feel such a conflict with her husband and was able to enjoy him. She then began talking about how much she loved to cook. She hated going to cooking classes, though, where they told you exactly how to do things, and she always dropped out. Both her parents still treated her like a child and she resented that. She felt bored and

> it seemed her life was going nowhere. Was it okay, she asked, to be her own person? She was taking a physics class at the university. It was pointless, she said, and even the teacher could not justify the reason for the class.

The patient began this session with a manifest reference to the adaptive context, which was the exercise I had assigned. By organizing her derivative communications around this adaptive context, the effect of my intervention became apparent. Through her encoded stories she was telling me about the questionable efficacy of my intervention. In giving her the exercise, I was treating her like a child, much as her parents did. As a result therapy was pointless and boring, and the treatment technique could not be justified. She much preferred to do things on her own, as with cooking, rather than being told what to do, in which case she immediately lost interest.

In addition to commenting on the treatment technique I had employed, she also spoke to my countertransference. As I listened I became aware of my own desire to take her under my wing and mold her into my child. In this instance she was much more cognizant of the dynamics of the therapy than I and she made derivative suggestions to set therapy straight: I should not treat her like a child and I should stop telling her what to do.

> I made the interpretation that in giving her advice (i.e., giving her the task), I, like her parents, was treating her as a child, which she did not like, and in so doing, I was undermining her sense of self. She was much happier when she did things on her own, such as cooking. When someone told her how to do things, she instantly lost interest and life became boring and pointless. She responded with a sudden remembrance of a present her husband had given her on Valentine's Day. She had wanted candy and was initially disappointed when instead he gave her a stuffed teddy bear. But when she thought about it, she realized that his gift was actually a very thoughtful, caring one because it was based on the fact that he knew that she really liked teddy bears. It meant a lot to her.

The patient thus validated the interpretation, telling me that this time what I had given her was the appropriate gift. Upon hearing a derivative communication like that, it became impossible to continue to blend my usual Gestalt–behavioral–Rogerian–psychodynamic approach with communicative therapy. My previous technique of assigned exercises (as well as confrontation and questioning) was shown to be incompatible with listening to and interpreting derivatives.

Other therapists agreed with me that the difficult part of this undertaking was that once the derivatives could be understood, it appeared that there was no room for compromise, no longer the option of using halfway measures or partially applying some of the previously described techniques. In short, there was no exit from the communicative approach unless one was prepared to don earplugs or bolster the ability to deny. The only way out was to move forward in learning the approach. For myself and other therapists who heard similar commentary from their patients, there was no turning back.

Calling on my Jungian background, I can best explain the difficulty in learning the communicative approach through the story of Adam and Eve. Jungians (e.g., Hannah, 1971) construe this story to be a tale of the development of consciousness. At first we are in the paradisical world of the unconscious, without knowledge. We are in harmony and at one with God and nature. But when we taste of the tree of knowledge, that is, when we gain conscious awareness, we are abruptly cast out of paradise and must make our way alone and unprotected through the harsh world. According to the interpretation, eventually there can be return to paradise (heaven in the myth), but *only* through consciousness, for once we have knowledge, we cannot disavow it and return to the unconscious uroboros of the womb.

Analogously, listening to Langs and listening to patients' derivatives introduce knowledge that effectively casts the therapist out of paradise. With regard to psychotherapy, paradise might be defined as listening on the manifest level; or the comfortable, complacent belief that all treatment techniques are equally salubrious; or perhaps the naive attitude that anything goes in therapy, especially if it is done through "intuition"; or the notion that the frame of therapy and proper ground rules are inconsequential. As Langs might explain it, learning the communicative approach—that is, honestly listening to the encoded feedback from the patient—means having to drop participation in the "psychotherapeutic conspiracy" that justifies symptom relief without examining the deeper issues involved in emotional illness. And since there is tremendous professional and patient support for maintaining the previously described "paradise" of therapy and the notion that symptom relief is sufficient, leaving the psychotherapeutic conspiracy is a sacrifice and a loss.

The solution to losing paradise, according to the tale, is not to attempt to reenter it by giving up the newly acquired knowledge and returning to the bliss of unconsciousness; rather paradise is found by developing awareness in order to make one's way to a new paradise that includes consciousness. From the standpoint of psychotherapy, eating the forbidden fruit is equivalent to listening to the patient's derivatives and taking seriously his or her perceptions that we, as therapists, may have caused injury. As in the myth, however, the solution to the trauma of being forced to recognize our own hurtful behavior is not to dispense with the cognizance of our negative practices and return to a state of ignorance. Instead we must continue to develop consciousness—the ability to comprehend and rectify our improper treatment techniques. Only then can we make our way to a new "paradise," which is an honest, intimate, incorruptible system of treatment that incorporates sound practice, proper ground rules, and the awareness of how we affect the patient.

SECURING THE FRAME AND ACTING OUT

New therapists, not yet having made it to the new paradise, must cope with the troublesome state of being somewhere between their old style and the new one. While therapists often employed healthful coping mechanisms such as writing, studying, or establishing informal supervision and study groups, it was not infrequent to find clinicians begin to engage in acting-out behavior. This usually took place as they began to secure the frame and had developed at least a rudimentary understanding of the principles of the communicative approach. For instance, several therapists I interviewed reported that they would use confrontation, answer direct questions, and respond to manifest content rather than interpret the encoded material, in full knowledge that these practices were in contradiction to the communicative approach. Other therapists were "forgetting" appointment times or arriving late unnecessarily, behaviors that typically surprised and embarrassed the therapist when they were retrospectively viewed. The following vignette will provide a more detailed example of a therapist's acting out following a validated interpretation.

> The patient, a woman with a primitive character organization and an impulse-control disorder, had been in treatment for several years with a male therapist. The therapeutic setting was replete with frame deviations, including acceptance of insurance

payments, the presence of third parties (a secretary and other therapists who shared the office suite), the past use of minor tranquilizers as an adjunct to treatment, and a reduced fee, which the patient paid when her insurance coverage expired. In the previous session, the therapist had made a successful interpretation and received validation for the first time. However, it was pointed out in supervision that he had failed to account for a serious indicator: the patient had thrown her glove at him.

The patient began this session with her usual barrage of complaints and berated the therapist for not returning her phone calls. She said that she felt sick, she hated his secretary, and that she needed stronger medication. She had been to the hospital that week to visit a sick friend and felt compelled to run down the halls yelling and screaming. She recited feelings of depression and said that she hated her mother and sometimes thought she would not be able to stop herself from hitting her. Then she took a pillow off the couch and threw it in the direction of the therapist. At this point the therapist intervened, saying, "Certainly things are chaotic and unsettled here but that does not give you permission to throw the pillow at me because you might be mad at me."

While this patient was indeed difficult to handle, the therapist's response in his hour was a blatant demonstration of acting out, that is, he engaged in action discharge via words (Bion, 1962; Langs, 1982b). He did not make reference to a specific adaptive context, nor did he wait for derivative material so that he could provide a meaningful interpretation. Instead he responded immediately in a manifest parental and authoritarian manner to the indicator of throwing the pillow, thus using words as the vehicle for "dumping" his anger at the patient rather than for enhancing communication and understanding. The patient provided instant commentary on his intervention:

She immediately denied throwing the pillow. She then spoke about her mother receiving dirt from a relative's grave and recalled that her parents used to put this dirt on her when she was little. She hated it. The night before she had "talked" with her dead aunt. (It was not clear whether this was a fantasy or an actual hallucination.) The rest of the session was nonderivative in nature. At the end the patient refused to leave the session and insisted on taking objects from the therapist's office with her. Despite his protest she managed to grab one of his business cards from his desk.

In her encoded remarks, the patient communicated to the therapist that his intervention was out of touch with reality and was dead; she would not hear it. It was like putting dirt from the grave on her and she (appropriately) hated it. Her last piece of behavior was most likely a reflection of the therapist's action–discharge response to her acting-in (throwing the pillow). He had communicated that he was afraid of her and suggested that he could not contain himself. In response she acted as though she could not contain herself either, and consequently her impulsive behavior in the session escalated.

Prior to learning the communicative approach, this therapist might have pleaded ignorance of proper technique. However, his successful intervention in the previous session suggested that his crude, punitive response in this session was not due to lack of knowledge: it was purely acting out. This antitherapeutic defensive response following a validated interpretation is typical of therapists at this juncture, and, according to Langs (1984), reflects a common fear of valid therapeutic work. "In almost all instances," he writes, "the intervention from the therapist that follows the validated interpretation is characteristically deviant, quite poor, and often at a level far below the recent general work of the therapist" (p. 9).

The peculiarity of the therapist's acting out following a validated interpretation and/or efforts at securing the frame is indeed a puzzling one. Ironically while, on the one hand, the therapist is struggling to honor derivative material and secure the frame, on the other hand, he or she typically engages in acting out behavior that destroys the secure frame. My own speculative explanation is that the acting out is a consequence of anxieties created by learning the communicative approach, and in particular is a reaction to securing the frame. When the frame is secured, it necessarily entails and end to therapeutic practices that serve to divert the focus of therapy from the patient's madness (unresolved unconscious conflicts) to the working over of the therapist's madness (i.e., deviations). With the unsecured frame, numerous diversions are created that act as barriers to intimacy and avert exploration of the deeper recesses of the patient's unconscious expressions. A home office, lateness, signing insurance forms, or changing appointment times focuses therapy on the therapist's behavior and the patient's reaction to it, rather than on the patient's madness. Other unsound practices, such as advice giving, confrontation, and dealing with manifest content, offer more direct methods of ignoring unconscious material.

With a secure frame, however, these avoidant techniques are no longer feasible. Moreover, the pathological gratification the therapist had previously derived from deviant techniques and the defensive use of action discharge must now be sacrificed. As an example, one new communicative therapist who had unresolved conflicts around money matters formerly engaged in reduced fees, bartering, and providing therapy "scholarships" for his less monied patients. In this way he engaged in action (the deviant fee arrangement) to resolve his monetary conflicts. Upon learning communicative psychotherapy, he was obliged to relinquish those practices, and, parenthetically, the pathological gratification of his narcissism that he had obtained by creating "grateful" patients. Thus it can be seen that the communicative approach asks the maximum in restraint of action on the part of the therapist and closes off numerous avenues of pathological gratification. The result is that the therapist's own anxieties and unresolved psychological conflicts (madness) must be controlled and contained, a requirement that creates tremendous psychological stress for the therapist—hence the motivation to escape the secure frame.

Langs (1984) elaborates further on the fear of the validated interpretation, and by extension, the fear of the secure frame. He posits that, in part, the therapist's anxiety stems from the narcissistic wounding that is inevitable in communicative listening and acknowledging the detrimental aspects of one's interventions. With a validated interpretation, however, the patient's defenses are modified so that stronger, less defended encoded negative perceptions of the therapist may now be revealed. Consequently the therapist is in peril of experiencing even greater narcissistic wounding.

In addition, continues Langs, by moderating the patient's defenses, a validated interpretation mobilizes instinctual drive wishes toward the therapist that may be experienced by both therapist and patient as threatening. Thus, if a therapist is fearful of his or her own primitive sexual or aggressive desires, he or she may well hope to avert these disclosures from the patient. The therapist feels endangered because, through the revelation of the patient's madness, his or her own subjective madness, primitive fears, and id impulses have become activated.

To be effective the therapist must be able to contain the patient's primitive wishes, impulses, and fears, an endeavor that seemingly threatens therapists with the terrifying awareness of their own primitiveness. Literature and mythology speak to the dangers and terrors of experiencing primitive unconscious expressions: Kurtz stayed too long and succumbed to the jungle and madness in Conrad's *Heart of Darkness*; Orpheus faced great danger and failure when he journied into the underworld to redeem Eurydice; and even Steven Spielberg's pop hero Indiana Jones had to confront the horrors of blood rituals, mass hysteria, and zombiism (loss of consciousness) when he descended into the madness of the Temple of Doom.

It is in this context that the therapist's acting out can best be understood. The therapist is faced with the frightening proposition of confronting and containing the patient's madness, and necessarily his or her own madness as well, but without the protection afforded by deviations and action discharge. For the vulnerable therapist, acting out may be seen as a way to discharge the unbearable feelings that subjective madness engenders; by *doing* something the therapist is attempting to rid himself or herself of those feelings, to discharge them rather than contain them. Additionally, acting out recreates the barriers and diversions and pathological satisfactions inherent in deviant frame treatment, thereby focusing therapy away from subjective madness and onto the madness of the therapist's errors once again, thus protecting the therapist from the patient. Certainly it is a paradox, for unless the therapist contains and interprets the patient's madness, there will be no true cure; on the other hand, that process itself is frightful for both therapist and patient, and acting out returns therapy to a seemingly safe equilibrium, albeit one that precludes true cure.

SURVIVAL

I have focused my presentation on the agonies of learning the communicative approach to psychotherapy. And indeed, for my own part, the transition has been at times tempestuous, terrifying, and, to use Langs' word, "mortifying." I have experienced each of the difficulties previously described, including guilt and acting out, and I honestly cannot remember the last time I felt so narcissistically bruised. Lest the reader begin to wonder at this juncture whether the communicative approach is attractive only to masochistic types, let us examine the other side of the coin. How have I benefitted?

Bit by bit I have begun to notice some subtle differences in the way I regard my patients. First of all, I have stopped blaming them for the failures of their therapies. Integral to the communicative approach is the belief that the therapist, and secondarily the patient, is responsible for the therapeutic interaction and the outcome of therapy. As a result there is no place for cruelty, hostility, or aggressiveness with patients, nor is there any justification for blaming lack of progress on the patient's inadequacies.

I contrast this attitude with one expressed at a clinic where I used to work, which I believe typifies a position held by many therapists. During a staff meeting, one of the therapists sarcastically remarked, "What we need here is a better class of clients." The other therapists shook their heads and laughed in agreement, and the implication was self-evident: if therapists could have "better" patients, then therapy would be more effective. In the therapy that Langs proposes, however, there is no tolerance for such an attitude, and rightly so, though the result is to deprive the therapist of major denial and projective defenses.

In learning the communicative approach, I have also discovered that I am not so angry about a patient's seemingly intractable symptoms. Instead I find myself optimistic about the success of treatment, even with the most difficult cases. Having had a glimpse of the powerful effectiveness of securing the frame and interpreting derivatives, I am convinced that once I develop the proper tools, I will be adept in a therapeutic technique that can provide lasting cure, almost regardless of the patient's diagnosis.

Again I contrast this attitude of cautious optimism with what I frequently hear from other therapists. As an example, a colleague of mine reported that she was assigned a borderline patient at the clinic where she works. She presented the case at a staff conference, and when the diagnosis of borderline personality disorder was substantiated, the rest of the staff, including the chief psychiatrist, moaned. The ensuing discussion focused on the impossibility of treating borderline patients and the therapist was left feeling discouraged and utterly helpless. On the other hand, I have never heard Langs speak disparagingly about the possibility of treating any patient—neurotic, narcissistic, borderline, or even schizophrenic. His optimism is infectious, thereby setting in motion a positive self-fulfilling cycle: if he believes a patient is treatable, then the therapist will, too, and as a result, the patient will receive treatment in a spirit of optimism about a cure.

Third, I find I am genuinely more respectful of patients. While working in a mental health center, I, too, often found myself participating with the other therapists in talking and joking about patients. Though we justified this behavior as a necessary evil for coping with the stress of our work, it was clearly inappropriate. Now, however, I find that it is virtually impossible for me to breech confidentiality or talk about my patients in such a way. I am appalled when, because of my lack of discretion in the past regarding strict confidentiality, any of my patients is identifiable to my colleagues or office partners. This attitude is not something I strive for intentionally merely because

Langs says I should keep strict confidentiality. Rather my reaction is visceral: I visibly twinge if I begin to speak about patients undisguisedly, critically, or without compassion.

On a more personal note, in planning an article about my supervisory experience, I had anticipated a humorous piece replete with laughable vignettes about my mistakes, insecurities, and absurd fantasies (e.g., that I should give up this business of therapy and move to Paris where I could sell bread in a little stand on the Left Bank). And yet when I honestly assess the learning experience, I see that it has had a surprisingly positive effect on the way I view myself, as well as on how I regard my patients.

Learning the communicative approach means leaving mediocrity and moving into the realm of therapeutic excellence. The patient asks for no less from us, as the derivative material confirms, and Langs' adaptive/interactional approach also demands the best from the therapist. In accepting this challenge of excellence, I find that I feel an increased respect for myself as a therapist. This is not so simply because I am accomplishing a difficult task. More important, it is because I have committed myself to a treatment approach that has integrity and is sensible; where the patient is afforded the deepest respect as the guide through the terrors and wonders of unconscious communication to emotional cure.

My conclusion, then, about this process of becoming a communicative psychoanalytic psychotherapist is as I stated in the beginning: The transition is not without its painful moments. It entails substantial injury to self-esteem as the therapist moves from being an expert to becoming a student again. The therapeutic setting must be altered and treatment interventions have to be modified. The new therapist is cast in a helpless role as he or she learns to decode derivatives but is as yet unable to formulate effective interventions. And even after the frame is secured, new fears are activated as the potential develops for revelation of the patient's madness, which concomitantly stimulates the therapist's awareness of his or her own subjective madness. Certainly the learning is arduous. The technique is a thorough, optimistic one, however, that offers deep respect and a profound appreciation for the patient. It holds that the wisdom of the patient's unconscious communications is to be trusted, and it honors that wisdom. Implicit in its design is genuine regard for the patient. I have concluded that despite the pain, a therapist who is faithful to a therapeutic process that honors and respects the patient can only honor and respect him or herself.

REFERENCES

Bion, W. (1962). Learning from experience. In *Seven Servants: Four Works by Wilfred R. Bion*. New York: Jason Aronson, 1977.

Hannah, B. (1971). *Striving Towards Wholeness*. New York: G. P. Putnam's Sons.

Langs, R. (1973). *The Technique of Psychoanalytic Psychotherapy*. Vol. 1. New York: Jason Aronson.

——— (1974). *The Technique of Psychoanalytic Psychotherapy*, Vol. 2. New York: Jason Aronson.

——— (1982a). *The Psychotherapeutic Conspiracy*. New York: Jason Aronson.

——— (1982b). *Psychotherapy: A Basic Text*. New York: Jason Aronson.

——— (1984). Making interpretations and securing the frame: Sources of danger for psychotherapists. *Int. J. Psychoanal. Psychother.*, 10:3–23.

Raney, J. (1984). Narcissistic defensiveness and the communicative approach. In *Listening and Interpreting*, ed. J. Raney. New York: Jason Aronson, pp. 456–480.

Searles, H. (1979). Feelings of guilt in the psychoanalyst. In *Countertransference and Related Subjects*. New York: International Universities Press, pp. 28–36.

11

HELAINE RUBINSTEIN, Ph.D.

DISCUSSION: *The Development of a Professional Identity as a Psychotherapist*

PSYCHOANALYTIC AUTHORS AGREE THAT THE DEVELOPMENT OF A PROFESSIONAL IDENTITY AS A PSYCHOTHERAPIST OCCURS THROUGH A PROCESS OF IDENTIFICATION WITH THE PSYCHOTHERAPY SUPERVISOR. IT WAS HYPOTHESIZED THAT THIS PROCESS OF IDENTIFICATION FOLLOWS AN OBSERVABLE CHRONOLOGY OF INCREMENTALLY ADVANCING LEVELS OF SPECIFIC EGO FUNCTIONS PROCEEDING THROUGH DISCRETE STAGES. THESE STAGES PARALLEL THE FIVE STAGES OF IDENTITY FORMATION CLAIMED BY MARGARET MAHLER TO OCCUR DURING THE FIRST THREE YEARS OF LIFE. THUS THE DEVELOPMENT OF A PROFESSIONAL IDENTITY AS A PSYCHOTHERAPIST WAS CONCEPTUALIZED AS A HIGH-ORDER REPRESENTATION OF A FUNDAMENTAL SEQUENCE OF PSYCHOLOGICAL GROWTH AND DEVELOPMENT.

AS A RESPONSE TO DR. PHYLLIS FRIEDMAN'S PAPER, THIS DISCUSSION APPLIES THE CONSTRUCTS COMPRISING THE HYPOTHESIS TO DR. FRIEDMAN'S STRUGGLES TO ACHIEVE A STABLE SENSE OF SELF AS A PROFESSIONAL PSYCHOTHERAPIST. ISSUES PECULIAR TO THE REENTRY STUDENT ARE CONSIDERED, AND THE KEY DYNAMICS OF THE SUPERVISORY RELATIONSHIP ARE DISCUSSED.

Becoming a communicative psychotherapist is a difficult task, indeed, involving extensive personal and professional variables. Overall it includes a view of human nature, a way of understanding mental disorders, and a stable definition of psychological change. Moreover, learning the approach involves a commitment to discovering the truth about oneself and others, a dedication to experiencing the integrity of its clinical methods.

As Dr. Friedman and her peers are well aware, learning how to help, how both to speak and be silent, how to contain, metabolize, and understand the material from patients, and how to design an intervention that will be in the service of cure, requires considerable mastery. It requires that a clinician know how to listen with therapeutic clarity on a moment-to-moment basis. It requires an ability to secure and maintain the ground rules, the framework of safety that enables the patient to move forward, the therapist to stand still, and the therapeutic relationship to endure. It requires, as well, a creativity, a unique ability to hear as others cannot, understand as others do not, and speak in a way that has interpretive meaning to a patient. Finally, learning the communicative approach requires a firmly fixed belief that this way of doing psychotherapy, this mode of relatedness and all it implies, constitutes the best that a practitioner can offer a patient. That is, if these requirements are to be met, if any substantial effort to master the communicative approach is to be sustained over time, the psychotherapist's labors must emerge from a special kind of devotion, a sector of the self-system that consistently assures the clinician that he or she is pursuing the only course of cure through insight.

Frequently the communicative therapist must work hard to relinquish the defense of measurable results, beginning with an acknowledgment that symptom alleviation can be effected by a variety of clinical methods. There need be no quarrel with the notion that responses can be extinguished, that ideas and behavior can be altered, at least temporarily, by any number of therapeutic manipulations. Cure through insight, through validated clinical truth, however, is a markedly different endeavor. Its effects are not always apparent, especially on the yardstick of manifest change. Its rewards are often long in coming. Yet the meaning of its successful enactment is profound in the actual and internal lives of both patient and therapist. To know that one stands for the pursuit of clinical truth is to know one's place in the world of other professionals. It means that the therapist is free to value him or herself and his or her work. It means that the therapist can remain the same regardless of the surroundings. It means that confronting the barriers to truth and meaning, struggling with the natural tendency to avoid pain, will be inherently pleasurable. And, finally, it means that a purpose higher than that which can be seen on the surface has become a firmly established part of the therapist's psychology, a sense of professionalism that will endure throughout the most difficult clinical intervals.

As a student of communicative psychotherapy, one is not simply learning a craft that is unrelated to one's personal identity, but is developing a professional identity that is intimately connected to one's very being. And just as the psychotherapist continually faces adaptation-evoking contexts in the work with patients, the student faces ongoing adaptation-evoking contexts in the struggle to learn from the teachers. To the extent that the student can adapt, can master whatever difficulties emerge as training proceeds, professional growth and development will continue. To the extent that adaptive mechanisms fail, the student will be overwhelmed. How best to understand the processes involved in becoming a communicative psychotherapist is the primary focus of this paper.

THE FUNDAMENTAL HYPOTHESIS

Several years ago the author completed a research study that was designed to explicate the intrapsychic and interactional properties involved in the development of a professional identity as a psychotherapist (Rubinstein, 1983). The study was based on the finding that, although psychoanalytic authors agree that the development of ego functions during clinical training occurred through the process of identification with the psychotherapy supervisor, there was nothing in the literature that definitively advanced a concrete theoretical framework by which to understand the specific dynamics of this process.

The hypothesis tested was generated in a series of studies that began with the author's examination of the clinical material obtained from the first few cases seen in psychotherapy during her first year of clinical training. These written records were examined for evidence of change in the therapist's level of cognitive functioning observed in her interactions with patients. This initial effort was followed by an observational study in which first-year psychology students participating in a clinical training program were evaluated in terms of professional maturation by four supervisors working with the students in a clinic setting.

Overall the results of the first study revealed that there were marked changes in the trainee's mode of relatedness with patients that could not be attributed to academic learning or the development of cognition. The results of the second study, however, demonstrated that despite significant differences in student/supervisor pairs in terms of age, gender, educational background, and nature of prior training, each student evidenced a strikingly similar progression of change during the training year studied. These observations suggested a pattern of ego development familiar to the investigator from prior studies of identity formation within the mother/child dyad during the first three years of life, leading her to conceptualize professional identity formation as a higher-order representation of a fundamental sequence of psychological growth and development. That is, it was finally hypothesized that the student's process of identification with the psychotherapy supervisor followed an observable chronology of incrementally advancing levels of specific ego functions proceeding through discrete stages. These stages parallel the five stages of identity formation claimed by Margaret Mahler to occur during the first three years of life (Mahler et al., 1975).

The hypothesis was tested in a single-case study of a clinical supervision. The method of inquiry included the analysis of audio recordings of the weekly meetings of a supervisor and a supervisee. The supervisor, Dr. Robert Langs, participated on the basis of his supervisory experience, ability to adhere to the demanding framework of human-subject research, and, of course, his facility with the communicative approach. The student was selected on the basis of her conventional academic background in psychology and interest in learning the approach. In addition, both subjects agreed to remain uninformed as to the nature of the study until its conclusion.

After all tape recordings were received by the investigator, they were transcribed and the transcriptions then analyzed by a team of four (blind) raters by means of five content-analysis scales. The rating scales were devised to measure the student's growth and development in five ego functions across five developmental stages. The ego functions tested were object relations, adaptive functions, anxiety level, defensive functions, and processes of internalization. Specifically, the progressively maturing manifestations of those ego functions, said by Blanck and Blanck (1974) to interact in the formation of identity in the first three years of life, were described according to the adult analogs of the five levels of development comprising Mahler's schema of separation-individuation. The stages were symbiosis, differentiation, practicing, rapprochement, and identity formation. The five functions and their corresponding stages were operationalized by means of the rating scales, and the scales then were applied to the supervisory situation, presented as an overall transition from "student" to "intern, resident, fellow, and doctor."

The results supported the validity of both the fundamental construct of professional identity formation and the method of measuring the growth and development of ego functions used. In addition they provided substantial credence for the notion that the development of a professional identity as a psychotherapist is a primary function of the supervisor/supervisee relationship, and within this framework, they shed considerable light on the intrapsychic and interactional struggles inherent in the learning process.

THE RESEARCH MODEL APPLIED

It is hoped that this model of professional identity formation, with its emphasis on the process of identification within the supervisory relationship, will be useful in understanding Dr. Friedman's efforts to become a psychotherapist. Specifically, it is suggested that the critical variable by which to distinguish her past and current efforts to find and keep a stable definition of herself as a professional had mostly to do with her inability to find a supervisor with whom she was able to identify constructively. That is, although Dr. Friedman cites concerns about "ineffectual technique" as contributing to her motivation to change professional tracks, from the viewpoint of the author, that concern could best be viewed as a "symptom," an end result of her associations with supervisors who themselves had not developed an enduring, cohesive, clinical stance. Effective technique is not to be found in any modality; rather it is to be learned from the practitioner of the modality and refined over time in one's work with patients.

In her history of clinical supervision, Dr. Friedman describes a series of liasons that, at best, were unfortunate in terms of providing her with a viable model for identification. Fundamental to the process of identification is the student's conscious and unconscious awareness of admired qualities, parts of the supervisor's professional persona and self-system that the student strives to make his or her own. As she notes her past efforts to learn from the poorly educated, ("my supervisor . . . explained that there simply were no answers to her situation . . ."), the clinically pessimistic ("because cure or even significant integration was not possible"), the acting out, ("he was constantly late for sessions . . . he spoke undisguisedly about patients . . ."), and the clearly aberrant role models in her learning environment ("he received a pornographic letter from a female client . . . he held it as a sign of the wonderful 'simpatico' between them . . ."), it is not difficult to understand Dr. Friedman's feeling of clinical unrest.

Although it is a sign of strength that she refused to identify in any lasting way with any of these haphazard mentors, it appears that Dr. Friedman's prior learning was punctuated by a series of trial identifications that surely represented her wish for a genuine professional role model. That she never settled in, never allowed herself to permanently internalize the viewpoints put before her, is a credit to her sense of self. Somehow she knew that the needs of her supervisors and the needs of her patients were at odds, that the search had to continue, that there must be some other sort of professional to be.

The trial-and-error method that continued, however, exacted a price that seems, in this case, to have taken the form of a non-person-specific identification with her past supervisor's collective clinical inadequacy. Moreover, although Dr. Friedman declines so harsh a judgment, there is a sense of her having been exploited, of having been unwittingly pressed into service as a repository for her supervisor's clinical ineptitude, pathological practices, and sadistic impulses. This variable is critical as such supervisory interactions notoriously prompt students to reenact this mode of relatedness with their patients in harmony with the very tenets by which students are expected to learn.

At this point in the development of the communicative approach, it is common to hear therapists such as Dr. Friedman speak of the devastation involved in the awareness that their patients have been wounded by the therapist's misguided clinical activities. But what of the knowledge that *the therapist* has also been wounded many times, and from many quarters? What of the awareness that one has repeatedly sacrificed oneself and one's patients out of fear of reprisal from the authority figures that all teachers represent, out of naiveté, guilt, or even for the sake of preserving the illusion of ego integrity in a defective mentor? Surely any such awareness or acknowledgment of the power to command held by such aberrant persons and futile enterprises, or the willingness to participate in so destructive a relationship, would be similarly devastating. Perhaps this touches some nuance of the persistent pain that Dr. Friedman and others label "stagnation," "bewilderment," and "ineffectual technique." Whatever constructs one uses to understand his or her own contribution to such pain, relinquishing its source and disavowing its attraction are the final liberation. That is, when one no longer is willing to sacrifice a sliver of reality for a slice of illusion, one is entitled to both the position of private strength and the sense of self-respect that Dr. Friedman has achieved.

From the author's experience with students, the story of Dr. Friedman's efforts to find an effective mentor is all too common. Once again, what distinguishes her and those like her from those who will either give up the profession or become the kinds of therapists her past supervisors would have them be, is an unwillingness to deny the validity of their ongoing clinical experiences, to submit to another's distorted self-system, and remain a party to a relationship designed for the overall purpose of avoiding truth and distorting meaning. As the vigorous pursuit of truth and meaning is a quality easily noted by any who are familiar with the work of Robert Langs, it seems evident that a supervisor who could offer some admired qualities with which to identify was finally found.

THE DYNAMIC MEANINGS OF CHANGE

Following this paradigm Dr. Friedman's efforts to become a professional psychotherapist take a markedly different turn. Rather than struggling to fend off a pathological supervisory introject or cope with the diminishment involved in discovering that a textbook is no worthy substitute for an object relationship, the issues now represent, in the language of the rating scales, a transition from a "student" identity to the level of identity formation named "doctor."

Although they are by no means alone, surely one problem that Dr. Friedman and her fellows share is that of their pursuit of current learning as a reaction to prior learning, rather than as the less encumbered action characterizing original learning. The author recalls the metaphor of the falsely constructed "foundation of the house" used by one of the clinicians in reporting his feelings to Dr. Friedman. This metaphor sounds apt, implying, as it does, the need to entirely renounce who one was and what one has been, so somehow integrate the hurt one has caused and one has suffered, to accept that all of one's assets are confederate, and still retain the impetus to rebuild. For the renewing clinician, this awareness is inevitable and is, in fact, the point at which many beginning students of the approach are lost, and many more established practitioners retreat with vengence. Although the author could cite many examples of this phenomenon, the most striking involved an advanced psychoanalytic candidate who could not tolerate even two hours of supervision in the approach for research purposes, and left midhour with the statement that his "world would fall down" if he stayed. Perhaps the failure of many to meet the challenge of learning the approach will be useful in understanding the intensity of the struggle facing those devoted to succeeding.

For the clinician who continues to work over the issues of professional redevelopment, however, the prognosis is good as, bit by bit, the fatalities of the past lose their power to elicit shame and guilt. Oddly, the author has heard only one student describe her rage at the realization that her professional upbringing had been so markedly defective. The absence seems significant when one considers the paradox, the perpetual double bind that characterizes the typical training situation in which a student is given responsibility without methodology, authority without knowledge, power without insight. Surely many trainees have experienced the perversion of their own good intentions and clinical optimism into an endurance test.

One gifted student of the approach, for example, conceded to her university's requirements by allowing a session of psychological testing with a child patient to be videotaped. Knowing that repercussions were inevitable, the student was hardly surprised to observe that the child's house/tree/person drawings included a man with binoculars hiding in a tree. Her assessment of this drawing as a representation of the video camera was roundly criticized as a "projection of her own self-consciousness," and she was graded poorly for her failure to appreciate the "early signs of paranoia" in her patient. Another student was dismayed to find himself one of 12 trainees observing a clinical interview behind a one-way mirror in a training clinic setting. With the principles of the approach in hand, he had little difficulty understanding the patient's communications, which began with talk about the "uselessness of group therapy, where no one is free to say anything important." His difficulty came, of course in trying to explain his views to a supervisor who understood the patient's communications as evidence of "problems with intimacy." Other students report that their unwillingness to tape, record, or take notes during sessions has branded them "resistant to learning," and in one training setting well known to the author, supervisors typically drop in on patient hours unannounced, explaining that they are monitoring the student's work, and asking to be "ignored."

Under these circumstances it is common to hear renewing students talk of guilt, mental confusion, and depression. The intrapsychic processes traditionally associated with mourning seem applicable here, including the stage in which the process ends, freeing psychic energy for new attachments. Perhaps there is a bit of truth along with the defensiveness involved in wondering whether a clinician without a traumatic professional history would ever be motivated to start anew.

The trials associated with starting anew, however, must neither be dismissed nor misunderstood. They add a unique dimension that transcends the academic and practical learning involved. For example, there is the pressure immediately to rectify the deviant frames and defective listening of ongoing clinical cases. There is the wish to do at least no further harm that typically emerges long before the new skills have been integrated. There is the need to relinquish the natural pull to insist that there was meaning in past mentors and past methods, that one's work was not all in vain. And, frequently, there is also the need to acknowledge the crimes and misdemeanors of one's personal analysis. A beginning student, one who has not been forced by circumstance to develop a superficial professional veneer and pressured by the realities of his or her work and life style to guard the surface jealously against attack from within or without, can only imagine the layers of meaning involved in the choice that Dr. Friedman and her colleagues had to make.

Another variable that should not be overlooked is the social isolation involved in learning the approach, the sense of being alone among one's peers that inevitably surfaces at the same time that the longing for a new professional community emerges. A rudimentary knowledge of the psychology of groups reveals that in every university, every training program, every mental health clinic or organization, a family exists that operates according to its own caste order, and is more or less unconsciously structured to meet its own needs for self-preservation. Dr. Friedman cites clear examples of such group dynamics in her description of the sanctioned discharge of hostility and aggression toward patients that she and others experienced in mental health settings. Such behavior, of course, has many connotations, not the least of which involves the pathological misuse of the professional hierarchy, resulting in a group that functions like a family fixated in adolescence. In such a system, family law ensures that the libidinal and aggressive issues between the generations will never be repressed and relinquished, but, will be endlessly displaced onto patients. One need hardly be a psychoanalyst to understand that any violation of the social order will be met with severe consequences. With little exception these consequences take the form of abandonment, which may range from denial of privilege within the family to actual banishment from the home. A therapist who has succumbed to the common tendency to replace his or her family of origin with colleagues and superiors, to be accepted by his or her peers, will be acutely sensitive to the spoils of transgression.

Rejection of the supervisor and the supervisory introject represents another aspect of both the intrapsychic and interactional isolation involved in learning the approach. Consciously or unconsciously, the supervisory relationship carries the expectation that the student will become like the supervisor in fundamental ways. If the student fails to do so, it typically will be understood as evidence of the student's psychopathology. Here, again is a point at which some students become depressed and lose the capacity to strive, while others decide that they have a resistance to learning that must be relinquished if professional activities are to continue.

Over the past few years, the author has heard many psychotherapists discuss these and other difficulties related to resuming a student role while still retaining a professional role in the mental health community. Invariably all of these discussions have involved the concrete concerns of floundering practices, loss of income, marital problems, and other personal difficulties. Although all of these surface manifestations are undoubtedly painful to those experiencing them, they scarcely touch the real meaning of practicing an approach that orders the conditions in which underlying madness emerges while sealing off all pathological means of defending the self, the patient, and the supervisor from experiencing it. That Dr. Friedman could so freely allow herself that knowledge is impressive. Many far more experienced practitioners would do well to learn that which she already knows: a commitment to learning the approach carries no lighter a burden than that of declaring the formerly revered objects mad, and coping with the loss of position, illusion, and protection that results, while still remaining a functioning professional.

Even with these caveats, however, that Dr. Friedman is making successive approximations toward her ultimate goal is clear. In her section on "The Bind," for example, she notes the difficult position of being able to hear derivative communication before the skills to organize such material usefully had been developed. Another student described the same position as the feeling that he "knew his train was leaving but had no idea how to board it." Disconcerting as such moments may be, they are also solid evidence that the learning process is working, that the therapist has moved to a higher level of ego organization, and has begun to internalize the supervisor and allow the patient his or her communicative due.

Similarly, Dr. Friedman seemed puzzled and displeased at her early "overdetermined" emphasis on ground rule and framework issues, noting her failure to anticipate the sort of communication that would emerge once the frame had been secured. This awareness, too, is a strong indication that the learning is proceeding as planned. The framework provides the first intelligible words of the common language, the first measuring device, the essential manifestation of the psychological boundaries needed to sustain a constructive relationship with the self, the patient, and the supervisor. The frame is fundamental to ego development. It is an operationalized metaphor for the beginning of all object relatedness in human life. Similar to patients who cannot afford meaningful communication in a meaningless environment, any student is entitled to withhold, like Dr. Friedman, his or her own confrontation with madness in the absence of a secure holding environment.

THE SUPERVISORY POSITION

An element of the approach that has required repeated clarification involves its emphasis on the therapist's responsibility to protect the patient from all destructive intrusion. This has somehow been misconstrued to mean that the therapist is the only potential contributor to the psychopathology of the bipersonal field. To avoid a similar misunderstanding of the supervisor/supervisee relationship, it is important to consider the special conflicts and anxieties facing the supervisor, as well as those faced by the student. The clinical supervisor, no less isolated than the psychotherapist, customarily approaches his or her supervisory tasks with no formal training and few, if any, constructive role models in his or her own professional history. Moreover, this supervisor consciously and unconsciously must accept a measure of responsibility for treatment hours over which he or she has limited influence and diluted, third-party authority. In some settings the supervisor may even be called to account for the results of the student's casework. All of these variables must be tolerated, along with the frequent observation that the skills of the supervisee are inadequate relative to the needs of the supervisee's patient.

In light of his or her position, surely the clinical supervisor can benefit from a supervisory framework at least as much as any student. Indeed, the salutory effects of a secure supervisory frame have been observed repeatedly by the author since 1983, when she concluded the final research study described earlier. Since that time the conceptual framework comprising the hypothesis has been used as the foundation for a supervisory training program in a training-clinic setting.

Initially all supervisors participating in the program were schooled in the developmental model involved, and continue to be trained to observe and interact with their supervisees according to an understanding of the student's changing level of ego development relative to professional identity formation. Although each supervisor had been trained in a different psychoanalytically oriented school, all ultimately accepted the tenets of the communicative approach and continue to report the benefits afforded by a framework within which their development as supervisors can safely proceed. The observations of supervisors and the ratings of students to date reveal that training the supervisor to hold the frame and allow the student to work over the issues involved in professional development has had a significant impact on the student's ability to tolerate the conflicts and anxieties attendant on reaching the first level of that development. It has also provided the supervisor with a theoretical model within which his or her effectiveness as a mentor can be monitored, and has begun to preclude the possibility of misuse of the supervisory relationship by either party. The model has increased each supervisor's ability to resolve the student crises that appear at now predictable intervals throughout the training year, and has, in turn affected both the frequency and the severity of incidents of acting out and other maladaptive behaviors within both the supervision and the student's casework. It is only a rational extension of existing clinical theory to note that a supervisor, a student, and a patient have similar needs for a secure hold, a containing environment in which the exercise of rational ego functions is mandated, so that the important work of teaching, learning, and psychotherapy with patients can proceed.

Overall, if one accepts that the learning of psychotherapy occurs within a relationship, then the burden of a student's failure to progress must be shared equally by student and supervisor. If this notion requires further validation, Dr. Friedman's shock upon discovering the difference between her self-image and the actual image she was conveying to her patients will be instructive. That is, the negative images she heard—"obnoxious . . . intrusive, competitive person . . . the critical boss . . . the aggressive, power-hungry wife . . ."—likely were portrayals of her interactions with patients at that time; they also, however, sound remarkably like her interactions with her former supervisors. By the same token, the new images—"his gift was actually a very thoughtful, caring one . . . a beautiful and expensive present . . . a lot of new clothes . . ." bespeak a different sort of interaction, an analysis of both her changing inner self and current supervisory relationship that surpasses the validity of any deliberate evaluation that either she or Dr. Langs could offer.

"THE REALIZATION OF THE DREAM"

It is apparent that Dr. Friedman is a communicative psychotherapist in the process of becoming. Her efforts to conceptualize and communicate the form and function of her evolving state of being are further evidence of her professional development to date. In her writing she has made herself available to other students and supervisors who have experienced similar struggles without the benefit of such diligent efforts to understand them. Perhaps it will serve a similar purpose to predict that Dr. Friedman will experience several more cycles in which the same issues will arise with increasing sophistication and spiraling intensity. More than once she will wonder who she is and what she is doing. The concept of psychological development, however, prescribes that with her mastery of each cycle, a higher order will be obtained that ultimately will provide her with an extension of the self-concept that will resemble its precursor mostly in reminiscence.

In his description of the mentor relationship, Daniel Levinson (1979) calls the final stage of professional development "the realization of the Dream." A developmental psychologist would call it "the achievement of professional autonomy." To the author's knowledge, the communicative approach has had neither name nor construct with which to define this stage. That is not to say that the need for such a construct has failed to emerge as time as passed and students have become teachers. For example, one clinician was startled to realize that he had introduced himself at a high-level professional meeting as a "communicative psychotherapist." When asked to define the term, he replied that "it used to mean Langsian." Another communicative therapist, when questioned by his supervisor about a specific framework management response, politely explained that his patient's material had provided sufficient consultation, and that, "on the basis of what I heard, I rectified my error. Listen. I think you'll hear it all."

A supervisor makes many promises each time he or she opens the door to a student, including the promise to function as transitional object in the student's professional development. To the extent that both student and supervisor can tolerate the repeated cycles of attachment, separation, and loss, that both can accept planned obsolescence, the relationship can provide each with the sense of personal integrity that legitimate work affords.

As Dr. Friedman's history states, to serve a developing professional, a beginning or continuing student of psychotherapy, one must offer the student a "good enough" hold, a theory that has meaning, a technique of psychotherapy that translates that meaning into clinical practice, and an object relationship that captures the essence of the practitioner that the student is striving to become. Only in this way will the student be given a genuine opportunity to become the best professional that he or she can be.

It is not that the learning ever stops, that one day Dr. Friedman will awaken to find that all of the conflicts have been resolved. It is not that the mentor relationship ever fully realizes its goal of peer relationship. It is more that the foundation of the house has been constructed, that the basis upon which professional identity as a communicative psychotherapist can be matured and refined over time is in place. It is more that the "hold," the organizing and containing functions of the supervisor and the theory, has been internalized by the student, and has finally become the student's own.

REFERENCES

Blanck, G., & Blanck, R. (1974). *Ego Psychology: Theory and Practice*. New York: Columbia University Press.

Levinson, D. (1979). *The Seasons of a Man's Life*. New York: Ballantine.

Mahler, M. S., Pine, F., & Bergman, A. (1975). *The Psychological Birth of the Human Infant*. New York: Basic Books.

Rubinstein, H. (1983). The developmental sequence of the acquisition of a professional identity as a psychotherapist (doctoral dissertation, Pacific Graduate School of Psychology, 1983). *Dissertation Abstracts International*.

12

STANLEY J. COEN, M.D.

The Analyst's Uses and Misuses of Clinical Theory: Interpretation

PSYCHOANALYTIC ATTENTION IS FOCUSED ON HOW THE ANALYST ATTEMPTS TO CONSTRUCT MEANINGS IN THE PSYCHOANALYTIC SITUATION. ANALYSTS' USES AND MISUSES OF THEMSELVES AND THEIR THEORIES ARE DISCUSSED. PSYCHOANALYTIC AND HERMENEUTIC APPROACHES TO UNDERSTANDING AND INTERPRETING ARE EXAMINED; BOTH EMPHASIZE THE PROCESSES AND PURPOSES OF UNDERSTANDING AND INTERPRETING. IN THIS PERSPECTIVE CRITERIA FOR VALIDATION OF INTERPRETATION ARE CONSIDERED. MOST IMPORTANT, THEY HELP THE ANALYST TO DETECT AND CONTAIN COUNTERTRANSFERENCES. EXAMPLES OF (COUNTERTRANSFERENCE) MISUSE OF CLINICAL THEORY ARE DRAWN FROM THE ANALYSIS OF DEPENDENCY.

This paper argues that psychoanalysts must continually examine the uses they make of clinical psychoanalytic theory so as to reduce their own subjective distress within the psychoanalytic situation. Once we separate our clinical theory from ourselves, from our own feelings, needs, and fears, within the psychoanalytic situation, we abandon a psychoanalytic perspective—on our theories and on ourselves. Once we stop asking ourselves why we need to believe what we believe, we stop being psychoanalysts and become rigid dogmatists. At issue here is not which clinical theory is better, but our uses and misuses of theory within the psychoanalytic situation for

Earlier versions of this paper were presented in December 1982 to the American Psychoanalytic Association, N.Y. and to the Association for Psychoanalytic Medicine, both in New York.

our own needs. Opening this question may permit further se… quiry and dialogue among psychoanalytic factions.

It will be argued that the rigidity of an analyst's clinical theory within the psychoanalytic situation reflects the analyst's own anxiety and insecurity and the need for dogmatic belief in and idealization of the theory. This advances a stance taken by Fliegel (1973), Polanyi (1974), Rothstein (1980), Basch :1981), and Coen (1981). Examples will be drawn from the current debate about the priority of interpretation in analysis versus the analyst as a new object, and between positivist, natural science and hermeneutic approaches to psychoanalytic interpretation. What we do with such theories within ourselves in the psychoanalytic situation and with our analysands will be examined. This approach should not be regarded as a nihilistic, subjectivist deconstruction of meaning in clinical psychoanalytic theory, but as a psychoanalytic expansion of our understanding of ourselves and the functions such theories have for us in the psychoanalytic situation. Neither psychoanalytic theories nor psychoanalytic theorists are under attack here.

The misuse of clinical theory within the psychoanalytic situation should be regarded as a form of countertransference, which may be hidden from the analyst's own introspection behind a defensive facade of rigid adherence to a piece of theory. Analysts are being reminded of something they should know very well—that when the "analyzing instrument" becomes stuck at the analyst's preoccupation with assumptions and theoretical formulations, something has gone awry. When attention to the analyst's hypotheses takes priority over listening to the analysand, the analyst needs to examine what is interfering within himself.

We need to be clear about the role of theory. Within the psychoanalytic situation, good psychoanalysts, of whatever theoretical persuasion, use their theories as guides in attempts to organize the clinical data, just as do other scientists and other interpreters. Theories are guides that enable us to organize our experiences into coherent, meaningful patterns. The first part of this paper examines the current debate within psychoanalysis about interpretation in terms of criteria for validity of psychoanalytic interpretations. The debate between natural science and hermeneutic approaches to psychoanalysis is refocused around the need for formal and functional criteria for validity of psychoanalytic interpretation. Guidelines for the assessment of the psychoanalytic process, although implicit, now require clearer statement.

THE SETTING OF THE CURRENT DEBATE

When Schafer argued at the May 1981 Panel on Interpretation of the American Psychoanalytic Association that the validity of a psychoanalytic interpretation could only be established by the subsequent course of the analysis, Arlow reacted with shocked surprise. Schafer was taking a stand against positivism, against the assumption that the analyst is automatically in a position to know what is correct. Arlow responded pragmatically that experienced analysts are likely to know which interpretations are correct. When students are taught the Rat Man, and modern commentary upon it, they ask how one decides the effects of Freud's speaking the words, "into the anus," pressing Lorenz for the name and photograph of his lady, or the famous herring meal. Lipton (1977) argued with passion that only functional criteria are relevant to the validity of an interpretation. That is, the furthering and deepening of the psychoanalytic process are the only standard upon which correctness of an intervention, or the lack of one, can be evaluated.

I believe that what has been most useful about hermeneutic approaches to psychoanalysis has been the attention directed to the theory of the psychoanalytic process, and especially to the emphasis on formal criteria for correctness of interpretation. Hermeneutics is the study of understanding and interpreting. It refers especially to discerning the meaning of written texts, of how this is to be established. Hermeneutic traditions, like those in any field, shift with time. Recently there has been considerable emphasis on the complexities of being a reader, on the reading experience, on what the reader does with the written text, and how this does or does not relate to what the author has created and intended (see Coen, 1982; (In press (b)).

Functional criteria for interpretation relate to their function of advancing the psychoanalytic process. Formal criteria can be used to evaluate an interpretation at the time it is made. Obviously how it will affect the subsequent course of the analysis remains to be determined, however much we think we can predict this. The hermeneutists have focused our attention on the logic and process of constructing our "understandings." These are human activities that serve human, personal, and communal needs. "Even in science," Heinsenberg (1958) writes, "the object of research is no longer nature itself, but man's investigation of nature" (p. 24). How, then, could psychoanalysts not become interested in the psychology of understanding, a relatively neglected area? Certain psychoanalytic proponents of a natural science perspective toward interpretation in the psychoanalytic situation have been unwilling to accept this shift toward a subjectively interactional interpretive paradigm, a subjective perspective within which observer and observed interact.

THE ANALYST'S THEORY OF INTERPRETATION

Understanding within psychoanalysis, as in any field, is constituted by our prior assumptions and communal agreements, whether formulations of oedipal phase conflict or of the most primitive repetitive behaviors. Validity in psychoanalytic interpretation cannot be established by appeal to the authority of other disciplines. We use knowledge and models from other fields as hypotheses with which to organize our clinical data within the psychoanalytic situation. The qualification here is how they fit, formally and functionally, into the ongoing psychoanalytic process. That is, such knowledge must be demonstrated to be valid *within* a given psychoanalysis. That a fact has been established in child development research, or even within psychoanalytic theory itself, does not per se establish its correctness within a given psychoanalysis. Kris and Kaplan's (1948) standards for esthetic interpretation are applicable to psychoanalytic interpretation as formal criteria: correspondence, intent, and coherence. Schafer (1980) offers a similar set of formal criteria for the validity of psychoanalytic interpretation: coherence, consistency, comprehensiveness, and "conformity with refined common sense." The analogy with esthetic interpretation, of art or of literature, is not unintentional. That is, we are seeking models for studying and evaluating the process of understanding and interpreting, of gauging the adequacy of our explanatory efforts. Thus when our colleagues in literature or philosophy study Freud's cases (e.g., Sherwood, 1969, on the Rat Man), they examine the organizing power, coherence, consistency, and comprehensiveness of the interpretations. Reasonable interpretive standards in psychoanalysis have to fit our underlying assumptions. They cannot be established once and for always. Our assumptions, needs, interests, and communal agreements change. This is what the hermeneutists emphasize about all understanding. It does not mean that all interpretations are equally valid or that the patient determines the validity of the psychoanalyst's interpretations. A subjectively interactional interpretive paradigm, wherein observer and observed interact, does not posit that all subjective responses have equal explanatory value.

Such a hermeneutic approach to interpretation emphasizes personal and communal needs, interests, and values as inherent, whether acknowledged or not, in our current beliefs, understandings, and explanations. Let us be absolutely clear, however, that this does not mean that theorists create primarily out of their own psychopathology or that we agree or disagree with them primarily out of our own psychopathology. A psychology of belief must be far more complex than such simple, hypercritical, anti-intellectual reductionism.

Functional criteria for the correctness of psychoanalytic interpretation have to do with our ideas about therapeutic efficacy. That is, does the interpretation lead to furthering of the analytic process and to the analysand's growth? As with formal criteria, functional criteria will depend on what we expect of the psychoanalytic process and what changes we expect in our analysands. This, too, has changed, and will continue to change with the history of psychoanalysis. Kris (1956) took an especially strong stand in favor of functional criteria for the assessment of interpretation. His emphasis on reconstruction related to his belief in its therapeutic efficacy in fostering the analytic process and leading to growth. Kris was critical of the continuing tendency to measure the outcome of psychoanalytic treatment by the memories recovered. He regarded this as a circular process involving changes in the structure of defense, strengthening of the ego, emergence of insight, and integrative functions of the ego. For Kris genetic interpretation was directed toward the anticathexis and not toward an actual event; this emphasizes the dynamic functions of interpretation. Kris (1951) earlier, in the context of the application of ego psychology and the analysis of resistance to psychoanalytic technique, had agreed with Freud (1937) that the correctness of interpretation is verifiable only by the patient's reaction. Kris' emphasis on functional criteria for interpretation had the pragmatic intention of reemphasizing Freud's stress on collaboration between analysand and analyst in contrast to unilaterally imposed interpretations. Nevertheless, here Kris and Freud are not supporting a stance against positivism but merely setting limits on the analyst's arbitrariness.

Fenichel (1938–1939), Kubie (1952), Brenner (1955), Ezriel (1956, 1957), Paul (1963), and Wisdom (1967) have offered clues for validation of an interpretation: new memories, fantasies, dreams, or associations that expand the interpretation; associations that parallel the interpretation; reduction of anxiety and symptomatic improvement, or the opposite with a negative therapeutic reaction; a feeling of surprise, recognition, or appropriateness by the patient; the sudden experiencing of the affect or urge interpreted. Brenner (1955) posited that an interpretation is correct if the ego becomes less afraid of the id, with relaxation of the ego's defenses, so that a derivative of the impulse defended against emerges. Langs (1974, 1976, 1978a, 1978b, 1982) has especially attempted to formulate criteria for validation of psychoanalytic interpretations. Guides to the probable correctness of the analyst's silent hypotheses include: further evidence for the same hypothesis in the latent meanings of the patient's associations in other contexts, from other derivatives; increasing coherence and comprehensibility of smaller hypotheses fitting together; elaboration through the analyst's own free associations. Direct validation of the analyst's spoken interpretations involves: derivative cognitive validation (unique, unexpected, surprising elaboration in fantasy and association, i.e., in its latent meanings); interpersonal validation (latent meanings of the associations include an introject of a well-functioning analyst); unique conscious insights and working through following the interpretation. Langs' model for validation of silent hypotheses involves formal criteria, whereas his direct validation involves functional criteria of correctness.

Although Langs does not explicitly use a hermeneutic model, he is exquisitely sensitive to understanding the patient's material, first, in terms of the analyst's actual contribution to it. Implicit in Langs' work is my own emphasis on the connections between criteria for validation of interpretation and the analyst's continuous self-scrutiny of his or her own contributions to the analytic situation and the meanings he or she attributes to it. Emphasis on criteria for validation especially alerts the analyst to examine the patient's responses to the "act" as well as the content of the interpretations. Nothing is to be taken for granted as correct. Functional criteria are paramount: What advances the analysis? Everything is to be understood. Why does the patient respond as he or she does? In traditional psychoanalytic terms, the patient is always right, and it is the analyst's task (in collaboration with the patient) to understand how and why this is so.

The hermeneutic approach to psychoanalytic interpretation emphasizes the relevance and consistency of meanings within the psychoanalytic situation. The central argument here is that psychoanalytic meanings are generated out of the psychoanalytic situation, out of interaction between analysand and analyst, from currently operative needs, wishes, desires, fears, defenses, and so on. Theories derived elsewhere must be demonstrated to be relevant to what is immediately at hand. Leavy (1973, p. 319) argues that psychoanalytic interpretation "precludes any recourse to means of validation drawn from sources not available within the psychoanalytic process." For Leavy

(1973, 1980), it is desire that keeps the past present and makes it interpretable through the present dialogue between analysand and analyst. All interpretation uses the imagery and language of the present to refer to earlier periods. Thus all interpretation, not only Kleinian, can be criticized as *Rückphantasierung*. That is, all interpretations are interpretations backward, from the present onto the past, using the fantasies and wishes of the present to refer to the past. Schafer (1976, 1978, 1980) and Leavy both argue that there are no a priori "facts" within the psychoanalytic situation. The facts are constituted by the analyst and analysand from what comes to life during the psychoanalytic process.

Functional criteria for interpretation must meet the same standards as formal criteria, with the addition of a vector of direction for change. That is, the psychoanalyst's interpretation not only must fit (narratively, esthetically) what has emerged in the psychoanalytic dialogue, but also is intended to move the patient in the direction of change agreed upon with the analysand. Skillful psychoanalysts, using a different language but the same hermeneutic principles, emphasize always beginning with the surface of the material to interest the patient in understanding his or her motivation in such a way as to maximize collaboration and minimize opposition. How to talk to an analysand, so that the analyst is heard and the patient is able to reflect on what has been said, is the art of clinical psychoanalysis. Although good narrative fit is essential, it is not per se the goal of psychoanalysis. When Spence (1982) warns us of the impossibility of the analyst and patient recovering the patient's actual experiences, and that these are immediately transformed in the psychoanalytic dialogue, he is overemphasizing "truth" at the expense of change. This overconcern tends to minimize both functional and narrative correctness. Psychoanalytic interpretations can, and should, be evaluated by both formal criteria (of narrative fit at the time the interpretation is made) and functional criteria of the effect on the process of the analysis and of intrapsychic change in the patient.

Sherwood (1969) points out that in the Rat Man case, Freud used three different psychodynamic theories of obsessional neurosis: aggression, anal erotism, and oedipal conflict. The theoretical part of the Rat Man discussion focuses exclusively on conflict over aggression. But evidence can be marshaled to support each of the three models, as Freud does. It is of interest that Freud could derive such a significant theory of obsessional neurosis just from the model of aggressive conflict. We could ask which theoretical model would best organize the original record of the case, and what would be most effective to interpret to the patient. Of course, these need not be the same. All kinds of factors within the patient will influence what we actually interpret after we have organized the material for ourselves. What has affective relevancy for the patient and what the patient is able to tolerate may preclude interpretation of some of what the analyst has understood.

However, some of the debate between hermeneutic and natural science approaches to the theory of the psychoanalytic process avoids recognition of the need for both formal and functional criteria for assessment of the psychoanalytic process. Like the literary critic, the clinical psychoanalyst is after the best "reading" possible of the material. And also like the literary critic, the clinical psychoanalyst is interested in using this "reading" to "influence" another to use the "reading" for certain purposes. All interpretation is motivated, subjective, and meant to use understanding for certain purposes, that is, to influence another to accept certain ideas. There are no unbiased readings, of analysands or of literary texts (Coen, 1985). From this perspective formal and functional criteria for psychoanalytic interpretation become conflated. The former are not more objective, or the latter more subjective. Our intentions with our analysands must influence our "readings" of the psychoanalytic dialogue. Attention to both functional and formal criteria for validation of psychoanalytic interpretation helps to maintain the analyst's stance on understanding. Nothing is to be taken for granted as already established by precedent; all is subject to new understanding. How and why the analyst and patient think, feel, and say what they do are to be understood. This is both a psychoanalytic and a hermeneutic perspective. The more a psychoanalyst is able to maintain such a perspective, the more able he or she is to utilize subjective responses, including countertransference, in the service of the patient's analysis. Thus attention to validation of interpretations, and criteria for validation, helps to contain the analyst's countertransference responses, by keeping the analyst's focus on his or her own contributions to the psychoanalytic situation.

From this perspective formal criteria for the validity of interpretation at the time it is made must also be functional. That is, the fit of an interpretation reflects not a static "reading," but the analyst's attempt to effect dynamic change within the analysand. An interpretation that will not potentially advance the analysis cannot be correct. Thus, again, Spence's (1982) overconcern with the truth of psychoanalytic interpretation misses the mark. We are interested in effecting intrapsychic change through an interpersonal transference experience, not historical truth; dynamic forces, conflict, and compromise formations take precedence over historical events. Although we can separate formal and functional criteria of validity of interpretation, I believe that both are functional. This, too, is both a psychoanalytic and a hermeneutic position—that all attempts at understanding serve purposes, needs, and interests, and are biased, and that this is best acknowledged rather than hidden.

Any clinical theoretical view of the psychoanalytic process can be misused defensively by psychoanalysts in their clinical work. At this point let us note that clinical theory, which allows for movement away from the immediacy of the patient's (and analyst's) subjective experiences to recourse to a model outside the immediate data, may especially invite such defensive misuse. That is, such theory invites the clinical analyst to justify what is happening between him and the analysand, without continual scrutiny of the experiences, of and between both parties by a hypothesis that cannot be validated within the psychoanalytic situation. On the other hand, careful attention to criteria for validation of interpretation helps to interrupt the analyst's defensive wishes for self-justification by recourse to an explanation not derived from the data of this particular psychoanalytic situation. For example, Gedo's (1979) model of hermeneutic interpretation in psychoanalysis stops with certain analysands' primitive, repetitive, "driven" behavior. Such phenomena, Gedo claims, are not subjectively experienced, and hence are not recoverable via introspection by the analysand. Gedo designates such phenomena as biologically determined "needs," outside of psychology, and here he shifts from hermeneutics to natural science. At this point the analyst, says Gedo, needs theory derived from biology as well as from developmental observation in order to understand and interpret. Gedo proposes that for "the more disturbed" analysand, what is most essential is to demonstrate his or her biologically determined need, and how the analyst has met it within the treatment situation, so that he or she can learn to perform such functions. He sharply differentiates such intervention from interpretation, which he limits to analytic efforts to "bring unconscious wishes into awareness" (p. 23). By biologizing needs and removing them from subjective awareness as well as unconscious conflict, Gedo does indeed remove such interventions from the class of analytic interpretation. The hermeneutists emphasize most the danger of theoretical constructions given to the patient that lie outside of subjective experience. Beyond the formal and functional criticisms of such interventions are the risks of defensive misuse of such clinical theory by other analysts in the psychoanalytic situation.

Others (Dorpat, 1976; Wallerstein, 1981; Coen, 1981) have argued against separating early needs from a psychology of conflict, in the belief that all needs and wishes are fated to become enmeshed in conflict. They are differentiated only by their urgency, and the patient's willingness to assume responsibility for them. For analyzable patients Schafer's (1976) argument in our clinical psychoanalytic work against erecting metapsychological motive forces, whether we call them drives or needs, is compelling. I understand this as a pragmatic hermeneutic argument to attend primarily to the psychoanalytic situation rather than to our theoretical constructs. When we speak of intensely driven behavior, as we do with patients with substantial preoedipal pathology, we are referring to the urgency and pressure (a contemporary energic model) to act that such patients feel. The risk is the analyst's use of metapsychological constructs in the clinical situation instead of what is affectively charged, experience-near motivation. For example, the self psychologists posit that the predominant motivation for behavior in relation to a self-object is a structural need for preservation of the cohesiveness of the self. I have argued elsewhere (Coen, 1981) that for most analyzable patients this is not a predominant motivation for behavior, even if they fear and fantasize such dangers. What is at issue here is not self psychology theory but the danger of analysts' resorting, under pressure in the analytic situation, to theoretical constructs that cannot be validated from their clinical data.

ANTIHERMENEUTICS: THE MISUNDERSTANDING OF UNDERSTANDING

I am concerned with how a hermeneutic approach to psychoanalytic interpretation has been misunderstood by many psychoanalysts. For example, Joseph (1979) states that only a natural science approach allows for therapy as its goal. This is a misunderstanding of the hermeneutic effort to clarify the process and criteria for understanding and interpretation. Although ostensibly critical of hermeneutics, Modell (1978) argues, following Polanyi, "beyond objectivity," toward a view of psychoanalytic interpretation not dissimilar from what I have outlined. He is impressed with Polanyi's psychological view of paradigm construction in science; that all paradigms fit human needs and values. What is most important is consistent perspective on the underlying needs and assumptions from which we constitute any paradigm and the consistency of our theory within the paradigm. Perhaps if Modell's critique of hermeneutics went beyond Ricoeur, Habermas, and Lacan, he would acknowledge that he has adopted a hermeneutic perspective. That is, there are more subjective and dynamic (more useful to the clinical psychoanalyst) hermeneutic theories of interpretation (in literary criticism) than those Modell reviewed; see Gadamer (1975), Bleich (1978), Fish (1980), and Coen (1982; in press (b)). Modell contradicts himself when he argues, following Polanyi, for different levels of meaning in psychoanalysis, while simultaneously regarding our theories of psychic structure as facts.

Coltrera's (1979) misunderstanding of hermeneutics contains its own correction. He criticizes hermeneutic approaches as overemphasizing the here-and-now of the transference and affective intensity at the expense of genetic interpretation, reconstruction, and understanding. This old debate within clinical psychoanalysis is exhumed by Coltrera for a straw-man attack. The self-correction then follows. Rapaport (1959) had understood Lewin (1937) as introducing a methodological warning about the probability of genetic interpretation and reconstruction. This is certainly consistent with an emphasis on the subjective creation of meanings. Coltrera then acknowledges that although Freud tended to see genetic reconstruction as causal explanation, Kris (1956), as we have seen, focused upon the "approximate" or probability value of a reconstruction and on its *function* of facilitating understanding through recall in the transference. Coltrera's entire argument, although unacknowledged, returns us to the problem of validity and efficacy of reconstruction and interpretation. At most we are left with a note of caution, always warranted in our work, of preserving balance, between understanding and affect, past and present.

ON THE PSYCHOLOGY OF THE ANALYST'S BELIEFS WITHIN THE PSYCHOANALYTIC SITUATION

Rangell, at the May 1982 panel of the American Psychoanalytic Association on the relationship between psychoanalytic theory and technique, argued that those who emphasize ambiguity in the psychoanalytic process defend themselves against knowledge of truth. He suggested that psychological factors (especially oedipal conflicts) led psychoanalytic revisionists to overemphasize the part over the whole, and to focus unduly on certain issues rather than on reintegrating these within the whole corpus of clinical psychoanalytic theory. Rangell here had the beginnings of a theory of the psychology of belief and investment in theory (see Rothstein, 1980; Polanyi, 1974). That he exempts his own position from such examination tends to undermine his concept.

My emphasis in this paper, however, is on the misuses that analysts make of clinical theory within the psychoanalytic situation so as to protect themselves from their own subjective distress. Rangell's approach may lend itself, in other hands, to facile impugning of unconscious conflictual motivation to all psychoanalytic revisionists. Let us instead concern ourselves with our own functioning as clinical psychoanalysts. Within the psychoanalytic situation, we need to be aware of the danger of rigid dogmatism in overstrong adherence to any theoretical position at the expense of suspended disbelief and evenly hovering attention. I have argued strongly in favor of the hermeneutists' approach against certainty, positivism, the possibility of objective meanings, the psychoanalytic situation as a closed system, and so forth.

Let us consider the hypothesis that it is the analyst's own distress within the psychoanalytic situation that causes him or her to move beyond interpretation and transference into biology mechanistic models, and extra-analytic interventions. Rothstein (1980) argued that Freud's biologizing was narcissistically invested, serving to reduce his anxiety. Fliegel (1973) suggested that the rigidity of Freud's female psychology derived from Freud's personal vulnerability during the 1920s. Basch (1981) proposed that theory is needed by the analyst in order to tolerate the emotional impact of the patient's needs. Just as oedipal conflict theory served to maintain the analyst's technical neutrality, the theory of self-object transferences, Basch argued, was needed for analysts to remain comfortable enough to analyze certain developmentally earlier issues. I have suggested (1981) that the self psychologists' overemphasis on empathy may have (usefully) served certain of its proponents to maintain an empathic stance toward intense preoedipal needs, fears, and wishes in their analysands as well as in themselves. That is, rigidity of theory is (unconsciously) used in the wish to overcome rigidity of character and to lessen the analyst's own subjective distress. When we get into trouble in our clinical work, we tend to move beyond psychoanalysis in the work and in the theories we employ to rescue us. This can happen whenever the patient's conflicts touch our own insufficiently resolved vulnerabilities and conflicts.

CLINICAL SKETCHES

Some Problems in the Analysis of Dependency, or What does the Patient Really Need from the Analyst?

• Professor A., an accomplished scholar, took great pride in his literary accomplishments. During his first analysis, he felt better about himself, became more secure about his talents, and seemed to be somewhat more at peace with himself. However, when his move to another university and city ended the analysis, he became depressed, self-tormenting, and doubtful about himself and his abilities. In his second analysis, he quickly tried to establish similar dependent ties with the analyst. He reported, and his transference behavior and fantasies with the second analyst indicated, that he derived considerable comfort and support from the analytic relationship. He sought to use this to attenuate his anxieties and insecurities. The first analyst (analyst A.) had emphasized strongly that Professor A.'s childhood deprivation and neglect were predominant factors in his hunger for attention and caring. As reported by Professor A., an analytic situation had been established in which he was shown the power of his dependent longings as primarily derived from real events (neglect, deprivation); ultimately he would have to renounce these wishes. Analyst A., an experienced and well-regarded person, seemed to have interpreted other defensive functions in Professor A.'s attachment to the analyst and other parental figures. However, what the second analysis indicated most was that Professor A. had become stuck in a satisfying, dependent relationship with analyst A., which apparently had not been systematically analyzed.

Professor A. fantasized and suspected that analyst A. had regarded him as a protege, enjoying his creative abilities and literary productions. During the first analysis, the patient had, in fact, written about areas that overlapped with his own original interests and those of the analyst. He guessed that certain childhood experiences and conflicts were similar in himself and in analyst A. According to his report, analyst A. seemed most irritable with him (a most unusual occurrence) when the patient suggested early in the analysis that analyst A. and he shared certain similarities of deprivation and neglect, as reflected in certain of the analyst's emphases.

Analyst B. was able to maintain a much more consistent analytic perspective on Professor A.'s dependency, questioning rather than gratifying it. Alerted by what the patient reported and indicated by his material, analyst B. emphasized the patient's willingness to settle for dependent attachments, including analysis, rather than understanding the defensive functions this served, especially in relation to hostile aggression. The patient's guess seemed plausible to analyst B., that analyst A. had, at times, tended to confuse himself with the patient and to enjoy a mutually shared dependent relationship. The problem for the reanalysis was to take apart the patient's willingness to "be in analysis," so as to make the analysis productive rather than a stalemate, in which the patient lived out certain childhood dependent patterns he had had with both parents. Various "seductive" interventions by analyst A. had added a quality of reality to Professor A.'s needs of the analyst, encouraging extra-analytic goals and emphasizing the patient's disability, rather than consistent psychoanalytic understanding of these.

• Ms. C., an unmarried artist in her 40s, was in psychoanalytic psychotherapy with a younger analyst who sought consultation. Ms. C. had been orphaned as a small child. After a brief period in an orphanage, she was raised by various relatives. She did not recall feeling wanted. The threat of abandonment additionally involved fears of being sent back to the orphanage. This added to her childhood terror of the intensity of her needs and her angers. The rapid development of an erotized transference surprised both patient and analyst. Well aware of the intensity of Ms. C.'s childhood trauma and neglect, the analyst tended, at times, to be overly warm and supportive, responding to the patient's emotional pressures on him. This tended to actualize the relationship between them, increasing Ms. C.'s feeling that the analyst was the parent she had never had and wanted so desperately. The analyst had alternated between being overly satisfying and attempting to interest Ms. C. in understanding her attachment to him. He was unsure of the cause of Ms. C.'s paranoid depressive responses to his interpretations of the uses she was making of the treatment: Did they derive from his own pressures, from the fluctuations that had actually occurred in this treatment between gratification and understanding, or from the interpretations per se? If the last, he was worried as to whether Ms. C. could tolerate interruption of the modus vivendi established in the treatment.

Consultation clarified that analyst C.'s inexperience, and theoretical view that more direct involvement and activity were required in the psychotherapy of a patient with such massive deprivation, was only part of the problem. When analyst C. was able to clarify, through consultation, where his own neurotic needs and fears had impinged on Ms. C.'s psychotherapy, she became less demanding, tolerated frustration in the treatment situation much more easily, and became interested in a more sustained way in understanding the dilemma of her attachment to the analyst. Analyst C. satisfied himself that the patient did not "really" need signs of his concern about her. On the other hand, sustained psychoanalytic understanding of the transference was hampered by the reality of what had transpired in the treatment, making it more difficult for Ms. C. to relinquish the illusion that analyst C. could provide her with the love she had missed; added to this was her terror of her angry destructiveness, which had to be hidden under a cover of positive feelings.

• Dr. D., a physician, had also had considerable childhood deprivation and trauma, which, however, alternated with considerable seductive involvement with her mother. In her analysis, under her cover of distance and anger, she intensely came to want closeness and contact with the analyst. She argued for more signs of his concern for her. Without much conflict, she spoke of wanting him to hug and hold her, to lie on the couch beside her. Like the previous two patients, Dr. D. wanted the transference actualized and her wishes gratified. Analyst D., however, insisted on understanding with her why she was willing to remain in such a childlike relationship with him (and others), and why she was so afraid of regarding herself as an adult. The point in this analysis at which the analyst especially emphasized the defensive functions of the patient's wishes to actualize a dependent transference not only interrupted the latter, but also dramatically opened up this woman's sexual (and further destructive) conflicts so that she became capable of having her first satisfying heterosexual relationship. When the analyst seriously questioned Dr. D.'s self-presentation as a little girl wanting only to be hugged, Dr. D. became interested in why she clung so tenaciously to this exclusive view of herself. In retrospect, analyst D. realized that he had tended too long to collude with the patient in her view of herself, and had not maintained a consistent enough focus on the defensive functions of her self-image and her dependent pressures.

• Lest it seem that patient's wishes for dependent supplies can and should invariably be analyzed, consider this brief vignette. It indicates the analyst's need for flexible responsiveness based on what is the patient's need and what is the analyst's need. Mrs. E. (reported in Coen, (1986; In Press (a)) as a young child had suddenly been transformed from a pretty girl into an ugly, weak child with disabling neuromuscular symptoms and bodily and facial disfigurement. Complicated surgery was performed to remove an endocrine tumor, although the family was not given a clear diagnosis. Her symptoms persisted, some for several years, while some disfiguring symptoms persisted permanently. Her illness, surgery, hospitalization, and multiple medical and surgical procedures left her dreading passivity and helplessness. Her analysis progressed satisfactorily, despite her extensive use of externalization, projection, and denial, and her difficulty with remaining passive (thoughtful) so as to reflect on the analyst's interpretations. However, when her son was reassessed as having much more serious psychological difficulties than first thought, Mrs. E. became more sadomasochistically embroiled with the son, leading the latter toward more destructive and self-destructive acts. In the analysis, she much more consistently focused what was wrong within her onto the son; she also attacked her husband, the analyst, and the son's analyst. She pleaded for direct guidance on what to do with the son. A guilty judgment of herself as bad and defective had been intensified by the son's difficulties. Analyst E. could not maintain his belief that Mrs. E.'s view of herself as defective as well as her demand for direct help with the son were analyzable within the present framework. His interpretations of Mrs. E.'s guilt, of her confusion with her son, of her responding as if she were now proved defective, did not help Mrs. E. Analyst E. had to work through his own disappointment, that he could not continue a standard analysis with Mrs. E., so that he could sit her up. The change was dramatic. Mrs. E. commented, over and over again, about her surprise that she could see (and believe) that the analyst leaned toward her, eager to help her, and certainly not repelled by her. The analyst shifted to a psychotherapeutic focus on what would help alleviate the crisis with the son. In this case, the analyst had continuously to monitor what Mrs. E. could and could not tolerate having interpreted to her. Gradually, over many months, it again became possible to work more consistently at understanding what was wrong within Mrs. E. herself.

APPLICATION: THE ANALYST'S USE AND MISUSE OF CLINICAL THEORY IN THE ANALYSIS OF DEPENDENCY

Do not expect to find here a review of the debate within psychoanalysis about the priority of interpretation versus the analyst as a new object. Nor will I attempt a critique of certain contemporary models of how analysands change. Instead, certain concepts about the psychoanalytic situation will be shown to be especially ripe for defensive exploitation within the psychoanalytic situation by certain analysts.

Analysts reading Loewald (1960, 1970, 1971, 1975, 1979), Greenson (1971, 1972), and Gitelson (1962) may come away unclear about the extent of the new real-object relationship with the analyst. Loewald (1979) emphasizes that the transference relationship is akin to drama, not to be actualized, and that the analyst is there as a new object for instinctual investment while consistently renouncing instinctual gratification (for self and patient) in favor of understanding and growth. While regarding the psychoanalytic situation as an interaction between two unequally positioned (especially in terms of level of organization) participants, Loewald does not advocate "interpersonalized mutualization of the transference" (Valenstein, 1979). When Greenson (1971) writes that the resolution of the transference neurosis occurs by its replacement by a real relationship, and that this does not occur "by interpretation alone," the ambiguity may lend itself to defensive misuse by other psychoanalysts. Brenner's (1979) criticism of Greenson, although extreme to my mind, has the virtue of preserving the analyst's task of understanding, or at least attempting to understand and interpret, instead of leaving the analyst free to waver between offering and withholding warmth and concern. That is, Brenner advocates consistent interpretation of conflict rather than the provision of warmth or concern.

Similarly, when Gitelson (1962) wrote that concern and care by the analyst are what tends to cure, do other analysts understand that he is describing only the first phase of analysis, and is not recommending the provision of anything extra, outside of standard technique? The diatrophic attitude, according to Gitelson, is implicit within standard technique; it does not require active intervention, support, or corrective emotional experience. Gitelson claims, paradoxically, that the analyst's diatrophic attitude leads not to increased infantile neediness, but rather to "the partial relinquishment of the anaclitic attitude" (p. 325), together with cooperation, identification, and collaboration. Friedman's (1969) warnings about the dangers of not interpreting transference longings in a first phase of analysis are relevant to Gitelson (1962), Kohut (1971, 1977), and Modell (1976). To the degree that illusions are accepted, that is, not confronted and interpreted, the more they tend to be regarded as reality rather than fantasy. With patients A., C., and D., the illusion of a special dependent relationship with the analyst had, to varying degrees, been actualized, making this more difficult to interrupt and interpret. There was no evidence that any of these patients had actually required a long period in which such attachment to the analyst was not interpreted. On the contrary, in each example, once the analyst could clarify his own needs and goals with the analysand and proceed to analyze the dependent attachment to the analyst, significant change occurred within the analytic situation and within the patient.

With needy, sensitive, anxiety-ridden patients with severe preoedipal pathology, as with anyone, the analyst must make the analytic situation tolerable so that an analytic process can unfold. The needier the patient, the greater may be the risk of behaviors that are common at times to analysts: warm encouragement, speaking more to alleviate the patient's anxiety and loneliness, occasional jokes, sharing of a common interest, reassurance, advice, telling anecdotes, and so on. The issue is not whether this is standard technique; witness Gedo's (1979) anecdote about Lowenstein—while whistling may not be an appropriate interpretive vehicle for the analyst, telling a Jewish joke is. The analyst's efforts to engage the patient emotionally, to provide some comfort, "support," a warm ambience, may tend to actualize the patient's illusion that the dependent relationship with the analyst is real. The more the analyst actually gratifies the patient's wishes for dependent support, the more this leads to a dependent enmeshment that is "beyond transference" because the patient has been encouraged by the analyst actually to seek the provision of the functions the patient feels unable to supply (as with patients A., C., and D.).

In contrast to Gitelson (1962), I believe that this may interfere with the patient's growth and further individuation, encouraging the feelings of inability to provide for him or herself, with a real rather than wishful turn to the analyst. The actualization of the patient's intense wishes for the provision of functions the patient feels unable to render (by an object on whom he or she is dependent) may interfere with their analytic resolution, actually attaching the patient to the analyst. The wishful transference setup that emphasizes so starkly the contrast between transference wishes and the reality of the psychoanalyst qua psychoanalyst is attenuated and replaced by a real dependent relationship. The more dependent the patient, the greater is this danger. We know from follow-up studies and reanalyses that it is not uncommon with patients who seem to complete analysis successfully that the apparent changes are in (large) part due to the actual presence of the analyst and the patient's emotional attachment (see Kohut, 1979; Oremland et al., 1975; Shapiro, 1976; Szalita, 1982; Levine, 1979). Later, without the analyst's presence, the gains soon fade.

The greater the patient's neediness, anxiety, demands, and sensitivity, the more difficult it may be for certain analysts to persevere with the analytic task. To relieve the analyst's distress caused by the patient and the reactivation of the analyst's own early conflicts that have been inadequately analyzed, extra-analytic interventions are used. To the degree that the analyst must rationalize these interventions and is unable to understand his or her own distress and conflicts, the patient may consciously or unconsciously believe (sometimes correctly) that the analyst actually wants to join in a mutually gratifying dependent relationship. This can be hidden from the analyst's own introspection under cover of a "friendly" analysis or by attributing the neediness entirely to the patient. That the patient unconsciously recognizes the analyst's gratification in their relationship further fixes the goal of actualization of dependent longings (as with patients A., C., and D.). It is not by the analyst's words alone that such patients move away from their demands for dumplings (Freud, 1915) to participate in genuine collaborative psychoanalytic exploration of their neurosis. Such patients do considerable testing of the analyst to determine what he or she is willing to do for them and really wants of them—psychoanalytic goals or otherwise.

Concepts such as the diatrophic attitude, holding environment, real realationship, and empathy may be used clinically to rationalize the analyst's interventions so as to lessen his or her own distress. When the analyst speaks more, it may be because the patient requires it, or because activity lessens the analyst's anxiety and reduces the pressure to do something for the complaining patient. The concept of the analyst as a new object is especially apt for exploitation by the analyst to handle any difficulties with preserving an analytic stance with respect to intense preoedipal neediness. It may be used to justify the provision of actual supplies for the patient because of the analyst's own emotional difficulties in the psychoanalytic setup with certain very needy patients. Not the analyst's theory, but the need to hide from him or herself his or her true intentions with analysands under the guise of theory, is the problem. Strachey's (1934) emphasis is relevant as to the sharp distinction between fantasy and reality in order for transference interpretations to be mutative. The danger is the analyst's becoming the good object the patient seeks, even if only at times, rather than helping the patient to work through transference wishes: inappropriate, impossible of fulfillment, serving multiple functions. In Strachey's terms the analyst here becomes not a good but a bad object. Certain functions, such as tension and anxiety reduction, may occur automatically in the presence of the analyst without the latter doing anything specifically. How the patient uses the analyst for this purpose, together with the wishes and fantasies about the analyst that come together here, become subject to analytic scrutiny. For the analyzable patient, the analyst does not ordinarily seek to fill in missing functions and structures but to join the patient in understanding him or herself. To do otherwise is to usurp the patient's own role. Thus there is danger in the analyst assuming the role of the analysand's tutor or provider of missing psychic functions. Such intrusion into the patient's life and mind may arrest further individuation during psychoanalysis, with the neurotic potential for sadomasochistic dependent submission to the authority of the analyst. If we believe, as we claim, that for analyzable patients there is complex defensive layering of preoedipal and oedipal conflicts, then whatever is currently on the surface for our patients must be treated as manifest content to be more thoroughly explored rather than accepted as fact. To regard the patient, even temporarily, as the incapable child the patient fantasies him or herself to be precludes the integration and understanding of its defensive functions within the totality of the patient as a competent adult. Even with seemingly infantile, demanding, dependent borderline patients in psychotherapy, far better results are obtained by confronting the aggression, impossible demands, entitlement, and masochism than exclusively "empathizing" with the patient's felt deprivation and disability (cf. Kernberg, 1975).

The analyst may feel pressured to speak, gratify dependent wishes, or alleviate the patient's distress, in order to disavow such intense aggression in the patient as well as in him or herself. The patient's pressure on the analyst to "do something" may be specifically related to making destructiveness in oneself disappear while "blaming" the analyst for the patient being stuck with the hatred. Or pressure on the analyst to "do something" may derive from envy and destructive spoiling by the patient of what the analyst does give. The danger here is the analyst's use of the concept of holding environment, diatrophic attitude, new object relationship, and so on, to sanction activity intended to avoid destructive feelings and wishes in the analysand and analyst. Of course, the clinical issue is to assess, sensitively and tactfully, what the patient can tolerate, and to respond to the patient's genuine need rather than the analyst's defensive need. Intense dependent wishes can certainly serve for defensive reassurance against dangerous (feared) destructiveness, so that dependency must be treated as a kind of manifest content to be explored for its functions. Even when we are certain that an analysand needs a little more gratification, we still have to understand what functions it serves. So long as we are able to preserve such an analytic stance toward introspection of our own responses to the patient, the analyzing instrument has not become stuck.

Actualization of the patient's transference fantasies toward the analyst may involve the latter more directly in becoming the bad object. Another example of defensive misuse of theory involves those analysts who overemphasize transference interpretation with certain mistrustful, guarded, controlled analysands with "more severe" pathology, insisting that the analyst be acknowledged as a person. Here the clinical theory that emphasizes transference interpretation as central for intrapsychic change during psychoanalysis is defensively (and angrily) overused when some analysts are unable to maintain sufficient perspective with certain rigid characters. The patient's fantasied dominance–submission struggle becomes actualized as the analyst forces the patient to acknowledge his or her importance. A power struggle rather than analysis may ensue.

Dr. F., a psychologist, was highly obsessional, rigid, suspicious, and guarded. Two prior analyses had foundered, with Dr. F. feeling angry, pressured, and threatened by the analyst's persistent interpretation of his fear of transference longings and his need to maintain emotional distance from the analyst. He felt locked in an unproductive power struggle with each analyst over the importance of transference. In contrast he felt that his present analyst helped him less by his warmth (which he had) than by the respectful space he granted Dr. F.; within this Dr. F. came to desire understanding of his conflicts (including his fearfulness of the analyst's importance to him), rather than feeling forced to do so by the analyst's own needs. Both earlier analysts were highly regarded in the analytic community.

The more unable we are to acknowledge our own anxiety as analysts in the analytic situation, the more we need to shift our attention to a theory to explain this away. If we can accept our own distress as analysts, then we can attempt to understand this in ourselves and in our analysands, and seek the clinical theory that will best organize our data. To the degree that we must defensively exclude our own subjective experiences, we will not use clinical theory to help us understand ourselves and our analysands but to justify ourselves. At that point we cease being psychoanalysts. As psychoanalysts we have to require of ourselves within the psychoanalytic situation a self-understanding that includes consideration of why we believe what we believe, and of how we use such beliefs and for what purpose.

SUMMARY

I have argued for further consideration of the psychology of the analyst's belief in and use of clinical psychoanalytic theory within the psychoanalytic situation. The analyst's own subjective distress in the psychoanalytic situation, when this must be hidden from the analyst's introspection, leads to defensive misuse of clinical theory. Examples of how theory may be misused defensively by the analyst have been drawn from the concept of the analyst as a new object for the patient; this may tend to interfere with the analysand's further individuation.

The rigidity of an analyst's clinical theory within the psychoanalytic situation, whether oedipal or preoedipal, positivist or subjectivist, exclusively focused on the patient or on the psychoanalytic dialogue, reflects the analyst's own anxiety and insecurity and the need for dogmatic belief in and idealization of theory. The analyst's own subjective distress with the analysand causes the analyst to move beyond interpretation, beyond transference, into biology, mechanistic models, and extra-analytic interventions.

REFERENCES

Basch, M. F. (1981). Self-object disorders and psychoanalytic theory: A historical perspective. *J. Amer. Psychoanal. Assn.*, 29:337–351.

Bleich, D. (1978). *Subjective Criticism*. Baltimore and London: Johns Hopkins University Press.

Brenner, C. (1955). The validation of psychoanalytic interpretation. Reported by J. Marmor. *J. Amer. Psychoanal. Assn.*, 3:496–497.

——— (1979). Working alliance, therapeutic alliance, and transference. *J. Amer. Psychoanal. Assn.* (suppl.), 27:137–157.

Coen, S. J. (1981). Notes on the concepts of selfobject and preoedipal object. *J. Amer. Psychoanal. Assn.*, 29:395–411.

——— (1982). Essays on the relationship of author and reader: Transference implications for psychoanalytic literary criticism—introduction. *Psychoanal. Contemp. Thought*, 5:3–15.

——— (1985). Freud and Fliess: a supportive literary relationship. *Amer. Imago*, 42:385–412.

——— (1986). The sense of defect. *J. Amer. Psychoanal. Assn.* 34:47–67.

——— (In press (a)). Superego aspects of entitlement (in rigid characters). *J. Amer. Psychoanal. Assn.*

——— (In press(b)). How to read Freud: a critique of recent Freud scholarship. *J. Amer. Psychoanal. Assn.*

Coltrera, J. T. (1979). Truth from genetic illusion: The transference and the fate of the infantile neurosis. J. Amer. Psychoanal. Assn. (suppl.), 27:289–313.

Dorpat, T. L. (1976). Structural conflict and object relations conflict. *J. Amer. Psychoanal. Assn.*, 24:855–874.

Ezriel, H. (1956, 1957). Experimentation within the psychoanalytic session.

In *Psychoanalytic Clinical Interpretation*, ed. L. Paul. New York: Free Press of Glencoe, 1963, pp. 112–142.

Fenichel, O. (1938–1939). *Problems of Psychoanalytic Technique*. New York: Psychoanalytic Quarterly, Inc., 1941.

Fish, S. (1980). *Is There a Text in This Class? The Authority of Interpretive Communities*. Cambridge, Mass., and London: Harvard University Press.

Fliegel, Z. (1973). Feminine psychosexual development in Freudian theory: A historical reconstruction. *Psychoanal. Q.*, 42:385–408.

Freud, S. (1915). Observations on transference love (further recommendations on the technique of psychoanalysis, III). *Standard Edition*, 12.

——— (1937). Constructions in analysis. *Standard Edition*, 23:255–269.

Friedman, L. (1969). The therapeutic alliance. *Int. J. Psychoanal.*, 50:139–153.

Gadamer, H. G. (1975). *Truth and Method*. New York: Seabury Press.

Gedo, J. E. (1979). *Beyond Interpretation: Toward a Revised Theory for Psychoanalysis*. New York: International Universities Press.

Gitelson, M. (1962). On the curative factors in the first phase of analysis. In *Psychoanalysis: Science and Profession*. New York: International Universities Press, 1973, pp. 311–341.

Greenson, R. R. (1971). The "real" relationship between the patient and the psychoanalyst. In *The Unconscious Today*, ed. M. Kanzer. New York: International Universities Press, pp. 213–232.

—— (1972). Beyond transference and interpretation. *Int. J. Psychoanal.*, 53:213–217.

Heisenberg, W. (1958). *The Physicist's Conception of Nature*. London: Greenwood.

Joseph E. (1979). Comments on the therapeutic action of psychoanalysis. *J. Amer. Psychoanal Assn.* (suppl.), 27:71–79.

Kernberg, O. F. (1975). *Borderline Conditions and Pathological Narcissism*. New York: Jason Aronson.

Kohut, H. (1971). *The Analysis of the Self*. New York: International Universities Press.

——— (1977). *The Restoration of the Self*. New York: International Universities Press.

——— (1979). The two analyses of Mr. Z. *Int. J. Psychoanal.*, 60:3–27.

Kris, E. (1951). Ego psychology and interpretation in psychoanalytic therapy. In *Selected Papers of Ernst Kris*. New Haven and London: Yale University Press, 1975, pp. 237–251.

——— (1956). The recovery of childhood memories in psychoanalysis. In *Selected Papers of Ernst Kris*. New Haven and London: Yale University Press, 1975, pp. 301–340.

———, & Kaplan, A. (1948). Aesthetic ambiguity. In *Psychoanalytic Explorations in Art*, ed. E. Kris. New York: International Universities Press, 1952, pp. 243–264.

Kubie, L. S. (1952). Problems and techniques of psychoanalytic validation and progress. In *Psychoanalysis as Science*, ed. E. Pumpian-Mindlin. Stanford, Calif.: Stanford University Press, pp. 46–124.

Langs, R. (1974). *The Technique of Psychoanalytic Psychotherapy*, Vol. II. New York: Jason Aronson.

——— (1976). *The Therapeutic Interaction,* Vols. I & II. New York: Jason Aronson.

——— (1978a). Validation and the framework of the therapeutic situation. *Contemp. Psychoanal.,* 14:98–124.

——— (1978b). The adaptational–interactional dimension of countertransference. *Contemp. Psychoanal.,* 14:502–533.

——— (1982). *Psychotherapy: A Basic Text.* New York and London: Jason Aronson.

Leavy, S. A. (1973). Psychoanalytic interpretation. *Psychoanal. Study Child,* 28:305–330.

——— (1980). *The Psychoanalytic Dialogue.* New Haven and London: Yale Universities Press.

Levine, H. B. (1979). The sustaining object relationship. *Ann. Psychoanal.,* 7:203–231.

Lewin, K. (1937). Psychoanalysis and topological psychology. *Bull. Menninger Clin.,* 1:202–211.

Lipton, S. (1977). The advantages of Freud's technique as shown in his analysis of the Rat Man. *Int. J. Psychoanal.,* 58:255–278.

Loewald, H. W. (1960). On the therapeutic action of psychoanalysis. In *Papers on Psychoanalysis.* New Haven and London: Yale University Press, 1980, pp. 221–256.

——— (1970). Psychoanalytic theory and the psychoanalytic process. In *Papers on Psychoanalysis.* New Haven and London: Yale University Press, 1980, pp. 277–301.

——— (1971). The transference neurosis: Comments on the concept and the phenomenon. In *Papers on Psychoanalysis.* New Haven and London: Yale University Press, 1980, pp. 302–314.

——— (1975). Psychoanalysis as an art and the fantasy character of the psychoanalytic situation. In *Papers on Psychoanalysis.* New Haven and London: Yale University Press, 1980, pp. 352–371.

——— (1979). Reflections on the psychoanalytic process and its therapeutic potential. In *Papers on Psychoanalysis.* New Haven and London: Yale University Press, 1980, pp. 372–383.

Modell, A. (1976). The "holding environment" and the therapeutic action of psychoanalysis. *J. Amer. Psychoanal. Assn.,* 24:285–307.

——— (1978). The nature of psychoanalytic knowledge (book review). *J. Amer. Psychoanal. Assn.,* 26:641–658.

Oremland, J., Blacker, K., & Norman, H. (1975). Incompleteness in "successful" psychoanalysis: A follow-up study. *J. Amer. Psychoanal. Assn.,* 23:819–844.

Paul, L. (1963). The logic of psychoanalytic interpretation. In *Psychoanalytic Clinical Interpretation,* ed. L. Paul. New York: Free Press of Glencoe, pp. 249–272.

Polanyi, M. (1974). *Scientific Thought and Social Reality: Essays by Michael Polanyi.* Ed. F. Schwartz. Psychological Issues Monograph 32, vol. 8, no. 4. New York: International Universities Press.

Rapaport, D. (1959). *The Structure of Psychoanalytic Theory: A Systematizing Attempt.* Psychological Issues Monograph 6. New York: International Universities Press.

Rothstein, A. (1980). Psychoanalytic paradigms and their narcissistic investment. *J. Amer. Psychoanal. Assn.*, 28:385–395.

Schafer, R. (1976). *A New Language for Psychoanalysis*. New Haven and London: Yale University Press.

——— (1978). *Language and Insight*. The Sigmund Freud Memorial Lectures, 1975–1976, University College, London. New Haven and London: Yale University Press.

——— (1980). Action and narration in psychoanalysis. *New Lit. Hist.*, 12:61–85.

Shapiro, D. (1976). The analyst's own analysis. *J. Amer. Psychoanal. Assn.*, 24:5–42.

Sherwood, M. (1969). *The Logic of Explanation in Psychoanalysis*. New York: Academic Press.

Spence, D. P. (1982). *Narrative Truth and Historical Truth: Meaning and Interpretation in Psychoanalysis*. New York and London: Norton.

Strachey, J. (1934). The nature of the therapeutic action of psychoanalysis. In *The Evolution of Psychoanalytic Technique*, ed. M. S. Bergmann & F. R. Hartman. New York: Basic Books, pp. 331–360.

Szalita, A. (1982). Further thoughts on reanalysis. *Contemp. Psychoanal.*, 18:327–348.

Valenstein, A. F. (1979). The concept of "classical" psychoanalysis. *J. Amer. Psychoanal. Assn.* (suppl.), 27:113–136.

Wallerstein, R. S. (1981). The bipolar self: Discussion of alternative perspectives. *J. Amer. Psychoanal. Assn.*, 29:377–394.

Wisdom, J. (1967). Testing an interpretation within a session. *Int. J. Psychoanal.*, 48:44–52.

13

ANNA ORNSTEIN, M.D.

DISCUSSION:

The Relationship Between the Method of Data Gathering, the Nature of the Transference, and the Interpretive Process: Reflections on Psychoanalytic Clinical Theory

STANLEY COEN'S MAIN THESIS IS THAT AN ANALYST'S CLINICAL THEORY MAY BE USED TO HIDE COUNTERTRANSFERENCE REACTIONS BY RATIONALIZING THE ANALYST'S UNCONSCIOUS, UNRESOLVED CONFLICTS. IN RESPONSE THIS PAPER ARGUES THAT CAREFUL ATTENTION TO THE RELATIONSHIP BETWEEN (1) METHOD OF DATA GATHERING, (2) THE NATURE OF THE TRANSFERENCE, AND (3) INTERPRETATIONS CAN SAFEGUARD THE ANALYTIC PROCESS, SO THAT THE ANALYST CAN REMAIN FOCUSED ON THE PATIENT'S SUBJECTIVE EXPERIENCES AND EXPLORE THEIR IDIOSYNCRATIC MEANING; THIS REDUCES THE DANGER OF COUNTERTRANSFERENCE "ACTING OUT" BY THE USE OF A PARTICULAR THEORY. THE PAPER ALSO SUGGESTS THAT THE RECOGNITION OF SELF-OBJECT TRANSFERENCES HAD ENABLED ANALYSTS TO DEAL WITH "PREOEDIPAL ISSUES" ANALYTICALLY, THAT IS, INTERPRETIVELY. THIS MAKES THE DISTINCTION BETWEEN "INTERPRETATION" AND THE USE OF THE ANALYST AS A "REAL OBJECT" ARTIFICIAL, NOT IN KEEPING WITH THE PATIENT'S SUBJECTIVE EXPERIENCES.

Dr. Coen raises some very important questions regarding the manner in which clinical theory may be used to cover up and rationalize the analyst's countertransferences.

An analyst may choose a particular theory because of its compatibility with her[1] own value system and personality; this may then conveniently serve to rationalize the analyst's unconscious and unresolved conflicts, and thereby compromise her neutrality. Since all psychoanalytic theories contain such hidden values and can serve to hide countertransferences, the analyst, Dr. Coen suggests, has to engage in an ongoing scrutiny of the nature of her own participation in the analytic process. I don't believe anyone could argue with such a position.

Psychoanalytic theories of all persuasion are value-laden. Freud's effort to free psychoanalysis from cultural and personally held values was only partially successful; the Vienna of his time and his personally held values became part and parcel of his theorizing. Had Freud been more successful in placing psychoanalysis into the realm of the natural sciences, which, theoretically at least, could have lessened the possibility of including personal values in psychoanalysis, we would then have to face the great limitation that the natural science approach has in explaining human behavior. Rather than "perfecting" the natural science approach, psychoanalysis has become, as Dr. Coen indicates, powerfully influenced by hermeneutics: the importance of understanding each patient, in terms of the unique personal *meanings* of his associations.

However, if we accept that *all* theories are value-laden and can be used for the rationalization of countertransferences, we have to ask a more fundamental question: Is there any aspect (or aspects) of psychoanalytic theory that protects the analysand from its misuse by the analyst? I believe that to answer this question we must examine the relationship between the practice of psychoanalysis and psychoanalytic clinical theory. I am suggesting that such an examination reveals that there had developed, over time, a divergence between the method (evenly hovering attention, empathy) and the other two aspects of psychoanalytic clinical theory: transference and interpretations. This divergence made clinical theory increasingly less useful

[1]In this discussion I shall refer to the analyst as she and to the patient as he.

in the organization of the data that could guide analysts in their interpretations. Instead, as can be seen from Dr. Coen's own clinical examples, analysts have been resorting to *explaining* clinical phenomena (such as dependency) without first *understanding* their meaning as this could be revealed in the nature of the transference.[2]

Since our therapeutic attention has to be focused on the meaning that our manner and action have on the patient, rather than on the actuality or reality of our manner and our actions, to grasp these meanings becomes the therapist's primary task. The question, then, is what method of data gathering could lead the clinician most reliably to the patient's subjective experiences that first will have to be understood and then, in the course of analysis, adequately explained in view of the patient's life history? The answer, I believe, lies in the relationship among the three components of clinical theory: method, transference, and interpretations.

The three components of clinical theory constitute a unit; changes in the view of one have consequences for the other two. It is the preservation of this interdigitating relationship among the three aspects of clinical theory that can support the analyst's efforts to remain in touch with the patient's subjective experiences and thereby arrive at an understanding of the meaning that the experience has for the patient. In addition, it is the preservation of this theoretical unity that can facilitate the analyst's recognition of her own participation in the analytic process. For example, selfobject transferences are characterized by the manner in which the analyst is being put to functional use by the patient; the analyst, therefore, has to be able to ascertain how she is being experienced by the patient—how her behavior, tone of voice, or choice of words affect the patient's state of mind. It is here that empathy as a mode of observation, attuned to the patient's

[2]In a recent publication (Ornstein & Ornstein, 1985), we had raised a question similar to the one Dr. Coen is raising; namely, how is it possible that psychoanalysts had not become interested in the psychology of understanding, a relatively neglected area? We had found that "for a variety of historical reasons, "understanding," which should have been alongside explaining as the two distinct steps in the interpretive process, has either been taken for granted or seriously underplayed as a specific and necessary intervention in psychoanalysis—in both clinical and theoretical discussions and writings. Hartmann (1927) and Eissler (1968) explicitly excluded understanding as a significant step in its own right in the interpretive process—for what appears to be ideological reasons. They considered psychoanalysis an "explaining psychology" to be sharply demarcated from "understanding psychology" which they regarded as nonanalytic and viewed with suspicion (1985, p. 49).

self-experiences, becomes linked to the recognition of selfobject transferences: the method (empathy) is intrinsically linked to observation (self-object transference), which, in turn, affects the wording and phrasing of interpretations. This is a circular process, which is why interpretations, in terms of their effect on the analytic process, can only be validated within the same analysis. Before embarking on my discussion, in which I emphasize the connections between the various aspects of clinical theory, I shall first briefly summarize the major points of Dr. Coen's paper.

Dr. Coen elaborated on the defensive use of psychoanalytic theory in relation to the following interrelated issues: (1) Fitting the patient's associations to the analyst's preferred theory interferes with evenly hovering attention. (2) Theory has an impact on interpretations, which are the analyst's major contributions to the analytic process. The analyst, therefore, has to be able to engage in continual scrutiny of her experiences as these evolve in the analytic process. (3) Psychoanalysis and hermeneutics have a great deal in common, primarily their emphasis on the importance of understanding of meanings: "subjectivity and countertransferences are better managed within a perspective that emphasizes continual attention to and understanding of the analyst's own attempts at understanding." (4) Considering that Dr. Coen focuses on the impact of clinical theory on the analytic process, he gives transference interpretations short shrift. Rather than examining the relevant transferences, Dr. Coen introduces his own theoretical biases to "correct" those of the previous therapists. His clinical examples, therefore, fail to buttress the thesis of his paper.

RELATIONSHIP BETWEEN THE METHOD OF DATA GATHERING AND THE NATURE OF TRANSFERENCE

One of the most potent safeguards of relative neutrality is the analyst's capacity to immerse herself in the patient's subjective experiences; that is, when the analyst is able to assume and maintain an empathic position and understand the patient from within his own perspective. Dr. Coen mentions empathy along with "diatrophic attitudes, holding environment, and real relationship." It is this gross misunderstanding of empathy that allowed Dr. Coen to suggest that "the self psychologist's overemphasis on empathy may have usefully served certain of its proponents to maintain an empathic stance toward intense preoedipal needs, fears, and wishes in their analysands as well as in themselves."

A listening position is assumed either from within the patient's perspective or outside of it. Analysts ordinarily do both. The capacity to understand the patient from within his own perspective is just as important for the patient who has revived "oedipal issues" in the transference as for those whose material indicates problems related to earlier phases of development. However, "intense preoedipal needs" may indeed be better understood from an empathic vantage point than from that of an external observer; they are more likely to be recognized as genuine expressions of reactivated selfobject needs for mirroring and idealization than resistances against oedipal (sexual and aggressive) affects. The assessment of the manifestly "preoedipal needs" in terms of their meaning to the analysand can only be made by assessing the nature of the transference. Identifying the patient's subjective experiences does not yet mean having discerned their meaning; empathy is only the method whereby the analyst can have a grasp of the patient's experiences. It is the transference that helps the analyst discern the meaning of these experiences: Why *now* in the analysis, and in relationship to *what*, had this particular set of experiences taken place?

Transference has come to serve as the single most important indicator of a psychoanalytic process in progress and as an organizer and guide for the analyst's interventions. The "transference neurosis," the reliving of the traumatic past in the present, is that phenomenon that combines the reactivated past with the manner in which the analyst is being experienced by the patient in the present. Because of the manner in which the changing views relative to the transference had affected interpretations, I shall briefly trace these changes.

The concept of the transference already had undergone important changes in Freud's own lifetime. Freud's original description of transference was that of a purely endopsychic process: Transference occurs when traumatically frustrated, and therefore repressed and unconscious, childhood needs and wishes become transferred across a weakened repression barrier and become amalgamated with a preconscious object or experience (the day residue). Transference toward the analyst was simply one of the many manifestations of this general psychological phenomenon.

Freud, himself, deprived the concept of this original metapsychological meaning when he distinguished between transference that facilitated the process of analysis (the unobjectionable, positive transference, an attenuated sexual attachment) and the erotic transference that had hindered the analysis. The latter constituted the basis for resistances and their analysis. However, transference and resistance (the targets of interpretations after the introduction of the structural theory) could be effected only as long as the analyst remained an obscure figure on whom the patient could project frustrated infantile sexual and aggressive wishes of his childhood.

Transference as a projection of frustrated sexual and aggressive needs has long been abandoned by psychoanalysts. This change in attitudes was made explicit by Sandler (1976): "Nowdays many analysts have the conviction (or at least the uneasy feeling) that the conceptualization of transference as the patient's libidinal or aggressive energic cathexis of a past object being transferred to the image of the analyst in the present, is woefully inadequate" . . . and that practicing analysts had long been aware that transference includes "not only the unconscious instinctual wishes but the whole gamut of unconscious (including preconscious) wishes related to all sorts of needs, gratifications and defenses" (pp. 44–45).

But more than a simple projection, transference has also been conceptualized as a displacement from the significant people of the patient's past to those in the present. Displacement from the past to the present *distorts* the analysand's perception of the analyst. Transference so understood calls for interpretations that aim at correcting this distortion and thereby improving the patient's reality testing ("I am not your mother" or "I'm not your father"). However, since this view of transference is tied to the dual drive theory, it is not sufficient to interpret the analysand's current distortions. Rather, the analyst has to take into consideration the *original distortion* of reality due to the child's progressive and changing drive needs. Distortions of reality had to occur in childhood as the child's experiences became colored and distorted due to his drive-related fantasies: oral greediness, anal hostility, and frustrated incestuous sexual wishes. The conceptualization of transference as a projection, displacement, and distortion in the present, as well as in childhood, in which the analysand could recognize his "true" intentions (drive needs), depended on the analyst being a "mirror," a nonparticipant observer.

But, as Dr. Coen indicates, this view of the transference in which the analyst is a mirror and in which transferences are truly spontaneous, uncontaminated by the analyst's personality and theoretical orientation, was abandoned by psychoanalysis some time ago. Arnold Cooper (1985), in the delivery of the 28th Sandor Rado Lecture, reminded his audience that long ago Rado pointed out that "no analyst had ever been a blank screen, that the therapeutic atmosphere of the analytic situation included the analyst's good will and concern, that transference always included two people in a transaction and that the analyst was a regulator, not only a receiver, of the patient's feelings and wishes" (p. 52). Placing the importance on the meanings that the manner of the analyst's communications have on the analysand, and not narrowly on the content of the communication, is one other way to highlight the impact of the analyst on the analysand's transference experiences.

Once we accept that transference manifestations are not exclusively of endopsychic origin, we have to consider the manner in which this changed view affects the process of interpretations. Transference can no longer be interpreted as an expression of projections, displacement, and distortions. Rather, the analyst's attention will be drawn to the manner in which her responses may, or may not, interfere with the more or less spontaneous evolution of the transference. Her questions not only will address advances in the analytic process in general terms, such as the state of the pathognomonic regression, recollection, working through, and insight, but will also be directed to the state of the transference; specifically, whether her comments had increased the patient's sense of safety that promotes self-reflection and insight, or had disrupted the evolving transference and increased the resistance to self-exploration and free communication.

THE IMPACT OF THE CHANGED VIEW OF TRANSFERENCE ON INTERPRETATIONS

When Dr. Coen refers to Robert Langs as being "exquisitely sensitive to understanding the patient's material, first, in terms of the analyst's contributions," he sees the importance of this emphasis in "the connection between criteria for validation of interpretation and the analyst's self-scrutiny of his or her own contributions." But what criteria is the analyst to use "to validate" her interpretations? To say that these criteria have to be functional, namely, that "the correctness of interpretation is verifiable only by the patient's subsequent reaction" (Freud, 1937), does not yet tell the analyst what it is that she ought to consider as a desirable change or an "advance" in the analytic process.

In a joint paper (Ornstein & Ornstein, 1975), we had examined this question, where, in agreement with Dr. Coen, we, too, had stated that "the individual interventions by the analyst can best be defined by their function'' (p. 265). In the same publication we examined the correspondence between the process nature of analysis and the analyst's interventions, and spelled out those criteria, which, in our view, signify an advance in the analytic process. We suggested that progress in psychoanalysis ought to be assessed in terms of the deepening of the transferences and their working through, rather than in relation to gross or sudden behavioral changes or symptomatic improvement. The points of orientation in the psychoanalytic process are provided primarily by the cohesiveness of the transference, ranging from their first fleeting appearance to their increasing consolidation, and finally to their resolution. By cohesiveness of the transference, we mean both ''its relative persistence throughout the process as well as its focus upon the analyst, i.e., the transference neurosis or the self object transference'' (pp. 338–339). To put it another way, we considered the function of any intervention (verbal or nonverbal) to be the facilitation of the analytic process by making pathognomonic regression, recollection, reconstruction, working through, transmuting internalization, and insight possible. Defining interventions by their function in this manner, and including all of the analyst's communications (verbal and nonverbal), establishes the individual interventions as components of a process—hence our emphasis on the interpretive process, rather than on single interpretations.

The dichotomy that Dr. Coen says some analysts maintain between ''the priority of interpretations versus the analyst as a new object'' is due, I believe, to the fact that even though, in practice, the concept of the transference had undergone changes, the consequences of this change for interpretations have not been made explicit. Once the transference is recognized as a dyadic experience rather than as purely endopsychic in origin, namely, that the transference is an ''organizing activity . . . [in which] the patient assimilates the analytic relationship into the thematic structures of his subjective world'' (Stolorow & Lachmann, 1984–1985), the patient's experiences can no longer be divided into two segments: repetitions on the one hand, and new experiences in relation to the ''new object-analyst,'' on the other. Such a division would be arbitrary and can exist only in the mind of the analyst. As far as the patient is concerned, the analytic experience is—as are all other human experiences, but more so—an amalgam of the old and the new. Clearly only a fraction of the possible meanings that the patient may attribute to his experiences in an analysis may become articulated by either or both participants. This, I believe, is due to the limitation of what can possibly be encompassed and verbalized in a meaningful human relationship. However, the analyst's aim is to bring as much from the patient's experiences into awareness as possible. This is why we have been emphasizing that, ideally, all communication by the analyst be in the "interpretive mode" (Ornstein & Ornstein, 1977, 1985). This reduces the likelihood of the patient attributing meaning to the analyst's communication that cannot be made explicit.

But another central question regarding the nature of the transference has to be clarified in order to illustrate the impact of this changed view of the transference on interpretation: Does the analyst view the presence of reactivated and pathologically elaborated childhood needs as being "the remnants" of inadequately neutralized and sublimated infantile sexuality and aggression, or does the analyst consider that her impact on the patient's transferences is related to the reactivation of *legitimate* childhood needs that have been traumatically frustrated by a nonempathic or only partially empathic environment? Much of the analyst's interpretive activity will depend on this crucial theoretical bias relative to pathogenesis. Dr. Coen touches on this fundamental difference in theoretical orientation, though not directly or explicitly. This is in keeping with his intent not to attack "either psychoanalytic theories or psychoanalytic theorists." This difference in theory, however, is highlighted by the clinical examples that are "drawn from the current debate about the priority of interpretation in analysis versus the analyst as a new object." They represent the problems of analysts in trying to deal with a preoedipal issue such as dependency, analytically, while using a clinical theory that encompasses only, or primarily, the psychoneurotic, that is, oedipal-level psychopathology. This may explain why, in all the cases Dr. Coen discussed, he had to introduce his theoretical bias that dependency, at least in relationship to patients in psychoanalysis, represents a defense or a resistance against aggressive or sexual wishes. Since these patients did not develop the expected oedipal transferences, their first analysts either introduced "parameters" or offered "warmth" to deal with the patient's clinginess, sense of entitlement, and "dependency."

COMMENTS ON THE CLINICAL EXAMPLES

Dr. Coen titled this section of the paper: "Some problems in the analysis of dependency, or what the patient *really* needs from the analyst" (italics mine). Two of the patients had been in analysis before; it was the second analyst who knew what the patient *really* needed from the analyst.

The Case of Professor A.

This patient experienced depression and self-torment after he moved away from the city where he was in analysis the first time. He felt well while he was still in analysis. When he attempted to establish "similar dependent ties with his second analyst," this was understood as the patient having "become stuck in a satisfying dependent relationship with the first analyst, which apparently had not been systematically analyzed. The second analyst wanted to correct this and he "maintained a much more consistent analytic perspective on Professor A.'s dependency, questioning rather than gratifying it."

Dependency is a social-psychological phenomenon. It describes the nature of a particular interpersonal relationships, and is not a statement regarding the nature of the transference. The analyst rather than attempting to understand the meaning of the dependency and interpreting it in the transference, *questioned* the patient's "willingness to settle for dependent attachments, including analysis, rather than understanding the defensive functions this served, especially in relation to hostile aggression."

In the material reported, there is no indication that "dependency" served defensive functions, nor that, if it did, it was erected "in relation to hostile aggression." Both these assertions appear to be based on theoretical assumptions: (1) that dependency here was defensive and did not indicate a genuinely reactivated transference need, which, in an optimal analytic climate, could have evolved into one of the selfobject transferences; and (2) that dependency was hiding hostile aggression. To these two Dr. Coen adds another assumption implied in questioning the patient as to why he "is willing to settle" for dependency. "Willingness" would mean that his dependency was a conscious decision; if his dependency served defensive purposes, could it have been under the patient's conscious control?

This clinical example and the others cited by Dr. Coen underline the timelines and significance of Kohut's contributions to clinical psychoanalysis: the identification and detailed descriptions of the various forms of selfobject transferences (Kohut, 1971). Since prior to that analyzability was linked to the patient's ability to develop a transference neurosis, based on the reactivation of an unresolved Oedipus complex, everything "preoedipal," such as dependency, had to be considered regressively defensive. The recognition of self-object transferences had enabled psychoanalysts to deal *analytically* (that is, interpretively) with those forms of psychopathology that were considered preoedipal and, therefore, on theoretical grounds, regressively defensive.

From this clinical example, it is unclear what exactly Dr. Coen meant by the patient's "dependency." He tells us that the first analyst created a stalemate "in which the patient lived out certain childhood dependent patterns he had had with both parents." However, he also reports that the patient's childhood was characterized by "deprivation and neglect" and not by "dependent patterns he had with both parents." The dependency, then, was not a repetition but a new experience for the patient in the analysis. Could it be that with a sense of safety in the analytic situation, dependency was the first tentative expression of trust and the nucleus for a transference experience that could have provided the patient with a genuine analytic experience? Such a view, as I indicated earlier, does not mean that the analyst views herself as "a new object" but that the selfobject transference experience provides the analysand with a transference experience that contains both—repetition as well as a new beginning; both of these are then the subject of transference interpretations and reconstructions.

The Case of Ms. C.

This was a supervised case of a 40-year-old woman who was an orphan, had lived in an orphanage briefly, and had been raised by various relatives. What Dr. Coen reports is a common observation in which analysts and psychotherapists "treat" the patient's history, rather than whatever the genetic impact of this history may have been on the patient. The therapist, under these circumstances, saw the therapeutic task to be to "make up" for childhood deprivations. Here, too, the assumption is made, without any evidence, that the patient was hiding "angry destructiveness behind a cover of positive feelings." This assumption, as was the case in the analysis of Professor A., indicates that the drive-defense model of explaining clinical phenomena may be so deeply ingrained in analytic thinking that they are assumed to be theory-free. Otherwise Dr. Coen could not have offered this as an example of processing clinical data without an a priori introduction of theory. The drive-defense model is fundamental to classical psychoanalytic theory; once the analyst uses this model to organize the data, interpretations such as were offered here are to be expected.

Case of Dr. D.

This case demonstrates the same points I had made with regard to the other two cases. I shall not repeat them here other than to question still another feature of Dr. Coen's approach to interpretation, which seriously undermines his earlier insistance on understanding the importance of meanings. This was a patient whose "self-presentation as a little girl wanting only to be hugged" was "questioned" by the analyst. One of the things the analyst questioned was "the defensive functions of her self-image and her dependent pressure." The question is this: Whose view of the patient shall the analyst consider as valid when she wants to comprehend the patient's psychic reality? Does the analyst offer her own view and dismiss the patient's "presentation" as a defense, or should she try to understand the meaning of the patient's own presentation of herself?

A further question arises in relation to this clinical vignette. Suppose the transference—which is not reported here—indicated that the wish to be hugged was a defense against adult sexuality. It is not clear why the analyst chose to use confrontation rather than the interpretive mode in dealing with this defense. The defense was confronted with such questions as "why she was willing to remain in such a childlike relationship with him" and "why she was so afraid of regarding herself as an adult woman." These questions, which are similar to the phrasing of questions in the other cases, also indicate an assumption that the motive for defense was "willful" or conscious to the patient. These questions, we are told, awakened the patient's curiosity regarding "this exclusive view of herself." Maybe it was at this point that the analytic process was set into motion; a report as to its evolution and the resolution of the transference would have been most illuminating.

The Case of Ms. E.

In this case Dr. Coen maintains a dichotomy between psychoanalysis and psychoanalytic psychotherapy—one that is commonly maintained in the psychoanalytic literature. It is of importance that the line of demarcation between the two forms of treatment is drawn in relation to interpretation, which is the mode of intervention in psychoanalysis, but not in psychotherapy. However, clinical observations favor the conclusion that whether or not an analytic process in the strictest sense of the word can unfold does not depend on the setting (whether the patient is lying down or sitting up), but on whether the therapist's interventions are in the interpretive mode or are instead "reassuring" and "supportive" in nature (Ornstein & Ornstein, 1977). Once noninterpretive modes of interventions are introduced into the process of treatment, introspection and self-reflection on the part of the patient cannot be promoted. It is then difficult to say whether the patient was not analyzable because of the way she experienced the analyst's interventions, or because of the nature of her psychopathology.

SUMMARY

Although I found myself in agreement with many of Dr. Coen's theoretical points, I also found that his clinical examples confirmed his own criticisms of other psychoanalysts who neglect understanding and thereby neglect the specific and idiosyncratic *meaning* of the patient's transference experiences. Instead, in the clinical examples, Dr. Coen uses his own theoretical bias to *explain* a particular clinical phenomenon, dependency. When Dr. Coen speaks of "the analysis of dependency," he is addressing a piece of symptomatic behavior. But can a symptom be "analyzed" without understanding its meaning to a particular patient—a meaning that can only be revealed in the transference?

In the last section of his paper, Dr. Coen's criticism becomes more clearly focused on the contributions of self psychology. For example, when he states that "for the analyzable patient, the analyst does not ordinarily seek to fill in missing functions and structures but to join the patient in understanding him or herself," he not only indicates a failure to understand the nature of selfobject transferences, but also indicates that his listening perspective is not from within the patient's perspective, i.e. empathic, but rather it is that of an external observer. The empathic, introspective mode of listening could have made it obvious to him that one cannot "seek to fill in missing functions and structures." The analyst cannot set herself up to be a mirroring selfobject; only the patient can determine the meaning that the analyst's verbal and nonverbal communications have for him, whether these are validating or questioning his self experiences. And it will be the patient whose rage reaction, haughty withdrawal, and increasing resistance will alert the analyst to the patient's unconscious expectations that had been frustrated by the analyst's responses. Once the analyst understands the nature of the transference, the patient's expectations can be acknowledged and accepted as reactivation of frustrated childhood needs, and interpreted and reconstructed as such. For the same reason, a therapist cannot "assume the role" of the analysand's "tutor, educator, or provider of missing psychic structures." However, it is up to the analyst to recognize in what capacity she is being used in order to join the patient in understanding himself. To do so she has to adopt an empathic listening perspective.

Dr. Coen faults these "other analysts" for their failure to deal with aggression and quotes Kernberg (1975) who recommends that "even with seemingly infantile, demanding, dependent borderline patients in psychotherapy, far better results are obtained by confronting the aggression, impossible demands, entitlement and masochism than exclusively 'empathizing' with the patient's felt deprivation and disability." It is in relation to statements such as this that I wonder why Dr. Coen so completely set aside in the second part of his paper the arguments he put forward in the first part, with regard to the need for understanding the meanings of the patient's experiences. Should the meaning of aggression and the sense of entitlement not be understood and interpreted but rather confronted because of their effect on the analyst and others in the patient's environment? Such a nonanalytic attitude toward certain parts of the patient's symptomatic behavior takes me back to Dr. Coen's original thesis that an analyst's choice of a particular theory and the fitting of the patient's material into that theory express countertransference. Confronting rather than understanding and interpreting speaks to the interpersonal aspect of a particular behavior rather than to its intrapsychic meaning; confrontations, therefore, especially with regard to certain "negative" aspects of the patient's behavior, appear to be expressions of countertransference on the part of the analyst. This kind of countertransference is no less dangerous than the one Dr. Coen describes in relation to Dr. F., whose various analysts had tried to force emotional closeness on him because of their own needs. I believe we would all agree that whether an analyst "forces" emotional closeness on her patients, or "confronts" them with their unacceptable behavior, we are dealing with serious countertransference issues, regardless of the clinical theory that the analyst may espouse.

I want to thank Dr. Coen for the opportunity to discuss this paper. It is the controversy surrounding these fundamental clinical issues (method of data gathering, the nature of transference and its effect on interpretations, and how this may introduce countertransference elements into the treatment process) that sharpens the clinician's thinking in daily work. Discussions related to such clinical concerns rather than those that are restricted to theoretical issues are the ones most likely to promote improvements in the practice of psychoanalysis.

REFERENCES

Cooper, A. (1985). The twenty-eighth Sandor Rado lecture—Changes in psychoanalytic ideas, the example of transference interpretations. *Bull. Assn. Psychoanal. Med.*, 25:51–57.

Eissler, K. R. (1968). The relation of explaining and understanding in psychoanalysis: Demonstrated by one aspect of Freud's approach to literature. *Sci. S. Child* 23:141–177.

Freud, S. (1937). Construction in analysis. *Standard Edition*, 23:255–269.

Hartman, H. (1927). Understanding and Explanation. *Essays in Ego Psychiatry*, pp. 369–403. N.Y. I.U.P.

Kernberg, O. F. (1975). *Borderline Conditions and Pathological Narcissism*. New York: Jason Aronson.

Kohut, H. (1971). *The Analysis of the Self*, New York: International Universities Press.

Ornstein, A., & Ornstein, P. (1975). On the interpretive process. *Int. J. Psychoanal. Psychother.*, 4:219–271.

Ornstein, P., & Ornstein, A. (1977). On the continuing evolution of psychoanalytic psychotherapy: Reflections and predictions. *Ann. Psychoanal.*, 5:329–370.

——— & ——— (1985). Clinical understanding and explaining: The empathic vantage point. *Prog. Self-Psychol.*, 1:43–61.

Sandler, J. (1976). Countertransference and role-responsiveness. *Int. Rev. Psychoanal.*, 3:43–48.

Stolorow, R., & Lachmann, F. (1984–85). Transference: The future of an illusion. *Ann. Psychoanal.*, 22/23:19–33.

II

Clinical Topics

14

SOPHIE FREUD, A.C.S.W., Ph.D.

Overloving/Underloving

WE KNOW FROM CYBERNETICS THAT OVERABUNDANCE OF ANY VARIABLE LEADS TO PATHOLOGY. THIS PAPER DISCUSSES THE DAMAGE THAT TOO MUCH LOVE CREATES IN ALL SIGNIFICANT RELATIONSHIPS, SUCH AS IN ADULT COUPLES, BETWEEN PARENTS AND CHILDREN, AND BETWEEN THERAPIST AND PATIENT. IT IS URGED THAT THE WORD "OVERLOVING" BE ADOPTED IN OUR LANGUAGE AND THINKING, AND SUBSTITUTED FOR MORE PEJORATIVE CONCEPTS, BECAUSE IT IS A PHENOMENOLOGICALLY CORRECT DESCRIPTION. SUCH USAGE WILL CLARIFY THE NATURE OF DAMAGING RELATIONSHIPS WHILE REDUCING GUILT. EXTREME FORMS OF UNDERLOVING, SUCH AS VIOLENCE, ARE CONSIDERED TO BE OFTEN ASSOCIATED WITH OVERLOVING. EXCESSIVE TRANSFERENCE REACTIONS IN PSYCHOTHERAPY ARE THOUGHT TO BE FORMS OF OVERLOVING BY THE PATIENT, USUALLY AS A RESPONSE TO AN OVERLOVING THERAPIST. PEOPLE IN ALL SIGNIFICANT RELATIONSHIPS ARE SEEN AS NEEDING TO MAINTAIN A DIFFICULT BALANCE BETWEEN ATTACHMENT AND FUSION VERSUS SEPARATENESS AND DISTANCE, BETWEEN OVERLOVING AND UNDERLOVING.

Our capacity to love each other seems to be our highest human achievement, possibly even the only salvation for humanity. It is therefore quite difficult to accept that the cybernetic principle that suggests that overabundance of *any* variable, including health or happiness, leads to pathology (Keeney, 1983) may also, or perhaps especially, apply to the emotion of love. Yet clinical experience and even ordinary daily observations leave no doubt but that many people damage others, and are damaged by others, more profoundly by too much love than by too little love.

I shall expand in this paper on the damage that is created by loving too much, and argue that the word and the concept of *overloving* can be theoretically and clinically useful to describe this process. I shall compare the process of "overloving" with the apparent opposite process of "underloving" in an attempt to see how they are related. I then want to reflect on the striking similarity between the mother–infant relationship and other intimate relationships, with emphasis on the similar ways in which overloving and underloving manifest themselves in all relationships. Finally, I want to reflect on the need to maintain some balance, however precarious, between overloving and underloving in all emotionally significant relationships.

THE CONCEPT OF OVERLOVING

There may be indignant protest against the use of the word "overloving" to connote the idea of "loving too much." In our effort to protect the notion of love in its beauty and purity, we try to find alternate names for expressions of intense love, perhaps calling it possessiveness, or narcissistic overinvestment in another person, or overprotectiveness. Yet the word "overloving" is phenomenologically correct for both the person experiencing the feeling and the person receiving it. Indeed, if the emotion that is expressed and received were not defined as *love* by common agreement, if would not create such havoc. Possessiveness that is not defined as love could be repudiated without guilt. And the person who feels overprotective or controlling would not be so hurt by a rejection if they had not defined their feelings as love. I think of overlove as one particular form of love that has grown toxic because it has grown out of bounds. We can equate it to the sorcerer's apprentice phenomenon, or to a cancerous growth that may have started from the body's efforts to heal a wound through new cell production. I know that many of my colleagues will object to the concept of overloving. The essence of love, they will say, is recognition of and respect for the partner's otherness and narcissistic investment is the opposite of love. Yet, opposites meet on the emotional continuum. I think of the Inquisition, in which people were tortured and killed to glorify God; or the enemies of abortion, who will kill to preserve the sanctity of life; or the arms race for the sake of peace. It seems that every ideal escalated to a fanatic level defeats itself. Why not love?

The word overloving is not only economical, graphic, and evocative, but is also extremely useful in clinical situations, as illustrated by the following vignette

> A woman whom I shall call Mrs. Kennedy consulted me regarding her adolescent son. She wanted me to recommend a

> group therapist. She had already arranged numerous tutorial and other therapeutic services for him, trying "to fix him" in every possible way, but he was not responding appropriately. I said she clearly loved him too much and that adolescents are allergic to mother love. Her next demonstration of love would be to release her control and let him mess up his own life. Mrs. Kennedy was very grateful to me for understanding her so deeply. She promised to follow through on this idea. She also explained that her former therapist had accused her of covert hostility toward her son, and that had missed the point completely.

The idea that too much love can be as destructive as too little love might seem absurd. Readers might point to such destructive phenomena as child abuse and other forms of family violence that appear to be the result of underloving, rather than overloving. Perhaps it is a question of semantics.

THE CONCEPT OF UNDERLOVING

We could agree on two meanings for the idea of underloving. One is the meaning of disengagement, lack of interest, and indifference. Indifference is quite a rare emotion among family members, although it may frequently arise as a defense against explosive rage.

The other meaning of underloving could be passionate hatred, as manifest in wife battering, for example. The abused child or the abused wife is not an object of indifference—on the contrary, violence happens in intensely fused relationships where the otherness of the loved/hated partner has been forgotten. We know to what length abusing parents may go to avoid removal of their abused child, and how desperately violent husbands cling to a battered wife, with protestations of undying love and ever-renewed promises of reform. Even more curiously, these feelings may be reciprocated. Actually we are all at home with crimes of passion. We may not approve of them, but we are not surprised when we hear that someone kills a partner out of excessive love, for example, in a fit of jealousy.

Scheflen (1972) suggests in the same vein that violence in the form of murder, suicide, or madness occurs when bound relationships—his word for overloving—become too much of a burden for the dominant partner and are suddenly cut off. This sort of underloving is so much like overloving, and one extreme can turn so easily into the other, that we must assume that overloving and this form of underloving are very similar emotions, or at least that love and hatred are two emotions that may coexist and rapidly alternate with each other.

Psychoanalytic theory has taught us that overloving is a cover for underloving, and that an overprotective mother, for example, "spoils" her child as a reaction formation against her hostile wishes. I have come to reject the whole concept of reaction formation associated with the assumption that one feeling is necessarily more basic than another, and, of course, it is always hateful feelings that are assumed to be more basic. One could also argue, as Searles (1965) has done, "that the most powerful driving force in human beings is the effort to express oneself in a loving constructive way" (p. 220). Indeed for some people the expression of loving feelings is more dangerous than hateful feelings, because they have learned to associate loving with dangerous consequences for self or other. Searles describes how some mothers of schizophrenic children treat them with indifference or hatefulness because they are afraid their love might damage their children. We might say in our language that they underlove their children out of fear of overloving them. In systems thinking the search for basic causes has been abandoned. We might need to give up on reaction formation in its usual meaning and agree instead that people have many conflicting simultaneous positive and negative emotions, all of which are probably equally authentic and should be acknowledged as such.

RECIPROCITY IN SYMMETRICAL AND COMPLEMENTARY RELATIONSHIPS

It is thus my impression that overloving and underloving take somewhat similar forms both in symmetrical relationships in which the two partners have equal social power, and in complementary relationships in which the two partners have unequal social power, but intermeshing needs. Although I find the concepts of symmetry and complementarity introduced by communication theorists (Watzlawick et al., 1967) heuristically useful in understanding relationship processes, these distinctions also have serious limitations that can obscure the deeper similarities and distort the preceptions that each relationship partner may have of his or her role in the relationship. Relationship partners may believe, for example, that they either have more power and less vulnerability or less power and more vulnerability than they actually have.

We can examine the three prototypic complementary relationships of parent/child, teacher/student, and therapist/patient in terms of emotional caretaking, rendering of instrumental services, and exposure to narcissistic injury, and look at the patterns of reciprocity and distribution of power that actually exist.

In terms of *emotional caretaking*, it often becomes dubious as to who takes care of whom. Early family therapy theory focused on the pathology of the "parentified child" who is expected to take care of his/her parents. More recently there has been recognition that family roles are flexible, and that "all the role functions in the family should be available to everybody in the family" (Whitaker, 1979, p. 111). A certain amount of emotional caretaking by children of their parents strikes me as an inevitable part of a parent–child relationship, and it is certainly the rule rather than the exception. I recently wrote an article (Loewenstein, 1984) in which I describe the ways in which I managed to take care of each of my three mothers, as one way of recruiting their love for me, and I found a most responsive accord with this idea, especially among women. I have the impression that it is daughters rather than sons who are selected for this vital caretaking task. Robert Langs (1982) writes about the emotional caretaking that patients do of their therapists, so that they can remain available to the patients, quite similar to the child's attempt at healing a parent in order to preserve a good enough relationship. Many patients never confront their therapists openly, not only because they have trouble with anger or assertiveness (which they also might have), but mostly because they do not want to hurt their therapist's feelings.

It is also often quite uncertain as to who renders most service to whom. I have heard of an experiment in which high school students with reading difficulties were enrolled to teach first-graders how to read, Of course, it was the teachers who made amazing progress in their reading skills, not primarily the students. If you want to learn something really well, it is best to become a teacher. It is also true that many of us become therapists in our quest for self-healing. Indeed, in order to get healed, it might be safer to become a therapist than a patient.

Caretaking must, of course, also be seen in a broader context. Others take care of us when they give us self-definition, and meaning and purpose to our lives. Now and then I remind my students, somewhat reluctantly, that I need them as much as they need me, or more accurately, much more so. It is one of my recurring teacher dreams—teachers have very characteristic nightmares—that I come to class and nobody is there, or that everyone leaves while I talk to them.

Relying on others for one's self-definition leaves one in quite a vulnerable position. Communication theory suggests (Watzlawick et al., 1967) that conflict in a complementary relationship results in disconfirmation of the one-down partner. While we must be acutely cognizant of the vulnerability of the one-down position, we who are in one-up positions also need to pay attention to the possibility of disconfirmation of our own roles. Children, clients, students, and employees can assault our self-definition as good enough parent, therapist, teacher, or boss. I have repeatedly seen classes of students kill off a teacher, and autistic children defeat a mother's readiness to love, let alone clients who disempower their therapists. I believe the narcissistic injuries inflicted in these admittedly Pyrrhic victories can be profound and lasting.

We must thus conclude that there is mutual vulnerability, reciprocity, interdependence, and subtle equality of power in all ongoing significant relationships.

LACK OF EQUALITY AND NARCISSISTIC CONTAINMENT

There are, however, admittedly important elements of inequality in relationships, aside from those obvious ones of social power. First of all there may be inequality of emotional investment. Often, between two partners, one partner is apt to be the actively loving one, and the other partner the loved one, thus creating an emotional inequality. Yet equilibrium might be maintained if the loved and loving positions change over time. Without such equilibration the complementary overloving and underloving positions may become entrenched, and eventually destroy the vitality of the relationship.

There is also the question of unequal responsibility. In an ideal world, the one-up person in the complementary relationships that I mentioned is charged with containing some of their narcissistic needs and maintaining the delicate balance between overloving and underloving. I want to reflect on the ways in which many of us fail in these two interrelated tasks, and especially on the ways in which we fail due to excessive good will rather than lack of it.

THE NEW "GOOD ENOUGH" MOTHER

It is my impression that clinicians reared in a theoretical climate of attachment theory, separation anxiety, and maternal deprivation may have propagated child-rearing advice that promoted maternal overloving. The new infant research has redefined the meaning of a "good enough mother" (Winnicott, 1963) and it is currently providing new parental guidance.

We could view the mother–infant relationship as a prototypic relationship that helps us to understand the functional and dysfunctional aspects of all potentially growth-producing relationships: We learn about the infant's need for physical contact, which later develops into the emotional, intellectual, and physical contact needs of adult life. The mother is asked to allow and promote the infant's self-regulation, as a first step in lifelong striving toward autonomy.

There is responsiveness to cues regarding the other's needs, rather than the assumption that they are similar to one's own. There is need for reliability and predictability in these relationships; one keeps one's promises and counts on one another in certain established ways. Just as with infants and mothers, there needs to be a balance of love relationships, or in teaching, or in therapy, between facing each other versus exploring the world jointly, between due attention to relationships needs versus learning new things together, with threat of sterility if either of these two poles is neglected. Infants do not absorb their food if it is given outside a relationship context, and teaching or therapy without relationship may also not truly nourish, yet there needs to be food, knowledge, content. Sometimes we tend to forget that the food, knowledge, gaining of insight, and the relationship dimension are not two separate poles that need to be alternately attended to, but that the two poles are really one pole, perhaps a cement pole in which water and sand become inextricably intermixed. I think the concept of transference is seen as too separate a dimension in psychoanalysis or therapy, without sufficient realization that not only is relationship created through intimate sharing, but the relationship then, in turn, shapes and colors everything that goes on in treatment, including the patient's reported dreams and free associations.

Above all, the infant, lover, student, client, must be seen as *other*, and not merely as an extension of oneself. The willingness to attend with care to one's partner's communications, to be responsive to cues regarding his or her needs, and to get to know him or her, infant or adult, in all his or her complexity and uniqueness is perhaps the highest expression of every kind of love.

Yet there is no need for perfection. In opposition to the very best mother, the good enough mother, teacher, lover, or therapist is not always attentive—sometimes she is casual, preoccupied, and turns her back to attend to her own needs. Sometimes he is in a hurry and imposes his own agenda—overlooks subtle cues and becomes unreliable and unpredictable. Lack of some unpredictability might even create stagnation in a relationship. I like to think we need unpredictability in a framework of predictability.

Flaws in loving, caretaking, teaching, and therapy introduce novelty and new learning. The child needs to learn that the mother is still there, even if she does turn her back, and that both goodness and badness belong to one and the same mother. Therapists commit empathic failures; teachers give unfair grades, or have favorite students, or are opinionated.

The good enough mother ultimately might be better than the very best mother, since the latter might set too awesome a model of perfection. Besides, I suspect the ambition to be the very best mother, teacher, and so on, is the first step toward overloving.

We even find occasional striking examples in which the relentless determination of one partner to become the "perfect caretaker" leads to madness or violence. Laing (1965) reports a case history in which a daughter becomes defeated by her inability to express her rage against her overdevoted selfless mother. "Julie's shreds of sanity . . . depended on the possibility of being able to lodge some bad in her actual mother. The impossibility of doing this, in a sane way, was one of the factors that contributed to a schizophrenic psychosis" (p. 194).

In a similar vein, it is my unproved fantasy that Virginia Woolf's marriage, in which an underloving wife was married to an overloving husband, followed a similar pattern. We learn that "the principal features of Virginia's ravings during her mad spells was criticism of others—of men in general, of Leonard [her husband] in particular . . ." (Spater & Parsons, 1977, p. 68). I believe that Virginia Woolf was in such a bondage of gratitude to her relentlessly oversolicitous husband, and unable to express her secret hatred against his overprotective intrusiveness, that she finally committed suicide as her only solution. Such apparently "perfect devotion" is the embodiment of what I have called overloving.

It is not the false step in a synchronous dance that is a danger to the partner, but the inability to acknowledge such missteps. Disappointments and frustrations seem to be an integral part of all relationships. Relationships become "good enough" not by being perfect, but when participants can meet the challenge of disappointed expectations through some sort of transcendence, some verbal or nonverbal communication, some understanding or forgiveness.

OVERLOVED CHILDREN

Overloving has been studied most extensively in the parent–child relationship, and there is considerable evidence that children can accommodate to casual or mildly neglectful treatment better than to consistently intrusive caretaking. Stern (1977) gives a frightening example of a mother who was so determined to be a "stimulating" mother that she was totally insensitive to her infant's needs for separateness.

> Whenever a moment of mutual gaze occurred, the mother went immediately into high-gear stimulating behaviors, producing a profusion of fully displayed, high-intensity . . . behavior. Jenny invariably broke gaze rapidly. Her mother never interpreted this temporary face and gaze aversion as a cue to lower her level of behavior, nor would she let Jenny self-control the level by gaining distance . . . after several weeks of visits . . . Jenny's avoidance of eye contact was almost complete, her face aversions more pronounced and continuous, and her face almost expressionless. (pp. 112–113)

Stern agrees with me that such overstimulation may not necessarily be a sign of covert hostility. He attributes it to inexperience coupled with interpersonal insensitivity, while I would seek a pattern of overinvestment.

Alice Miller (1981) is the most recent and vocal author who draws a link between "overloving" parents (not her word) and narcissistic vulnerability in children. Her book was received with enthusiasm by mental health professionals, apparently because so many readers recognized themselves as overloved children. Such children are narcissistic ornaments, loved conditionally for being obedient, smart, attractive, and generally a source of pride for their parents. Thus we have few adults who take their self-worth for granted, as an integral part of the self. Self-worth has to be laboriously earned, over and over, and self-esteem regulation becomes a source of lifelong preoccupation for most men and women.

Actually I think we could redefine the ambiguous concept of narcissism as a condition in which one simultaneously overloves and underloves onself, without being able to strike a harmonious balance.

Parents who have suffered in extreme ways, such as those who have lived in great poverty or discrimination, or who have survived the holocaust, are especially vulnerable to overloving their children. They are determined that their children will lead better lives than they had led. It is tragic that such desperate determination, like overloving in general, carries the seed of its own defeat. Such parents, and of course many other parents as well, exert tight control over their children "for their own good." They may feel a sense of deep betrayal and extreme rage if their children fail to live up to their expectations. Their children understand that they are expected to make up for their parents' missed youth, disappointed dreams, and years of despair. The children feel exploited and oppressed, but their hostility appears to them as baffling and unjustified. They know how much their parents have sacrificed for them, and they feel like ungrateful monsters. Children desperately want their parents to have contented lives. Loyalty and gratitude to parents are basic human emotions. These children, and overloved children in general, may split off their angry feelings, and thus inevitably loving feelings as well, perhaps becoming emotionally impoverished in the process. Other overloved children may direct their unexpressed disowned anger against others, in eruptions of violence, or against themselves, in depression. It is a great hardship when children feel too precious to their parents and when the meaning of their parents' lives rests exclusively with them. Parental love, or rather parental overlove, may exact a high price.

The taboo against accusing parents does get broken, and I believe it is sons who have been most bitter and eloquent in accusing their overloving mothers in what I call the Portnoy syndrome. However, I believe daughters are in even greater danger of being overloved by either parent. I have just suggested that prevalence of depression among women in our society is partially due to maternal overloving. Fathers' overlove of their daughters may be expressed in a continuum from subtle seductiveness to outright incest, leading to various forms of psychic injury.

OVERLOVING IN THE THERAPEUTIC RELATIONSHIP

While the parent–child relationship is particularly vulnerable to overloving patterns, I have already suggested that it can be almost equally prevalent and equally toxic in other significant relationships. "Intrusiveness," the transgression of personal boundaries for presumably benevolent reasons, might then take different forms. In therapy, for example, such intrusiveness might be in the form of premature or otherwise misguided interpretations.

Maintaining the delicate balance between overloving and underloving is a constant juggling act in the therapeutic relationship, and indeed different schools of therapy seem to swing the balance from one side to the other—such as from the strict therapeutic neutrality recommended by traditional psychoanalysts to the whole-hearted empathy of self psychologists. I am a little concerned regarding emphasis on the expression of *warmth* in some recent feminist thinking in psychotherapy, rather than need for atunement or attentiveness, for example, and I see this as a swing of the pendulum that will right itself. The therapeutic experience seems to lend itself to the development of overloving feelings, and this has emerged especially in the male therapist–female patient encounter.

Just as Miller (1981, 1983) takes on the cause of children who are emotionally exploited by their parents, Robert Langs (1982) is an outspoken advocate for patients who are emotionally exploited by their therapists. I suggest that some form of overloving by the therapist is one example of such exploitation, as shown both by available autobiographical literature (e.g., Mitchell, 1973; Ferguson, 1973) and by my own work. In research I have done on the passionate love experience (Loewenstein, 1980) I have interviewed a number of women who had overloved their therapist and consequently experienced various emotional disasters. Sometimes these women had gone into therapy in the first place because of a loss related to some overloving experience in their life. While these women could be described as either hysterical or borderline, a closer look, or at least a different perspective, confirms Langs' contention that the therapist bears serious responsibility for such "therapeutic passions," even if not blatantly seductive. The following situation in which I acted as a consultant illustrates such subtle collusion.

> A professional married woman in her early 50s returned to a therapist whom she had seen 12 years earlier, over a three-year

> span, to get help with her depression. Although her depression had not abated, the therapy had been an emotionally positive experience for her. This time she told her therapist of a brief extramarital affair in which she had been quickly rejected, leaving her with a sense of inadequacy and isolation. The therapist had expressed great pleasure in seeing his old patient again. He compared her life situation with his own midlife loneliness and disappointment in his marriage. These confidences precipitated a flood of passionate emotions in the woman, leading to various forms of acting out. She felt these emotions had been stored in her for many years and that she had now received permission to express them.

Freud sanitized the strong emotions that arise in therapy by calling them transference, but he admitted, perhaps in a weak moment (he later retracted this, probably for political reasons) in his paper on transference love (1957/1915), that transference love with its irrational infantile projections, addiction, dependency, and obsessional longing for fusion was not much different from other kinds of love.

The most recent book documenting the problematic nature of transference love is called *A Secret Symmetry*, edited by Carotenuto, an Italian Jungian psychoanalyst (1982). The book consists of actual diary entries and letters of a young Russian woman, Sabina Spielrein, which had been found in the basement of a Swiss clinic. She had been brought by her parents to Burghölzli, the Swiss sanatorium in which Carl Jung started his psychiatric career, to be treated for an emotional illness. Spielrein became Jung's patient and her diaries and letters describe her desperate passion for her therapist, which, it seems, was cautiously reciprocated. Carl Jung had rescued Sabina Spielrein from her emotional illness—she later became a productive psychoanalyst—but at the price of her feeling much tormenting love for Jung for many years. Carotenuto comments on the dilemma: "If the analyst is happy and his love is outside the analysis, then he is 'dead' for his patient. If instead he wants to experience love in the analytic relationship, then death is imparted by the dissolution of the analysis" (p. 172). Carotenuto thinks that Spielrein inspired Jung with some of his most creative ideas, reminding us of Anna O. who invented the "talking cure."

The power and drama of addictive transference love do not seem to me to be primarily around sexual desires. In a recent 60-year follow-up of Freud's "most famous case," the Wolf Man, we find that his entire long life had been overshadowed by his love–hate dependency relationship with this famous analyst. He had a lifelong passion for Freud, quite as intense, in its own totally different way, as Spielrein's passion for Jung. Perhaps it is hard to be analyzed by people with such strong personalities.

Actually the life history of the Wolf Man, one of the most written about insignificant men of the 20th century, is a stunning example of Langs' point that the therapeutic relationship can repeat, and even reinforce rather than resolve, certain earlier relationship conflicts. We might say, stretching the point a bit, that from an overloved child, the Wolf Man became an overloved or overloving patient. Actually he was both underloved and overloved by his mother, whom he describes as very cold, yet very possessive, and maybe he was both underloved and overloved by Freud as well. In any case he transferred his unresolved dependency needs from his parents to Freud and on to a series of other psychoanalysts, never growing toward a sense of wholeness or of being in charge of his own emotional life.

RELATIONSHIP GOALS

We thus expect therapists, teachers, and parents to control their narcissistic needs, and yet the demands of these roles are so great that we surely could not meet them adequately without some personal narcissistic investment, by which I mean involving our self-esteem in the success of these relationships. When others are used to meet our needs for emotional nourishment, for self-affirmation, for feeling alive rather than dead, for feeling useful rather than useless, for being in control rather than being controlled, then the relationship is in danger of becoming one of emotional exploitation. Yet it is hard to imagine a situation in which some of these factors do not exist. It is thus more of a problem of balance, and it is the tipping of the balance in the direction of too much narcissistic investment that I call overloving.

There are, however, widely divergent opinions on the degree to which one should use one's own power to influence others for their own good—one form of narcissistic enterprise.

Cybernetic theorists warn us of too much "conscious purpose" (Keeney, p. 187) that does not respect the whole ecology of a context. They urge us to "become oblivious of any reward to be gained . . . [and] of any fame to be acquired . . ." (p. 201). In a similar Taoist spirit, Fingarette (1963) opposes any form of overloving relationships. He believes that "detachment is the essential ground out of which relationships among genuinely autonomous individuals can arise" (p. 272). His solution to the balance of overloving and underloving is detachment without indifference, respect without envy or expectations, love without possessiveness, caring without control. "Sentimentality and portentousness arise out of the using of things and persons in the service of a fixed idea of one's own, whether it be 'to care,' 'to create,' 'to love' or 'to save' " (p. 282). Other people are not to be used for one's own psychic purposes or narcissistic gratification. Some people would characterize his ideal relationship goals as underloving. Relationship work in general thus seems to have two major components:

1. The gradual withdrawal of projections and consequent differentiation of self within the relationship.
2. The examination, acknowledgment, and tempering of one's narcissistic needs within the relationship.

When this process is completed in therapy, we can assume that treatment is finished.

Is there also danger that total differentiaton is a relationship, such as Fingarette suggests, means the end of love? Is lack of differentiation perhaps the glue that holds our social fabric together? Will mature detachment extinguish the fire and spark and life-giving passion that are nourished by one's narcissistic needs, and lead to the death of creativity?

I come to the conclusion that significant relationships are forever suspended in the delicate balance that I have called underloving and overloving—detachment that may border on indifference and sterility, or passionate engagement that may become intrusive and destructive. We can embrace this creative act of tightrope walking as a lifelong pursuit.

All through this paper I have first said one thing, and then the opposite. I would like to end similarly with two quotes that alternately celebrate underloving and overloving. The first is from the German poet Rilke, on the nature of love, taken from Rilke's *Letters on Love* (see Mood, 1975).

> I hold this to be the highest task of a bond between two people: that each should stand guard over the solitude of the other . . . a good marriage is that in which each appoints the other guardian of his solitude. . . . A togetherness between two people is an impossibility, and where it seems nevertheless to exist, it is a narrowing, a reciprocal agreement which robs either one party or both of his fullest freedom and development. But, once the

> realization is accepted that even between the closest human beings infinite distances continue to exist, a wonderful loving side by side can grow up, if they succeed in loving the distance between them which makes it possible for each to see the other whole and against a wide sky. (pp. 27, 28)

The second is from Mary Wollstonecraft who was a great feminist and a woman of great passions. By ending with *her* quotation, rather than with Rilke's, and saving the best for last, I am giving away where my own weight falls in this balancing act. She wrote, in 1795:

> Love is want of my hear. I have examined myself lately with more care than formerly, and find, that to deaden is not to calm the mind—Aiming at tranquility, I have almost destroyed all the energy of my soul—almost rooted out what renders it estimable . . . The desire of regaining peace (do you understand me?) has made me forget the respect due to my own emotions—sacred emotions, that are the sure harbingers of the delights I was formed to enjoy.

REFERENCES

Carotenuto, A. (1982). *A Secret Symmetry*. New York: Pantehon Books.

Ferguson, S. (1973). *A Guard Within*. London: Chatto & Windus.

Fingarette, H. (1963). *The Self in Transformation*. New York: Harper & Row.

Freud, S. (1957). Observations on transference love. *Standard Edition*, 14.

Keeney, B. P. (1983). *Aesthetics of Change*. New York: Guilford Press.

Laing, R. D. (1965). *The Divided Self*. New York: Penguin Books.

Langs, R. (1982). *The Therapeutic Conspiracy*. New York: Jason Aronson.

Loewenstein, S. F. (1984). My three mothers. *Radcliffe Q.*, 70(4):14–17.

——— (1980). Passion as a mental health hazard. In *The Evolving Female*, ed. C. Heckerman. New York: Human Sciences Press.

Miller, A. (1983). *For Your Own Good*. New York: Farrar, Strauss, Giroux.

——— (1981). *Prisoners of Childhood*. New York: Basic Books.

Mitchell, S. (1973). *My Own Woman*. New York: Horizon Press.

Mood, J. L. (1975). *Rilke on Love and Other Difficulties*. New York: W. W. Norton.

Obholzer, K. (1982). *The Wolf-Man. Sixty Years Later*. New York: Continuum.

Scheflen, A. E. (1972). *Body Language and Social Order*. New York: Prentice-Hall.

Searles, H. F. (1965). *The Collected Papers on Schizophrenia and Related Subjects*. New York: International Universities Press.

Spater, F., & Parsons, I. (1977). *A Marriage of True Minds*. New York: Harcourt, Brace, Jovanovich.

Stern, D. (1977). *The First Relationship*. Cambridge, Mass.: Harvard University Press.

Watzlawick, P., Beavin, J., & Jackson, D. (1967). *Pragmatics of Human Communication*. New York: W. W. Norton.

Whitaker, C. (1979). On family therapy (interview with Bruce Howe). *Pilgrimage* 7:107–114.

Winnicott, D. W. (1965). *The Family and Individual Development*. New York: Basic Books.

Wollstonecraft, M. (1795). (Quoted by Ellen Moers. Vindicating Mary Wollstonecraft. *NY Rev. Books*, February 19, 1976.

15

HAROLD F. SEARLES, M.D.P.A.

DISCUSSION:

"Overloving"—A Misnomer

THIS DISCUSSION OF SOPHIE FREUD'S PAPER ASSERTS THAT "OVERLOVING" IS NOT A VALID CONCEPT. MANY PEOPLE BELIEVE THAT THEY ARE OVERLOVING; BUT, BEING PREDOMINANTLY NARCISSISTIC RATHER THAN MATURELY OBJECT-RELATED, THEY ARE LARGELY UNCONSCIOUS OF THEIR HATRED AND OTHER NEGATIVE EMOTIONS. DR. FREUD ONLY BELATEDLY STARTS TAKING NARCISSISM INTO ACCOUNT, AND SHE SEEMS UNAWARE OF THE HIGHLY RELEVANT MECHANISM OF PROJECTIVE IDENTIFICATION. BUT THIS DISCUSSANT FINDS ADMIRABLE HER COURAGE IN EXPLORING SO VAST A PROBLEM AS THE DEFINING, ESSENTIALLY, OF THE NATURE OF MATURE LOVE. MOREOVER, HE FINDS HER PAPER HIGHLY PERSONALLY INVOLVING AND EVOCATIVE, STIMULATING OF MUCH THINKING ON THE READER'S PART, NOT ONLY ABOUT RELATIONSHIPS WITH PATIENTS PAST AND PRESENT, BUT ALSO ABOUT THE MOST IMPORTANT RELATIONSHIPS IN HIS OR HER PERSONAL LIFE. HER PAPER BESTIRS THE READER TO BECOME CLEARER ABOUT HIS OR HER OWN VIEWS, NO MATTER WHETHER THESE BE PREDOMINANTLY CONSONANT WITH, OR MAINLY OPPOSED TO, THOSE OF SOPHIE FREUD.

My initial reactions to this paper were critical, and even scornful. I was, and am, convinced that there is no such thing as "overloving." Many people feel that they are overloving, but they are largely unconscious of their hatred and other negative emotions. They are not maturely object-related, but narcissistic. I have written repeatedly of the therapist's so-frequent readiness to assume that he or she is the only genuinely loving person to come upon the patient's life scene, and of such a therapist's unconscious investment in narcissistic pursuits, largely unfettered by any detailed and accurate awareness of the patient as a fellow human being separate from him or her.

I write as one who has gone through much self-disillusionment in this regard. Early in my career as a therapist (at a VA mental hygiene clinic), I assumed my helpfulness and kindliness to be basically without flaw and, more often than not, I felt generally good about my therapeutic devotion. But shortly thereafter I began my training analysis, and as I became less narcissistically self-absorbed and able more readily to identify with my patients, I would typically feel good only for a few moments after a session with a patient. I then would be struck with the realization, "My God! Did I say *that*?"—thinking how hurtful (or whatever) some comment of mine must have sounded, must have felt, to the patient.

All this did not change quickly, however (and I am sure that one's conflicts about important things like this are lifelong, for that matter). It was probably at least one or two years later that I felt puzzled by a comment from my training analyst at the end of one of my sessions with him. He had said something about the kindly person who goes about leaving a trail of destruction in his wake. I failed to hear that the word "kindly" was said ironically; my analyst was not above speaking cryptically, and this was one of his more cryptic times. I indicated that I did not understand the point he was making, whereupon he said simply, with scornful impatience, "dissociated hostility." This enabled me to understand.

To return to this paper and my early reactions to it, by the end of a few pages I was becoming convinced that it is written quite amateurishly, as by a layperson for lay readers, rather than by a professional for professional colleagues. But later I found that I was admiring the author's courage in taking on so vast and fundamental and humbling a problem as the defining, essentially, of the nature of mature love. Further, as I read on, I found that the paper stimulated a good deal of thinking and, more important, personal reminiscence in me—about not only my own work with patients, but my relationships with my wife and children, and my friends. I finally came to realize that a paper so personally involving as this is by no means to be scorned out of hand.

My comments will be in the order of the contents of the paper, and will serve to show something of my mixed reactions to it as I read along.

First, with regard to the abstract, I found it unfortunate that I know next to nothing of cybernetics, although I well remember the stir made by Norbert Wiener's (1948) book introducing this branch of science to the world. I think it would be a mistake for this paper's readers to be so cowed by a lack of knowledge of cybernetics as to lead them to disqualify themselves from judging its merits. In this spirit, while feeling duly inferior for not having the author's acquaintance with cybernetics, I did (and do) take vigorous issue with her central thesis that "many people damage others, and are damaged by others, more profoundly by too much love than by too little love."

In her vignette at the beginning of the paper, where she writes, in reporting upon her consultation with a Mrs. Kennedy, "I said she clearly loved him too much and that adolescents are allergic to mother love. . . . Mrs. Kennedy was very grateful to me for understanding her so deeply. . . .", I found relevant the opening paragraph of a paper I wrote nearly 30 years ago (Searles, 1958), entitled "Positive Feelings in the Relationship Between the Schizophrenic and His Mother":

> My experience in the psychotherapy of chronic schizophrenic patients has convinced me that, in the patient's relationship with his mother, the basic feelings, those which more than any others determine the structure of the relationship and the development of the patient's illness, are positive—fondness, adoration, compassion, solicitude, and loving loyalty and dedication. In this relationship, which is regarded by many psychodynamically oriented researchers as being of central importance in the aetiology of most cases of schizophrenia, I have found that it is not the often-emphasized mutual hatred and rejection and self-seeking dependence which forms its foundation, but rather genuine love for one another—love largely maintained in the unconscious through intense denial mechanisms, and love which finds extremely warped expression, but love nonetheless. Further, I have found that it is essential for the patient to become aware of the presence of this love between his mother and himself, in order to develop both a healthy self-esteem and a thoroughgoing resolution of his schizophrenic illness.

The author reports that the grateful Mrs. Kennedy "explained that her former therapist had accused her of covert hostility toward her son, and that had missed the point completely." The word "hostility" here reminded me of what I still feel was a major error on the part of my late training analyst: he incessantly interpreted my "hostility" (a word I kept hearing from him over and over), and did not interpret my *fear of* my hostility, which was much more descriptive, in retrospect, of the state I consciously was in, in those early years of my analysis, and would have been a focus crediting me with some degree of essential goodness. His approach proved effective, however; I remember vividly my realizing one day, after I had left his consulting room at the end of a session and walked through his reception room and started to open the door to the hallway, "I guess I really *am* hostile"—and realized this in a quiet but inescapable, deeply accepting way.

I regard the vignette concerning Mrs. Kennedy as a poor one to illustrate the paper's central thesis, if we keep in mind that we are professionals, trying to understand psychodynamics of great complexity. The vignette refers to Mrs. Kennedy's "former therapist"; but the author was not Mrs. Kennedy's therapist in any enduring and thoroughgoing therapy. Otherwise she could not have gotten by with this largely pathology-denying dismissal of Mrs. Kennedy's own problems. If we were to embrace uncritically Dr. Freud's main thesis, we would be selling out to those patients generally who manifest a comparable degree of unconscious denial of psychopathology within themselves.

The author ends the Kennedy vignette with the comment, "Perhaps it is a question of semantics." Here I want to say that it is important that the *therapist* utilize, and not lose touch with, a definition of the word "love," which is different from the *patient's* definition of it. Further, I had the tributary recollection of my realization, many years ago, that schizophrenic patients attach different (and often idiosyncratic) meanings to many common words (such as the word "crazy") than do most of the rest of us. This was one great reason why I came to rely more and more on nonverbal participation (on my part) in the therapy, and, when I did interpret, I learned to use as few words as possible, as otherwise the risk of being misunderstood is compounded exponentially. Another tributary line of thought went to my very-long-term work with a chronically schizophrenic woman; for many years my work with her has consisted mainly in my getting in touch with her delusional world, and keeping in touch with it, while not losing touch with my own world (Searles, 1972).

Later, the author goes on to say: ". . . we are not surprised when we hear that someone kills a partner out of excessive love, for example, in a fit of jealousy." I react strongly against this. The "we" may hold true for lay people, but not for experienced therapists. But in the next paragraph, by contrast, I commend her saying that ". . . we must assume . . . that love and hatred are two emotions that may coexist and rapidly alternate with each other." Similarly, I feel that the author's following statements express well the view I have come, in relatively recent years, to hold:

> I have come to reject the whole concept of reaction formation associated with the assumption that one feeling is necessarily

> more basic than another. . . . We might need to give up on reaction formation in its usual meaning and agree instead that people have many conflicting simultaneous positive and negative emotions, all of which are probably equally authentic and should be acknowledged as such.

But it does seem to me that, in the long run, loving feelings must be predominant over hateful ones in any lasting and predominantly constructive relationship.

Then, while continuing largely to reject vigorously the main thrust of her paper, I feel again a grudging admiration of her for taking on so basic an issue as to discuss this matter (to which I have just been referring). I do feel, however, that even at this early point, she should have introduced the topic of narcissism.

In her reference to Langs' (1982) writing about the caretaking that patients do of their therapists, she does not cite my (Searles, 1975) relevant paper, "The Patient as Therapist to His Analyst." Incidentally, it occurred to me at this juncture that I do not feel at all thoroughly clear, myself, as to the difference between love and hate. This particular matter may best be regarded as an ever-intriguing, basically unknowable or incomprehensible subject in any full and detailed and final sense, and the exploration of this subject may be one of the basically fascinating and inspiring aspects of the practice of psychotherapy or psychoanalysis.

Still regarding the issue of semantics, I wish to emphasize the importance of the therapist's realizing that the patient is a layperson—a subjectively truly loving (or attemptedly loving) one—and that it is important not to talk to the patient as to a professional. I do not mean to imply that the author seems to use professional jargon too much in her work as a therapist, as I get no such impression, but her paper brought this topic to my thoughts. I was reminded of the complications that tend to ensue when the patient *is* a fellow professional; I have analyzed some 30 psychiatrists (including psychoanalysts), and a considerable number of psychologists, psychiatric social workers, and other professionals in the mental health field. In general, even when working with these professionals, I think it well to be sparing in one's use of professional jargon. This makes it all the more crucial, however, that one be able to maintain in one's own thinking a definition of, say, the word "love" or the word "hate" that is significantly different from that to which the patient is, as yet, able to give expression.

When Dr. Freud says, "Communication theory suggests (Watzlawick et al., 1967) that conflict in a complementary relationship results in disconfirmation of the one-down partner. . . . I believe the narcissistic injuries inflicted in these admittedly pyrrhic victories can be profound and lasting," I was reminded of an experience I had, years ago, in working for several years with a woman whose nursemaid had been a black woman whom the patient remembered, at the beginning of the treatment, with conscious feelings of predominant fondness. Her largely unconscious feelings toward me as the personification, in the transference, of this black woman, who had been held in contempt by the family and by the wider social community, were so subtle, and so resistant to interpretation, that they took an unusually heavy toll on my self-esteem. For years in the work with this woman, I felt that during the sessions I became less of a person, in my life as a whole, by reason of the work with her. The treatment eventually went sufficiently well so that I became free of that countertransference reaction.

At this same juncture in the author's paper, I recalled my realization, some years after leaving Chestnut Lodge Sanitarium 25 years ago, after having been working there for nearly 15 years with preponderantly chronically schizophrenic patients, that I had come largely to lose sight of their collective transference to me as being an inadequate or worthless mother (therapist). I had come to feel, that is, so *really* ineffective with them, so low in my own self-esteem, that I was not able to keep in focus their *transference-based assumption* that I had nothing useful to offer them. I am overstating this appreciably, here, to make the point. As my self-esteem has recovered through work with preponderantly much less ill patients, I have come to see more clearly how central was that self-esteem-vitiating factor of these patients' "worthless-mother" transference to me during the years at Chestnut Lodge.

To proceed with the Freud paper, I strongly endorse her statement: "We must thus conclude that there is mutual vulnerability, reciprocity, interdependence, and subtle equality of power in all ongoing significant relationships." But I would emphasize the enormous role of the *unconscious* in both participants.

When the author, in her discussion of lack of equality and narcissistic containment, says, "First of all there may be inequality of emotional investment," I was reminded of my previously mentioned work, over many years and still continuing, with the chronically schizophrenic woman. For more than ten years after I became her therapist, I felt that the devotion to the relationship was mine alone. I felt that if at any time I were to become so discouraged as to quit, she would feel no loss, but would count it as a victory, and not even an important victory, but only a very minor one. As I thought about this, however, in response to this paper, I realized that I had probably been striving unconsciously, during those years, to keep exclusive possession of the treatment situation, reacted to by me, unconsciously, as a mother whom I was determined not to share with the patient. This possibility occurred to me because, in remembering those years of my consciously lonely devotion to this woman's treatment, I was reminded of how similar to mine was the orientation of a narcissistic man whom I treated for several years, beginning nearly 20 years after I had begun with the woman. This man, as became evident as his treatment went on, was unconsciously invested in keeping the analysis totally to himself. The analysis seemed to represent to him a parent figure whom he was determined to share as little as possible with me, with me representing, in the transference, the rival parent or one of his jealously regarded siblings. With regard to my work with the chronically schizophrenic woman, it is noteworthy, also, that during those years when I felt that only I cared about her treatment, my narcissistic gratification at an unconscious level was probably maximum (my qualifying, in my own eyes, as the selflessly devoted saint).

It was at such a point as this, in my reading of this paper, that I sensed that any paper that is so evocative of the reader's clinical experiences and ideas, whether the reader agrees or disagrees with the author's views, is inherently stimulating and worthwhile. If nothing else, it bestirs the reader to become clearer about any opposing views.

When the author says, in continuing her discussion of the lack of equality and narcissistic containment, "there is also the question of unequal responsibility," I was reminded of my continuing difficulty with this aspect of my practice. Time after time, it is my exercise of what I feel to be my professional responsibility that impels me to responses that prove untherapeutic for the patient. At one point in my work with the chronically schizophrenic woman, my feeling of responsibility as a therapist caused me to make an interpretation that proved to be distancing and disruptive. Her reproach was memorable: "When you say things like that, I feel that I've been riding in an airplane with you and I've just been dropped to the bottom of the ocean."

One of the valuable contributions of this paper is the author's statement (in the section on the "good enough mother"): "I think the concept of transference is seen as too separate a dimension in psychoanalysis or therapy, without sufficient realization that not only is relationship created through intimate sharing, but the relationship then, in turn, shapes and colors everything that goes on in treatment, including the patient's reported dreams and free associations." I was reminded of my (Searles, 1984) paper, "The Role of the Analyst's Facial Expressions in Psychoanalysis and Psychoanalytic Therapy." Further, I was reminded of my having come in recent years to note, increasingly, the subtle affective intonations in verbal comments—not only from the patient, but my own as well. Recently, for example, during a session with the schizophrenic woman, after a brief silence I reported to her, "I just had the thought that you and I are going to be buried in different cemeteries. I notice that in saying that I sound *determined* that it will be so, don't I?" As I recall, she concurred with my impression and showed some mild interest.

The author makes an important point in saying, "Above all, the infant, lover, student, client, must be seen as *other* and not merely as an extension of oneself. . . ." But many years ago I introduced (Searles, 1959) the concept of therapeutic symbiosis (a concept I have elaborated on in a series of subsequent papers, and a view I still hold strongly). I postulated that symbiotic relatedness constitutes a necessary phase in psychoanalysis or psychotherapy with either neurotic or psychotic patients, and I introduced the term "therapeutic symbiosis" for this mode of patient–therapist (or –analyst) relatedness.

But when Dr. Freud says, "I suspect the ambition to be the very best mother, teacher, and so on, is the first step toward overloving," she sounds amateurish again, like the layperson writing for laypersons. It is eminently clear to me, on the face of it, that anyone who is determined to be the very best mother (for example) is struggling to preserve a narcissistic image, with an inability to have any significant degree of regard for, or awareness of, the needs of the other person.

She notes that "Laing (1965) reports a case history in which a daughter becomes defeated by her inability to express her rage against her overdevoted selfless mother." I would assume, until was demonstrated otherwise, that the daughter's rage was being projected into her, to a significant degree, by her mother—unconsciously, of course.

Dr. Freud also says, "Relationships become 'good enough' not by being perfect, but when participants can meet the challenge of disappointed expectations through some sort of transcendence, some verbal or nonverbal communication, some understanding or forgiveness." Here I was reminded of the phenomenon, in basically strong marriages, of the two persons' mutual cherishing of shared past experiences, whether or not those past experiences are predominantly happy or predominantly stressful; the experiences are mutually cherished because they were shared, were lived through together.

The author, in her discussion of overloved children, cites Stern's "frightening example of a mother who was so determined to be a 'stimulating' mother that she was totally insensitive to her infant's needs for separateness." What both Sophie Freud and Stern failed to see, here, is that this mother is projecting her own schizoid or autistic unrelatedness, her unconscious interpersonal deadness, into the child.

Dr. Freud writes that "we could redefine the ambiguous concept of narcissism as a condition in which one simultaneously overloves and underloves oneself, without being able to strike a harmonious balance." I am far from sure that I subscribe to this redefinition, but I feel envy, and a grudging admiration, of her ability to take on this, to me, awesome task. I am reminded of my similar feelings toward a certain analytic writer for his seeming willingness to give papers about practically any psychodynamic topic.

Next I want to call the reader's attention to the long paragraph in the same section that begins, "Parents who have suffered in extreme ways, such as those who have lived in great poverty or discrimination, or who have survived the holocaust, are especially vulnerable to overloving their children." In her discussion of this topic, the author seems, as usual, unaware of the element of the parents' projecting their unconscious anger into the children. I begin to doubt how well she comprehends the presence and working of the unconscious. Certainly she does not seem to take into account the mechanism of projective identification, whereas for me (as for so many others) this is one of our most helpful psychodynamic concepts. It is this kind of naîveté on her part that makes her article seem amateurish in many respects.

Incidentally, I begin to wonder, in reading this same paragraph, whether perhaps most authors who write about the holocaust are unaware of the presence of the survivor parent's unconscious identification with the aggressor (oppressor), and the projection of that unconscious identity into the offspring. Relevant here is a clinical vignette from a recent paper of mine (Searles, 1985) entitled "Borderline Psychopathology as Revealed by the Patient's (a) Pauses and (b) Ungrammatical Word Order." This is an example of the significance of ungrammatical word order.

> A young Jewish woman says, "I had been told about *the pogroms by my parents*" [my italics], which revealed a quite different mean-

ing from the consciously intended one, "I had been told by my parents about the pogroms." The analysis was coming to plumb the depths of her paranoid grandiosity, and of her subjectively omnipotent malevolence, malevolence which involved unconscious identifications with her parents—perceived as being innumerable, persecutory mass murderers.

When Dr. Freud writes that the "prevalence of depression among women in our society is partially due to maternal overloving," and that that "fathers' overloving of their daughters may be expressed in a continuum from subtle seductiveness to outright incest, leading to various forms of psychic injury," my gorge continues to rise at her use of the term "overloving." These examples are *not* of over-*loving*, and it is both naîve and clinically harmful to use such an amateurish and grossly inaccurate term.

But a bit later, in her discussion of overloving in the therapeutic relationship, she makes a good point in stating that " 'intrusiveness,' the transgression of personal boundaries for presumably benevolent reasons, might . . . take different forms. In therapy, for example, such intrusiveness might be in the form of premature or otherwise misguided interpretations." I was reminded of a session with the chronically schizophrenic woman, when we were sitting in chairs placed in front of, and near, my desk. A few moments after I had made some comment meant to be helpful, she, remaining silent, suddenly reached across my desk (on which there were many letters and various personal items), picked up some item (I don't recall which one), and started examining it. My first reaction was to feel antagonized by her intrusiveness; then I realized that she intended me to feel how intrusive my comment had seemed to her.

Later in the paper, under "Relationship Goals," the author writes wisely of the inevitability of personal narcissistic investment:

> We . . . expect therapists, teachers, and parents to control their narcissistic needs, and yet the demands of these roles are so great that we surely could not meet them adequately without some personal narcissistic investment. . . . It is thus more a problem of balance, and it is the tipping of the balance in the direction of too much narcissistic investment that I call overloving.

When she wonders, "Is there also danger that total differentiation in a relationship, such as Fingarette suggests, means the end of love? Is lack of differentiation perhaps the glue that holds our social fabric together?," I am reminded again, of my papers on therapeutic symbiosis. I largely endorse her writing:

> I come to the conclusion that significant relationships are forever suspended in the delicate balance that I have called underloving and overloving—detachment that may border on indifference and sterility, or passionate engagement that may become intrusive and destructive. We can embrace this creative act of tightrope walking as a lifelong pursuit.

But I do take issue with the emphasis upon the delicate balance, and the tightrope walking. To me this is more the stuff of which obsessive–compulsiveness and catatonia are made than the feeling orientation of mature love. To me a happy marriage, for example, is one in which the partners rediscover, and fall in love with one another, over and over again. A relationship of mature love is not a tightrope, but a broad plain where both partners are free to range widely through realms of hate and contempt (and, for each, times of privacy that may partake of autism), as well as passionate love and mutually enjoyable companionship.

I read this paper twice before setting down my thoughts about it, and I noticed that I liked it appreciably better during my second reading—although I was still far from approving of everything Dr. Freud was saying. The paper is sufficiently stimulating and evocative, sufficiently involving of the reader's thinking and feeling, to warrant anyone's second reading.

REFERENCES

Searles, H. F. (1958). Positive feelings in the relationship between the schizophrenic and his mother. *Int. J. Psychoanal.*, 39:569–586. Reprinted in *Collected Papers on Schizophrenia and Related Subjects*. New York: International Universities Press, 1965, pp. 216–253.

——— (1959). Integration and differentiation in schizophrenia. *J. Nerv. Ment. Dis.*, 129:342–350. Reprinted in *Collected Papers, Ibid.*, pp. 304–316.

——— (1972). The function of the patient's realistic perceptions of the analyst in delusional transference. *Brit. J. Med. Psychol.*, 45:1–18. Reprinted in *Countertransference and Related Subjects—Selected Papers*. New York: International Universities Press, 1979, pp. 196–227.

——— (1975). The patient as therapist to his analyst. In *Tactics and Techniques in Psychoanalytic Therapy, Volume II: Countertransference*, ed. P. L. Giovacchini. New York: Jason Aronson, pp. 95–151. Reprinted in *Countertransference, Ibid.*, pp. 380–459.

——— (1984). The role of the analyst's facial expressions in psychoanalysis and psychoanalytic therapy. In *International Journal of Psychoanalytic Psychotherapy Volume 10*, ed. R. Langs. New York: Jason Aronson, pp. 42–75.

——— (1985). Borderline psychopathology as revealed by the patient's (a) pauses and (b) ungrammatical word order. Presented at the 31st Annual Chestnut Lodge Symposium, Rockville, Md., October 4, 1985.

Wiener, N. (1948). *Cybernetics*. New York: Wiley.

16

JANIS KROHN, M.S.W.

The Meaning of Pain: A Developmental Pathway

THIS PAPER PROPOSES A DEVELOPMENTAL APPROACH TO UNDERSTANDING THE DIFFERENT INTRAPSYCHIC MEANINGS AND FUNCTIONS OF PHYSICAL PAIN AND DISCOMFORT. FOR THE TYPICAL CHILD, PAIN IN INFANCY IS SEEN TO PLAY AN IMPORTANT ROLE IN ESTABLISHING A REALITY-BASED, CONCRETE BODY SCHEMA, PARTICULARLY A BODY BOUNDARY. IN TODDLERHOOD PAIN IS EXPERIENCED IN THE CONTEXT OF THE DEVELOPMENTAL TASKS OF SEPARATION AND INDIVIDUATION, WITH SEPARATION ANXIETY AND PHYSICAL DISCOMFORT SEEMING TO BE EXPERIENCED AS IF INTERCHANGEABLE. THE EXPERIENCE OF PAIN IS ALSO PROCESSED AND INTEGRATED PARALLEL TO THE TODDLER'S EVOLVING CAPACITY TO ACKNOWLEDGE AMBIVALENT FEELINGS TOWARD PRIMARY OBJECTS. FOR THE PHALLIC AND OEDIPAL CHILD, PAIN BEGINS TO FUNCTION AS A SIGNAL OF BODILY INJURY, AND TYPICALLY EVOKES CASTRATION ISSUES. EXAMPLES ARE DRAWN FROM OBSERVATIONS OF NORMAL TODDLERS AND PRESCHOOLERS AS WELL AS FROM CLINICAL DATA. THE IMPACT OF EXTREME OR PROLONGED EXPERIENCES OF PAIN DURING EARLY DEVELOPMENT, AS WELL AS CASES OF CONGENITAL ABSENCE OF PAIN, ARE ALSO NOTED.

The typical child encounters tummy aches, knee scrapes, mosquito bites, doctors' shots, sore bottoms, twisted ankles, and so on in the course of the early years. Much of the task of mothering can involve soothing a crying, uncomfortable infant, or kissing a toddler's "booboo," or helping a preschooler deal with anxiety over an upcoming vaccination. For most children these kinds of experiences become almost a routine part of life. For a few, painful illness, parental abuse, or other unfavorable circumstances put the child in the position of having to cope with and integrate continual, intense, or overwhelming physical pain. When these children come for treatment, we discover the many ways in which these painful experiences have been woven into their sense of themselves and their libidinal and aggressive life. From these children we have learned much about the role of pain in psychic development. From observing normal children and working with children in treatment who do not have a history of unusual physical pain, we can learn more about the role of pain for the typical child as well. This paper proposes a developmental sequence to organize our understanding of the intrapsychic significance of intermittent physical pain. The hypotheses proposed include, in broad outline, the intrapsychic significance of bodily discomfort and pain for children of different ages, as well as the varying relationship between physical pain and mental pain, or anxiety, as it changes through various stages of development.

While physical pain is typically the experienced response to injury or body damage, it is also an affect, an experience connoting emotional and ideational components in addition to physical sensation. Because both physical sensation and unpleasurable affect are components of the experience of pain, the task of distinguishing among physical pain, emotional pain, and anxiety is a continuing conceptual problem. The task of sorting out the subjective experiences of anxiety, pain, and other negative effects also constitutes a developmental problem for the infant and young child, who, like the adult, must begin to understand and interpret the differences and similarities in his or her experiences of the various unpleasurable and uncomfortable affects. In using a developmental framework, we assume that the child experiences physical pain in ways integrally related to the dominant tasks and conflicts of each developmental phase. Positing a developmental line for the meaning of pain therefore necessarily involves hypotheses about the development of body image, roots of anxiety (Deutsch, 1959; Mushart, 1975; Szasz, 1957; Weiss, 1934; Engel & Schmale, 1967), and unfolding ego capacities (Hoffer, 1949, 1950; Ferenczi, 1913), in addition to vicissitudes of aggression.

In this paper I discuss three major developmental hypotheses, which distinguish different functions and meanings of physical pain according to three major phases of normal development. In the first year, discomfort and physical pain, I propose, have a function in developing the infant's sense of the body as a cohesive unit separate from the bodies and body parts of others, and in contributing to the infant's growing capacity for reality testing. During toddlerhood, bumps, bruises, and minor illnesses appear to play a significant role in the unfolding of the child's attachment to important people. Pain plays a role in how the toddler processes loss and separation from these objects, as well as in the child's gradual acknowledgment of an ambivalence toward these objects. For the oedipal child, pain is experienced as a threat to the child's sense of body integrity, and as a signal of bodily injury, often triggering or manifesting castration anxiety.

INFANCY

The newborn and young infant do not know their bodies as their own, nor do they have a sense of where they stop and the rest of the world begins. This picture of the infant has been described by Freud (1929) and others, most recently by Nagera (1980). Pain, in early infancy, seems to be merely a sensation devoid of unconscious or conscious meaning and significance, and not yet an affect. As the infant begins to mature, however, various body states and sensations, including pain, begin to be associated with events in the infant's environment. Pain, like other bodily sensations, begins to have psychological meaning beyond a purely sensory experience, and to be associated with the emerging ego's relationship with the body, the body's needs, and the external world. Our understanding of how the infant's sense of his or her body and its boundaries evolves therefore includes an understanding of how the infant processes pain.

In the early weeks, the infant seems to experience pain as a sensation that comes and goes without meaning, and is felt in different parts of his or her as-yet-unintegrated body. Gradually, it appears, the infant develops a sense of a "body ego," a sense of his or her own body as separate from others, with a more definite boundary between what is part of the self, inside, and what is part of the environment, outside (Hoffer, 1950; Freud, 1923; Fisher & Cleveland, 1968; Schilder, 1935). Freud (1923) referred to this process in the following statement:

> Psychophysiology has fully discussed the manner in which a person's own body attains its special position among other objects in the world of perception. Pain, too, seems to play a part in this process, and the way in which we gain new knowledge of our organs during painful illness is perhaps a model of the way by which in general we arrive at the idea of our body.

Because we cannot speak to an infant to check our theory, we rely on inferential data. Sources of evidence do exist, however, that point to the crucial role played by pain in the establishment and evolution of the body image. Perhaps the most convincing is the work done with people who have accidentally or surgically lost a limb, and thus have suffered a radical and sudden change in their body contours. Almost universally these people retain a subjective experience of sensation in the area, now beyond their body boundaries, in the "phantom limb." Further, as Szasz (1957) has pointed out, those who have had the most difficulty adjusting and accepting the loss of their body part also suffer most frequently from a sensation of pain in their phantom limb. This finding led Szasz to the hypothesis that the physical sensation of pain may serve as a psychic defense against recognition of the loss suffered. In a sense it is as if one says, "I can feel my arm hurt, so it must not be gone; it is still part of me." Perhaps a related kind of experience is expressed in the saying used when one is not sure if what one is experiencing is real or not; that is, "pinch yourself to see if you are dreaming." The ability to feel pain is the ultimate test to establish the reality of an experience. We assume that if we can feel pain, what we are experiencing is a real part of ourselves and not a fantasy.

An extreme example of the role of pain in establishing a sense of bodily reality may be seen among some patients who repeatedly mutilate themselves. In treatment we find that these patients are sometimes trying to enact, through a severely regressed mode, a definition and experience of their bodies, and themselves, as real, as concrete objects with definite shapes and boundaries (A. Krohn, 1980–1981). Might we view these patients, in part, as using cutting, scarring, and so on to "pinch" themselves in a dramatic and extreme way to make sure *they* are real? Since many of these patients manifest with severe pathology rooted in earliest development, understanding the role of pain in establishing a body schema in infancy helps us to understand them as harking back to an early, infantile understanding and use of bodily pain.

Similarly, patients who show signs of obliviously putting their bodies or specific body parts in danger, exposing themselves to severe injury or pain, often present with corresponding difficulties in early body image and primary narcissism. Their image of their physical body does not fit their subjective experience of who they are, of what constitutes the "I" or self. Just as some of us might say "this is part of me, I know because it hurts," for these patients the opposite is expressed: "This arm, foot, etc., feels no pain as it is injured, therefore it confirms my sense that it is *not* part of me."

Infants who suffer from an abnormal, organically based *absence* of pain have also been found to develop severe problems in body boundaries, body image, and ego boundaries. Roiphe (1973) presented a case of a psychotic child who seemed not to experience pain, and who also displayed symptoms that indicated an inability, or perhaps refusal, to acknowledge where her body began and ended. Dubovsky and Groban (1975) reported a case of an 18-year-old youth who was born without the physical capacity to feel pain, and with only a minimal capacity to feel any bodily sensations. They reported that he felt anxiety and other unpleasant affects. His most striking deficits appeared in a lack of clear body and ego boundaries. This example, though inconclusive in itself, lends weight to the hypothesis that pain sensations play a crucial role in developing body boundaries in early development, separate from experiences of anxiety, frustration, or other forms of unpleasure. Frances and Gale (1975) also reported a case of a boy with congenital absence of pain. The boy had a severe symptom of head banging, which continued into adolescence. Based on observations of this boy, as well as published accounts of other cases of children born without the capacity to experience pain, Frances and Gale hypothesized that the boy's ability to establish a firm sense of his body boundaries was severely impeded by the absence of pain sensations. The head banging was seen as a way of establishing bodily reality based on rhythmic, kinesthetic feedback and a hypercathexis of inner bodily sensations and rhythms.

TODDLERHOOD

By the time the typical child reaches toddlerhood, he or she has solidified a basic feeling that his or her body is his or her own and that it is intact. In toddlerhood pain gradually plays less the role of establishing the reality of the child's body boundary and begins to take on other meanings and functions. During this phase the child becomes increasingly attached to significant others and begins to acknowledge and struggle with both his or her separateness and dependence on them. The child also comes to value his or her body and increasingly discrete, autonomous sense of self. Simultaneously with these developments, the toddler begins to establish a more complex body schema, which includes separate body parts that the child can begin to name, special attention to body products, some sense of the internal organs, and a schema of a whole body that fits all these parts together in some kind of cohesive unit. For the toddler, however, the distinction between bodily and mental pains appears to be very fuzzy; experientially the border between emotional and physical discomfort appears highly permeable. These characteristics of toddlerhood work together to determine the typical ways in which the toddler understands and responds to pain. Small injuries seem to trigger anxiety about the continued, protecting presence of loved objects, and, conversely, the absence of the beloved caretaker seems to highlight physical discomfort or injury for the toddler.

The emergence of the importance of attachments to loved objects and consequent fears of the loss of those objects coincides with the toddler's relative inability to distinguish the sources of pain and the distinctions between bodily pain, emotional pain, and anxiety. In this phase physical pain transfers quickly into fear or anxiety, and vice versa, reflecting a fluidity of emotional and physical experiences that typifies the toddler's rudimentary understanding of his or her body and feelings. This is what, I believe, Freud (1926) was describing when he referred to pain as the reaction to the loss of a loved object in his addendum to *Inhibitions, Symptoms and Anxiety*. He explained this apparent puzzle in the following way:

> For the intense cathexis of longing which is concentrated on the missed or lost object (a cathexis which steadily mounts up because it cannot be appeased) creates the same economic conditions as are created by the cathexis of pain which is concentrated on the injured part of the body. . . . The transition from physical pain to mental pain corresponds to a change from narcissistic cathexis to object-cathexis. (p. 171)

The intimate connection and ready transfers between bodily pain and the fear of loss of a loved object during toddlerhood can be seen in the typical repertoire of reactions to minor hurts demonstrated by toddlers, as illustrated in the following vignettes. There is nothing remarkable about any of these incidents; they represent typical reactions to minor physical hurts among normal two-year-olds. What is remarkable is the universality and repetition of the same sequence—the wish for mother or acceptable mother substitute triggered by the "hurt," independent of a wish for mere relief of the physical discomfort or pain.

- A two-year-old child, running along the beach, trips and falls flat on his face near some strangers. He begins crying, looking around for help. When a stranger (a woman) goes to offer assistance and comfort, he cries even harder, screaming, "No, I want my mother!" and looks around more frantically until his mother arrives and comforts him.

- A young child (three years old) in the nursery falls in the gym and cries. He is picked up by a staff person and comforted. He calms down, but then cries again and says, "I want my mommy."
- In the toddler room, S. (age 2½) bumps her head. The staff person asks if she is okay. S. says "yeah." The staff person replies, "Did you bump your head a bit?" S. responds, "Yeah, but I have my blankie." Teacher replies: "You're okay if you have your blankie?" And S. says "yeah."
- K., age 2½, in the toddler room hurts himself on the slide. He quiets a minute and then initiates playing peek-a-boo with a well-known adult (mother is far away). Peek-a-boo is not a typical game for K. to play, except in response to separations from important objects.
- J. falls and bumps his knee. He comes running to mother, who asks if she should kiss it to make it better. Tearfully J. nods. As soon as mother has kissed the hurt, J. calms, and goes on to play with the toys.

How do we make sense of the magical kiss, illustrated in the last vignette, which is so typical of toddlers? We must look at what pain means to a two-year-old. Physical and emotional injuries and fears of loss are so intimately connected in the toddler's experience that mother's magical kiss works, I think, because it symbolically and ritualistically restores her loving attention to the child. With the kiss she repairs the rift experienced between the child and her, and thus eliminates, or significantly reduces, the felt pain. This is why the mere physical caring for a minor scrape during this phase is usually not enough—the caring must be provided by mother, or mother substitute, and with reassuring calm. The ministrations of a stranger, although well intentioned and physically effective, will often not effectively calm the child, and may even make the experience seem more painful.

Observations of the toddler and nursery school programs at the University of Michigan have also provided data showing the converse of these illustrations, that is, toddlers reacting to separations from mothers with attention to physical distress. Responses to separations vary among toddlers, and at different times for the same toddler, more than is seen in the above situations, where the toddler gets hurt and seeks comfort and reassurance from mother or mother substitute. It is not unusual, however, to see a toddler complaining of a physical hurt or "accidentally" hurting him or herself soon after mother's departure, or sometimes shortly after her return. Many of these incidents provide examples of a process of turning aggression against the self, in response to anger at the mother's departure. With mother gone the toddler uses the self as the target of frustration, anger, and aggression. The incidents also add confirming evidence for the hypothesis that for the toddler the pain of separation from mother and the pain of the body are interrelated, and indeed experientially interchangeable—the one can stand for and express the situation of the other. In these cases it is as if the toddler is saying, "When mother is gone it is like something were wrenched from my body, for see how I ache, or bruise, etc." In these situations we may also see the toddler's beginning use of pain as a signal to get needs met by mother. Here is an example:

> T. (age 2½) is in the toddler room. T.'s mother has left the room for a moment. While T.'s mother is gone, T. turns for comfort to another mother whom T. knows well, and sits on her lap. T. is calm but checks the doorway repeatedly for mother. When mother returns T. goes to mother for a greeting. Mother does not greet T. warmly, being distracted by something else happening in the toddler room. After a moment T. leaves mother's side and rides on a toy truck, falling and bumping her behind within seconds. T. then goes to mother for reassurance and comfort.

A dramatic example of this sequence came to the author's attention during an evaluation of a child referred because of concern about his teenage mother's ambivalence and uncertainty about mothering him. D., age two, showed little manifest attachment to the mother while she was there, seemingly oblivious to her as he played with the interviewer and the toys in the office. Within five minutes of his mother's leaving the room, however, D. was in tears, calling inconsolably for "mama." He then suddenly experienced a nosebleed. This was a typical sequence in response to her departures, according to D.'s mother. It was only through D.'s dramatic, ultimately physical reaction to mother's departure that he showed his attachment to her and the depth of anxiety, or fear, he experienced in her absence.

For the toddler pain can thus serve to express an injury to the body, to a body part, or to a relationship with an important object. All these experiences, fears, and anxieties become interchangeable through the language of pain. In cases of severe developmental arrest, we would, taking this view one step further, expect to see physical and emotional distress being experienced and defended against in parallel ways. In her book *Insights from the Blind*, Selma

Fraiberg (1977) reports a case of a nine-year-old blind boy who presented like a borderline child, with severe delays in his psychological development. Two of the most striking manifestations of this boy's pathology were his apparently complete lack of anxiety at separating from his mother and his apparent lack of response to pain, even in the face of quite serious injuries. During the course of treating this boy, Fraiberg found that the boy's ability to respond to physical pain emerged *simultaneously* with his manifesting anxiety upon separations from his mother. In this clinical example, we see a temporal correspondence between the acknowledgment of physical and mental pain—at first neither is felt, and then, when they do emerge, they emerge at the same time. In this case whatever blocked the boy's awareness of physical pain seems to have worked in tandem with the blocking of emotional distress, or anxiety, at separations from mother. This example adds credence to our idea that the two are processed intrapsychically in very similar, if not identical, fashion. Perhaps this is also an illustration of the connection between the child's incapacity to cathect another person and his inability to cathect and care for his own body. Not enough information is given by Fraiberg in this particular case to determine whether the boy failed to cathect his mother as well as his body, or whether he was impervious to pain and separations because of an illusion of oneness, of symbiosis, with mother so that he never, before treatment, *experienced* separation as being apart from mother.

In the report of an unusual analysis with a dying patient, Norton (1963) reports a converse phenomenon. In visiting her dying patient in the hospital for regular sessions, the analyst discovered that when the patient was experiencing the analyst as a loving, caring mother in the transference, the patient's pain from her cancer would subside. When the patient did not experience this feeling of being in the presence of "mother," her physical pain continued. This case report illustrates the intimate connection between physical comfort and the feeling of being in the presence of and cared for by mother, even to the point of diminishing chronic pain. Surely the caring mother's ability to soothe her infant physically continues into toddlerhood in her ability to soothe her toddler through her caring attention and presence. It is this comfort that seems to have helped Dr. Norton's patient feel some relief from her physical pain during their sessions. Although this was an unusual treatment situation, it echoes experiences in the course of treatment of many patients for whom physical pain triggers, or is triggered by, longings for a nurturant, caretaking, omnipotent mother. In the author's work with children, an announcement about an upcoming vacation or interruption has frequently been followed by the child's "accidentally" bruising a finger, knee, toe, and so on. The response is especially predictable when the child is struggling at the time with issues of separation rooted in the toddler phase.

For the toddler, then, there seems to be an intimate connection between mental and physical pain, and between pain and anxiety. The two are not felt by the child as separate and distinct. Pain is experienced in response to both internal, bodily injury and object loss. It is important to stress here that it is not clear what aspects of the object loss are most important to the toddler; that is, whether the toddler is responding to the separation from the loved object per se, or is experiencing anxiety at an anticipated unpleasure and danger in the absence of a need-satisfying object. Both processes are most likely at work in varying degrees during the toddler's development.

Anna Freud (1965, p. 103) speaks of the potential for ego regression inherent in the face of the stress of bodily pain. Conversely, bodily pain, psychogenic or "accidentally" inflicted, can itself be a manifestation of ego regression, using physical sensation to express emotional fears, anxieties, and wishes in disguised form. Thus a tendency to hurt one's self, either accidentally or deliberately when faced with loss, can represent in some patients a regression to a "two-year-old" way of processing separation and pain. This constitutes a regression to a time when the child experiences physical and emotional painful sensations as not easily distinguishable, and when ruptures in the integrity of the relationship with important objects is experienced as akin to ruptures in body integrity. It is in this phase-specific permeability between mind and body that we may eventually find more complete explanations of some pervasive psychosomatic and hypochondriacal reactions.

Another aspect of the toddler's experience of pain is its relationship to the toddler's need to maintain an illusion of omnipotence. Every experience of pain threatens this illusion, although the reverse is not the case; not every threat to the toddler's sense of omnipotence is experienced through physical pain. Mothers often respond to the toddler's need *gradually* to abandon this illusion by using the magical kiss. As the child feels more equipped to manage events, the child is able gradually to individuate his or her own from the mother's power, and to feel less vulnerable, thus diminishing the need for an omnipotent stance. As this happens the older toddler can correspondingly feel less vulnerable to the jarring experience of suddenly feeling helpless in the face of pain or injury; we see the child finding ways to cope with these experiences and begin to see the emerging ego's defensive repertoire. Some toddlers insist on a Band-Aid, for example, as a badge of their bravery and a certificate of their being able to be repaired when injured. Others run to mother for a hug, refuel, and then can go off for more adventure. Some toddlers and mothers hit upon the gimmick of blaming something external, "bad chair," for being in the way and hurting "little Johnny." Here mother and child collude in using projection and externalization to confirm the toddler's defensive illusion that he or she is not caught in a world full of unnameable or unexpectable dangers, but has only to deal with one "bad chair" at a time.

The last example raises another issue that is crucial to the toddler period: the function of pain vis-à-vis the toddler's struggle with ambivalence. A major task for the toddler is to acknowledge anger at a loved object. Being able to hate and love the same person—achieving object constancy despite frustration of needs—is a major accomplishment for late toddlerhood and the early phallic-oedipal period. When the mother and child agree that the chair is the "bad guy," they are making an implicit pact that pain, blame, and rage exist only outside of their relationship. They are saying, in effect, "Mommy is not to blame, and baby is not to blame, but it is the chair that is the source of attack and aggression. Pain and aggression will be deflected outside of us and will not come between us." Just as the infant needs gradually to own pain as part of the self, so the toddler/mother dyad must gradually allow anger, aggression, and pain to enter their cocoon. The toddler must move from a position of seeing the causes of hostility and pain as outside the self and mother to being able to acknowledge when he or she is frustrated and angry with mother, or wishes to hurt mother, and when mother is angry or displeased. If this process takes place gradually, with a mother helping her toddler to modulate and find appropriate channels for any sadistic wishes, the toddler can begin to understand that rage and pain between him or herself and mother will not mean that the mother is lost as a caring object. In cases where the toddler is the victim of unremitting pain, or in an environment that is abusive or neglectful, this gradual acceptance and integration of ambivalence may be aborted. This child may then find one of several maladaptive solutions: he or she may retain the fantasy that all aggression and pain are extruded from an idealized, omnipotent mother/child dyad; or the child may place the source of the pain and the rage totally within him or herself, protecting mother from imperfections; or he or she may posit the source of rage and pain within the mother, whom the child then fears and loves simultaneously. These various solutions may, in addition, accompany a primary reliance on maladaptive defenses of splitting, projection, denial, and idealization.

PHALLIC-OEDIPAL PHASE

As the child enters the phallic-oedipal phase, new understandings of pain emerge. Physical pain functions in an ever more differentiated and symbolic fashion. The experience of pain begins to acquire the role of a signal that "something" is not right with one's body. This "something" is in the form of an organized conception or fantasy rather than a reference to an undifferentiated, unorganized feeling state. The attainment of a signal role of pain occurs simultaneously with the child's increasing cognitive ability to differentiate between somatic and emotional pain, among physical pain, anxiety, and fear. It also occurs when the child is becoming more aware of the complexities of his or her body and feelings. The oedipal child begins to establish a distinction between bodily and mental events, and his or her understanding of both becomes more complex. The child's body image now begins to include some conception of various processes occurring inside the skin, building on the foundation of a firm sense of a body boundary established earlier. We find the typical four-year-old, for instance, very curious about the various body parts. He or she wants to know how the body works—how the bones hold the body up, why the blood moves, where the air goes that is breathed, and so on. He or she has the capacity to conceptualize parts of the self that cannot be seen or felt, to imagine them and incorporate them into a more refined body image. Concerns about the body are also more differentiated and less global than before. At the same time, upon entering the phallic phase, the child is adding sources and areas of pleasure to the libidinal repertoire. The phallic-oedipal child experiences anxiety that these phallic pleasures will be denied, and that the source of such pleasures (the penis for the boy, the clitoris for the girl) will be, or has been, injured or taken away.

The emergence of these various developmental trends is well illustrated in the case of K., a member, as mentioned earlier, of the toddler program at the University of Michigan. When K. was 2¾ years old, his mother reported that over the course of a few weeks, he seemed more grown-up and less toddlerlike, and that certain things had seemed to coalesce for him. For the first time, he was able to put together the pieces of a face to make a reasonable gestalt, with the eyes, nose, and mouth in the right places. He also had begun to pick up sticks and other long objects he found and to use them as pretend swords, guns, and so on, obviously enjoying newly found phallic pride and prowess. At the same time, K. seemed more concerned about tiny scratches he found on his body than he had been before. He periodically would come up to his mother and show her a scratch, saying, "Mommy, look at this," with some concern in his voice. This mother's perceptive observations of her child illustrate the concurrent emergence of a more organized body (represented by his new ability to draw a face), preeminence of phallic activities, and anxious attention to small hurts. The emergence and intertwining of these developmental trends as the child enters the phallic and phallic-oedipal phases, illustrated in this example, are probably a typical, though often unnoticed, aspect of this phase of development.

In the realm of feelings, the preschooler typically makes similar strides toward greater complexity of understanding. The global temper tantrum and affect storms of infancy and toddlerhood give way to experiences of distinctly different feelings, which begin to be labeled more carefully by the preschooler. Anger, frustration, excitement, disappointment, jealousy, love, and friendship, as well as pain and fear, enter the vocabulary in some form. If helped, the child can begin to go beyond labeling feelings to describing and distinguishing them.

A parallel process occurs in the preschooler's experience of pain. He or she can begin to describe much more carefully than before *where* something hurts, *how* it got hurt, what the hurt *feels* like, and so on. The preschooler also develops the capacity to understand the difference between "hurts" that have a somatic source and "hurts" that have an emotional source. For example:

> F. (4½ years old) had watched a frightening program on television, and at the same time was coming down with the flu, diagnosed the next day. In talking about the scary TV program, his mother tried to help him understand the difference between real and pretend, something he had down pat for cartoons. At the end of the conversation, F. said, "I wasn't scared at the TV movie; my tummy was scared, and that's why it hurts. I'm not scared of TV programs, just my tummy is. I am strong and never scared."

Although F.'s tummy ache was probably a symptom of the flu, he showed in his comments a beginning understanding that uncomfortable affects can get translated into uncomfortable sensations in one's body—even in a part of the body, the "tummy," which is only "known" in the abstract until it hurts. In addition to this cognitive advance, we also see the beginnings of the role pain can play in the child's emerging defensive structure, as this child struggled to maintain a sense of himself as strong and brave by assigning his psychic discomfort to an uncomfortable part of his body. With the phallic-oedipal phase, pain and its psychological correlates can, for the first time, become part of a conflict that is truly intrapsychic. Pain now functions truly as an affect, with emotional and fantasy concomitants; it no longer can be solely a physical sensation as in infancy, or a reactive response, as in toddlerhood.

When a child reaches the developmental point where pain functions as a signal, a confusion is reflected, and perhaps fostered, by common usage in our language, as to whether such hurts signal physical pain, physical injury, or emotional pain. This common usage may reflect a blurring of distinctions that goes beyond a semantic problem to an affective and cognitive difficulty everyone faces in development, and which lingers unconsciously in adulthood.

Confusion arises from the use of "hurt" for another meaning: hurt feelings as opposed to physical hurts. This is a distinction with which the young child begins to come to terms. A child who complains, "You hurt me," usually means physically, but gradually begins to understand that one's feelings can be hurt. For example, a four-year-old complained, after being reprimanded by her mother, that her mother had "hurt her ears." Her mother explained that her scolding probably had not really hurt her daughter's ears, but perhaps it was her feelings that had been hurt, because the scolding indicated that mother was mad at her. The little girl was very interested in this new verbal distinction. The next time she was reprimanded, she indignantly told her mother that she had "hurt her feelings." The difficulty posed by the child's concreteness of thinking leads the child to think in terms of physical, palpable hurts, in trying to understand and explain experiences.

Castration Issues

It should not be surprising to see the many meanings and implications of a "hurt" for a preschooler. Imagine a typical conversation with a four-year-old. The child falls and explains that his or her knee hurts, but that he or she didn't *get* hurt—in other words the child feels pain but has determined that no injury was sustained. By asking "Did you hurt yourself?" the mother is really asking two questions—"Is there pain?" and "Is there an injury that needs to be tended to?" As young children come to understand pain as a signal, they also begin to look for or worry about damage whenever they feel pain, so that they simultaneously contend with two sources of discomfort—the sensation of pain itself and the anxiety about injury.

We have a taste of this as adults when we find our tolerance for pain affected inversely by the degree of anxiety we feel about the source or consequences of the pain we are experiencing.

Pain also evolves as a signal of injury in the context of the preschooler's phallic concerns. Since children at this age are becoming more attached to pleasurable feelings in their genitals, the key injury they begin to fear is an injury to the genitals. When an oedipal child experiences pain, the understanding that this can signal injury or bodily damage typically raises the level of castration anxiety. Pain and increased anxiety may be responded to in various ways, which are all seen repeatedly in nursery school: The boy with a "daredevil, macho" attitude that denies any pain or concern at all; a quick visual or tactile check of the genitals to make sure they're still okay, even when the child has in fact hurt only a finger; an excessive concern with a particular aspect of the hurt, perhaps a drop of blood or a forming scab, in an attempt to gain reassurance about the main, largely hidden concern of what this might mean for the safety of the genitals; and so on.

Typically, for the boy, such concerns are seen in terms of an expression of castration anxiety through displacement and an expression of fears of retaliation for oedipal fantasies of hurting or eliminating the father and father's phallus. For the girl the role of pain and concerns about bodily injury have perhaps been less well understood. Castration anxiety, for the girl, takes the added form of trying to figure out what she *does* have and what she does *not* have, and why. Here the theories of Nagera (1975) and Brenner (1979) on female development are very relevant. If a girl experiences her anatomy as representing a body already castrated, then it makes sense that pain as a signal that physical injury has occurred may play a significant role in a girl's coming to terms with her castration complex. I would like to illustrate the connection between pain and castration anxiety for the phallic-oedipal girl, using case material from the treatment of a six-year-old.

Clinical Example—Phallic-Oedipal Phase

B. was an extremely bright, creative child referred for treatment due to a learning inhibition in school, excessive anxiety at mother's departures from her side (although B. was quite happy to leave mother to go play with friends), fearful fantasies that seemed extreme to the mother, and psychogenic stomachaches. Throughout the early months of her treatment, B. focused on many minor hurts and little injuries, such as mosquito bites, scratches, and loose baby teeth. She seemed to experiment through action to find out if something could be lost from her body without her knowing about it through a signal of pain, or whether she could feel pain in minor accidents and still sustain no lasting injury or damage. Through her attempts to understand her aches and pains, B. seemed to be trying to reassure herself that she was not "broken" or castrated, contrary to her unconscious belief, as evidenced in her play and fantasy material, which centered on the "broken" or missing parts of various clay animals she made or puppets she played with in therapy sessions. Making sense of her "hurts" and of her anatomy, and of the connection between the two, was a recurring theme in B.'s treatment. Here are some examples:

> *Session A*: When she came to her session, B. was nursing some scratches on her leg that she had received in a fall. They were bleeding slightly. B. asked, "Did I tell you about the cut on my toes?" She then proceeded to describe a previous cut on her toe. She made snakes out of Playdoh and cut one in two, saying it was too long. She played with the part she had cut off and said it looked like a unicorn's shell or horn. In the ensuing discussion of how the horn had become separated from the unicorn, B. said, "If you took a hammer and really hit it, then it would come off; it would bleed and it would hurt." After awhile B. talked about the baby tooth that she had pulled out recently and remarked, "It didn't hurt at all." B. talked about the first time she had lost a tooth, about eight months ago, and how she had been surprised. She had not expected to lose it. She then pondered the idea that that tooth also had not hurt when it came out.
>
> *Session B* (the following month): B. lost another tooth yesterday; she had pulled it out herself. She has another one that is loose. She showed her therapist the bottom teeth that had come out during the summer and pointed out that you couldn't tell that there had been a tooth because there was such a very small space. The therapist asked about other things that one could lose and B. replied, "Well, you can lose hair when you brush it, and fingernails." As this session came in the context of a series of sessions about differences between boys and girls, and B.'s concerns about being broken, the therapist said that sometimes little girls wonder why it is that boys have a penis and girls don't, and that perhaps B. wondered if she might have lost one somehow, like the teeth. B. checked the chair out that she was sitting on, and asked, "Is this the broken chair?" (She had discovered a hole in the bottom of the chair the previous session.) B. then put her head down to look under the chair, hang-

ing down from it, and said, "Well, underneath it's ripped." She sat up again and said that her head hurt, that the blood was all over it.

Session C (the following month): B. began fixing the clay superheroes she had been playing with in therapy for awhile. She said one had become a bit "squished" in the locker. She said they had to be fixed; if they were not fixed, they would begin to hurt. B. explained that they did not hurt yet, but they had looked into the mirror and could tell that they were not made right. They knew that if they didn't get fixed, they would begin to hurt.

Here we see B. struggling with the issue of injury and pain, a central theme in her castration complex. She seems to be continually trying to figure out if she could have lost a part of her body without it hurting, like the baby teeth. Or was it possible that if she were not the right shape, like the clay superheroes, she would eventually feel pain? As B. came to understand her castration worries and her wishes for a penis like her younger brother's, her accident proneness and attention to hurts subsided, and eventually disappeared, only to make a brief reappearance in the termination phase of her treatment. The stomachaches, for which B. was originally referred, also disappeared in the course of her treatment. These represented, primarily, oral impregnation fantasies, as well as a physical way of experiencing sadness over loss, which B. had had to deny, despite significant losses experienced around the age of 3½.

SUPEREGO CONSOLIDATION AND PAIN

Finally, pain takes on another significance with the consolidation of the superego and with the waning of the oedipal phase. This is the pain that is experienced when there is an intrapsychic rift between the ego and the superego. This is the meaning of pain as punishment for imagined or real transgressions unacceptable to the superego. Precursors for this role of pain are seen much earlier than the oedipal stage and latency, just as precursors for the superego are seen much earlier. For example, we often see young toddlers hit or bite another, and then immediately hit or bite themselves, in an early expression of internalizing limits and turning aggression against the self. The common experience during illness or severe physical pain of thinking "what have I done to deserve this?" expresses this meaning of pain as punishment. In cases of self-injury through frequent "accidents," or deliberate attempts to hurt oneself, the physical pain may symbolize an attempt to appease a superego by punishing the self.

CONCLUSIONS

As with any symptom, self-injury, accident proneness, or recurrent psychogenic pain must be carefully analyzed to understand precisely the meaning and function of the pain in a particular patient's development and current psychological functioning. Such symptoms might reflect self-punishment impelled by superego pressures. They might, in other patients or at other times, represent a response to an experienced loss of an important object, using the language of bodily pain to express mental anguish, harking back to separation issues of toddlerhood. They might, in other cases, represent an attempt to establish a firm, concrete bodily reality in the face of subjective experiences of self- or bodily disintegration. Or, finally, painful psychosomatic symptoms or accident proneness might reflect fantasies about potential or accomplished castration. It is my hope that by viewing the many meanings of pain in a developmental framework, we will be better able to interpret the role that small injuries and discomforts play for each patient, in the context of that patient's development and intrapsychic dynamics.

REFERENCES

Brenner, C. (1979). Depressive affect, anxiety, and psychic conflict in the phallic-oedipal phase. *Psychoanal. Q.*, 48:177–197.

Deutsch, F. (1959). Symbolization as a formative stage of the conversion process. In *On the Mysterious Leap from the Mind to the Body*, ed. F. Deutsch. pp. 75–97.

Dubovsky, S. L., & Groban, S. E. (1975). Congenital absence of sensation. *Psychoanal. Study Child*, 30:47–75.

Engel, G. L., & Schmale, A. H., Jr. (1967). Psychoanalytic theory of somatic disorder: Conversation, specificity, and the disease onset situation. *J. Amer. Psychoanal. Assn.*, 15:344–369.

Ferenzi, S. (1913). Stages in the development of the sense of reality. In *Sex in Psychoanalysis*. New York: Dover Publications, pp. 181–203.

Fisher, S., & Cleveland, S. E. (1968). *Body Image and Personality*, 2nd ed. New York: Dover Publications.

Fraiberg, S. (1977). *Insights from the Blind*. New York: New American Library.
Frances, A., & Gale, L. (1975). The proprioceptive body image in self-object differentiation: A case of congenital indifference to pain and head-banging. *Psychoanal. Q.*, 44:107–125.
Freud, A. (1965). *Normality and Pathology in Childhood*. New York: International Universities Press.
——— (1952). The role of bodily illness in the mental life of children. *Psychoanal. Study Child*, 7:69–81.
Freud, S. (1929). Civilization and its discontents. *Standard Edition*, 21.
——— (1923). The ego and the id. *Standard Edition*, 19.
——— (1926). Inhibitions, symptoms, and anxiety. *Standard Edition*, 20.
Hoffer, W. (1949). Mouth, hand, and ego integration. *Psychoanal. Study Child*, 314:49–56.
——— (1950). Oral aggressiveness and ego development. *Int. J. Psychoanal.*, 31.
Krohn, A. (1980–1981). Some clinical manifestations of structural defects in a borderline personality. *Int. J. Psychoanal. Psychother.*, 8:337–361.
Mushart, C. (1975). Mind-body-environment: Toward understanding the impact of loss on psyche and soma. *Psychoanal. Q.*, 44:81–106.
Nagera, H. (1980). Self and object. In *The Developmental Approach to Childhood Psychopathology*. New York: Jason Aronson, pp. 81–110.
——— (1975). *Female Sexuality and the Oedipus Complex*. New York: Jason Aronson.
Norton, J. (1963). Treatment of a dying patient. *Psychoanal. Study Child*, 18:541–560.
Roiphe, H. (1973). Some thoughts on childhood psychosis, self, and object. *Psychoanal. Study Child*, 28:131–144.
Schilder, P. (1935). *The Image and Appearance of the Human Body*. London: Kegan Paul, French, Frubner, & Co.
Szasz, T. (1957). *Pain and Pleasure*. New York: Basic Books.
Valenstein, A. F. (1973). On attachment to painful feelings and the negative therapeutic reaction. *Psychoanal. Study Child*, 28:365–391.
Weiss, E. (1934). Bodily pain and mental pain. *Int. J. Psychoanal.*, 15:1–13.

17

B. M. BIVEN, Ph.D.

DISCUSSION: *Pain: Psychoanalytic Perspectives*

IN THIS PAPER THE CONCEPT OF DEVELOPMENTAL PATHWAYS AND THE GATE CONTROL THEORY OF PAIN ARE SEEN AS COMPLEMENTARY THEORIES THAT PROVIDE A FOUNDATION FOR THE CLINICALLY OBSERVABLE FACT THAT PHYSICAL PAIN HAS A VARIETY OF EMOTIONAL MEANINGS, BOTH NORMAL AND ABNORMAL, AT DIFFERENT PHASES OF DEVELOPMENT, AND ARE BEST SEEN AS DIFFERENT STRANDS COMPRISING A COMMON DEVELOPMENTAL PATHWAY. EXAMPLES FROM INFANT OBSERVATION, CHILD PSYCHOANALYSIS, AND NORMAL DEVELOPMENT ARE DISCUSSED IN SUPPORT OF THESE VIEWS.

At the turn of this century, most scientists believed that physical pain was purely a matter of sensation. Pain was believed to occur when a stimulus activated pain receptors in the skin. These receptors then carried the message to a pain center in the brain. In the minority were those who believed that pain was essentially an emotional issue, and that no sensation could be called painful unless it had an emotional meaning.

These views have largely persisted to the present day. The first theory, that pain is primarily a sensory quality to which there are secondary emotional and cognitive reactions, is held by the majority of neurophysiologists. The second theory, which maintains that psychological factors determine the nature of pain, is held by some, but by no means all, psychoanalysts. This controversy about pain has at times become heated, probably because it is possible to prove that each extreme position is incorrect. Until recently, however, it has not been possible to reconcile them in a way that is scientifically rigorous.

With regard to the first theory, one need only observe that an infant will receive an injection with minimal protest, while an oedipal child will complain bitterly of the pain. The pain experienced by the oedipal child is clearly and decisively colored by the castration anxieties typical of that stage of psychological development. The infant, who harbors no such anxieties, experiences only mild discomfort. Other psychological factors, such as the degree to which one is relaxed, anxious, or depressed, also influence the experience of physical pain. In medicine the use of placebos, suggestion, and coping skills to reduce pain have been so useful that "there is no longer any doubt that it is possible to reduce many kinds of clinical pain by means of different psychological therapies" (Melzack, 1973).

I shall return to the topic of psychological factors that intensify or diminish pain in the discussion of Janis Krohn's paper. For the present I wish only to establish that these psychological factors do exist, and that they often account not only for the intensity of pain, but sometimes for its presence or absence. It is, therefore, incorrect to say that physical pain is always a sensory issue and that psychological factors are always secondary.

The second theory veers close to a mind–body duality that is scientifically untenable. Emotion and cognition, no less than physical sensation, result from functions of the central nervous system (Brenner, 1955). The difference between them is that we have a better understanding of the physiology of sensation than of emotion and cognition. It was this limitation that caused Freud to abandon his efforts to link psychological processes with brain functioning (Freud, 1895), and to turn his attention to metapsychology. In the intervening years, knowledge of brain functioning has not progressed sufficiently to allow for an understanding of the neurophysiological processes that accompany the subtle psychological processes one encounters in psychoanalytic work. For this reason psychoanalysts still rely upon metapsychology and base their theories of the mind upon psychoanalytic data alone.

As it happens, much of Freud's early psychoanalytic research concerned hysterical conversion symptoms. Indeed, it was from observations of a colleague, Josef Breuer, that Freud's ideas first took shape. Breuer had treated a hysterical patient through hypnosis. When she recalled the experiences and emotions associated with her physical symptoms, they disappeared. Upon further study Freud concluded that hysterical conversion symptoms were a somatic expression of emotional conflict. In other words, psychological conflict caused the physical symptoms.

If one were more precise, one would say that the brain dysfunction that causes the emotional conflict of the hysteric is also responsible for the physical symptoms. If we were able to isolate and treat the brain dysfunction, presumably psychoanalysis would not be necessary. As things stand we are ignorant of the physiology involved, and can only treat the physical and emotional pathology in accordance with our theories of metapsychology. For this reason the mind–body duality, erroneous though it may be, has gained momentum in some psychoanalytic circles.

Within these circles one sees a tendency to expand upon Freud's studies on hysteria, and assert that many, even all, physical symptoms are caused by psychological factors. A metapsychological explanation of this extreme position was proposed by Eduardo Weiss in a paper called "Bodily Pain and Mental Pain" (1934). Weiss was a follower of Federn, an analyst who elaborated upon Freud's assertion that the ego is first and foremost a body ego. Federn believed that the mental concept of the body (body ego) is central to psychic life. In elaborating on this theory, Weiss asserted that the body ego allows us to experience physical stimuli as bodily pain. He argued that in altered states of consciousness, such as sleep or psychosis, the body ego is also altered, or even absent. In these altered states of consciousness, physical stimuli are often experienced as psychic pain. Thus Weiss concluded that when the body ego is intact, excessive external stimuli result in a painful physical sensation. When the body ego is not sufficiently intact, the external stimuli will produce mental rather than physical pain. As clinical support Weiss cites a case of a patient who dreams of being humiliated, and upon waking realizes that she has had menstrual pains during the night. He also writes of a schizophrenic patient who experienced a laceration of the forehead as psychic pain.

In his theories Weiss endeavored to explain the riddles of hysterical symptoms, and of physical and mental pain in general, by making them functions of the body ego. Plausible as it might appear, however, Weiss's theory cannot explain the development either of the physical sensation of pain or of the body ego. Even if one grants that Weiss is correct in saying that once the body ego is established, it determines whether pain is experienced as physical or mental, one must ask how the mental concept of the body comes about in the first place. It is difficult to imagine how one might gain the concept of the body without sensation, yet Weiss writes that we do not experience physical sensation (pain being one variety) unless the body ego is intact. It is upon this circular argument that Weiss's argument founders.

Regardless of how one views psychological influences upon the experience of pain in the older child and adult, one must admit to the existence of physical sensation and pain in the development of the body ego. As I observed in an earlier paper (Biven, 1982), "Within the framework of the basic principles of psychoanalytic theory, it can be seen that such authors as Spitz, Anna Freud, Mahler, Ribble, Winnicott, Ramzy, Wallerstein, Ritvo, Solnit, and others, are in broad agreement regarding the importance of the acquisition of [physical] pain as a developmental step. This developmental step . . . has the task of delineating and structuring an image of the body. Such images are contained within the emerging ego." Thus, paradoxically, the psychoanalytic studies of infant development insist upon the primacy of physical sensation.

Recent studies also indicate that while psychological factors contribute to the adult's experience of pain, they do not appear to be the reason why pain occurs in all cases. A study by Melzack and colleagues (1982) of injured patients who were pain-free makes three observations. First, the type of injury was an important factor in determining the presence or absence of pain. Deep-tissue injuries were more painful than those limited to the skin. Second, somatic endogenous analgesic effects were operative in pain-free patients. Third, these pain-free patients were not stoical personalities. These findings indicate that the absence of pain was not necessarily a psychological phenomenon as others (Beecher, 1959) have contended.

The authors did note, however, the similarities in the quality of pain from one injury to the next and concluded, "The paucity of information regarding the nature of the injury suggests that acute pain has the function of signaling possible injury without carrying much information about the nature of the injury" (Melzack et al., 1982). Thus there is ample room for psychological factors to play their part after the initial painful registration. This study indicates, however, that psychological factors are not the only reason we feel pain, as the extreme views of Weiss and others would maintain.

It seems clear that neither of the two radical views of the origins of pain is correct. The decisive influence of psychological elements upon the subjective experience of pain indicates that it is not purely a matter of sensation. At the same time, developmental considerations of the infant and clinical data regarding pain in adults indicate that painful sensation, in the traditional sense of the word, often plays an all-important role beyond psychological considerations. This state of affairs might place one in an unsolvable quandary regarding the cause of pain, except for some thought-provoking discoveries by Melzack and Wall (1965) known as the "Gate Control Theory." This theory emphasizes *parallel* processing systems to sensory and affective/cognitive (psychological) brain centers. This means that "cognitive capacities such as attention and suggestion can influence pain by acting at the earliest levels of sensory transmission" (Melzack, 1973).

Thus the Gate Control Theory provides neurophysiological evidence for the integration of sensory and psychological factors in the experience of pain. This model is of value in helping us to integrate Janis Krohn's ideas on the development and meaning of pain.

By using my concept of developmental pathways (Biven, 1980), Ms. Krohn offers a model whereby one can trace the fate and meaning of pain at different phases of development. The concept of developmental pathways is an elaboration of Anna Freud's formulation of developmental lines that proceed or regress in a two-dimensional fashion. I found it useful to envision development in terms of strands that converge into common pathways, and later may separate and converge into different pathways. The convergence, separation, and regrouping of strands over time may be seen as a developmental network.

This paper will focus upon the strands which, at various levels of development, contribute to the experience of pain, which is a developmental pathway. In most instances the author and I are in agreement, but on one or two important points we see things differently. The paper will also focus upon these points of agreement and disagreement.

INFANCY

One of the difficulties in understanding the meaning of pain for an infant is that there are no first-hand reports. Infants cannot tell us and we cannot remember. In addition, constitutional factors may predispose infants to vulnerability or resistance to pain in ways that we cannot discern from their responses. In short, we cannot know the infant's subjective experience of pain. We infer from their responses that they are distressed, but beyond this we can only interpolate, possibly incorrectly, from our own adult experiences.

Ms. Krohn suggests that the infant's response to pain accounts for the capacity to experience his or her body as real. To support this point, she cites examples of adult amputees who retain the sensation of a phantom limb in order magically to deny its loss. She also cites cases of self-mutilation in adults and older children, and postulates that these patients hurt themselves to affirm that they are real and to dispel, thereby, the anxiety aroused by their pathological regression to an undifferentiated state. These explanations, while plausible, are not possible to prove—and, frustrating as it may be, I think it best to acknowledge that one cannot reconstruct infantile experiences from those of adults. The theoretical rationale for such reconstructions is that the adult is in such a regressed state that he or she is having an infantile experience. Such reasoning is circular and tells us nothing.

This reasoning also assumes that the infantile, undifferentiated state is one that is actively pleasurable, which is to say that one regresses to it much as one might regress to a pleasurable, instinctual fixation point. There is, however, no evidence that lack of differentiation is a state one actively experiences. It may well be that lack of differentiation represents the absence of ego, a state of emotional nothingness, out of which ego differentiation and active experience emerge. Until more evidence exists, we have no access to the infant's fantasy life, nor do we know if the infant even has a fantasy life. Therefore, we cannot say that the experience of pain allows the infant to experience the body as "real." Indeed, we have no way of knowing what meaning, if any, pain has for an infant.

Given this insurmountable limitation of infant observation, what can one say about the meaning of pain to a small baby? Observation does reveal two points. First, the infant can often discover the painful site. Colicky babies will bring their knees up to their stomachs to relieve tension, and they will flail their arms and hands about the thoracic region. This latter response occurs also when babies are very hungry. Infants with ear infections will bring their fists up to the sides of their heads, rubbing and hitting the afflicted area. Second, though it is difficult to know if a newborn can distinguish between kinds and severity of stimuli, this is a capacity that quickly develops in the infant. As the baby grows, he or she responds differently to different kinds and intensities of stimuli. For example, the mother of a four-month-old can distinguish between the vehement hunger cry and the disgruntled whimpering that may precede sleep.

From these two observations, it is reasonable to assume, as Ms.

Krohn does, that pain allows the infant to distinguish between different parts of the body, and later to distinguish between different types of sensation. It is worth remembering here that pain is just one category of sensation, and cannot be singled out as the only beacon of physical reality. Pleasurable sensations can have the same effect. All that is necessary is that the baby experiences the sensation involved as emanating from the body.

These capacities—to discover the site of the stimulus on the body and to differentiate kinds and intensities of stimuli—are observable strands in the experience of pain. Though we can say little about the infant's subjective experience, we do know that these two strands are central to it.

TODDLERHOOD

Toddlerhood extends roughly from 15 to 30 months of age. It has been described in terms of the toddler's anal sadistic fantasies (Freud, 1905), of fantasies of omnipotence (Mahler et al., 1975), of fears of object loss and loss of love (Brenner, 1982), and, by the author, of the newly emerged capacity to love and hate. How do these forces operate in the toddler's personality? My preference is to examine the toddler's omnipotent fantasies vis-à-vis the immature ego. By using this orientation, I shall try to integrate the other characteristics of toddlerhood.

There are two ways in which the toddler leans toward omnipotent fantasies. First is the tendency to see the self and others as omnipotent. The toddler's dependence upon his or her parents accounts for the view of them as omnipotent. Parents are the all-powerful beings who gratify or punish, and for reasons that are, at best, vague for the child. During toddlerhood the child first encounters attempts at discipline, or, to be more precise, is object related enough to understand restrictions as discipline. Inevitably the child identifies with the disciplinary parent. It is difficult to assess to what extent the toddler simply imitates the parents as opposed to identifying with them. Here again we are up against the problem of child observation and our limited access to the child's fantasy life. Certainly the young toddler cannot speak his or her mind and the child's immature motor coordination makes it difficult always to understand his or her body language. Both capacities improve in the course of toddlerhood, but it is not easy to say when identification proper begins for the child as opposed to when we are able to discern it.

In any event one can usually see signs of identification by two years of age. When discipline imposes unpleasant restrictions upon the child, the parents are seen as hostile, and discipline appears to be punishment. Anna Freud (1971) coined the term "identification with the aggressor" to describe the child's tendency to identify with those aspects of parental behavior that appear to be hostile. In this way the child turns a passive experience into one that is, in fantasy, an active one. By identifying with the aggressor, the child no longer feels the helpless brunt of parental hostility, but instead feels powerful and aggressive. One regularly sees little children spanking and shouting at their dolls and stuffed animals, playing the angry parent to the hapless toy. Sometimes identification with the aggressor goes the route of role reversal, as it did with two-year-old Grace who would march about the house, with her chest puffed out, chanting, "Big Grace!" and then cringing and taking tiny steps, she would finish, "and tiny little Mommy."

Although identification with the aggressor, by definition, focuses upon questions of hostility, it appears equally true that the toddler identifies with the parent's power to love, protect, and nurture. When an aunt with a new baby visited the home of two-year-old Timmy, he was astounded and enthralled when his aunt breastfed her infant. The following day, Timmy's mother saw him cuddling his Teddy bear against his naked chest. "I can feed my Teddy," he asserted, his tone leaving no room for contradiction. In the days that followed, he would join the new mother and minister to his Teddy bear when she cared for her baby. He was touchy and sullen if anyone appeared to talk down to him, and he joined league with his aunt only after he was sure she would not laugh at him.

While mothering his Teddy, Timmy felt himself to be the powerful, nurturing mother. In this way he identified with the caring behavior of his own mother. One wishes there were a phrase as pleasing as "identification with the aggressor" to use for this equally universal phenomenon of identifying with the nurturing parent. Until there is we can only take note that the phenomenon does exist, and that the child sees the nurturing parent as omnipotently powerful.

To summarize this first aspect of omnipotence—namely, the toddler's tendency to see both self and others as omnipotent—we understand that the child's dependency upon the parents causes the child to regard them as omnipotent figures. In fantasy the child turns his or her experience of being the passive child into one of being the active, powerful parent. The child achieves this transformation by identifying with the omnipotent parent. The toddler identifies with those aspects of the parents seen as aggressive as well as with those aspects seen as nurturing. In both cases the act of identification allows the child to feel omnipotent, as he or she believes the parents to be.

The child's identification with the parents is healthy and desirable. By identifying with the aggressor, the toddler reverses a sense of helplessness and weakness. By identifying with the nurturing parent, the child overcomes the feelings of incompetence. If parents overpower or belittle the toddler in these identifications, the child will be thrust back into the painful feelings of fear, shame, helplessness, and anger. This child will see the parents as doubly powerful, because they are able to impose such painful feelings. Such a child will then identify with the belittling parent, who is seen as the aggressor.

The second reason a toddler feels omnipotent can be understood when one considers that the child's immature ego has poor control over his or her impulses. As Ms. Krohn points out, these impulses now are ones of love and hate for parents or guardians. It is beyond question that the toddler does indeed experience these newly emerged capacities to love and hate. The tantrums and negativism of the "terrible two's" are legend, and the exuberant hugs and expressions of affection are no less evident, if they are less bothersome. When the toddler experiences these feelings of love or hate, they are apt to overwhelm an immature ego, and in the midst of the emotional flood, the child may lose sight of reality, of which he or she also has only a partial grasp, again due to the immaturity of the ego. When a child loses sight of reality, we say that the child believes in the omnipotence of his or her wishes because he or she mistakes them for reality.

Consider a typical example of a toddler who does not want to put on his shoes. If mother maintains her composure and plays a waiting game, she will probably get her way in the end. If, however, she is in a hurry or she becomes angry herself, a battle may ensue. In such battles the child's aggression often reaches the proportion of a tantum, where he or she is convinced that mother is the enemy, and so may call her names, or hit, kick, or even bite her. When we describe this kind of emotional state as an omnipotent one, we are not speaking of the child's identification with an omnipotent parent. We are, instead, explaining the power of strong emotion to distort or obliterate one's grasp of reality and make the fantasy seem real.

What is the fate of such powerful emotion? What effect does it have upon the child's personality? Clearly, if the emotions have the stamp of reality, the child will have expectations of the environment that are in keeping with the child's wishes. For example, the little boy who refused his shoes will believe that mother is sadistic and cruel even though she might, in reality, be reasonable and caring. As therapists we caution parents of an angry toddler not to overreact. Excessively angry responses from parents will exacerbate the child's rage, cementing the conviction that the parents are really cruel. This, in turn, may build up the child's hatred of the parents and a consequent fear of punishment.

There is also danger when parents fail to react to the child's emotional state. For example, if a parent ignores an angry child, the child may feel abandoned, or might feel doubly provoked and even angrier. This anger will, in turn, engender a greater fear of punishment. In either case the parent who overreacts or underreacts will increase the toddler's fear of punishment or of loss.

As the author points out, powerful emotion is not always hostile. The toddler also experiences overwhelming affection. Here parental failure to respond is the more common problem. When parents do not respond to a child's love, the child either will clamor for it, or, if rejection is habitual, will experience the rejection as punishment. An example of the former occurred when a family had just moved. Everything had gone wrong, and at the end of the day the mother was irritable and exhausted. She was uncharacteristically unresponsive when her affectionate 18-month-old, Judith, climbed on her lap while they were watching television. The mother tolerated the baby on her lap, but waved off other attempts at embrace. The child renewed her efforts, which mother absentmindedly rebuffed, concentrating instead on the television program. Undaunted, Judith insisted on a hug, which mother accepted, but did not return. The next moment the child "accidentally" fell off the mother's lap. Now in tears, Judith finally got the affection she craved.

Less common is the parent who overreacts in kind to the toddler's displays of affection. Toddlers usually experience the too-loving parent as intrusive. A mother who continually hugs her baby will just as continually interrupt his or her developing autonomy. The child will not be able to walk, explore, or discover the environment in peace. Toddlers will react to excessive demonstrations of love with irritation, or, more ominously, may regress and abandon the activity so essential to development. One should note in this context that motives other than love usually account for a parent's intrusively affectionate behavior.

To summarize this second aspect of omnipotence, the toddler experiences powerful feelings of love and hate that are mistaken for reality. Thus we say his or her fantasies are omnipotent. When parents overreact to underreact to the toddler's emotional upheavals, the child will experience the parents' behavior as a hostile attack, a withdrawal of love, an abandonment, or an intrusion.

To return to the subject of pain, the toddler will experience pain in the context of his or her emotional realities. Pain may represent physical retaliation, loss of love, abandonment, shame, or intrusion, depending on the child's experiences with the parents. No doubt this emotional meaning also depends upon the nature of the pain. For example, a sharp pain lends itself to fantasies of physical punishment, whereas a chronic ache may appear to be an ongoing intrusion. These kinds of meanings are the strands that constitute the developmental pathway of pain in toddlerhood.

Ms. Krohn emphasizes the toddler's "inability to distinguish the sources of pain and the distinctions between bodily pain, emotional pain, and anxiety," and adds that "physical pain transfers quickly into fear or anxiety, and vice versa." With this point I would disagree. There is much evidence that the toddler retains the infantile capacity to locate the site of pain, and to understand that it is physical rather than emotional. For example, a two-year-old who was "helping" with household renovation suddenly cried in distress. "Knuckle!" the child shouted. He had gotten some paint remover on his knuckle, and though he could not see a laceration, he could pinpoint the painful place on his body.

I would agree with the author that all pain has an emotional meaning. I would agree further that powerful emotions engender somatic response that the child might experience as physical pain. For example, shame may cause blushing and headache. Anxiety may cause intestinal distress. It is also true that physical or emotional pain can overwhelm the toddler to the point where he or she cannot coherently distinguish between mental and physical pain. To assume, however, that the inability to make such a distinction is an inherent aspect of toddlerhood seems to me to be a mistake.

If physical and emotional pain are not interchangeable, how can one explain the fact that emotional issues can worsen or alleviate the subjective experience of pain? This is a point that Ms. Krohn documents with extensive and convincing clinical vignettes. These vignettes indicate that the toddler experiencing pain appeals to the loving and nurturing aspects of the parents. When parents comfort the child in pain, this diminishes the impact of the pain. When a parent is absent, unconcerned, or punitive, the child's experience of pain increases. Why emotion causes fluctuations in physical sensation is a question that we could not answer until the advent of the Gate Control Theory. This theory allows that emotional factors can influence the sensation of pain "at the earliest levels of sensory transmission" (Melzack, 1973). Thus while physical and mental pain are not interchangeable, they can exert a decisive influence upon each other. Clinical evidence and the Gate Control Theory are compatible with each other, and the Gate Control Theory provides the physiological rationale for psychoanalytic observation.

PHALLIC-OEDIPAL PHASE

The oedipal period is in full flower from 2½ to five years of age. If infant observation provides a dearth of subjective experience, the oedipal child provides a plethora of clinical examples that tell us how the child feels. How are we to organize such an abundance of material in a coherent manner? Here my preference is to examine the child's maturing ego in the context of instinctual development. From the side of the instincts, the oedipal child has sexual desires. The little boy lusts after his mother and wishes to be rid of his paternal rival. The little girl, at first, has sexual wishes that are identical with those of the boy. With the realization that she does not have, and will never have, a penis, she shifts her affections to her father while mother is her rival.

We can generalize that the oedipal child experiences feelings of love, lust, murderous rivalry, bitter disappointment, and inadequacy. These feelings are every bit as powerful as those of the toddler. For example, the adoring child will be crushed to realize that he or she cannot marry the parent of the opposite sex. Children regularly deny this well-known fact, and insist that they will marry their parents. We know also that the murderously rivalrous child will fear retaliation from the parent of the same sex. Ample testimony to this fact is seen in the thinly disguised nightmares so typical of the oedipal phase. Similarly, the child who feels the disappointment and inadequacy of sexual immaturity takes little comfort in knowing that he or she will eventually grow up. The wish to be big in the here-and-now is so pressing that its postponement is intolerable.

If oedipal children have similar instinctual drives and conflicts, their egos exhibit great variations in individuality. Indeed, as analysts, we know that these individual variations usually persist into adult life. They occur because the oedipal child's ego is more mature and has greater capacity to function than does the toddler's ego. For this reason oedipal children do not appear to be overwhelmed by emotion as the toddler is. We have said that the toddler's emotions are so strong that they are mistaken for reality. This is why we say the child's wishes are omnipotent to the child. The situation with the oedipal child is more complicated. Oedipal strivings do not always bear the stamp of reality for the child. This does not mean that oedipal strivings are weaker than the toddler's emotions, but that the oedipal child's ego sometimes has the capacity to modify and transform the experience and expression of oedipal strivings. Consider 4½-year-old Billy who feared that his neighbor's house would burn down. He had known for some months that the neighbors had no smoke alarm, but this knowledge had not bothered him. Then Billy had a fight with the neighbor's son, an older boy whom Billy viewed as an oedipal surrogate. That night Billy began to worry that the house next door might incinerate at any moment. Clearly his wish to murder the neighbor's child played a decisive role in this worry. His ego defended against this wish by transforming it into its opposite, namely, a dreaded fear that he hinged upon a fragment of reality. The toddler's ego is too immature to institute such elaborate defenses. While toddlers are notorious for their straightforward expressions of murderous intent, the oedipal child is more apt to defend against such impulses.

One sees similar defenses against libidinal impulses. Five-year-old Stacy developed a passion for baking and loved to prepare treats for her father to eat when he came home from work. Analysis revealed that Stacy had heard father refer to mother's pregnancy as a "bun in the oven." Though she realized this expression referred to a real pregnancy, she defensively latched onto it and in displacement fashioned many "babies" of her own to give to her father. Here, again, the instinctual impulse is defensively transformed into more acceptable wishes and behavior.

The variety of ways in which oedipal children defend against their impulses depend upon their experiences, the nature of their identifications, constitutional factors, and so on. Each child's ego is different. This is why one sees such variety and individuality in oedipal children.

Before discussing the meaning of pain for the oedipal child, we must consider one more important feature of the child's development—the superego. The superego is the psychic seat of morality. Though one can see superego precursors in toddlerhood, it is not until the end of the oedipal phase that the superego is clearly apparent in the personality. A child develops a superego largely through identifications with the parents. Its intrapsychic function is to serve as an internal inhibitor of unacceptable thoughts and actions. The child who disobeys his or her superego feels guilty. Thus guilt, as opposed to fear of punishment by external agents, is the hallmark of superego formation. As Ms. Krohn points out, the guilty child may sometimes seek out pain, which is seen as punishment. Thus the pain would replace and alleviate the even more painful sense of guilt.

Because oedipal children exhibit such a variety of personality traits, pain has an equal variety of meanings. These meanings derive not just from instinctual impulses, but from the manner in which the ego and superego defensively transform instincts into acceptable wishes. One child, for example, may see pain as castrating punishment for forbidden sexual impulses. Another may see it as a rationale for demanding the exclusive love of the oedipal parent. Still another may see it as penance that alleviates the sense of guilt. The variety of meanings is endless because no two egos or superegoes are exactly the same. Nevertheless all varieties will be on an oedipal theme, because instinctually we are all so similar. These variations are the strands that constitute the developmental pathway of pain during the oedipal phase.

With regard to instinctual considerations, I agree with the author that pain is experienced within the framework of oedipal strivings and conflicts. It is with regard to ego considerations that I take exception to some of her concepts that stem from her belief that physical and emotional pain are interchangeable in toddlerhood. With this premise she contends that the oedipal child's superior cognitive ability enables him or her to distinguish physical from emotional pain. She argues that this distinction goes hand in hand with the oedipal child's greater awareness of body parts and sensations, as well as the capacity to distinguish among a variety of affects. As I pointed out with regard to toddlerhood, clinical evidence opposes the notion that physical and emotional pain are interchangeable. If they are not interchangeable, then one would explain the child's concerned awareness about the body in terms of phallic-oedipal conflicts. The capacity to distinguish shades of affect occurs partly because of increased cognitive capacity, but, more important, because the oedipal child's affective life is far more varied and subtle than it was in toddlerhood. This variety of affect takes place because of the newly developed ego and superego capacities to transform the expression of instinctual wishes in the manner described. Thus the variety and subtlety of affect is a new development that is caused by the child's maturing ego.

For these reasons I disagree with the view that the oedipal child's body awareness and capacity to distinguish a variety of affects are functions of the newly acquired capacity to distinguish physical from mental pain. I believe that the capacity to make such a distinction happens very early in life, that the child's awareness of the body results from oedipal concerns, and that his or her affective capacity is the result of ego maturity.

Given this point of disagreement, how can my views account for the well-established fact that emotional factors aggravate or minimize the experience of pain? Again I turn to the Gate Control Theory, which allows for the mutual influence of emotional and somatic factors. This mutual influence does not mean that physical and mental pain are interchangeable. It does, however, explain the clinical phenomenon, well documented by Ms. Krohn, that emotion can decisively influence the experience of physical pain.

CONCLUDING REMARKS

If we try to understand pain as a developmental pathway in early childhood, we are struck by the problems of child and infant observation. We can know little of the infant's subjective experience. Our observation of toddlers allows for more insight, but our understanding of their fantasy life is still rudimentary. Only with oedipal children do we gain a full view of their fantasies, and hence the meaning that pain has for them.

Within the confines of our method, we can say that pain, along with other sensations, allows the infant to gain a concept of the body (body ego). For the toddler pain is seen as punishment by an omnipotent parental force. The oedipal child experiences pain in the context of oedipal desires, fears, and conflicts.

The concept of developmental pathways in the meaning of pain fits in well with the Gate Control Theory, which allows for parallel processing of sensory and cognitive activities. The Gate Control Theory provides neurological evidence that is consistent with clinical psychoanalytic data illustrating that emotional factors influence the degree of pain, or even its presence at times. This does not mean that physical and emotional pain are interchangeable. Such a theory cannot account for the development of the body ego, and is also inconsistent with much clinical data. What the Gate Control Theory does offer is a physiological rationale for the clinically observable fact that physical pain has a variety of emotional meanings that can, at different phases of development, be seen as strands in a common pathway.

REFERENCES

Beecher, H. V. (1959). *Measurement of Subjective Responses*. New York: Oxford University Press.

Biven, B. (1982). The role of skin in normal and abnormal development with a note on the poet Sylvia Plath. *Int. Rev. Psychoanal.*, 9:205.

——— (1980). The concept of a developmental network: Developmental pathways. *Int. Rev. Psychoanal.*, 7:113.

Brenner, C. (1955). *An Elementary Textbook of Psychoanalysis*. New York: International Universities Press.

——— (1982). *The Mind in Conflict*. New York: International Universities Press.

Eland, J. M., & Anderson, J. E. (1977). The experience of pain in children. In *Pain: A Sourcebook for Nurses and Other Health Professionals*, ed. K. Jacox. Boston: Little, Brown & Co.

Freud, A. (1963). The concept of developmental lines. *Psychoanal. Study Child*, 18:245–265.

——— (1971). *The Writings of Anna Freud*, Vol. VIII, 1970–1980. New York: International Universities Press.

Freud, S. (1895). Project for a scientific psychology. *Standard Edition*, 1:283–399.

——— (1905). Three essays on the theory of sexuality. *Standard Edition*, 7:193.

Mahler, M. S., Pine, F., & Bergman, A. (1975). *The Psychological Birth of the Human Infant*. London: Hutchinson & Co.

Melzack, R. (1973). *The Puzzle of Pain*. New York: Basic Books.

——— & Wall, P. D. (1965). Pain mechanisms: A new theory. *Science*, 150.

——— ——— & Ty, T. C. (1982). *Acute Pain in an Emergency Clinic: Latency of Onset and Description Patterns Related to Different Injuries*. New York: Elsevier Biomedical Press, pp. 33–43.

Spear, F. G. (1964). A study of pain as a symptom in psychiatric illness. Unpublished M.D. Thesis, Boston University.

Weiss, E. (1934). Bodily pain and mental pain. *Int. J. Psychoanal.*, 15:1–14.

18

RUTH RIESENBERG MALCOLM

Melanie Klein: Achievements and Problems (Reflections on Klein's Conception of Object Relationship)

THIS PAPER DEALS WITH ONE OF KLEIN'S MOST IMPORTANT THEORIES, THE THEORY OF THE EARLY OBJECT RELATIONSHIP. THE FIRST PART OF THE PAPER IS CONCERNED WITH HOW THIS RELATIONSHIP DEVELOPS FROM BIRTH, AND HOW IT INFLUENCES THE DEVELOPMENT OF BOTH THE EGO AND THE SUPEREGO. THE EARLIEST MENTAL MECHANISMS ARE EXAMINED IN THE LIGHT OF THE BABY'S RELATIONSHIP TO THE MOTHER. IT IS EXPLAINED HOW ALL EXPERIENCES OF THE BABY DERIVE THEIR MEANING FROM THIS RELATIONSHIP. IN THE SECOND PART OF THE PAPER, A CLINICAL EXAMPLE IS USED TO ILLUSTRATE HOW THIS EARLY OBJECT RELATIONSHIP IS EXPERIENCED IN THE TRANSFERENCE; SOME TECHNICAL PROBLEMS ALSO ARE DISCUSSED. FINALLY, THE THIRD PART OF THE PAPER CONTAINS THE EXPOSITION OF EIGHT PROBLEMS DERIVED FROM KLEIN'S IDEAS THAT INVITE FURTHER RESEARCH.

Melanie Klein's creation in the 1920s of a technique for the analysis of children started her on a voyage into the known and unknown territory of psychoanalysis, which resulted in many discoveries that have enlarged and enriched the analytic conception of the human being. Klein conceived of herself as a follower and admirer

This paper was read to the British Psycho-Analytical Society in commemoration of the 20th anniversary of the death of Melanie Klein (October 1, 1980).

of Freud. She was like Freud in the absolute rigor with which she studied mental phenomena, in her bravery in formulating new conceptions, and in her integrity in defending these conceptions. She used Freud's psychoanalytic technique and applied it vigorously. She not only accepted wholeheartedly many of Freud's findings, but she applied and developed them in her own practice and writings.

Yet it is also true that Klein departed from some of Freud's ideas and moved in new directions. Some of these departures were stated explicitly by her; others can be deduced from her writings; and with still others it is a matter of controversy as to whether or not they are in agreement with Freud.

In this paper I will focus on what is, for me, the cornerstone of Klein's technique and theory, namely, object relationship. I will give a brief account of my understanding of Klein's views of the earliest beginning of object relationship, and how it affects and relates to ego development. By means of a fragment of case material, I will try to illustrate how the relation to the object gives meaning to anxieties, defenses, and feelings. I will then refer to psychoanalytic technique, and go on to present some problems arising from the theory of object relationship.

BEGINNING OF OBJECT RELATIONS

Klein's conception is that psychically, as well as physically, a relationship between baby and mother exists from birth. This conception has centered our understanding of mental phenomena on what is always an interaction between people; at first, mother and child, increased later by father and other members of the immediate family. Impulses, anxieties, feelings, defenses, and their results always exist in a relationship, either externally or internally. They have no meaning in isolation.

A baby at first feels a pain, a gratification, hunger, and so on, as caused by the mother. As soon as the baby has its first contact with mother, it is with her or through her that the infant feels everything.

In analysis patients relive their early experiences with their original objects in their transference relationship with the analyst. By understanding the transference, the analyst can understand the patient's emotional life.

In infancy the mother provides for the infant's physical needs. She also, by sensing, mainly unconsciously, the infant's feelings, can minister to her child's emotional needs, through what Bion (1962) called "reverie." She contains and transforms those feelings through her own feelings, rendering them bearable, and thereby making it possible for them to evolve into something else.

The analyst is not the patient's parent, yet does something that is close to reverie. The analyst uses a knowledge of psychoanalysis; that is, theory and technique. His or her own analysis enables the analyst to understand what is being perceived emotionally from the patient's affective communications, which is the countertransference. The analyst then works through this intellectually by means of his or her knowledge of him or herself, of the patient, and of the analyst's theory. The resulting synthesis is the interpretation.

For the emotional relationship between infant and mother to take place from birth onward, the baby has to have an original capacity of relating to an object. From her analytic observations, Klein inferred that the baby is born with a rudimentary ego, that is, a capacity to feel anxiety and to react defensively because of it. This reacting is toward the mother, and it begins simultaneously with the development of the ego and the object relationship.

Klein's postulation of a rudimentary ego has caused no end of controversy among analysts. Though it seems to contradict some of Freud's statements, yet it appears from *Instincts and Their Vicissitudes* (1915), *Beyond the Pleasure Principle* (1920), and other writings, that Freud was conceiving of the existence of an early ego. Together with this rudimentary capacity to sense anxiety and react to it defensively, Klein, following Freud, postulates the inborn existence of life and death instincts. The operation of destructiveness and the conflict between it and love are sensed by the child as anxiety. This conflict, which persists through life, is the cause of all anxieties.

Here we touch upon a frequent area of misunderstanding and controversy—the way in which Klein used the concept of instinct. My view of this is expressed by Baranger's (1971) remark: "When Melanie Klein speaks of life or death instincts, she refers to 'great polarities' or 'great tendencies' that govern psychic life."

I think that the ideas of energy and cathexis as quantities do not play any role in Kleinian thinking today, even if Klein herself used it differently in her thinking. To state it simply, I think Klein's view is that the life instinct (or love) is a tendency toward integration and the death instinct (or hate) is a tendency toward disintegration. According to this line of thought, the baby feels the conflicting forces of the life and death instincts as anxiety, and because of it relates emotionally to the mother, who becomes the psychological object for the baby, and this relationship is the foundation for the meaning of all mental phenomena.

Probably the first experience of the infant is what could be called, for lack of a better word, a "bad" experience. The loss of the protection of the womb exposes the infant fully to the internal pressure of the death instinct, which is felt as anxiety or terror. The presence of the mother and the first feeding reestablishes the well-being of the baby; we could say that it has a "good" experience. But the mother, in feeding the baby, not only has given the child emotional goodness, but has removed the pain of the bad experience. The baby has gotten rid of something and has taken something in. Both experiences take place in conjunction with the mother, and it can be said that the baby has a *divided* contact with the mother, or with her breast. In translating this into ordinary psychoanalytic language, it is obvious that I am speaking of introjection, projection, and splitting.

The first months of life are a struggle for physical and psychio survival. The mother helps toward this survival by her love and ministrations to the baby. Babies put things out and take things in. I use the word "things" on purpose, as it is body products, mother's milk, and physical contact that go out and in. The experiences are bodily felt and shaped, but by the fact of being experiences, they, by definition, are mental. Introjection is an experience of the baby with its mother, who is taken in; in projection an experience of the baby is put into its mother.

EARLY MENTAL MECHANISMS

Because introjection, projection, and splitting seem to be the earliest and most mental activities of the baby in relation to the mother, I would like to remark briefly on how they evolve into the much more complicated events with which analysts are familiar, and on their relation to identification. I want especially to emphasize that all three are the bases for development, as well as defenses against anxiety.

I should mention that I often use the word "mother" rather than "breast," which would be more accurate when speaking of the very early stages of development, to emphasize the emotional quality of this part object. Melanie Klein, in describing the first defensive maneuver against the death instinct as projection, follows Freud's idea of deflection. Freud also used the term projection in this context. Klein adds to and modifies Freud's idea by giving it a more psychological implication. Freud says the "organism" deflects the death instinct, whereas Melanie Klein says the baby does this, and a baby is much more than an organism. Also, Klein says that the baby projects the destructive impulses into the mother or her breast. In other words, she is more precise than Freud about where such impulses go—namely, into the mother. The projecting of the bad experience into the mother frees the baby from the horror, and the mother is felt as bad. And also, as we shall see presently, since the baby tends to take everything in, the badness is taken back into the baby.

Am I speaking now of projection or projective identification? When Klein describes projective identification in her paper on schizoid mechanisms, she speaks of it as a mechanism deriving from projection. I think that projection and projective identification are the same thing. The baby, by projecting the death instinct, is turning out a horrible destructive feeling, perceived as anxiety. In doing so, however, what is being put into the mother is that bit of the baby that had that feeling so as to allow the rest of the baby to feel better. Thus the baby has split and entered the mother with the split-off part. The mother is now felt as bad. This mother, or breast, felt as bad, is often reintrojected into the baby. As the baby grows and develops, this projective identification, as well as other mental mechanisms, becomes progressively complicated, acquiring manifold aims and results, and influencing the development into normality or pathology.

With regard to the introjection of a good feeding experience with the mother, this fuses with the child's loving feelings and starts a good relationship with her. She becomes established in the child's mind as a good breast; and the relationship becomes double, one with the external mother and one with a variety of internalized mothers or breasts. Thus an internal world is built up, populated by good and bad objects. These objects are mental phantasies; that is, the breast and other parts of the mother or father are what they were felt to be when the introjections took place. They are highly personalized perceptions to which the child goes on relating.

Though the external object is at first one, internally there are many objects. The reason is that there are many introjections, and also the splitting processes divide or fragment the object into many bits. Later on other people are included in this world.

In my view all introjections affect the ego in either of two ways. In one way they are assimilated into the ego; that is, the child's ego becomes identified with the qualities of the object that has been assimilated. The repeated assimilation of the good object into the ego allows the ego to develop and become more differentiated. It becomes stronger. I think one can say that the ego develops through continuous processes of identification.

The other way is that the introjection of an object in a bad experience affects the ego by weakening it; that is, the ego again feels an increase of anxiety, against which it has to defend. The defenses are mainly based on splitting, which is used now to attack the bad object inside. But, as I said before, by splitting the experience, the ego severs that bit that has it, and is itself split. Thus its strength is reduced. To regain strength the person has to have good experiences again, and introject good objects and assimilate them.

Splitting

It seems to me that splitting is one of the earliest mental mechanisms, and is connected at first with projection. The self has to split itself to project the first impact of the death instinct. Therefore, splitting is a precondition for projection.

One can also see that splitting, by facilitating this first projective maneuver, creates the germ in the mind of what develops into an ordering factor, that is, the keeping apart of the good from the bad feelings, experiences, and objects, and so allows the individual to enlarge his or her ego and internal world through accumulation of good experiences with objects. Splitting is also used to attack objects.

To Summarize

Baby and mother relate from the start of life. The prevalence of either instinct over the other will influence the ways in which this relationship will develop. The mother's personality will help or hinder this development.

At first, because of the omnipotent character of mental phenomena, the perception of the mother by the baby will be more determined by the baby's feelings. The continuous operation of projective and introjective processes will make her, in the baby's mind, the cause of every feeling. The continuous presence and ministration of the mother will slowly help the baby, by assimilating her into the baby's self, and progressing from the fragmentary mother into an integrated mother, which in turn will allow the baby to increase the perception of separateness from the mother and to start recognizing his or her own feelings toward the mother.

THE INNER WORLD

I have been trying to concentrate almost exclusively on the factors involved in the very early relations between baby and breast, which result in both the development of the ego and the formation of an inner world. This inner world is a world of objects, at first part objects. They are part objects because of limited perceptions and because of splitting processes. It is a world of good and bad objects; the good part objects are more whole than the bad ones, which tend to be in pieces. At first it is a world of horrors and marvels. Good equals ideal; bad is a persecutor. The difference between this inner world and the external world is at first minimal and ephemeral. The child's early perceptions of feelings, as well as of objects, are closely connected to body sensations and body products.

I have been speaking of the ego and of its objects. But what about the superego? My not mentioning it has nothing to do with the fact that I am concentrating mainly on the first few months of life. For me the superego *is* the internal objects. One might wonder whether some of these objects have a special character in their relationship to the self, which could be called the super ego. I don't think so. In my view, when one calls something a superego reaction, one is speaking of some internal objects pressurizing the ego in some way. I think, however, that in psychoanalysis we will go on speaking about superego, because the word has a place in our language in reference to specific types of behavior and reactions. That is, it has a legitimate place as a description, but not as a component of the inner world that is different from internal objects.

CLINICAL ILLUSTRATION

The following clinical material illustrates how the basic concept of object relations is the center of analytic work. It is based on two sessions from the analysis of a man in his sixth year of treatment. The man is 40, married, and has a family, and is the fifth child among sevel siblings. A clergyman in a congregation outside London, he originally came to analysis because of a sexual perversion: exhibitionism. He is a tall man with a reddish complexion and speaks with a marked Scottish accent.

At the Friday session, the first third of the session appeared very muddled. The patient was complaining about one thing after another; he felt very disgruntled, and had the flu. He reported quarrels with several people. He complained especially about someone called Rowena, who should have been more helpful in a crisis in his congregation, pointing out she did not support him enough when the situation there was breaking down.

My attempts to say something were brushed off. He seemed irritated by my speaking, and at the same time seemed to become more impatient in expecting to get something from me. During this time I was feeling a mixture of things. I felt inept and irritated, and I had a sense of danger. I did not know how much of what I said had been actually heard by him. He returned to the subject of Rowena, complaining how unsupportive she was in such a collapsing situation, and that it had felt to him very frightening.

Finally I managed to tell him that something was going on in which we did not seem to be able to meet. I said that most of my attempts to say something had been interrupted and discarded by him, and that his preventing me from talking, by bombarding me with words, must make him feel that I was not understanding and was totally unsupportive. He felt angry and under pressure, and very much feared that he might break down with no one to help him.

Then Mr. L. relaxed, his posture and manner changed, and he became thoughtful for a moment. In a markedly different manner, undisturbed and animated, he started speaking about someone whom he thought had severe problems, and he feared might have a mental breakdown. From this association and my interpretation, we seemed to become involved in a dialogue in which whatever I said—whether interpretation, elaboration, or just repetition of what he had said—was accepted, agreed with, and immediately applied to somebody else and expanded in the context of that person's experience.

After a little while, I felt weary and unclear. The idea of parallel lines came into my mind. I said that it did not matter what I said, since it was immediately applied to somebody else, only slightly changed; and that in this way he prevented any direct contact between himself and me, a contact that might allow me to give him some understanding about what he felt. Still he seemed interested in something of what we said, and tried to keep us going. I said that to link directly with me felt to him both hateful and frightening. He stiffened in his position, as if forcing himself to speak, saying "it is like Peter when . . ." He seemed to me to be embarking again on the same type of exercise. I interrupted him here, and pointed out that what he was actually doing at that moment was exactly what I had been describing in this part of the session. He nodded, and this time listened. I started interpreting, saying that breaking the connections with me and applying what I said to all those different people did not allow him to take the understanding for himself. As I was about to continue, he interrupted and, sounding very depressed, said that what I was speaking about was schizophrenic thinking, that should he have to name it, that would be the name he would use.

I interpreted that he felt that I was speaking about something very dangerous, namely, the breakdown he mentioned at first, but that he felt that all I could do was to describe it, but not help him. He agreed, saying, "Aye." I continued, explaining that when he prevented any direct contact with me or severed it and located it in those people, I felt to him to be useless, while he felt he was about to collapse. He said he could see what I meant, that he felt sad, like crying. A tear came from his eye. In what remained of the session, the direct contact with me was maintained, and we could work on his actual behavior and feelings and link them to the relationship to his mother, and also to a quick dispersal of himself into and confusion with his siblings.

The following session he arrived 20 minutes late. He said that while waiting for me to open the door he felt awful. He thought that I must be fed up and angry, and that I would say, "Enough of chopping bits of sessions and wasting time." But when I came to fetch him I smiled and, he said, looked much younger than I had for ages.

He proceeded to discuss the weekend. He had been ill, and had relatives staying in the house. Then he talked about his wife's complaints and her resentment of his being unwell, and her having to take the children out.

I interpreted how he felt me inside him being angry and resentful because of what he called chopping. And I linked it to his behavior regarding my interpretations in the previous session, especially when he cut them out of context, not allowing a direct connection from me to him. That is why he expected me to look old; that is, worn out by his behavior. He said "Aye," and that he regretted being late, since he had a dream that was very much on his mind and felt an urgent need to tell it to me.

The dream was about Jean, whose parents are in his congregation. She took an overdose on Friday. She is 14 years old. He went on to say that her parents came to see him on Friday night. They were very upset. He learned that Jean was "in care" of the Social Services.

The parents talked about what a lot of fuss and agitation had gone on—GP, social workers, a lot of people, but nothing very effective. They talked for quite some time, and he said he felt very angry that the parents were not allowed to be proper parents. They asked him to intervene, and he contacted some friends in the community. Jean is to go to a small ward in the mental hospital. He knows some nurses there, who are good. He said he feels that Jean is one of those people who either make it now or remain broken down. He had related all this with an unusual straightforwardness and sense of helpfulness, in a rather quiet and thoughtful way.

In the dream he had decided to have sex with Jean, as he thought that this would be good for a person with a mental condition. When he woke up, he wondered if he were feeling sexual; he also wondered why he should have such a dream. He spoke a bit more about Jean, whom he had met only twice. The contact she made with him felt strange. He went on talking about the meeting with the parents. While he was telling me the dream, what was most striking to me was the way that he was doing so. For years we had often had the problem of highly eroticized sessions. This time he was reporting it as a problem instead of acting it out. I interpreted this to mean that apparently he had felt in the previous session that we were speaking about something important, which we had seen many times, but it seemed to him now that it was a make-or-break situation. He seemed to realize that we had a problem in making contact with each other; that is, that he gets excited, and this excitement makes him feel that treatment is sex.

He said he feared he might get an erection here; that he often does fear it when I speak. What would I do then? I pointed out that in listening to me and getting excited, he becomes confused and fears that I am confused by it and will be equally excited, or frightened. He nodded slightly. I continued, saying that in situations like the one we had yesterday, he felt that we were having an agitated conversation about several people's problems, which made for a lot of fuss and nothing done. He was a bit tearful. I linked it to a relation with early experiences with his mother, in taking the breast—that he might have become excited, and felt that his mother was carried away by this, or was unhelpful. The result was that she was not allowed to or could not be a proper parent.

He proceeded to describe some thoughts of when he was very little and had erections while on his mother's lap. Also, she seemed to like very much his being funny, making noises, and playing with her. It seemed to make her livelier. She used to tell him what a happy baby he was, always doing something. He spoke of memories of his mother as being severe, quiet, and distant. The session proceeded along these lines for a while. It changed later.

DISCUSSION OF THE CLINICAL MATERIAL

Let us follow the movement occurring in those sessions. At the beginning of the session, Mr. L. feels very persecuted and hostile; the world he speaks about is now in the consulting room, and he attacks and fears me. Because of his bombardment of me, he feels that I am useless and cruel for not helping him. I am like the Rowena who allows a situation to break down. Eventually it seemed that I could provide a bit of understanding that acted as containment. He felt relieved and better about me. But new feelings seemed to set in. He feared that the content of his anxieties was too painful, and he felt too insecure to face it. He also resented that I might be able to deal with it. This led him to a new way of relating to me. By multiple projective identification, we both became split. There we were, he and I, talking animatedly and in a friendly way to each other, but the issues we talked about (that is, his feelings and problems) were spread among many other people. Through this behavior he felt he could control me, and feel safe and friendly toward me. But the relationship is sterile, and new anxieties come to the fore—about disintegration and further collapse.

This could only be modified by persistent work of mine, showing the patient, in the very moment he was doing it, what he was doing, and how he did it. When the patient finally could take this in, he could look more directly at his fears. In his mind apparently I was stronger and more supportive. He now could give his anxieties a name. He spoke about what he called "schizophrenic thinking," and talked to me about his fears. Though this feeling about me as stronger was still very precarious, and, as we see from the beginning of the following session, he felt me to be accusatory, he also felt me as "younger." I was now a better object, and had also been introjected into his ego in this better version. This resulted in an increased capacity for symbolization. He could express the problem in a dream, which he brought for analysis, and tried to work with in the session.

Through the dream of Jean and its linkage to previous experiences in the analysis (and I am not referring only to the previous session), we could get a more precise understanding of his problem, as expressed in his difficulty of taking my interpretation directly, that is, his early problem at the breast. The relevant thing, in my view, in this session was that the patient felt aware and could verbally acknowledge what the problem was. As can be imagined, I had often interpreted this type of behavior and linked it with early experiences, but though he listened, or sometimes even paid lip service, to the interpretations, they never were fully felt by him. Instead these problems were acted out by him, with no lasting modification.

From what I have been describing in the transference, one can deduce from these two sessions, which were actually the culmination of a long period in the analysis, a very disturbed relation to the breast, in which excitation seemed to have interfered with a steady feeding. It is not clear in my mind what the reason for this early excitability was. Envy appears to have played a role in it, but does not seem to cover it completely. The mother, who had emerged through the analysis as a very disturbed person, overwhelmed by so many small children, gave me the impression that she did not know how to cope with his excitability.

When describing the onset of object relations in the early part of this paper, I continuously tried to bring together the development of the ego and the internal world, and the interrelations between object and ego. I hope that I have been able to illustrate this in my clinical presentation.

I wish to turn now to some observations on technique. From my understanding of object relations and our knowledge of transference, it follows that my main emphasis in the work with patients in the session is put on the here-and-now of the transference. When we talk to our patients about their present experience with us, however much that experience is transfered from the past, we should talk about what is going on now, before relating it to the past. Therefore, I think the way to acquaint the patient with this experience is by speaking in the adult language to which the patient is accustomed; only when the present situation in the session is felt by the analyst to be sufficiently recognized by the patient is the link to the early situation meaningful.

In my clinical illustration I spoke mostly about what was happening to the contact between the patient and myself, and of what it turned into because of what he was doing, and so on. Only when I was confident that the patient was aware of and felt all of this did I link it to the archaic object that was being projected.

Here I think there is a real difference among Kleinian analysts, and I do not think it is just an idiosyncratic difference. For example, in the part of the session in which I kept interpreting to the patient how he was breaking direct contact with me, some analysts, assuming that they agreed with my interpretation, would have interpreted directly in an archaic, anatomic language (for instance, that the patient was biting the nipple, or not allowing the nipple into his mouth, and so forth).

I, too, accept this model, but it is my contention that however much the original experiences were felt physically and were linked with the breast and the baby's body, those original experiences are now felt and thought in the patient's adult language, and it is in terms of this language that the analyst must try to bring about the patient's insight into the archaic background. I believe that too prompt a use of what has been called "symbolic" language runs the danger of short-circuiting the achievement of awareness of the connection between the present and the past, thus preventing the patient from fully benefiting from the understanding of that connection.

However, I do not want to give the impression that I think that all the problems involved in object relations have been resolved, either by Melanie Klein or by the many Kleinian analysts who have worked with her ideas on this topic since 1960.

SOME PROBLEMS DERIVING FROM KLEIN'S THEORY OF OBJECT RELATIONS

To conclude this paper, I would like to refer to some of these unresolved problems. I have chosen eight problems. Some I will state as open problems for which I have no answer; with regard to the others, I will venture some suggestions that might be helpful toward their solution.

1. The first problem concerns splitting of the personality, which allows some areas to develop while others remain stuck in very primitive and pathological modes of relation to archaic objects. Since object relations are the base of all mental phenomena, what remains fixated are pathological internal relations. But more often than not, this fixation only includes some area of the personality, while other areas can continue development. If we look at the patient discussed here, we can see that he studied, married, and worked, and that in spite of whatever difficulties he might have had in those areas, one can say he functioned. On the other hand, a whole range of very hostile and terrifying relationships to early objects is encapsulated in his exhibitionism. How such a splitting occurs, and what maintains

it, is in my view an open question, but a very important one for our analytic work.

2. What happens in psychic change? Do the internal objects change? This is a controversial problem that requires further investigation. I think that since the internal objects are mental phantasies, perceptions of the ego, the change in its perceptions is a change in the internal objects. As a result the ego now relates differently to the newly perceived objects.

3. Does this change in the objects remain permanent after the termination of the analysis? One knows that often it does not. Why should this be so?

4. How does the phenomenon of psychic change relate to the instinctual forces of love and destructiveness? If we refrain from thinking of those forces quantitatively, what could it *mean* to say that *they* "change"? Is it meaningful to conceive of those forces as existing in abstraction from the objects?

5. How does this newly created situation of psychic change relate to the instinctive forces? In my view those do not change, but can be dealt with in such a way by the individual that constructive integration will predominate over destructiveness. But what causes such a development in object relationships to last, if it does last, and to counteract the destructive impulses?

6. It is known that the patient projects his or her internal objects into the analyst. Paula Heinmann (1956) described the role of the analyst as that of a supplementary ego, which I think is an accurate description. But by the fact of the patient's projecting into the analyst his or her internal world, the patient hears more often than not, not what the analyst actually means, but the patient's version of it. What happens in the patient so that, as a result of interpretative work, the patient withdraws projections, the omnipotence of the early mechanisms lessens, and he or she actually changes? Most of us will have answers and descriptions of what happens in the consulting room. All of us will speak of introjection and its results, correctly in my view. Still I think there is much to be learned of how this happens, of the more minute changes that take place and that facilitate the intake of the analytic interpretations.

7. This problem is related to the previous one, but looked at from a different angle. If we accept Heimann's postulation of the analyst as a supplementary ego, a question immediately arises: How does a supplementary ego operate? I wonder if it would not be helpful to look at the analyst's work with the patient as creating a new and artificial splitting, which permits the individual, at one and the same time, to project into the analyst, to distort his or her perceptions of

the analyst because of these projections, and still keep another area related to the analyst relatively free from the projections.

8. My last problem is a more general one. Melanie Klein's contributions to the understanding of early object relations have immensely widened our understanding of psychoses. But we are still very much in the dark as far as treatment of psychoses goes. Do we need, I wonder, more answers in the areas about which I have raised questions, if we are to perfect our technique so as to improve our results in the treatment of psychotic illnesses?

SUMMARY

In this paper I have addressed myself to one of the main contributions of Melanie Klein, namely, object relations. I have illustrated how I view our analytic work from the standpoint of the object-relation theory, and how it affects transference and countertransference. And I have ended with a selection of problems we need to understand better.

REFERENCES

Baranger, W. (1971). *Posicion y Objeto en la obra De Melanie Klein*. Buenos Aires: Ediciones Kargieman.

Bion, W. R. (1967). Differentiation of the psychotic from the non-psychotic personalities. In *Second Thoughts*. London: Heineman Medical Books.

——— (1962). *Learning from Experience*. London: Heineman Medical Books.

Freud, S. (1911). Formulation of the two principles of mental functioning. *Standard Edition*, 12:213–226.

——— (1915). Instincts and their vicissitudes. *Standard Edition*, 14:109–140.

——— (1917–1915). Mourning and melancholia. *Standard Edition*, 14:237–258.

——— (1920). Beyond the pleasure principle. *Standard Edition*, 18:1–64.

——— (1924). The economic problem of masochism. *Standard Edition*, 19:155–172.

——— (1923). The ego and the id. *Standard Edition*, 19:1–59.

Heimann, P. (1952). *Functions of Introjection and Projection in Development in Psycho-Analysis*. London: Hogarth Press and Institute of Psycho-Analysis.

——— (1956). Dynamics of transference interpretations. *Int. J. Psychoanal.*, 37:301–310.

Joseph, B. (1975). The patient who is difficult to reach. In *Tactics and Techniques in Psychoanalytic Therapy*. New York: Jason Aronson.

Klein, M. (1946). Notes on some schizoid mechanisms. In *Writings of Melanie Klein*, Vol. III, 1–24. London: Hogarth Press and Institute of Psycho-Analysis.

——— (1948). On the theory of anxiety and guilt. In *Writings*, Vol. III, pp. 25–42.

——— (1952). Some theoretical conclusions regarding the emotional life of the infant. In *Writings*, Vol. III, pp. 61–93.

——— (1957). Envy and gratitude. In *Writings*, Vol. III, pp. 176–235.

Laplanche, J., & Pontalis, J. B. (1973). *The Language of Psycho-Analysis*. London: Hogarth Press and Institute of Psycho-Analysis.

Segal, H. (1957). Notes on symbol formation. Int. J. Psychoanal, 38(VI).

——— (1979). Klein. Glasgow: Fontana. Collins. Modern Masters.

——— (1981). Notes on symbol formation. In *The Work of Hanah Segeil*. New York: Jason Aronson.

19 T. ESKELINEN DE FOLCH

DISCUSSION: *Melanie Klein*

IN THIS PAPER RUTH RISENBERG MALCOLM CONSIDERS SOME FUNDAMENTAL ACHIEVEMENTS AND PROBLEMS IN KLEINIAN THEORY AND TECHNIQUE. SHE DOES IT WITH THE CLARITY AND SIMPLICITY TO WHICH WE ARE ACCUSTOMED IN HER WRITINGS. THESE TWO QUALITIES ALSO SHOW HER DESIRE TO BE UNDERSTOOD BY DIFFERENT SCHOOLS OF PSYCHOANALYTICAL THINKING. AT THE END OF HER PAPER, SHE UNPRETENTIOUSLY RAISES EIGHT PROBLEMS SHE FEELS SHOULD BE INVESTIGATED FURTHER. THESE PROBLEMS OR QUESTIONS ARE CLEARLY SET AND THUS GIVE US SOME INDICATION OF THE DIRECTION OF HER OWN THINKING, BUT SHE LEAVES THE READER FREE TO USE HIS OR HER OWN EXPERIENCE IN CONSIDERING THEM. IN MAKING USE OF THIS FREEDOM, I SHALL CONSIDER SEVERAL POINTS: VICISSITUDES OF INTROJECTION IN THE ANALYTICAL SESSION, IMPORTANCE OF THE CONCEPT OF PROJECTION AND PROJECTIVE IDENTIFICATION IN THE PARTICULAR WAY IN WHICH THE PATIENT OBSERVES THE ANALYST, VERBALIZATION OF THE INTERPRETATION, AND CHANGES OR NONCHANGES IN INSTINCTUAL FORCES AS A RESULT OF ANALYSIS.

Ruth Malcolm describes some aspects of Klein's concept of ego—how ego gains in strength when it introjects an object as a result of a good experience, and how it loses force with the introjection of an object resulting from a bad experience. She then illustrates this by describing fragments of two sessions with a patient, showing us some vicissitudes of introjection of the analyst interpretations, and how the patient understands these but then uses them to deal with other people, for example. The author describes this and other ways the patient uses to avoid the real impact of her interpretations and she persistently interprets this for the patient, who finally makes contact in a more stable, solid way. He then becomes more capable of introspection and symbolization—instead of perverse acting out, the patient brings any problems to the session in the form of a dream that can be discussed and understood.

I think that very many analysts would have been quite happy to see their patients understand their interpretations and to use them outside. This analyst felt that something had gone wrong and showed this to her patient.

What would have happened if she had not done so? To my mind her interpretations would have been somehow understood and taken in. They would have gone to the defensive part of the patient's ego, which would have been engrossed in its apparent ability to deal with the problems of others. Probably his narcissism would have been inflated by this very quick identification with the analyst and by taking over the analyst's understanding functions. As this part of the patient's ego felt that it could not face the anxieties—and thus avoided matching the interpretation with the real need—the patient would have seen the analyst as somebody who too is unable to face his anxieties and impulses, as the patient seems to have seen the mother: pleased and relieved when he behaved as "a happy baby." When the analyst struggled with the patient's anxieties and defenses in the face of her interpretations, she became somebody who could face up to them. The patient not only introjected her interpretations, but introjected and identified with the strength and persistance of the analyst in facing the problems. He could consequently do it himself; for example, face their seriousness ("schizophrenic thinking"). This then helped him both to differentiate himself from her (the subject from object, signifying from signified) and at the same time to contain his anxieties within his ego, both of which are fundamental for a capacity for symbolization (see Segal, 1981). I have wanted to lay stress on Malcolm's close observation of the patient's way of responding to her interpretations because this is quite commonly overlooked in many technical publications. And when the analyst fails to observe in the course of the session the way the patient is relating to the work and his or her interpretations, he or she is in danger of losing the most valuable possibility of observing the actual interaction between analyst and patient. He or she can also be led to think misguidedly that the patient is making real use of his or her interpretations, when in fact the patient is doing no more than incorporating them into his or her customary defensive organization.

One cannot stress sufficiently the importance of Klein's concepts of the functions of the early ego, of such mechanisms as introjection, projection, and projective identification, for a more conceptual understanding of what happens in the consulting room between the patient and the analyst, and which is often thought accessible with no other tools than personal intuition. And yet this is—as far as I know—the first Kleinian paper that discusses the nondifference between projection and projective identification. As soon as we consider, as Malcolm does, that in all projection there are parts of the ego that are split and projected into the object, we have gained some understanding of how the patient experiences hir or her observations of the analyst's reactions. For example, when a patient mainly functions with projective identification and projection (in the paranoid-schizoid position), that patient appears to be convinced that he or she "knows" why and in what mood the analyst interprets this or that. Sometimes these "perceptions" are almost entirely tinted with the patient's own projections, but not always. The patient has also learned to observe from within the analyst (as if in the analyst's skin) what responses the projections cause. Thus there is a double observation: the part of the ego that observes and speaks to the analyst with a certain awareness of separateness and distance, and another part of the ego that is projected into and fused with the analyst and that observes from within. B. Joseph (1983) has investigated these areas of communication from the paranoid–schizoid position in her last papers, such as "On Understanding and Not Understanding: Some Technical Issues." (IJ 1983, vol. 64) R. Langs (1981) also discusses this area of transference relationship in his paper "Modes of 'Cure' in Psychoanalysis and Psychoanalytic Psychotherapy." He describes a technical approach, a way to listen to the patient that takes into consideration the patient's unconscious and conscious perceptions of the analyst's responses.

Ruth Malcolm points out differences of technique within the Kleinian school itself, especially in the formulations of the interpretations. She shows us, through the description of her relationship with the patient and by technical explanations, how important it is for the patient to be able to experience his or her anxieties and feelings in the relationship with the analyst on the same level at which he or she establishes actual contact. If, for example, the analyst reconstructs the patient's history too quickly, then this patient could use that history against the actual experience: could look at this history as an observer, not as a person who is actually experiencing a past conflict in a present relationship. In her case history the author is speaking to an intelligent adult who seems to have developed in many areas of his personality (family, work, etc.), while his early, horrific, pathological relationships were enclustered in his perversions. Ruth Malcolm describes to us—and I agree with her—how the early experiences with the mother and her body are now felt in an adult way and acted out in the way an adult acts and thought about, if at all, in adult language: biting the nipple, for example, is now a severing of contact with the analyst in different adult ways.

The author shows how she uses models of early relationships to understand how her patient is relating to her. But she builds a detailed, unique picture of this patient by observing his present, personal ways of relating to her during this particular session. Then she attempts to convey her understanding to her patient in a language in such a meaningful way that it becomes an experience and not a discussion of problems. In this way of applying the technique, not only the infant in the adult, but also some previously unattainable pathologies (such as perversions), have become more observable in the transference relationship. I mention this pathology because one of this patient's symptoms is exhibitionism, and I was curious, in reading the description of the sessions, to find out how this exhibitionism could be observable in the transference.

This brings us to my last point: Do instinctual forces change in the analysis or not? The author thinks that they do not change but are subjugated to a constructive integration. My experience suggests that when an individual is able to emerge from a pathological, destructive experience of satisfaction and begins to enjoy—even partially—more loving libidinal relationships, then this changes the nature of the destructive impulses. The change is both quantitative and qualitative. There seems also to be some kind of correlation, a vicious circle, between the destructive impulses and the ego's inability to bear anxiety. When the individual feels unable to face anxieties, he or she also feels invaded by unbearable suffering, which then increases the impulse to destroy, to inflict suffering on others, and on him or herself. When the ego grows stronger in its ability to face anxieties and to modify some of their causes, the resulting libidinal satisfaction is such that it can break the vicious circle. Ultimately the patient's experience, however momentous it may be, of feeling able to face up to anxiety and destructive impulses is the experience of being loved, and being able to love in turn.

REFERENCES

Segal, H. (1981). Notes on symbol formation. In *The Work of Hanna Segal*. New York: Jason Aronson.

Joseph, B. (1983). On understanding and not understanding: Some technical issues. *Int. J. Psychoanal.*, 64.

Langs, R. (1981). Modes of "cure" in psychoanalysis and psychoanalytic psychotherapy. *Int. J. Psychoanal.*, 62.

*The True and the False Essay on the Logical Structure of Psychoanalytic Interpretation**

Chapters 1, 4, and 5
Translated from the Italian by
Marion Palmedo, in consultation with
Paolo Migone, M.D.

With an introduction by Paolo Migone†

Introduction

Enzo Codignola prefaces his book with the following acknowledgment:

> The theoretical elaboration of this essay began in 1962 within the study group that at present is connected with the Italian Journal Psicoterapia e Scienze Umane. In particular, the theme

*The original Italian edition of the entire book was published under the title *Il vero e il falso. Saggio sulla struttura logica dell'interpretazione psicoanalitica* by Boringhieri, Turin, Italy, in 1977.

A german translation of the complete book, entitled *Das Wahre und das Falsche. Essay über die logische Struktur der psychoanalytischen Deutung*, with an introduction by Paul Parin, M.D., has been published by S. Fischer Verlag, Frankfurt/Main, Germany, 1986.

†Paolo Migone, M.D., was trained at New York Medical College and is a Fellow of the American Academy of Psychoanalysis. He currently practices in Italy. Via Palestro 14, 43100 Parma, Italy.

> was developed initially in discussions with Pier Francesco Galli and, later on, also with Marianna Bolko, Giambattista Muraro, and Berthold Rothschild. The collaboration with this group in more general areas has been decisive in helping me to identify the specific direction that my research was to pursue.

With this statement in mind, I feel that Codignola's essay is best introduced by first discussing the author amid the cultural atmosphere in which he lived, and by explaining some of the characteristics of the group of analysts to whom he is referring in his acknowledgment. I will then give a brief summary of the book itself, focusing especially on those chapters that do not appear in this translation. Only three chapters, in fact, have been translated: Chapter 1, in which the author introduces his research, and Chapters 4 and 5, which are central to the thesis of the book.

THE AUTHOR AND HIS CULTURAL ENVIRONMENT

Enzo Codignola was born in Genoa, Italy, in 1930. He was graduated from medical school in 1954 and completed his residency in nervous and mental diseases in 1957, at the University of Genoa. In 1960 he went to Kreuzlingen, Switzerland, to work at the Psychiatric Institute "Sanatorium Bellevue," directed by Biswanger, where he stayed for three years and completed his psychiatric and psychotherapeutic training. At the same time, he received his psychoanalytic training in Zurich.

Upon his return to Italy, he entered private practice, while continuing to study and to do research in psychotherapy and psychoanalysis. In 1967, together with other analysts, he founded the quarterly journal *Psicoterapia e Scienze Umane*, of which he was to remain coeditor—with Pier Francesco Galli—until his death. He died, prematurely, in 1977, shortly after the publication of his book on interpretation. Fortunately he was able to finish the essay; however, even though during the writing of the book he did not yet show any signs of his illness, it seems that he wrote it in a hurry, almost knowing that he may not have time enough to complete it. It must be pointed out, on the other hand, that he always intended this book to be only the beginning of a much greater and more elaborate line of research, which he had meant to develop in future years.

The period in which Codignola spent the last and most productive part of his life, from the early 1960s to 1977, was a very intense and stimulating phase in the cultural life of Italy, as well as that of other European countries. The movement of the 1960s, for example, brought about a wave of change in many areas of cultural and intellectual life, and the interest in many disciplines, including psychoanalysis, began to spread as an outgrowth of this wider sociocultural movement. As a matter of fact, the specific area in which Codignola was operating—psychoanalysis, psychotherapy, and the so-called behavioral sciences in general—was still a virgin sector in Italy: the state of psychiatry was very much underdeveloped and rigidly attached to old academic traditions, and psychotherapy was virtually in a primitive state. As we well know, the development and growth of psychoanalysis in Europe occurred in a way very different from that in North America. While in the United States the rapid growth of psychoanalysis reached its boom in the 1950s (and the crisis of the social image of psychoanalysis that we experience now in the United States is surely a reaction to some exaggerated aspects of that boom), in Europe—and particularly in Italy—psychoanalysis became really popular only in the late 1960s. The reason why psychoanalysis in some European countries assumed the characteristics of being "progressive" or somehow culturally provocative at that time was in large part due precisely to the fact that this discipline for decades had to remain outside of the academic establishment and the universities.

All these facts were making it very challenging in those years in Italy to work for the advancement and development of psychotherapy, especially for analysts such as Codignola and others who had been trained abroad (mostly in Switzerland, but some also in the United States). Thus we see this group of analysts—who in the early 1960s had worked together in Milan and had founded the "Gruppo Milanese per lo sviluppo della psicoterapia" (Milan Group for the Advancement of Psychotherapy), and later the journal *Psicoterapia e Scienze Umane*—intervene actively in the Italian situation as an important outside stimulus, for the Italian Psychoanalytic Association as well as other professional organizations, universities, and various public institutions. A particular area of intervention was the improvement in psychological and psychotherapeutic education of mental health professionals, particularly the drive toward an improvement of the training in psychotherapy for psychiatrists, and the training of physicians in the psychological approach to the medical patient. The group included, among others, Marianna Bolko, Enzo Codignola, Pier Francesco Galli, Emanuele Gualandri, Giambattista Muraro, and Berta Neumann.

At this point it is well to acquaint the reader with some of the initiatives taken by members of this group: they organized the first teaching hospital in Italy, as a pilot experiment, to demonstrate the possibility of improving psychiatric training (Gruppo milanese per lo sviluppo della psicoteria, 1966); in 1970 they sponsored the Eighth International Congress of Psychotherapy in Milan (Galli, 1973), as well as several other meetings and conventions; they contributed to the diffusion of many important foreign texts on psychiatry, psychotherapy, and psychoanalysis, by arranging for their translation into Italian and by organizing the publication of important series of books with some of the major publishers in the field; and so forth.

A characteristic of this group was its interest in diversified areas of intervention. For example, this interest was not solely confined to classical psychoanalysis, but also embraced the psychotherapy of psychosis (part of the original group worked with Gaetano Benedetti in Basel on the psychotherapy of psychosis); group and family therapy (the founders of what later evolved into the Milan School of Family Therapy—Selvini-Palazzoli et al.—originally were members of the group); psychotherapeutic work within institutions; the new psychiatric movement toward de-institutionalization; and similar activities.

It was in this environment that Codignola worked and pursued his research. His book *The True and the False: Essay on the Logical Structure of Psychoanalytic Interpretation* may be considered the most important contribution to psychoanalytic theory by an Italian author. It shows not only the author's multidisciplinary perspective, but also his continuous concern with the most theoretical and methodological aspects of psychoanalysis. Codignola tries to place the problem of psychoanalytic interpretation within a wider perspective; for example, he takes into serious consideration authors who are not specifically psychoanalysts, such as Habermas and Lorenzer, but who, in their way, established a bridge between psychoanalysis and other behavioral sciences and philosophy. Codignola's main contribution, however, in his investigation of interpretation is that he took as his starting premise the actual, concrete situation of the psychoanalytic treatment. What he did, in essence, was to link the process of interpretation itself closely to the so-called "setting." The term "setting," which in English has a slightly different meaning (referring largely to the place of the therapy), in the Italian psychoanalytic jargon has assumed the meaning of "set of the ground rules" or "frame" of the therapy: fees, length and frequency of sessions, use of the couch, and so on.

The concept of setting in recent times has grown more and more important in the psychoanalytic literature, to the extent where we may now say that it has become a pivotal point in every discussion of the theory of psychoanalytic technique. Indeed it would almost seem that the place held by interpretation in defining the psychoanalytic method has been taken over by the concept of setting: after the major changes in the recent history of psychoanalytic theory (the change of perspective on the importance of the Oedipus complex, for example), it seems that interpretation has lost its central role in identifying the psychoanalytic method, and many authors now appear to shift toward the concept of the setting—or frame of the therapy—in their search for a new way to define an essential element of the psychoanalytic method. For this reason the work of Codignola is a path-breaking one, as he links the process of interpretation directly to the psychoanalytic setting in a logical structure—and this may open the way to future research.

The concept of setting as a set of ground rules for the therapy seems a very simple one, but indeed, as Langs (1981, p. 429) correctly said, no aspect of the therapeutic experience has proved more controversial or more difficult to conceptualize. This led Lorenzer, for example, to say erroneously in 1973:

> The fact that the analytic setting has only rarely been object of discussion . . . may suggest that it corresponds perfectly to the needs of the psychoanalytic method. (cited by Codignola, 1975b, p. 2)

Many authors have entered into this discussion, but only after the 1950s. Freud, in his five papers on technique (1912a; 1912b; 1913; 1914; 1915), conceived the ground rules simply as a means of establishing a workable therapeutic situation, and a safeguard for the transference. In the years following, there appeared articles in the literature of classical psychoanalysis that basically followed this view. In 1952 Milner tried to extend the conceptualization of the ground rules by likening them to the frame of a painting, which defines the painting and distinguishes it from the world outside. Eissler, in his important 1953 paper, which is a milestone in ego psychology literature, stated that the ground rules may be modified at times, according to the deficits of the patient's ego structure, and under specific conditions. Eissler's pivotal paper, as we will see, is greatly taken into consideration and discussed by Codignola in his essay.

But the line of thought begun by Milner—the metaphor of the ground rules as a frame, with its own functions and qualities—was continued by other authors, many of them of the Kleinian school.

Bleger (1967), for example, spoke of the "psychoanalytic frame" as the setting of the analysis and suggested it is the essential representation of the early mother–child relationship. Langs (1975) also stressed this view and pointed out how sometimes the deviations from the ground rules—or, according to Eissler's term, the introduction of "parameters"—supposedly justified by the condition of the patient's ego, may be countertranference-based, and may have major consequences on the transference.

An important contribution to the study of the analytic setting is the one by Winnicott (1956), who spoke of its holding qualities and functions as a background of safety. Modell (1976), in a paper that shows a noteworthy effort to integrate certain Kleinian contributions into more classical or North American views, elaborated Winnicott's concept of "holding environment" by stressing the object relationship aspects of the therapist's hold. Langs (1978a, 1978b) further elaborated the function of the setting, which is penetrated by fantasy and is an important part of the conscious and unconscious communicative interaction between patient and therapist. In another pivotal study, Bion (1977) formulated the concepts of "container" and "contained" in a setting in which the patient may grow and resolve any intrapsychic and interpersonal conflict.

The authors just mentioned are not, of course, a complete list of those who contributed to the subject of the analytic setting; as a matter of fact, they give only a partial view of this intricate problem. The state of psychoanalytic theory—on both the level of metapsychology and the theory of technique—today is a very complex one, articulated on many different planes and in the context of more or less differing schools.

How does Codignola approach the problem of the setting? As I mentioned earlier, he links the setting to the process of psychoanalytic interpretation, and, more precisely, suggests that it acts as the element that supports the logical structure of interpretation. I shall not go into detail in developing his thesis; the reader will see the unfolding of Codignola's thought through the passages of the chapters that are here published. They are thought-provoking and extremely stimulating.

SUMMARY OF THE BOOK

In Chapter 1 (Psychoanalysis and Interpretation), the author discusses the need on the part of psychoanalysis today to clarify and reaffirm its scientific status; he suggests that among the different theories, terminologies, and areas of application, the original, most solid and stable nucleus of psychoanalysis is to be found in the area of methodology. And within this area, interpretation gives psychoanalysis its most precise identity. The method of interpretation, elaborated by Freud in 1899 in *Interpretation of Dreams* (1900), constituted the crucial moment of departure of Freudian thought, the point of reference of his entire theoretical edifice. Albeit so, the problem of interpretation is a very complex one, which may, for example, involve the realm of philosophy. But even if we see interpretation as a clinical intervention embedded in a theory of technique, it is highly likely that while we are learning, using, and teaching this intervention, we do not necessarily know in depth what interpretation really is. For example, as concerns communication within the profession itself and transmissiblity of the technique of interpretation, Codignola observes that what is being transmitted appears to be a logical structure inherent in the interpretive process, irrespective of whether or not the participants in the transmittal (e.g., teacher and pupil) are aware of this. In fact psychoanalysis is transmitted not simply through the study of the theory, by means of written texts, and so forth, but through direct transmission, which constitutes the typical model of psychoanalytic training.

After considering some of the implications of the two approaches to this problem (a more abstract and philosophical approach as compared with the one that links it to concrete psychoanalytic practice), the author concludes that, in order to understand the essence of psychoanalytic method, namely, interpretation, it is necessary to abandon the idealistic view with which all Freudian hermeneutics are so heavily burdened, and to start from the practical procedure, from the realistic surroundings in which the interpretive process takes place.

In Chapters 2 and 3, Codignola reviews the literature of the major contributions to the problem of interpretation.

The author begins Chapter 2 (Interpretation in Psychoanalysis and Scientific Psychology—Literature on Interpretation, Part 1) by

*For the bibliography pertaining to this summary, please see the References following the three chapters by Codignola.

pointing out that analysts have often spoken about interpretation, but in different contexts: either within the context of technique, or within a more theoretical one. And indeed, to define interpretation is no clear-cut task, because the concept is tightly linked to both the theory of the technique and metapsychology. Ricoeur (1965), for example, shows how difficult it is to discuss interpretations without discussing all of Freud.

Codignola, however, wants to concentrate his study on interpretation as a practical procedure, within the analytic setting. To this end he feels that we have to look closely at two significant moments in Freud's work in which he dealt with this problem: first, in the seventh chapter of *Interpretation of Dreams* (1900), and, so many years later, in *Constructions in Analysis* (1937).

Between 1900 and 1937, Freud developed most of his ideas. Codignola stresses that in *Constructions in Analysis*, Freud concludes that interpreting does not mean merely the decoding of a symbol by the analyst, that it is not simply a "translation." As the author points out, Freud here abandoned his previous attempt at reaching complete factual knowledge, but at the same time rejected the idea of reducing analysis to pure hermeneutics.

In his endeavor to avoid the danger of arbitrary interpretation, Freud tried to link the analytic process to the "cure" of the patient, and to his relationship with the analyst. For example, concerning the interpretation of dreams, he used to say that we always interpret a patient, not a dream. The problem, then, with which Codignola is deeply concerned is the specificity of the interpretive method.

If we consider the definition of interpretation according to Laplanche and Pontalis (1967), we find that interpretation can be understood in two different ways: in a methodological one, which derives from the *Interpretation of Dreams* and which concerns Freudian hermeneutics, and in a clinical one, that is, interpretation as a clinical intervention. This may be an artificial distinction, but it is useful. In fact, if we look at the literature on interpretation, we come across authors who study interpretation in its first meaning, from the viewpoint of a philosophy of science and epistemology (interpretation as a fundamental method of psychoanalysis), and we come across those who study interpretation as a specific clinical intervention, in a concrete psychoanalytical practice.

Codignola first discusses the latter group of authors, then (in Chapter 3) the former group, and states that his own investigation may be considered in the middle between the two.

The group of studies dealing with interpretation as a clinical intervention tries to break up this intervention into different steps, and then to classify these steps. Various "frames of reference" have been used for this classification. Codignola reviews some of these frames of reference by means of the authors who have used them:

1. "Efficacy versus nonefficacy" of interpretation with regard to the therapeutic goals. This frame of reference has been taken into consideration by Strachey (1934) with his concept of "mutative interpretation," which the author discusses.
2. The second frame of reference is "what to interpret"—is it the content, the resistance, the transference, and so on? The "problem of priorities" was the subject of many studies and discussions that began in the 1930s. The authors discussed here are W. Reich (1927, Kaiser (1934), Fenichel (1935, 1941), Menninger (1958), Isaacs (1939), Sandler et al. (1973), and Devereux (1951), among others.
3. The third frame of reference deals with the conceptual difference between interpretation in the narrow sense (*sensu strictiori*) and other interventions, more or less related to it. Some of the authors mentioned here are Sandler et al. (1973), Strachey (1934), Greenson (1967), Eissler (1953), Menninger (1958), and others.
4. A fourth group of authors examines the general logical structure of psychoanalytic interpretation. This group is close to the next group, discussed in Chapter 3, which deals with the more methodological and epistemological aspects of interpretation. Within this fourth group, Codignola mentions the Minnesota Studies on Philosophy of Science, particularly Carnap (1956) and Feigl (1956), and discusses in detail the contributions of two major authors who worked on the subject: Paul (1963), with a more psychoanalytic viewpoint, and Levy (1963), with the viewpoint of scientific psychology. In line with Levy's study, the author also discusses the theory of cognitive dissonance of Festinger (1957).

After having reviewed, in Chapter 2, the literature of the authors who deal with interpretation from a more clinical point of view, Codignola approaches, in Chapter 3 (Contributions to the Theory of Interpretation as a Method—Literature on Interpretation, Part 2), those authors who deal with interpretation from a more methodological and philosophical perspective. Here he chooses to discuss four authors: Rapaport (1960), then Ricoeur (1965), Lorenzer (1973), and Habermas (1968). In reviewing the work of these authors, Codignola offers some critical comments on certain aspects of their contributions, a detailed discussion of which is not feasible within this brief summary. At the end of the chapter, Codignola stresses again the main purpose of his investigation, which is to study the inextricable ties that link interpretation to the concrete psychoanalytic practice.

Chapter 4 (The Psychoanalytic Setting in the Interpretive Process) is wholly devoted to the issue of the psychoanalytic setting, as the author feels that this setting forms an essential component of the logical structure of interpretation, as he will clarify later on. He defines the setting as all those elements within the psychoanalytic situation that are not interpreted, emphasizing that only the deviations from, or violations of, this setting may be interpreted at times. Consequently he includes in the concept of the setting not only the traditionally accepted elements—that is, the realistic, preestablished, contractual conditions under which the analysis proceeds (frequency of sessions, hourly schedule, fees, etc.)—but also, for instance, the roles assumed by the analyst (citing, in this respect, Loch, 1974), since these roles, too, are not interpreted under normal conditions. The author then discusses the fact that the setting thus defined is closely tied to historical-social contexts and may undergo variations in different sectors of applications. In other words he suggests that the setting is more mobile than assumed in the traditional view of it as an ideal, static element whose existence and delineations one may take for granted and forget, as it were.

In looking at the setting in this light, Codignola concludes that there exists between it and the interpretive process a close rapport that is logical and structural in nature, rather than a bond based on banal circumstances. This means that the neat division between setting and interpretive process collapses, or at least that the division must be approached from a completely different angle.

This the author proceeds to do in Chapter 5 (The True and the False), where he suggests that the logical structure of interpretation rests on two poles, which he names the "true" and the "false." Roughly speaking all elements that are interpreted compose the category of the "false," while all elements that are not interpreted compose the category "true," which functions as a frame of reference for the "false" elements. But, and that is his point, there is not necessarily an a priori stipulation as to what belongs into which category; it is, rather, the interpretive process itself that dictates what elements qualify for either.

Citing Eissler (1953) as the first to point out the falsity of the dichotomy between the interpretive process and the concrete elements of the psychoanalytic situation, Codignola takes Eissler's introduction of "parameters" as an example and a point of departure in elaborating his own hypothesis. He argues as follows, for instance: The analyst may introduce a parameter to assuage the patient's anxiety, otherwise the treatment would come to a standstill. This means that the patient's anxiety (or, for that matter, any other datum of analytical diagnosis) may, at a given moment, become an element that is impossible to interpret, but on which, instead, it becomes necessary to act in a concrete, realistic fashion, as on any other presupposed, factual element of the setting. (Let me point out that the author emphasizes that the dissimilar origin of the two elements—here, the psychic state of the patient; there, practical circumstances—is irrelevant. What counts is the way in which they are *treated*.) In other words whenever the needs of the interpretive process demand it, a particular element may have to be shifted from one category to the other.

To sum up, then, the logical structure of interpretation that Codignola hypothesizes consists of two essential components—the "true" and the "false"—which, however, are not to be identified as "setting" versus "process," but which are interlocked in a mobile, interdependent relationship, furthering the aim of the interpretation itself.

The author begins Chapter 6 (Concerning Reality Testing) by restating that the antinomy true/false was not chosen by him at random, but to serve a specific function—to shed light on the logical structure of interpretation. However, as he alerts the reader, there is the risk of its creating ambiguities, confusion, or overlapping with other antinomies, such as that of real versus fantasized, the Freudian antinomy of outer world/inner world, or reality principle/pleasure principle. Here the author raises an important question: What is the relationship between the reality testing concept and the analytic situation? Is reality testing simply a descriptive psychiatric concept, and in that case, would it lie outside of interpretation? It is quite probable that the therapist may see reality testing in analysis in a descriptive or objective way, as, for instance, orientation. In other words what is the place of reality testing within the analytic situation and within the interpretive process? Reality testing is an important element of the structure of interpretation itself. Strachey (1934), for example, said that in the mutative interpretation the patient becomes aware of the distinction between the fantasy object and the real object.

The reality of the outside world enters into analysis via the person of the analyst, the elements of the setting, and the roles, all of which are accepted and bilaterally validated by both partners in the analytic relationship. It may seem that the analyst deals only with the symbolic, the interpretable—in other words, that the analytic work is encompassed in the realm of the "false." But this is only apparently so. The fact is that the "true" is always present, for the imputation of a meaning derives only from its logical interlock with the true elements; otherwise psychoanalytic interpretation would become an arbitrary, and potentially authoritarian, operation. As the author points out, there is always the risk of using the transference to "brainwash" the patient with a psychoanalytic ideology, to force the patient to accept a dogma.

In conclusion Codignola reiterates his contention that psychoanalytic interpretation is strictly linked in a logical structure with the elements that surround the analytic situation (the setting, the ground rules), and that only in this situation is it possible to verify the validity of interpretation. Outside of analysis (for example, in applied psychoanalysis, in interpretations of social, political, cultural, or anthropological phenomena) it is certainly possible to make use of psychoanalytic theory to make propositions. However, unless we respect the specificity of its interpretive method, an obvious danger must be borne in mind: that psychoanalysis may become the banal undertaking of imputing abstract meanings.

In Chapter 7 (Remaining Problems) Codignola draws some conclusions from his work, while positing some remaining problems. He stresses again that his essay has tried to deal with the problem of the logical structure of psychoanalytic interpretation not from an abstract or ideal perspective, but from a practical one, that is, the analytic situation. The whole analytic procedure has been seen as a complex of operations basically contingent upon interpretation. This point of view, coherent with that of many other authors, allows us to see the connections between method and technique. Only if we approach interpretation from this perspective will it be possible to render some remaining problems visible and to embark on their further exploration. The problems are, among others: the issue of the relation between the analytic setting and the analytic method, which is still relatively unexplored, especially regarding the attempts to apply alternative psychoanalytic techniques; the problem of the "search for truth" in analysis, with regard to psychoanalytic determinism (there have been many studies on this subject, but mostly from an abstract and theoretical point of view); or the problem of the relation between psychoanalytic technique and metapsychological theory. Such explorations, Codignola feels, are indispensable for psychoanalysis today.

REFERENCES

Ancona, A. (1979). Introduction to a discussion on E. Codignola's essay, "The true and the false." *Psicoterapia e Scienze Umane*, 2:62–66.

Bion, W. (1977). *Seven Servants*. New York: Jason Aronson.

Bleger, J. (1967). Psychoanalysis of the psychoanalytic frame. *Int. J. Psychoanal.*, 48:511–519.

Bolko, M. (1979). Introduction to a discussion on E. Codignola's essay, "The true and the false." *Psicoterapia e Scienze Umane*, 2:66–69.

Codignola, E. (1971). Formazione e funzione culturale nelle scienze umane. *Psicoterapia e Scienze Umane*, 1:1.

——— (1972). Appunti sull'interpretazione. *Psicoterapia e Scienze Umane*, 1/2:1.

——— (1975a). Nota sulla relazione d'oggetto e la costituzione dell' io. In *Amore Oggettuale e Realtà*, A. H. Modell. Turin: Boringhieri, pp. IX–XVI. (Introduction to the Italian translation of A. H. Modell, *Object Love and Reality*. New York: International Universities Press. Reprinted in *Psicoterapia e Scienze Umane*, 1975, 1:1–3.)

——— (1975b). Una metateoria? Nota su Lorenzer. *Psicoterapia e Scienze Umane*, 4:1–2.

——— (1977). *Il Vero e Il Falso: Saggio sulla Struttura Logica dell'Interpretazione Psicoanalitica*. Turin: Boringhieri. (English translation of Chapters 1, 4, and 5 in this volume.)

——— (1978). 23 settembre 1930–10 ottobre 1977. *Psicoterapia e Scienze Umane*, 1:1–3.

———, Galli, P. F. (1977). Modelli concettuali e pratica della istituzione psicoanalitica. In *Il Modello Concettuale della Psicoanalisi*, D. Rapaport. Milan: Feltrinelli, pp. VII–XIV. (Introduction to the Italian translation of *Collected Papers of David Rapaport*. New York: Basic Books, 1967.)

Eissler, K. R. (1953). The effect of the structure of the ego on psychoanalytic technique. *J. Amer. Psychoanal. Assn.*, 1:104–143.

Freud, S. (1912a). The dynamic of transference. *Standard Edition*, 12:97–108.

——— (1912b). Recommendations to physicians practicing psychoanalysis. *Standard Edition*, 12:111–120.

——— (1913). On beginning of the treatment (further recommendations on the technique of psychoanalysis, I). *Standard Edition*, 12:121–144.

——— (1914). Remembering, repeating, and working-through (further recommendations on the technique of psychoanalysis, II). *Standard Edition*, 12:145–156.

——— (1915). Observations on transference-love (further recommendations on the technique of psychoanalysis, III). *Standard Edition*, 12:157–171.

Galli, P. F., ed. (1973). *Psicoterapia e Scienze Umane. Atti dell'VII^mo Congresso Internazionale di Psicoterapia*. Milan: Feltrinelli.

Gruppo Milanese per lo Sviluppo della Psicoterapia (1966). La formazione degli psichiatri nella situazione italiana. In *La Psicoterapia in Italia. La Formazione degli Psichiatri*. Milan: Centro Studi di Psicoterapia Clinica, 1967, pp. 101–136.

——— (1967). *La Psicoterapia in Italia. La Formazione degli Psichiatri. Contributi*

di Balint, Benedetti, Cremerius, Galli, Müller, et al. Milan: Centro Studi di Psicoterapia Clinica.
Langs, R. (1975). The therapeutic relationship and deviations in technique. *Int. J. Psychoanal. Psychother.*, 4:106–141.
——— (1978a). Interventions in the bipersonal field. In *Technique in Transition*. New York: Jason Aronson.
——— (1978b). The adaptational-interactional dimension of countertransference. In *Technique in Transition*. New York: Jason Aronson.
———, ed. (1981). *Classics in Psychoanalytic Technique*. New York: Jason Aronson.
Lorenzer, A. (1973). *Über den Gegenstand der Psychoanalyse, oder: Sprache und Interaktion*. Frankfurt: Suhrkamp.
Milner, M. (1952). Aspects of symbolism in the comprehension of the not-self. *Int. J. Psychoanal.*, 33:181–195.
Modell, A. H. (1976). The "holding environment" and the therapeutic action of psychoanalysis. *J. Amer. Psychoanal. Assn.*, 24:285–308.
Redazione di Psicoterapia e Scienze Umane (1975). Psicoanalisi e psicoanalisti. *Psicoterapia e Scienze Umane*, 4:20–31.
Winnicott, D. (1956). On transference. In *Collected Papers*. London: Tavistock Publications, 1958.

Translation

CHAPTER 1
Psychoanalysis and Interpretation

Within the past two decades, the cultural and operative horizon of the so-called behavioral sciences has changed drastically, and in the midst of these changes, the debate of psychoanalysis has taken on new directions as well. For example, we are today recognizing more and more that linkages are possible, on various planes, between the new ideas existing in psychiatry and psychology on the one hand, and psychoanalysis on the other. Thus we are witnessing a growing tendency to discuss psychoanalysis not so much on the basis of various theoretical hypotheses as, rather, on the basis of its methodology. This, of course, was inevitable, for the debate on whether or not psychoanalysis can be applied in situations other than the traditional ones was bound to lead eventually to a reexamination of the method involved, it being an indivisible part of the whole theoretical-practical structure of psychoanalysis. Now, if in the course of such a reexamination we seek to protect a certain scientific rigor, we must, in turn, eventually arrive at the search for a clearer definition of what exactly it is that is to be protected. The theory is less in need of such protection; for, as Lorenzer (1970, p. 9) states:

> The most important theoretical issues—as for example the role of infantile sexuality or the existence of unconscious contents—have been widely recognized and have, to a considerable degree, even become part of the common domain. Today's oppositions and . . . discussions are far more concerned with the systematic classification of psychoanalysis as a science and a therapy.[1]

As we see, an old issue has emerged once again. As psychoanalysis has been called upon to account for itself in more specific terms and within more specific contexts, it has become evermore pressing to reaffirm and clarify its scientific status. Beyond that which Habermas has called the "scientistic self-misunderstanding" of psychoanalysis (Habermas 1971, p. 246), there are still certain claims awaiting clarification. A discussion of metapsychological theories could be extended to include the most recent developments and could also bring to light the mutual incompatibility between certain individual hypotheses as compared to others.[2] We are also witnessing today the formation of scientific languages that, although departing from a common matrix, have become so differentiated as to appear totally separated from one another—a case in point, for instance, is the diverse developmental theories in psychoanalysis. Yet, if we trace the problem back to its very roots, it becomes obvious—as researches of a philosophical nature have shown—that the original, most stable

[1]Actually, in recent years German members of the profession have been particularly sensitive to the attacks on and criticism of psychoanalysis that arose in the wake of the students' movement of 1968. Lorenzer himself (1970, p. 15) cites that movement as the incentive for his own interest in the discussion of psychoanalytic theory. A discourse on the criticisms of psychoanalysis stemming from various sources is also offered by Horn (1974). Contributions to the subject, if perhaps not as systematic and strictly defined as the German ones, have appeared also in other European countries. Certain issues were dealt with in a debate published by the Psychoanalytisches Seminar Zürich in Switzerland, including contributions by P. F. Galli, B. Rothschild, and myself (Codignola et al., 1974).

[2]With regard to this issue, see my introduction (1975a) to the Italian translation of A. H. Modell's *Object Love and Reality* (Turin: Boringhieri, 1975).

and solid nucleus of psychoanalysis is to be found in the area of methodology. The experiences of recent years have taught us that psychoanalysis may be approached from various points of view; but even if we choose the most banal viewpoint—that is, the applicability of its therapeutic technique in one sector of work or another—the one issue that is indispensable (or should be regarded as such) continues to remain the same: the method.

Within the area of methodology, it is the structure of interpretation that bestows on psychoanalysis its most rigorous identity. We must therefore study the interpretive process—understood as the modes, the criteria, the characteristics of interpretation—if we want to grasp the fundamentals of the scientific legitimacy of psychoanalysis, and the keystone of its structure as a theory and a therapy. This idea, of course, does not originate with me: we need but recall Ricoeur, the author who developed it at greatest length, as well as other psychoanalysts who have confirmed it in isolated instances. But there exists an even older, and certainly more original source: Freud himself. There are frequent statements in Freud's work on the provisory status of all the metapsychological hypotheses he was developing (not to mention the anthropological ones). He maintains that each one of them may have to be revised, corrected, or modified; and we know how often he did just that. But there is one element that Freud elaborates only once—namely, in the *Interpretation of Dreams* (1900)—and that is the method of interpretation. From that moment on, this method would remain unaltered throughout and was to constitute the point of reference for his entire theoretical edifice, in the sense that he used it for constructing, criticizing, and restating every successive hypothesis. To do this, as it happens, Freud availed himself of clinical observation; but it is clear that this does not imply "objective" observation, but the use of data recovered from the analytical situation—in other words, data already "treated" by the interpretive process. And as the discussions on the scientific structure of psychoanalysis have demonstrated abundantly,[3] the lack of "objectivity" of such data, far from constituting a reason for doubting their demonstrative and evidential efficacy, is instead embedded in the very nature of the theory, in that it is a psychological theory; as such, the theory has the right to claim a position *sui generis*, so to speak, among scientific theories. It has also been shown[3] that the

[3]Many authors could be cited in this respect; all in all, it is perhaps best exemplified by the arguments developed by H. Feigl (1956) and R. Carnap (1956) in the well-known *Minnesota Studies in the Philosophy of Science*, and, of course, by D. Rapaport, especially in his *Structure of Psychoanalytic Theory* (1960).

scientific verification of the use of interpretation as a source of "observables" is to be sought within the internal coherence of the theoretical system rather than in the claim to a naturalistic neutrality of the observation itself. Thus, in reality, interpretation is the most coherent instrument of observation at the disposal of the analyst and, at the same time, the analyst's therapeutic agent *par excellence*. In this sense interpretation constitutes the hinge that links, and operates on, the two members of the psychoanalytic structure—the theoretical-epistemological one and the clinical-applicative one.

After Freud, practically every psychoanalyst has been guided by these criteria, if perhaps not always with full awareness. It is noteworthy, for instance, that Anna Freud (1965, p. 22 ff.) makes a point of distinguishing among the ego functions some that she finds assessable (in their development) *also* through objective observation, thereby confirming that these cases are in some way exceptions to the general rule of analytic observation. At present there are but a few analysts who still insist in the use of "direct observation" of the child to confirm their hypotheses.[4] One may take exception to this, however, on the grounds that the behavioral patterns of the child, in order to be usable in psychoanalytic reasoning, must be recorded in specific ways. That is to say, one must accomplish that transcription of language, from ordinary to theoretical language, which Levy[5] describes as a part of interpretation. What this means, once again, is that data are being used that have already been treated by interpretation, not raw, so to speak "objective" data. And if this were not so, after all, psychoanalysis would become a science of objective truth in psychology—something, that is, which since Freud and ever after it has never sought to be.

If, on the other hand, we expand our horizon to an overall view of Freudian thought, we find that it was precisely the structure and physiognomy of his interpretive method that formed Freud's first point of differentiation. In other words, what constituted the identity

[4]I am referring to the movement that arose out of the publications of *The Psychoanalytic Study of the Child*: the intention that had originally fostered these studies—in itself irreproachable—seems to me to have been exaggerated by some analysts, especially those of the Kleinian school, who insist that the "direct" observation of the child may be brought in as evidence for the hypotheses developed by them. In my opinion the scientific legitimacy of such hypotheses is not refuted by the fact that a "pure" or direct observation of the child is obviously impossible in psychoanalysis. The question here is simply to discuss a possible error in the method.

[5]Levy's work (1963) is discussed in greater detail in Chapter 2 [not translated here—*translator's note*].

of psychoanalysis as compared to the ideas prevailing at Freud's time was not so much the progressive construction of the theory as rather the early establishment of this method. In this sense Ricoeur relates Freud to Nietzsche and Marx:

> If we go back to the intention they had in common, we find in it the decision to look upon the whole of consciousness primarily as "false" consciousness . . . The Philosopher trained in the school of Descartes knows that things are doubtful, that they are not such as they appear; but he does not doubt that consciousness is such as it appears to itself; in consciousness, meaning and consciousness of meaning coincide. Since Marx, Nietzsche, and Freud, this too has become doubtful. After the doubt about things, we have started to doubt consciousness. (Ricoeur, 1970, p. 33)

And again, further on:

> Thus the distinguishing characteristic of Marx, Freud, and Nietzsche is the general hypothesis concerning both the process of false consciousness and the method of deciphering. The two go together. . . . (Ibid., p. 34)

We shall return to the thoughts of the French master later on; he is quoted here because in those passages he confirms the primacy of psychoanalytic interpretation also on the historical plane, and shows that it was indeed this interpretation which, as mentioned before, constituted the crucial moment of differentiation of Freudian thought. Ricoeur thereafter concentrates on a comparison between Freudian and other possible types of interpretation; he examines closely the "conflict of interpretations" and, finally, discusses psychoanalysis in strictly hermeneutic terms, as a decipherment of the symbol. All this, it seems to me, concerns the philosophical problem in which Ricoeur is interested, and it diverges, at least in part, from the subject here proposed. For Ricoeur, also the study of psychoanalytic hermeneutics (which inevitably ends up being a study on Freud as a whole) evolves on strictly theoretic planes. It is indeed the theory that is the true object of his research. However, to arrive at an understanding of the internal, concrete logic of psychoanalytic interpretation is possible only if we start from the specific, that is, from the practical procedure involved. The philosophical works of recent years have shown that the route toward a perception of the methodological nucleus of psychoanalysis passes through the study of interpretation. It therefore becomes necessary now to place the problem within its own, very specific and concrete frame. But what happens, in actual fact, when a method that has constituted such a momentous instance in Western culture is found to be embedded in its practice? Up to which point does its structure remain recognizable; at which point does it instead get lost in the thicket of technical precepts? The study of interpretation, that much is clear, may serve to make comprehensible not so much that which psychoanalysis is claiming, but rather the characteristic manner in which it is treating things; and it is precisely in the latter sphere that obscure areas seem to persist. Since the analyst does indeed interpret, one often acts as though it could be taken for granted that the operation is known in all its elements, its internal logic, and the course that it follows. But a closer inspection is likely to reveal that this may very well be a false conclusion: doing something does not necessarily mean having a thorough knowledge of the logical structure of that which is being done.

Clinical psychoanalysis is amply studied and discussed today. Numerous are the contributions on particular aspects of technique and metapsychology, presented with examples from clinical situations. The same cannot be said about issues concerning the method, above all that of interpretation; the many years of psychoanalytic literature yield a rather scant amount of research dedicated to this subject, as we shall see in the chapters following.* If such scarcity is, in fact, a manifestation of the general belief that the physiognomy of the psychoanalytic operation may be accepted as a known factor, let us call to mind that now, as much as ever, certain problems persist that would belie such a belief. If we want to approach these problems, we might begin by discussing the question of communication within the profession itself.

One often hears—in seminars, for instance—that it is factually impossible to reconstruct exactly what occurs in a clinical situation. The variables at play are too numerous, ranging from the analyst's countertransference upon the patient as well as upon colleagues, to other sources of resistance. Other variables concern the diversity of theoretical positions, the differing ways of conceiving or describing one and the same phenomenon, and so forth; and this happens even within homogeneous professional groups. In sum we are faced here with a complex problem: the mutual exchange and elaboration of information that is scientifically coherent and, by preserving an appropriate rigor, thus usable in practice. And it seems that such an

**Translator's note*: This refers to Chapters 2 and 3, not translated here; see summary in the introduction by Paolo Migone.

exchange is encountering continuous difficulties. Yet, and this is an interesting fact, it has been observed that points of consensus and collective verification are actually being reached with relative ease, especially in a situation where practical action is involved. In professional circles this fact is usually considered the resultant of certain group dynamics, in the sense that the emergence of a leader ensures the group's rallying around the line of thought advocated by that leader.

Factors of this kind are doubtless at work; still, the feeling remains that they do not completely elucidate the problem. It is a noted fact that a consensus is reached more easily among analysts of experience than among the younger ones, and that the homogeneity of theoretical views appears to be a variable of relatively minor importance. On the other hand, one cannot simply reduce the whole problem to a question of experience; in reaching a consensus, even in seemingly chaotic psychoanalytical discussions, the paths that are being followed are more elusive. It is as though everyone felt that a point of collective reassurance exists, while no one succeeded in identifying it with sufficient clarity. There are, of course, attempts to localize it within metapsychology. But such attempts often lead to no more than an ideological use of metapsychology itself, serving the cohesion of one group or another. This often happens, for example, with certain "schools of thought" that in reality represent local groups of analysts and an established model of exercising professional power in the particular area. But quite aside from such reflections, it is precisely the attempt to unite around the theory of metapsychology that is destined to fail in the end, if for no other reason than that the need for a dialectic is inherent in that part of psychoanalysis. After all, a total unity of thought around a "definitive" metapsychology would be tantamount to the claim on the part of psychoanalysts to have arrived at the ultimate anthropological truth; but this would be a flagrant contradiction of the very foundations of the psychoanalytic method. What other solution is available? Within recent years, various attempts have been made—including through the study of the literature—to find a solution within the sphere of the technique. The object of such researches into the technique was perhaps to counteract certain centrifugal tendencies—spawned by the growing expansion of the discipline—by positing some fixed points of universal value; the fact that many more manuals on analytic technique have been published within the past decade than during any previous ones[6] may very well be evidence of that assumption. And yet it seems

[6]Let me but mention at random that the texts by Racker (1958), Menninger (1958), and Greenson (1967) all appeared within the short span of a few years.

that when an author writes a text of this type, when he tries to establish once and for all what psychoanalysis is to be for everyone—at least on a technical level—he succeeds merely in rekindling the most ardent polemics (like the ones that ensued after the appearance of the work by Greenson, 1967); and the more precise the elaboration, the more minute the codification in such discourses, the more violent do these polemics become. Time ago Eissler (1953) had argued that the gap between metapsychology and technique was still very wide and far from being bridged; it appears that his argument is still valid today, considering the discord that exists on certain levels.

To recapitulate, then, one may uphold the belief that all analysts are doing, or should be doing, the same things; but understanding exactly what these things are is another matter. As we have seen, it is extremely difficult to track down a common denominator within the area of metapsychology and, even more so, in the field of the technique alone. But there is another path, less beaten but for all that no less promising.

It is quite possible that, all the predicaments notwithstanding, a true point of consensus does exist, and is in fact active, as it were, but that it has not yet been satisfactorily conceptualized. That is to say, it is possible that something is being made use of even while it cannot be clearly distinguished. Perhaps the nucleus in which theory and practice are united, and with which every analyst seeks to identify, has not been made sufficiently explicit with regard to its internal structure. And it may be this lack of a thorough explicitness that constitutes the ambiguity in the whole argument.

Let us, therefore, approach the problem from the point of view of the transmissibility of psychoanalysis as a practical procedure among the members of the profession. It is well known that there are essentially two ways in which psychoanalytic skill is passed on: one, through the study of the theory—that is, the texts; and two, through direct transmission, which includes the passing on of knowledge from artisan to apprentice, as well as the exchange of knowledge among analysts in general. The second way is the one that is discussed most extensively, the reason being, among others, that it constitutes the typical model of psychoanalytic training, and because it is founded on a specific—namely, psychoanalytic—view of the cognitive activity. In other words the direct transmission is an operation that takes into account the psychoanalytical theory of cognitive activity and exploits it for the purpose of elaborating as well as transmitting certain information. But what is it specifically that is being transmitted? It certainly is not metapsychological theory—for that, there are abundant texts available for study. Neither is it, in a certain sense, the theory of technique, nor the technique in its details—for these, too, textbooks exist for easy consultation. Perhaps, then, we should ask the question differently: What exactly is it that causes the need for a direct transmission? This need, as it happens, arises not merely from considerations regarding cognitive activity, but also from the fact that it is *exclusively* the logical structure of the interpretive process that is being transmitted, regardless of whether the participants in the transmittal (for instance, teacher and pupil) are aware of this or not. And this logical structure has obviously not been conceptualized clearly enough to be treated in a textbook. Thus, in effect, it is held that the interpretive process cannot be passed on by any other means than that of craftsmanship, the typical example of which is the psychoanalytic training.

In explaining this phenomenon, the idea of inexpressibility is usually invoked (for instance, interpretation is said to be an "art," and therefore not teachable by common methods). But what is at work here, more likely, is that interpretation is being discussed as a process, while no one is succeeding in establishing a cognitively viable concept of the process itself. We teach, we transmit, we learn how to interpret, and, to a great extent, we continue to be unaware of what psychoanalytic interpretation really is. To be sure, during training, the rudiments of a technique of deciphering symbols are being provided. But a more generalized conceptualization of the issue of interpretation, when it is attempted, immediately becomes an operation in abstracts. As much as one may resort to particular concepts in an attempt to make the process comprehensible (for example, the relationship between interpretation and transference, the evolution of interpretation that accompanies the development of the analysis, the "clinical judgment" as an instrument for obtaining concrete contexts, and so forth), something continues to be elusive. And the impression remains that the logical nucleus of interpretation is not clear, even though we know how to pass it on to others. During seminars and discussions, one invariably has the feeling that the discourse revolves around a secret, yet characteristic and irreplaceable core. But the secret may not lie so much in something that is deliberately concealed, but rather in the obscurity in which the logical-operational nucleus of interpretation is still enshrouded.

This obscurity is recognized by Menninger (1958, p. 129), for example, when he writes that speaking of interpretation in analysis means using a "rather presumptuous term," and it is no coincidence that he points out the risk "young analysts" may run of considering themselves "oracles, . . . wizards, . . . linguists . . . [or] great wise men" (and, one might ask, is this not perhaps equally true even in the case of the older analyst?). But why is the act of interpreting immediately linked to magic, and why does it so readily evoke illusions of omnipotence? Again, this is possible only because of the lack of an adequately defined and conceptualized system of interpretation itself.

On the other hand, it must be admitted that we are confronted with a difficult set of problems. Faced with these problems, many have stopped short along the way and have escaped into vagueness or romanticism (like those who insist in the "art" of interpreting, or in making use of their own unconscious).[7] Few have succeeded in advancing beyond the first steps, and it is not by chance that their treatises immediately became classic texts. The subject is a complex one, and it is easy to wander off into spheres that are not strictly pertinent to psychoanalysis. To speak of interpretation may mean, for example, seeking to establish what interpretation *is*; but that is a task for the language philosopher. In trying to understand why it works, the question, also with regard to its anthropological implications, embraces so widespread a sphere that psychoanalysis can make no claim to finding an answer.

It is, therefore, necessary that we demarcate the area of investigation. If we want to start from the premise of the practical procedure, we must seek to comprehend above all the realistic surroundings in which the interpretive process takes place, and the specific modalities of its execution, all the while keeping in mind the characteristics peculiar to the psychoanalytic interpretation. If we succeed in advancing a few steps in that direction, the task of future researchers sharing this orientation will be greatly facilitated. A vision thus oriented could begin by shedding that idealistic ballast with which the concept of psychoanalytic interpretation, and, in more general terms, all of Freudian hermeneutics, is so heavily burdened. As a matter of fact, one often notices the misgivings that certain of the traditional views of these concepts are causing in the minds of some analysts; yet it is not easy to recognize what the error in perspective rests in, not to mention demonstrate it. For years we have been accustomed to considering these methodological aspects an untouchable inheritance, discovered by the genius of Freud and known only to some

[7]Discourses on the "art" of interpreting appear in numerous texts of various origins. Regarding the use of the analyst's own unconscious as a therapeutic tool, see reference to Susan Isaacs (1939) in Chapter 2 [not translated here—*translator's note*].

erudite philosophers or linguists. The analyst often succeeds only in employing the tools that were handed down, without ever touching on these methodological foundations; beyond that both the psychoanalytic technique and metapsychology provide sufficient justification to practice the craft. But the theory as such offers no foothold that would allow the freeing of the concept of interpretation from the encrustations of the ideas of the Enlightenment, nor from the idealistic, distorting views to which it has often been subjugated. In reality the idealistic view—to which I shall return later for a more detailed discussion—does not stand up to clinical verification; interpretation is not, as is often suggested, a "pure" operation that develops under ideal, abstract conditions.

But if things are not what they seem to be—above all, if interpretation does not function in the way it is often believed and taught—what is it then that is going on? What are the logical operations that determine the act of interpreting, and what sphere do they embrace—the symbolical one, or perhaps a sphere of which the symbolic is only one part? What are the mental workings that involve both analyst and patient during the interpretive process, when they are not imagined in ideal terms but reduced to the actual modes of expression? This is the area of research to which the present essay wants to address itself. My contribution will only be a partial one, but that does not diminish the importance of the problem as such. I believe the time has come to open up a perspective different from those implied in many previous studies. Given that the psychoanalytic method is certainly not of an idealistic cast, and given its internal dialectics, it seems to me that such an effort is to be encouraged.

Many of the issues I have touched upon have been the subject of previous researches. Other studies on interpretation in psychoanalysis have cleared up certain problems. In the following chapters,* I shall discuss the most important contributions that have appeared so far. In this chapter I have tried to present the reasons for this study and the directions it will take, but it is only by examining the more precisely drawn horizons provided by the existing literature that these reasons and directions will become clearly visible.

**Translator's note*: This refers to Chapters 2 and 3, not translated here.

CHAPTER 4
*The Setting in the Interpretive Process**

One of the most basic material components of the analytical situation, in my opinion, is that which goes under the name of *setting*; that is, the sum of all the realistic conditions under which analysis takes place. If these conditions are treated as a fixed entity—as is done in certain traditional literature—whose sole function is to aid the method, then the setting is rendered abstract. Consequently, also the method—interpretation—is inevitably treated as an abstract operation, which evolves within an ambit that is invariable and ahistoric—namely, a setting that has been preestablished once and for all. Certainly it is convenient to work on the basis of such a "pure" image of psychoanalytic practice: everything is clear-cut and positive, and the analyst is but the methodical interpreter of a text that is presented to him within a uniform and neutral environment. In my opinion it seems evident that this view is idealistic in character in more senses than one. Even if this assumption is only roughly sketched out here, it appears to me that it does present the elements for a critical examination of certain accepted concepts of analytical practice. Since, as I assert, the setting is of crucial importance to the interpretive process within that practice, such an examination must begin by trying to establish a more practicable definition of the concept of setting.

The setting is rarely the subject of discussion. It appears mostly in studies on technique, and then almost solely for the purpose of stressing the importance of observing the stability of the setting, and of intervening analytically when attempts are made to disrupt it. As we know such attempts on the part of the patient may range over a vast array of possibilities. The patient may demand that the analyst modify the initial "pact" with regard to its contractual conditions, which he or she wants to be more flexible, or may argue about the schedule of appointments, say, or the payment of fees, or other agreements of that type. Or else the patient may simply not observe those agreements, as in the classic case of coming late for sessions;

**Translator's note*: The first paragraph of this chapter as it appears here is actually a passage from Chapter 3 in the Italian original. Since the author at the beginning of the present chapter refers to that passage, I thought it necessary to include it in this chapter. Because of the omission of Chapters 2 and 3, other editorial changes had to be made, but they are unimportant for the thesis of the book and will not be mentioned specifically.

on the other hand, the patient may cathect elements of the setting rather than the analytical process, as in the case of obsessive ritualization of the formal procedures of the analysis, and so forth. In these cases the analyst must bring those of the patient's demands which on occasion seem to hide an "ulterior" need back into the orbit of the analysis—that is, of interpretation. By proceeding in this way—as both the theory of technique and clinical experience are teaching us—it is almost always possible to uncover certain current conflicts in the patient, which, depending on the specific transference situation of the moment, find their expression in one of the manners mentioned.

Thus at first glance it seems that we may define the setting exclusively in terms of the concrete working agreement between patient and analyst; in other words, it would be no more than the sum of the conditions of contract, clearly stipulated at the beginning and to be upheld for the entire duration of the analysis (as an example, see the discourse on the analytical contract by Menninger, 1958, Chapter II). However, the term "setting" does not point so much to the contractual aspects as to the physical circumstances of the therapeutic situation (appointment schedule, length of sessions, fees, the analysand's position on the couch, and so forth). These circumstances, inasmuch as they are elements of the "ideal" analytic situation, should stay perfectly uniform throughout the duration of the treatment. We know, however, that it is never as simple as that. Indeed the uniformity of the setting, be it from one analysis to another or within one particular case, is a desired goal rather than a reality; or at least it is not so obvious and invariable a reality as to allow us to forget about it, so to speak. On the other hand, to the extent that we seek to analyze each single deviation from the postulated setting, we are turning the setting into a sort of analytical rule. The deviation is considered indispensable by most analysts for permitting the flow of free associations on the part of the patient.[1] There is a contradiction here. On the one hand, we are suggesting that the patient be allowed the greatest possible freedom, for the purpose of fostering the play of associations; on the other hand, we confine the patient to a frame of rigidly stipulated boundaries, and we interpret (basically as something deviant) any variation the patient tries to introduce. Yet, in

[1]Among the numerous authors who support this view let me but mention the classic work by Fenichel, *The Psychoanalytic Theory of Neurosis* (1945). As is well known, Fenichel offers a meticulous investigation into the metapsychological justification of psychoanalytic technique. An original treatment of the method of free association is that by Hermann (1934).

spite of this contradiction, the analyst knows that a clear and stable setting is indeed necessary. But such a necessity cannot possibly arise merely out of a regard for convenience, or for practical reasons. If we see the setting only as a body of contractual conditions, it does not reveal all of its importance for the analytical process; the setting also acts as a basic frame of reference on the cognitive plane. If the analyst realizes that he or she is no longer able to interpret the patient's "acting out" toward the elements of the setting, there is no other choice but to interrupt the analysis, precisely because the cognitive activity that characterizes the analysis itself is no longer possible.

I have chosen an extreme example, not a typical one (as a matter of fact, situations of this type are being handled in various ways—for instance, by introducing "parameters," to use a term coined by Eissler, which will be discussed in the following chapter). Still, the example is useful for obtaining a more precise definition of setting. This definition not only must take into account the agreement or contract that makes the encounters between patient and analyst practicable and regulates them conveniently, but also must do justice to the setting's role as a frame of reference with specific cognitive functions. However, not even these functions may be posited as the setting's defining criteria, since the institution of the setting does not serve this purpose exclusively.

To determine what it is that all the elements of the setting have in common, we must, in my opinion, turn our attention back to the analytical process. Within this process these elements may be defined above all in a negative way; that is to say, by clarifying what they do not participate in. While it is true that they represent the material aspect of the analytical situation and are indispensable for its existence, and while they do perform certain functions within interpretation (as points of reference), their foremost characteristic is that they are excluded from the analytical activity true and proper—that is, from interpretation. In other words, they are things that are not interpretable, and that is the only criterion by which the elements of the setting may be defined exclusively. They are treated as extra-analytical facts.

In the traditional view of the setting, all this is considered as taken for granted. One acts as though the analytical process were connected with the setting merely through fixed and, in a certain way, negligible ties. The setting is seen as a preestablished and static framework. If anything, as we have seen, it is the deviations from this frame that are worked upon analytically, for they leave the frame proper (which is posited as one and the same throughout) and enter the realm of interpretation.

A good example of this view is the dispute among those who support the idea that the analyst should "conceal himself," and those who advocate the theory that the analyst should "reveal himself." Both positions have had their staunch supporters, as we know, and the argument involves directly the issue of the setting. Meltzer (1967), for instance, in arguing that analysis is a "search for the truth," claims the following:

> In order for this search for the truth about the patient's mind to proceed, it is necessary that the setting should minimize those interferences with the unfolding and elaboration of his transference such as would be caused by the intrusion of external realities upon the setting. Common sense would predict that this was impossible as regards the age, sex, appearance and character of the analyst. (p. xii)

The justified aim of not wanting to disturb the unfolding of transference drives Meltzer, as we see, to the point of desiring that analysts conceal themselves as much as possible from the eyes of their patients. To him it seems already a disadvantage that the patient knows the sex and age of the analyst. Others assume the opposite position, arguing that it is desirable that the analyst "reveal himself." But both sides, as this example clearly demonstrates, consider analysis a kind of completely abstract situation, in which it is possible to search for the psychological "truth" without taking into account its ties with the so-called "external reality." This implies, then, that it is possible for analysts to decide whether to conceal themselves, or to what extent to reveal themselves, to the patient—until one arrives at the blatant absurdity of prescribing, as does Meltzer, simple demeanors and clothing (p. xiii). In looking at things realistically, it is obvious in any case that the patient possesses all kinds of information about the analyst, regardless of the latter's decision. The point thus is not whether to conceal oneself from the patient—which remains a pious hope anyway—nor whether to reveal oneself—which is a disputable undertaking in regard to the analysis itself (for the analyst's problems obviously have no business in the analysis). The issue must be assessed differently. Inasmuch as the patient's curiosity, as we have said, may be satisfied no matter what the analyst's decision (even the analyst's endeavor to create an anonymous setting may offer precious information to the patient; what it might signify to the patient is anybody's guess), the point to be discussed is how to handle analytically any possible probing forays on the part of the patient, or the use of information about the analyst. To act differently, on the part of the analyst, would mean ignoring certain signs the patient is giving and which are connected with the patient's desire to gain knowledge; a desire, by the way, that may reveal important conflicts and is connected to the "real" elements of the analytical situation (but then, what behavior on the part of the patient is not so connected?).

To return to the problems implicit in the traditional view of the setting, they may be summarized as follows: (1) Seen as a fixed and negligible element, the setting becomes abstract and untouchable; this is indeed the attitude held by many analysts. The setting, namely that described by Freud, has never again been revised on the theoretic plane, but has always been tacitly considered the absolute optimum for the correct development of the analytic process. (2) This fact proved to be a momentous obstacle at the moment that psychoanalysis began to expand its field of action. The advent of the treatment of psychoses, for instance, forced analysts to modify the setting; in doing so, however, they preferred to speak of a "psychoanalytically oriented psychotherapy," or use other circumlocutions, rather than speak of analysis in a nontraditional setting. (3) Psychoanalysis thus became enclosed in a narrow confine that was in contradiction with its very possibilities. I realize, of course, that all this did not happen in regard to the setting alone; however, what happened to the setting has been of great relevance to the very problem in question.

If we now return to the definition of the elements of the setting reached so far, we will realize that the list of these elements must be extended. Beyond the contractual conditions, there are in fact other components that are indispensable to the analytical situation and that possess the same characteristics of fixedness and extraneousness as regards the interpretive process that I have used as criteria for defining the setting. The most salient example is that of the roles typically assumed in analysis, especially on the part of the analyst. Hence for reaching a more precise and comprehensive definition of setting, we must discuss some of these roles, all the while keeping in mind the traditional view of the analytical process.

The issue is taken up by Loch (1974) in a short study that examines the roles played by the psychoanalyst and the exercising of power within the analytical situation. Loch appears to detect a contradiction here or, as he says, a paradox. On the one hand, psychoanalysis purports to open up a type of communication that is freer than a prescribed power structure would permit; on the other hand, to reach this goal, it launches a process in which the analyst takes on the roles of legislator and pedagogue. In other words, the search for the patient's freedom is pursued in a situation that is essentially unfree. Putting forth his argument meticulously on the metapsychological plane, Loch concludes that these roles are being legitimized by the ethics inherent in the research activity that is the overall purpose of psychoanalysis. The research project, in other words, provides the justification for the analyst's exercise of power. On the other hand (and on this point Loch is very decisive), the analytical process is only made possible precisely through the assumption of these roles by the analyst. Psychoanalysis, he argues, aims at reaching a relative truth, in the sense that it is ultimately subject to the patient's consent, which fact provides further justification for the pedagogical and authoritarian aspects of the psychoanalyst's roles. The author suggests that it is only at the end of the analysis that the unfree situation will be resolved, by the analyst's relinquishing his or her roles and the restoration of equality between analyst and patient.

Loch thus shows that the roles of legislator and teacher represent conditions of reality that are indispensable for the development of the psychoanalytic process. Moreover, they are obviously not temporary roles, occasioned by a particular phase in the patient's development; thus for Loch they are not "parameters" in Eissler's sense. Now, since these roles evidently possess the same characteristics of fixedness and extraneousness in regard to the interpretive process that I described earlier, there is no reason why they should not be considered elements of the setting. Proof of this lies in the way in which Loch treats the question. If the thesis advocated here is correct, then these roles belong even more so among the elements of the setting: they are being "acted," not analyzed. And, in fact, Loch looks upon them in just that way: to the extent that they connote the "real world" acting on the part of the analyst, they must be facts just like the typical elements of the setting. From there it follows that the roles cannot be interpreted; that is, they may not be reduced to anything else (as, for instance, experiences of transferences or countertransference) that is not the pure and simple efficacy of the analyst's activity. If this were not so, Loch's initial premise would collapse. But if it is true, then we may draw the following conclusions:

1. Being elements of the setting, the analyst's roles of teacher and legislator are not resolved by means of the analysis itself (in the same way that the role of interpreter, for instance—another element of the setting—is not resolved). In other words, they have no recourse to analytic solutions; they are not interpreted, for example, as are the

patient's childhood experiences and conflicts that have been transferred onto the analyst, for it was the analyst who assumed these roles, and not the patient who bestowed them onto the analyst. True, at the end of the analysis the roles cease to exist, but this happens only because, in fact, the analysis comes to an end, in the same way that the analyst ceases to interpret at the end of the analysis. Hence these roles are inherent in the practical act of carrying out the analysis; they are not internal transferential aspects of a person's psychic process. Even though the patient manages to internalize these roles, inasmuch as they may be instantly reinstated if the patient should decide to resume the analysis, such internalization is not interpreted and thus relegated to the realm of fantasy, but is considered concrete proof of the success of the analysis.

2. Within the psychoanalytical process, the patient does, through transference, reproduce elements and conflicts inherent in the relationship to power and authority. All these are interpreted, with the aim of clearing up the problematic areas in the traditional sense of analysis. But the roles of which Loch speaks are something else. If they are part of the setting, they cannot be reduced to other matter, as we stated before. That is to say, if the analyst acts to a certain degree as legislator and teacher for the reason of furthering the development of the psychoanalytic process, the analyst certainly cannot renounce these roles without compromising the process itself; and trying to interpret the roles during the analysis would mean just that. We may recall, in this connection, the analyst's role of auxiliary superego that Strachey (1934) points to in his discussion of interpretation. These aspects of the problem of freedom in analysis, as we see, cannot be confronted on the real-world level, that is, they find no solution within the analytic situation. The patient remains tied to a system of rules and standards that limit freedom in a very precise manner. These ties may be undone only by the concrete fact of the conclusion of the analysis, because any prior attempt at dissolving them would mean jeopardizing the setting, the theory of the technique, and, ultimately, the analytical process itself. The fact is that the analytical situation does not offer the patient a model of freedom that is any better than the one offered by life; on the contrary, in certain respects, the patient is far less free in analysis—aside from enjoying a kind of abstract freedom, namely, being able to say all sorts of things in a situation in which he or she is forbidden to do them.

3. All this by no means implies that we should search for a different setting or a situation that offers more freedom. On the contrary, it is folly to think that analysis, in its character as an

institutionalized activity within a certain social and economic structure, might offer something that other institutions within that structure are not able to offer. The analytic setting, including the roles that the analyst assumes, are given us today by the society in which we live; their legitimacy is tied in with the nature of the analytical process, on the one hand, and, on the other, with the real-world conditions in which this process takes place. There is no reason to look for other justifications, even less so if it involves factors substantially removed from the analytical process, such as the ethics of research projects. Admittedly, though, we would do well to reflect upon the fact that in our present society, something that touches so closely the internal life of a person as analysis does should have to be carried out at the price of such authoritarian working conditions.

All these considerations open up a further line of reasoning. The structure of the setting and the nature of the roles were formed step by step, during the history of psychoanalysis, on the basis of empirical findings gathered by Freud and his followers during their analytical activity. Those empirical findings have always provided a feedback on the development of the theory; but as regards the formation of the setting and the assumption of the roles, these have produced a description of the concrete conditions for the practical applicability of the method. To return to the example of the therapy of psychoses, we know that the psychoanalysts who have tried that therapy have gathered data that have had a decisive feedback effect on the initial theories, modifying them in significant ways (the famous Freudian discourse on the interpretation of paranoia in the Schreber case was recognized as partially untenable only at the moment that analysts began to work with psychotics). But at the same time, it had been necessary to construct a different setting, which would take into account the new psychopathology and with it the altered circumstances under which the analytic activity took place. This, as mentioned before, has also been a source of gross misunderstanding; one avoided speaking of "analysis" of psychoses not so much because in the case of psychotic states the structure of interpretation is different from that in cases of neurosis, but above all because the setting was different, which is almost like claiming that analysis is reocgnized by the fact that the patient is lying on the couch, or succeeds in free-associating. It is interesting to note, in this connection, that the same phenomenon has not occurred with regard to the analysis of children, even though the change in the setting has been equally notable. In any case the contributions made since then by psychoanalysis toward understanding and treating psychotic states should be sufficient to settle this issue.

To return to Loch's argument, it is evident that the discussion of the institutionalized roles of the analyst and, more generally, the setting, is a discussion of psychoanalytic practice in reference to its method and the realistic conditions under which that method is applied. Clinical psychoanalysis—be it conducted in connection with one or another psychopathological situation—is the model of the practical application of psychoanalytic theory, realized through the execution of a profession. There is no reason to believe that the profession of psychoanalysis should escape the social and historical shackles with which other professions are bound. Nor may we claim that such shackles are entirely extraneous to the psychoanalytical process; in fact, the deliberation here presented intends to show the opposite to be true. To claim that the current psychoanalytic setting is the way it is only for methodological reasons—that is, that it is absolutely the only precondition possible for analytical interpretation—would be equivalent to believing that the analyst chooses certain roles and operational situations not because historical and social factors do in fact compel the analyst to do so, but in the name of certain theoretical principles. This, in my opinion, is an ideological view that must lead to the following observations:

1. We are upholding, and passing on, an ideal vision of psychoanalysis that is rooted in metapsychology. Such a vision may easily be used to perpetuate the age-old isolation and aristocratic detachment of psychoanalysis from other disciplines, and, even more so, to ignore the realistic circumstances under which psychoanalysis actually takes place.
2. This view prevents us from recognizing the historical and social determinants responsible for the fact that in our present occidental culture, the psychoanalytic process can only be realized at the price of such a strict pedagogical setting. To be sure those determinants are active in each of us and make it difficult for us to imagine a different type of setting. But we must remember that the setting as we know it cannot have an absolute value, bestowed on it by science. Granted that it represents the best model so far, that simply means that it is the only setting in which psychoanalysis can be applied in the here and now.

After this short digression, let us return to the issue raised at the beginning. A given setting, we stated, is by no means the particular element that distinguishes analytic activity from other forms of psychotherapeutic work. It might seem obvious to say that analysis does not owe its character solely to the typical material conditions under which it is conducted, and yet it is difficult to come up with an adequate conceptualization of the problem. Within recent years, for example, we have seen an expansion of the applicatory possibilities of psychoanalysis. However, this is still being approached in the traditional way. Specific modes of application of psychoanalysis of one type or another have often been considered as totally extraneous to true psychoanalytic method; in fact, they have been seen as sources of potential danger to orthodox doctrine. In other words, one continued to believe that a method, itself immutable, had to grapple continuously with circumstances that were sometimes more and sometimes less favorable to its application, and that any incorrect application might distort this method. The ideal model, from which one was to deviate as little as possible, was exemplified by the analysis of neuroses, and in particular by the setting of this analysis. One may object, above all, that there are other ways to guarantee "orthodoxy," ways less stodgy than those that assume a predetermined setting as the point of reference. Furthermore, a change of the setting may be a necessity for reasons that are fully compatible with the terms of analytic theory; for instance, in the case of children or psychotics it may become necessary to take into account the altered conditions of the ego structure—a datum that is doubtless analytical. To determine whether certain applications of psychoanalysis are correct or not, from the point of view of scientific rigor, one must enter into complex discussions. For instance, it might be demonstrated that a certain technique is incorrect by proving that it is radically removed from psychoanalytic theory as well as practice. That may not be impossible, but neither is it an easy task, because, as far as the theory is concerned, important parts of it are being revised continually, and as far as practice is concerned, one can always claim that it changes according to the new modes the revised theory is offering (implicitly) for dealing with diverse situations. In other words, one may derive from the theory a series of technical modalities that differ radically from one to the next, according to what this theory itself considers to be dissimilar clinical situations.

Be that as it may, it cannot be denied that a modification of the setting creates great difficulties for the analyst. No matter what the causes, any modification of the setting is necessarily accompanied by a change in the physiognomy of interpretation, and this may have far-reaching repercussions on the analyst's view of the process. Those who work in psychiatric institutions are very sensitive to this problem, so much so that some prefer coining new terms—for example, "socio-analysis"[2]—whereas one may justifiably suspect that they are really trying to use the analytical instrument in a situation—that is, a setting—that is very different from the traditional one. It is evident that, from the point of view of a theoretical systematization, these are still unexplored and open problems. However, what interests us here is not so much to find answers as to suggest some premises for possible research, so that we may avoid the risk of accepting only one single type of setting as the absolute ideal model (which, in point of fact, is almost never to be found in practice; see the discussion on Eissler in the following chapter).

But if it is true that any variation in the setting is necessarily accompanied by variations in the interpretation, then there must be bonds between setting and interpretation that are of a different, and indeed much tighter, nature than we have believed them to be. Perhaps we are beginning to discover that between analytical interpretation and the material elements of the situation in which it is realized, there may exist a grid of structural bonds, rather than a banal, circumstantial relationship. This assumption is the main reason why I felt it necessary to include the problem of the setting in this discussion about the logical structure of interpretation. As a matter of fact, interpretation does not exist apart from the setting, as I shall try to show; on the contrary, interpretation encloses the setting within the very core of its logical structure—and it could not be otherwise.

Before moving on to the next phases in our examination, it will be useful to recapitulate what we have established so far with respect to the setting. I started with a description of the traditional view, which confines itself to the analysis of any possible deviations from the predetermined setting. This served as a preliminary, rather narrow definition of the elements that make up the setting, seeing them as mere parts of the analytical contract. At this first approach, it already became evident that the elements of the setting also function as a frame of reference on the cognitive level during the treatment; thus the setting, initially seen only as the material contract, was now also considered in its function as a frame of cognitive reference that

[2]I am referring specifically to the work of Elliott Jaques. Leaving aside for the moment a critical discussion of its intrinsic worth—which would offer interesting starting points for debate—it seems to me that the terminology adopted by that author and by some of his followers is a compromise between the need to acknowledge at all cost the psychoanalytic matrix of certain techniques and theories, and the difficulty of defining them explicitly in psychoanalytic terms.

is indispensable to the analytical operation. Finally, in the search for a more precise definition of the setting, I singled out the one characteristic that is common to all the elements of the setting, and only to them: their noninterpretability.

The definition thus obtained permitted us to expand the concept of setting, for the attributes of fixedness, cognitive function, and nonanalyzability that characterize the setting are also present in other components of the analytical situation—albeit implicitly, in contrast to the explicit contractual elements. To illustrate this point, I referred to a work by Loch on the roles typically assumed by the psychoanalyst. These roles were seen to satisfy the criterion established earlier: they remain outside of interpretive activity, for they are not products of the fantasy of patient or analyst—to be resolved by an analysis of the transference or countertransference—but real-world factors, which, through their very existence in reality permit the analysis to proceed. Since these roles may thus be likened in every sense to the elements of the contract, they were included among the components of the setting.

Next I placed the setting thus extended in an ambit that is more versatile and more concrete than that to which a tacit tradition of psychoanalytic thought had relegated it. Being dissatisfied with the abstractness of the traditional view of the setting, I tried for a new, more materially oriented perspective, in which I looked at the variations of the setting on two planes—which I may call the vertical and the horizontal planes. On the vertical, historical plane, one type of setting became fixed—fixed, though, by definite, material factors—and it very quickly came to be the ideal setting, and was to remain such, whereas in reality it was the only one possible, within a particular historical-social situation, for the treatment of neuroses. On the horizontal plane, the variations of the setting are seen in the areas of application of psychoanalysis that exist at present. In these applications, in other words, the setting is always subject to modifications, and that fact opens up problems, not limited only to the theory of the technique, that are more complex than one might have assumed.

Finally, I offered a hypothesis that is still tentative for the moment, far from being proved. I suggested that there exists between the setting and the interpretive process an interrelationship of a logical-structural nature, rather than merely banal, circumstantial ties.

Extending the attributes of the elements of the setting to cover all other "real" conditions, materially speaking, of the analytic practice means treating these conditions as variables that are in a specific way connected, on the one hand, to the historical and social determinants at work in that practice, and, on the other hand, to the theoretical models of the doctrine. Of this double correlation, the latter is of immediate interest here. Dealing with the first one, in fact, would lead us to the reconstruction of a history of psychoanalysis on epistemological lines—certainly an important task, which, however, lies beyond the scope of this essay. The second correlation, concerning the links between the variables and the theoretical models, is more pertinent to the issue raised here. Many analysts argue that there are very precise connections between analytical practice and the theoretical and methodological concepts of psychoanalysis, but the argument has really remained very vague so far. Now, inasmuch as the method in analytic practice is primarily expressed through the use of interpretation, it became essential, in my opinion, to redefine certain aspects of the material conditions under which this interpretation is conducted, in order that we may rid the analytic practice of some of its abstract and idealistic traits. It was for this reason that a discussion of the setting seemed crucial to me.

Perhaps we can see our path somewhat clearer now: once we have examined the factual conditions involved in analytical activity, it is now our task to investigate the possible links between these conditions and the method employed in analysis. In the following discussion, we shall see the neat division between setting and analytical process collapse; or at least we shall see this division in a radically different light.

CHAPTER 5
The True and the False

The analytic method is often treated as if it could exist by itself, independent of its practical surroundings, and as if it were connected to that reality by circumstantial ties only. Hence the issue of the setting is reduced to a search for the optimal situation in which to apply this method. This approach produces the view cited earlier, according to which all problems disappear, once the best possible setting has been found. Once it has been decided that a method may only be applied in one particular concrete situation, it becomes pointless to ponder over any deeper meaning of the connection between the method and that situation; it must be a matter-of-fact connection, because the concrete situation is simply a set of preestablished facts that permit the application of the method. This type of circular reasoning may even lead one to believe that the problem of the setting—if a problem at all—may at most be a matter of revising the definition of the setting as such, as indeed I have tried to do in the preceding chapter. In this idealistic view of the analytical situation, the same argument can be applied also with regard to the inner workings of the analytic process. In analysis we certainly do take into account the *hic et nunc* and, in fact, even use it in interpretation. For example, the patient's factual relationship with the analyst is carried back to its possible symbolic meanings. But while it is true that elements of the setting are employed as points of reference for interpretations of other data, they are still considered circumstances that are in themselves irrelevant for the interpretive process; they are seen as facts that are perhaps interesting on a historical or social level (such as the variations of the setting), but have in substance nothing to do with the method.

In other words, in this ideal vision of the analytical situation, the analysis can proceed once the optimal conditions for it have been established, while the conditions themselves become no more, and no less, than fixed, factual data, irrelevant to the goal of the analytical process. The conditions may be reintroduced to the process, but only in the event that they should emerge with a different meaning—attributed to them, for instance, by the patient's conflicts. In that case, however, the conditions themselves are surely not being discussed—since they are considered irrelevant givens—but rather the shift of their meaning. The setting, in this type of view, is merely a supporting frame that allows the interpretive activity—that is, analysis—to be conducted on a practical level; and with that the setting has exhausted all its possible functions.

From such a viewpoint, I think, substantially two implications may be derived: (1) analysis is interpretation; (2) since psychoanalytic interpretation is all-encompassing—that is, it acts upon "everything" that is happening—anything that remains outside of the ambit of interpretation is by definition merely a set of factual data, without importance for the aims of the analytical process.

Before agreeing with point 1 and disagreeing with point 2, I would like to call to mind that this viewpoint has many supporters, whether they themselves are aware of it or not. For instance, all those who see analysis as a form of hermeneutics are lined up along these positions. They state—or, in any case, imply—that only those things that are symbolic, or reducible to a symbol or some symbolic text, serve the ends of analytical interpretation. All that which cannot be placed on a symbolic level is considered a banal fact; or, at the most, is allowed to participate in the analytical activity only when it is felt that its banal, literal meaning has been falsified by the corruption of a vocabulary (I am thinking of Lorenzer), but that analysis can restore it to its original significance. But if, as Habermas (1971) states, "psychoanalysis appears . . . as a special form of interpretation. It provides theoretical perspectives and technical rules for the interpretation of symbolic structures" (p. 214), and if it "unites linguistic analysis with the psychological investigation of causal connections" (p. 217), to arrive at a "depth hermeneutics" that "deals with texts indicating self-deception of the author" (p. 218), then it is not clear what other than the restoration of the corrupt text could be the objective in such an operation. This is equivalent to assuming that in clinical analysis interpretation is exclusively concerned with, and applied to, the symbol. The situation in which analyst and patient interact is thus assumed to be entirely symbolical—hence entirely interpretable—or else to be insignificant regarding some of its factual features. The only concern of importance is the text to be interpreted and the ways in which this text is being produced, that is, the play of resistances. Once again, the setting is being disposed of as a substantially negligible circumstance, and interpretation is settled exclusively within the symbolic sphere; it is an interpretation of symbols, and nothing else.

Habermas, who is being cited here only because of the expressiveness and conciseness of his phrasing, is not concerned with these aspects. But to get an idea of the possible consequences of a view such as just described, we need only consider the work of those authors who have carried psychoanalytic interpretation out of its natural—the clinical—habitat. For these authors it does indeed merely seem to be a question of interpreting this or that symbolic phenomenon, which attitude evidently has given rise to the legitimization of arbitrary—at times frankly mad—psychoanalytical interventions in a vast range of issues, from political to anthropological ones. What the authors, who claim to be speaking as psychoanalysts, do not always realize, however, is the fact that such an extension of the concept of psychoanalytical interpretation, and its use without any ties to a setting, diminishes, perhaps even annuls, the possibility to preserve the logical structure of interpretation, for it deprives interpretation of a precise and concrete frame of reference. It is true, of course, that the results of psychoanalytic theorization may be carried beyond the clinical ambit; however, that only means that the application of some of the theory's statements—at times perhaps a generalization of such statements—may be more or less tenable also in other areas. But interpretation true and proper, when outside of its own natural sphere, loses every scientific legitimacy; such legitimacy, in fact, arises solely out of the use of its method. And if we delude ourselves into thinking that we can actually exploit that method's total range of effectiveness, instead of being satisfied with its results, we will end up trying to interpret, say, a society, a single or collective behavior, or whatever else, without any points of reference other than symbols or the translation of a language. Obviously, if we did this in psychoanalysis, we would soon find ourselves accepting the symbolic as an ontological fact. Such a manner of proceeding can have its legitimacy in other fields—we need only think of the work of Cassirer.[1] But with regard to our concerns, it transforms the analytic method into something that is as abstract as it is indiscriminate and, finally, arbitrary.

On the other hand, it is not enough to stress once again the importance of what I have tentatively called the "frame of reference"; one might be led to think that all that was necessary was to base psychoanalytic interpretation on something like empirical confirmation. But this means skirting the issue here, which, I repeat, is the logical organization of interpretation itself. I will try to clarify this by choosing the most symbolical of phenomena—the dream. It presents itself classically as a text upon which the interpretation forged by Freud can proceed without recourse to anything else: what else is necessary for a dream's interpretation but the gathering of associations and all the contextual phenomena, such as the patient's elaborations and resistances?[2] And anyway, can one not understand a dream, at least under certain circumstances, even outside of the concrete references that we have been discussing? Perhaps one can; yet the methodological foundation was laid down by Freud (1900) himself when he spoke of associations:

> When I instruct a patient to abandon reflection of any kind and

[1]I am, of course, referring to the well-known work of Cassirer, *The Philosophy of Symbolic Forms* (1923–1929). It is hardly worth mentioning that the anthropological method, profoundly different from the psychoanalytical one, fully legitimizes the direction taken by this and other authors. But it is something else entirely to adopt these directions when dealing with the symbolic in analysis.

[2]In this section, as well as in the following ones, I am not treating the interpretation of resistances—and hence the work on defenses—as being separate from the interpretation of symbols. True, the concept of defense is by no means close to that of the symbol, nor may we claim that defenses, in their clinical manifestations as resistances within transference, are always expressed in symbolic form. But from the viewpoint of the logic of interpretation, symbolic productions as well as resistances are being treated as things that are interpretable, and they are in fact interpreted by the same technique. Thus, in order to simplify the argument, I am restricting my discussion to the interpretation of the symbol.

> to tell me whatever comes into his head, I am relying firmly on the presumption that he will not be able to abandon the purposive ideas inherent in the treatment and I feel justified in inferring that what seem to be the most innocent and arbitrary things which he tells me are in fact related to his illness. There is another purposive idea . . . one relating to myself. The full estimate of the importance of these two theorems, as well as more detailed information about them, fall within the province of an account of the technique of psychoanalysis as a therapeutic method. (pp. 531–532)

In a body of work as comprehensive as that of Freud, one single phrase is certainly not determinant. But the passage quoted contains a direction that Freud, it seems to me, followed throughout his entire research. It was this path, signaled by the "purposive ideas," which led him to the discovery of transference. One might suggest that he was here constructing the background against which the symbolical figure becomes visible; or, if one prefers, that he was stating precisely what, in psychoanalysis, the referent of the symbol consisted in. That which Freud calls "purposive ideas" are elements removed from the purely symbolical sphere, inasmuch as they are taking on the role of logical, factual elements, which are not interpretable—be it in the interpretation of dreams or in that of every other phenomenon—yet are posited as such.

This was to remain Freud's range of perspective whenever he would discuss technique, or construct this theory. True, he was to depart from it in works like *Totem and Taboo* (1912–1913) or *Civilization and Its Discontents* (1930); but he was always conscious of the fact that in studies of that type it is not the analytical method that is under discussion, but the theory of man, which may be derived from that method. This is the reason why Freud repeatedly refers to certain anthropological theses as tentative, problematic, and incomplete. One thing only is accepted by him as stable: the structure of the interpretive process. He felt that its use in practice—that is, in the clinical situation—leads to the construction of theoretical (metapsychological) propositions that are in a continuous state of development and revision. Freud is ready to discard any hypothesis if the application of the interpretive method proves it to be inexact, incoherent with the general theory, or incongruous with the data obtained through interpretation; the method itself, however, remains preserved to the last. Within this method the elements here described as points of reference are indispensable to the interpretive operation.

All this can only serve as confirmation of something I have pointed out earlier—the preeminent place of interpretation in psychoanalysis. It must be stated categorically that every metapsychological assertion and every rule of technique are subject to their permanent verification through the interpretive method. It is clear that this is the only path that psychoanalysis can pursue, if it does not want to descend to the level of one of the many anthropologies that are so readily available on the market of ideas. But here we must concern ourselves with the logic of this interpretive process, which I posit as the stable nucleus of psychoanalysis, and clarify the role and importance that the elements of the setting take up within it. I think that another look at the study by Eissler (1953), which I have cited only in passing so far, will help us decisively in this direction. Eissler's approach to the issue of psychoanalytic technique is indeed different from the traditional one; thus we find him among the first to demonstrate the falsehood of the existence of a dichotomy between the interpretive process, on the one hand, and the concrete elements of the analytic situation, on the other.

We need not embrace the whole of Eissler's research here, but its basic points must be mentioned. The author not only affirms the preeminent position of interpretation in psychoanalysis, but even goes so far as to make it the nucleus of analytic technique. At the same time, he notes that it is not true that deviations from the model technique—that is to say, noninterpretive procedures—are necessary only in the therapy of psychotic or prepsychotic patients. On the contrary, Eissler feels that the model of "orthodox" technique—the one limited to interpretation exclusively, which is followed in the traditional setting—ends up being very restricted. He believes that it is necessary to include in that technique a series of procedures that are usually considered deviations from that model, but that are nonetheless part of most analytical treatments. Eissler therefore sets out to reappraise what he calls the "basic model technique," and then proceeds to define the deviations from it (which he calls "parameters"). Finally, recognizing the necessity to admit these parameters into the therapy, he stipulates certain criteria for this admission, so that it be done in the correctest way possible. I shall now examine Eissler's discourse more closely and, disregarding for the moment his conclusions, I shall try to extract some points of contact between his argument and the discussion at hand.

The basic model technique, according to Eissler, is that which adopts interpretation as the exclusive model of the analyst's activity and which has a "zero" level of parameters throughout the treatment. "In the ideal case the analyst's activity is limited to interpretation"—that is how Eissler (1953, p. 108) expresses his view of the predominance of interpretation. At the same time, however, he recognizes that it is almost never possible to limit oneself to "pure" interpretation, since the "ideal case" is extremely rare, all but nonexistent. Very often it becomes necessary to introduce "parameters," that is to say, to adopt procedures that are in no way interpretation, nor are they, in the strict sense, preparatory measures for interpretation. As a classical example, the author cites that of Freud imposing commands on his phobic patient in order to prevent the analysis from coming to a standstill.

Eissler, in other words, accepts the possible need for parameters ("based . . . on clinical observation," p. 110), and emphasizes that "(1) a parameter must be introduced only when it is proved that the basic model technique does not suffice; (2) it must never transgress the unavoidable minimum; (3) it is to be used only when it finally leads to its self-elimination; and (4) the effect of the parameter on the transference relationship must never be such that it cannot be abolished by interpretation" (pp. 111, 113).

As we see, Eissler arrives at conclusions that are without doubt acceptable on the practical plane, especially from the viewpoints of technique and the control over countertransference. However, if his clinical experience leads him to these conclusions, his argumentation appears to contain some incoherency. Namely, with regard to definitions, both his concept of "basic model technique" and that of "parameter" remain ambiguous. Eissler defines the basic model technique as "pure" interpretation, and the parameter as that which is not interpretation. But in doing so, he is reestablishing, as the author himself says, the ideal model of analysis: a model in which two categories are neatly separated. One is interpretation; the other, something totally extraneous to it, introduced for "therapeutic" reasons. In other words, in order to permit the proper development of the process, one resorts to measures that are deemed extraneous to that process. The problem lies precisely here: Is a concrete situation in which "only" the interpretive activity is performed really imaginable? Or, more to the point, can psychoanalytic interpretation ever be conceived of in these "ideal" terms? It should be clear by now that to maintain such a claim would be equivalent to imagining an analytical situation devoid of any setting—that is, an interpretive activity that takes place in a vacuum. Instead, what really does happen in an analytical situation, even at its very beginning? When putting down the conditions of contract, what is the analyst doing if not introducing a full-grown set of "parameters"? What, indeed, is the difference between Eissler's "parameters" and the other elements of the setting?

As a matter of fact, Eissler does his best to establish differences. It is no coincidence that he is so obviously aware of the importance of the setting, even if his approach will not allow him to plunge into the heart of the matter. He sees the parameters as something like necessary but temporary impurities, to be resolved in the successive development by analysis itself, as his aforementioned criteria demand. In that sense the parameters might indeed be considered different from the other elements of the setting. The difference would be twofold: one regards duration—the setting elements are permanent, as was confirmed with regard to the roles cited by Loch, the parameters are temporary; and one regards analyzability—the parameters are interpretable, the other setting elements are not. However, this is a deceptive difference, for let us consider this: When introducing a parameter as an indispensable measure during a particular phase of the analysis, the analyst certainly turns this parameter into an element of the setting, at least until such time as it will be possible to analyze it. This means that it is made one of the real conditions that permit the development of the analytic process. This is, in fact, the very purpose of the parameters, for I will call to mind that in Eissler's own argument, to introduce a parameter means, for example, to offer the patient reassurance, and this must be done only when it is indispensable for the continuation of the analysis. At that moment, in other words, the reassurance (a noninterpretive gesture, behavior on the part of the analyst) is considered the only thing that will render the analysis workable. Otherwise, to stay with the example, without the reassurance, the patient's anxiety, in certain conditions of the ego, would interrupt the treatment. But that means that anxiety (or the conditions of the ego, or any other analytic diagnostic datum) assumes the role of one of those elements that, at any given moment, cannot be interpreted, but upon which it becomes necessary to act. That, in turn, means that it is treated like one of the preestablished facts of the analysis, exactly like any one of the elements of the setting. Admittedly, the origins are different—in the case of the setting elements, the origin is the practical circumstance under which the analysis is conducted; in the other cases, instead, it is the patient's psychological state. But that is irrelevant. What counts is not the provenance of the phenomena, but the way in which they are treated in the analysis.

If this argument is correct, then the vision of the analytic process as "pure" interpretation collapses, since the "basic model technique" of Eissler does not exist. On the other hand, it is difficult to disagree with Eissler (or, for that matter, with all those who preceded him) when he states that analysis is interpretation. How is it possible to reconcile this contradiction? The only way, it seems to me, is to admit that it is the concept of interpretation that must be revised. For it is altogether probable that the analyst operates within a logical pattern that is much more complex than the one traditionally accepted under the term of interpretation. Of that logical pattern I have so far only elucidated one characteristic: that it is not separable, in an absolute sense, from what I have called the setting in the broadest acceptance of the term, nor from that which Eissler considers impurities of the process and which he calls parameters. These features cannot be wrenched from the interpretive process, because they are an integral part of it. Only by accepting this fact can we pass from an abstract view of the analytical situation toward a realistic one. It is now in order to discuss this in greater depth.

From the perspective of analytic technique and its theory, there is only one difference between the analytic elements that we consider factual or circumstantial—including Eissler's parameters—and the interpretable "texts" (to speak with Habermas). This difference is certainly not to be found in the intrinsic nature of these elements. Taken one by one, they all reveal themselves, in particular contexts, as reducible to a symbolic meaning, and one class of these elements melts into the other. In certain situations, not only the parameters, but any given element of the setting may be treated not as a factual datum but as an interpretable text. Nor does the difference lie in the fact that one class of elements is considered indispensable for the material existence of the analysis, while the other class makes up its content; in fact, as we have seen in regard to the setting, the things that are indispensable are not always the same. The only difference that can be traced with any assurance, from one moment to another, is pointed out by the interpretive process itself. That is to say, in every analytical situation there are elements that at a particular moment are not interpreted (because they are considered noninterpretable), and others that are. I shall now try to show that this difference in treatment is the pivotal point of the interpretive process, and that on this point hinges its very logic.

All those who have concerned themselves with the issue of interpretation are united on one obvious premise: to interpret means to attribute to something a meaning that is different from its explicit and apparent meaning; to decipher a message; to identify the duplicity in a discourse. But in practice this attribution of an ulterior meaning does not extend to *all* that happens in an analytic situation. As we have seen, there are elements, and by no means insignificant or casual ones, whose meaning is taken literally. They perform the well-defined function of a frame of reference for the interpretation of the symbolic text. Certainly the analyst does not always know why he or she ascribes a meaning that is different from the manifest one only to part of the phenomena that he or she is observing. Yet the analyst knows that if one did not proceed in that fashion, the interpretation would be senseless, would be an abstract and arbitrary operation.

Thus, in an analytical situation, the interpretive method establishes a division; it continually separates phenomena into two categories. One category contains all the things that are being interpreted; the other one, all the things that, in contrast to the former ones, are taken at their face value and can thus be used as a frame of reference. In other words, two different types of treatment of the analytical elements form the poles of a distinct opposition—or, we might say, divide these elements into *false* ones and *true* ones. And it is interpretation itself that determines that that which is being interpreted is partially false, otherwise it would lose its reason for being. In psychoanalysis the falsity as such, as we know, is, of course, the outcome of a falsification (a famous example is Freud's work on dreams or on the mechanisms of remembering). Conversely, in this logical system, things that are not reducible to anything but themselves are deemed noninterpretable and assume the roles of "true" elements (e.g., the fact of the patient's illness and the figure of the analyst in the excerpt from Freud). I hope it will be clear by now that by the terms "true" and "false" I do not want to imply that these things are different in a phenomenological sense, much less in an ontological one. The fact that the analyst will treat some things as false and others as true arises from the method and is independent of any actual attribution of a nature of "truth" to any one fact in the analysis. The issue of "truth" in that sense, which will be taken up later, has nothing to do with the argument at hand. The logical structure that I am suggesting here pertains to the interpretive process: it is that process, not common sense or verisimilitude, which dictates the proper conditions for the bestowal of a "true" character on some things and a "false" one on others. In fact, we may even posit a definite reciprocity: the true is that which is not interpreted, the false that which is interpreted. (This is quite aside from the fact that, in practice, of all the interpretable elements, only some are actually interpreted from time to time. I should therefore say, more precisely, that the false corresponds to the interpretable; the true, to the noninterpretable.) The potential transparency of the phenomena that are treated as false is counterbalanced by the stark impenetrability of those that are accepted as true; and the dialectic of the psychoanalytical process includes both of these poles.

As I have said, it is the psychoanalytical process that dictates the proper conditions for ascribing the attributes of "true" and "false." This must not be understood to mean that analysis holds an agnostic attitude with regard to external reality and proceeds by the dictates of some kind of abstract convention. Clearly certain elements that are endowed with the role of the true in analysis—we need only think of the setting—have in fact very precise ties with that reality. What is meant here, rather, is this: External reality enters analysis *only* through the interpretive process. Analyst and patient may discuss this reality as long as they wish—their discussion will have no bearing on the analysis at hand, unless it is concerned with elements that are treated as true *within*, not outside of the logic of interpretation. That is why any attempt on the part of the analyst to defend the setting against certain attacks is destined to fail. Not that the setting as we know it here and now is indefensible (see preceding chapter), but it can be defended only on the basis of that logic—certainly not on the basis of what is considered justified or correct in a scientific sense. I shall return to these issues in my discussion of "reality testing" in the following chapter.* For now, let us remember that the anatomy of the "real" in psychoanalysis rests in history and is determined by it to such an extent that it varies together with that history; and let us furthermore remember that the objective of psychoanalysis is the relation between the conscious and unconscious (this, too, being subject to the vicissitudes of history), not the formulation of a theory of anthropological truth.

But to return to the logic of interpretation: How does psychoanalysis handle the interplay between its two components; that is to say, between the elements postulated as "true"—not further decomposable—and the elements postulated as "false"—decomposable by analysis, and inherent in the psychic makeup of the two members of the analytical relationship? I have claimed that both categories of elements are equal components of the interpretive process, thereby opposing the view that sees this process as a method evolving in an abstract context. If my claim is true, then there exist, at any given moment of the analysis, two distinct, but connected, logical areas—to wit, the true and the false. Now, in the traditional view, this division is rigid and static. In essence the view accepts as true only the elements of the setting, which are assumed to be unalterable; they are, in other words, the only elements that are not interpreted, being considered outside of the process, and fixed. On that view I voiced my doubts, in the preceding discussion of the setting, by pointing

**Translator's note*: Not translated here.

out a variability of the setting that I may call latitudinal: the setting has neither always been the same throughout the history of the psychoanalytic movement, nor is it the same today from one country to another, and this—now we can see it more clearly—cannot be devoid of importance for the purposes of the formation of psychoanalytic theory. But to demonstrate the variability of the setting is not enough for proving my argument correct; after all, one might object that whatever version of the setting we look at, it nevertheless remains the same throughout a single analysis and is thus the only thing that is treated as true. I shall therefore suggest that there is another variability, one that does in fact exist within each single analytical situation, and which I shall call longitudinal. In any given analytical treatment, individual elements may be shifted from one category to the other, according to the needs of the interpretive process. Elements that up to a certain moment were treated as true, may have to be interpreted after that moment, hence treated as false (the inverse transit, which probably exists, is more obscure). It is likely, in other words, that even within a single analysis, there is never a constant body of "true" elements, but that at any given moment at least part of these elements may be transformed along a gamut of possibilities. To give an example, let us return to Eissler's discussion of the parameters.

There is no doubt that Eissler considers the parameter a "true" element at the moment in which the analyst introduces it. Now, as he states, the parameter must be introduced in such a way that it can be eliminated by succeeding interpretations, at which time, in other words, it moves into the realm of the "false." But if the logical structure of interpretation is as I am describing it, the displacement of an element from the logical sphere of the true to that of the false cannot occur without the void being filled; that is, the element that is being interpreted must be replaced by a new "true" element (remember that the "true" elements exist because they fulfill a definite need on the part of the process). Indeed, just that occurs. Following Eissler, we know that if a parameter was introduced correctly, and is thus effective, it renders possible a development of the ego; the new ego condition eventually makes it possible for the parameter itself to be interpreted. We must therefore admit that the new element taken on as true is the postulate of the altered condition of the patient's ego structure. It is a datum that is not decomposable, but simply accepted as an existing fact, and treated as such.

The same line of reasoning may be applied to the scheme of interpretation proposed by Strachey (1934). Strachey calls psychoanalytic interpretation "mutative" because it reaches a turning point—namely, the moment in which the patient acquires cognition and succeeds in distinguishing between the object of his or her fantasy and the object of reality. The "reality" here seems to refer to the person of the analyst, while in my opinion it can be demonstrated that it is a "true" element within the true–false antinomy. In fact, if the problem were merely for the patient to distinguish a bad, internal object from an external one that is good, then we would arrive at the paradox of an analyst who must be good by profession (and those who see in this the "neutrality" of the analyst do at times arrive at that paradox). But my point is this: The patient accomplishes the fundamental task of cognition at the moment when the analytic situation and the conditions of the ego permit him or her—by using the analyst as a "true" element—to recognize the "false" component he or she had projected onto the analyst. For this to occur, it is not at all necessary that the analyst be good, or bad, or neutral. Even supposing for a moment that, for some absurd reason, the analyst were nasty with the patient: under adequate analytical conditions, the patient would be able to distinguish the analyst's nasty behavior from the badness of his or her own internal experience; the same applies equally, of course, to kindness or any other behavior. The pivotal point of the mutation involves both the true as well as the false element within the interpretive process.

According to Strachey, this interaction is repeated over and over, since mutative interpretation provokes a long series of minute mutations throughout the entire analytical process. Once a mutation has occurred, it cannot but be accepted immediately as a new "true" element. Thereupon it assumes its logical role within successive interpretations, which take into account the alteration of the ego brought about by preceding interpretations. If this were not so, the analysis would have no longitudinal development; one would be facing an analytical stalemate. Besides, the entire contemporaneous school of ego psychology speaks of interpretations "appropriate to the phase of development" of the patient. This concept implies not only that interpretation may change from moment to moment in an analysis, but also that the true–false relationship itself may have a series of evolutionary moments.

The real function of this true–false relationship in interpretation thus begins to reveal itself: it makes it possible for cognition to occur. The moment the analyst interprets, he or she places that which is being interpreted into the sphere of the false; but whether the analyst is aware of it or not, this cannot be done without postulating a "true" element as a mark of cognitive reference. To return to Freud's example cited above, the interpretation of dreams cannot treat the patient's "purposive ideas" regarding his or her illness and the figure of the analyst any differently. It is easy to extend this concept to encompass not only all the elements of the setting but the whole analytical situation of any given moment, which, when taken as "true," makes it possible to understand the interpreted phenomena. I don't know whether these concepts may be extended also to areas outside of the psychoanalytic confine—including interpretation in a general sense—nor is it my task to study that possibility. I feel certain, however, that in the psychoanalytical situation this is indeed the logical structure that sustains the process of interpretation. In this structure the components "true" and "false" evidently interact as members of one single category and are therefore indivisible; this realization is the reason that the entire preceding elaboration seemed necessary to me. The traditional approach, although it did not resort to a terminology such as I have coined here, tended to separate these components and to invest them with different, literal meanings between which there were no logical points of contact.

Throughout the preceding discussion, we have seen the progressive broadening of the realm of the "true." At first it seemed to comprise only the elements of the setting; later certain roles adopted by the analyst were included. An examination of "parameters" resulted in their inclusion as well. Finally, I found myself having to admit to the realm of the "true" even certain postulates that are properly part of metapsychological theory—for instance, those on ego development. This must cause us to reflect for a moment: Could it be then, that even metapsychological theory is really but an element of the logical structure of interpretation and thus plays an instrumental—and to a certain degree variable—role within the analytical process? Or is it perhaps too belittling to think of the grand construction of metapsychology in such terms?

These questions require a step backward. In our discussion of Ricoeur* it was observed that the autonomy of psychoanalytic interpretation, with *its* roots in metapsychology, has been demonstrated convincingly. We may, therefore, look upon metapsychology in two ways: on the one hand, as the theoretic scaffolding that supports the interpretive method and gives it its typical character; on the other hand, as the sum of all the postulates that constitute a general theory of human psychology—to wit, a metapsychology. And it is exactly in these two ways that the theory enters into the interpretive process. As its underlying supposition, it forms the foundation of the process

**Translator's note*: This refers to a discussion in Chapter 3 of the Italian original, which has not been translated.

and supports it; as a general, affirmative theory of human psychology, it fits itself into the realm of the true within the interpretive process. Of course, the analyst uses metapsychological theory in an implicit way, at least partly (for example, in judging the patient's current phase of regression or development), but the logical role assigned to it is assuredly that of a true, nondecomposable element. If this is so, the theory, thus fitted into the realm of the true, should also be subject to the factors of historical variability that I pointed to earlier. This would imply that the general theory encompasses two different functions: one, unchanged to date, which consists in supporting the structure of interpretation; and the other, acting as one of the true elements within the interpretive process itself. That the theory in the latter function is subject to a series of historical variations should not cause surprise; on the contrary, this perception enables us to understand how it happens that the cognitive efficacy of analysis tends to remain relatively unchanged, even in the presence of the modifications and the developments of the metapsychological theory. The postulates put forth by psychoanalysis are obviously subject to all the changes that a continuous process of revision may generate. Even within a single treatment, these postulates are likely to display a certain longitudinal variability. However, even if today we do not interpret the way we did 30 or 50 years ago, the logical structure at work is probably the same as then.

The concept of the true–false antinomy and the inclusion of metapsychology as an affirmative participant in the logic of that antinomy may have more far-reaching repercussions. It may lead us to a better understanding of the reasons for the criticism launched at those who would turn psychoanalysis into a commodity and reduce it to a set of static and finite statements. Shedding light on the structure of the method may allow us to propose the theory anew as something radically open and discussible. Moreover, my examination of the method ended up in a discourse on interpretation, in which I have tried to trace the factual modalities by means of which psychoanalysis bestows on itself its own character, that is to say, removed from the idealistic distortions and ideological uses of its theory. My aim, in starting from the analytical practice, was to get at the meaning of things as it expresses itself in the activity of interpretation in all its real components.

The logical structure of interpretation thus began to reveal its shape. Even in this first approach, it seems to me, this structure shows much less contradiction with the material-dialectical component of analysis, which we have to acknowledge no matter how we see things. It is true that this perspective may open up more problems than it solves, but that must not mean that we should close our eyes to it.

REFERENCES*

*Alexander, F. (1925). A metapsychological description of the process of cure. *Int. J. Psychoanal.*, 6:13–34.

*Bernfeld, S. (1932). Der Begriff der Deutung in der Psychoanalyse. *Z. Angew. Psychol.*, 42:448–497.

Carnap, R. (1956). The methodological character of theoretical concepts. In *The Foundations of Science and the Concepts of Psychology and Psychoanalysis. Minnesota Studies in the Philosophy of Science*, 1. Minneapolis: University of Minnesota Press.

Cassirer, E. (1923–1929). *The Philosophy of Symbolic Forms*. Trans. Ralph Mannheim. New Haven, Conn.: Yale University Press, 1953–1957.

Codignola, E. (1975a). Nota sulla relazione d'oggetto e la costituzione dell'io. In *Amore oggettuale e realtà*, A. H. Modell. Turin: Boringhieri, pp. IX–XVI. (Introduction to the Italian translation of A. H. Modell, *Object Love and Reality*. New York: International Universities Press, 1968). Reprinted in *Psicoterapia e Scienze Umane*, 1975, 1:1–3.

——— (1975b). Una metatoria? Nota su Lorenzer. *Psicoterapia e Scienze Umane*, 4:1–2.

——— Galli, P. F., & Rothschild, B. (1974). Intellektuellen- und Klassenkampf am Beispiel der Psychoanalyse. *Arbeitspapiere zur Psychoanalyse*. Zurich: Psychoanal. Seminar Zürich.

Devereux, G. (1951). Some criteria for the timing of confrontations and interpretations. *Int. J. Psychoanal.*, 32:19–24.

Eissler, K. R. (1953). The effect of the structure of the ego on psychoanalytic technique. *J. Amer. Psychoanal. Assn.*, 1:103–143.

*Ellenberger, H. (1970). *The Discovery of the Unconscious; The History and Evolution of Dynamic Psychiatry*. New York: Basic Books.

Feigl, H. (1956). Some major issues and developments in the philosophy of science of logical empiricism. In *The Foundations of Science and the Concepts of Psychology and Psychoanalysis. Minnesota Studies in the Philosophy of Science*, 1. Minneapolis: University of Minnesota Press.

Fenichel, O. (1935). Concerning the theory of psychoanalytic technique. *Int. Z. Psychoanal.*, 21:78–95. Reprinted in *Psychoanalytic Clinical Interpretation*, ed. L. Paul. London: Collier-Macmillan, 1963.

——— (1941). *Problems of Psychoanalytic Technique*. New York: Psychoanalytic Quarterly.

——— (1945). *The Psychoanalytic Theory of Neurosis*. New York: W. W. Norton.

*This is the complete bibliography as it appeared in the original text. Those references preceded by asterisks are not cited specifically in the material presented here.

Festinger, L. (1957). *A Theory of Cognitive Dissonance*. Stanford, Calif.: Stanford University Press.

Freud, A. (1965). *Normality and Pathology in Childhood. Assessments in Development*. New York: International Universities Press.

*Freud, S. (1895). Project for a scientific psychology. *Standard Edition*, 1.

——— (1900). The interpretation of dreams. *Standard Edition*, 4, 5.

*——— (1911a). Formulations on the two principles of mental functionings. *Standard Edition*, 12.

*——— (1911b). The handling of dream interpretation in psychoanalysis. *Standard Edition*, 12.

——— (1912). Recommendations to physicians practicing psychoanalysis. *Standard Edition*, 12.

——— (1913a). Totem and taboo. *Standard Edition*, 13.

*——— (1913b). The claims of psychoanalysis to scientific interest. *Standard Edition*, 13.

*——— (1922). The Ego and the Id. *Standard Edition*, 19.

*——— (1926). Inhibitions, symptoms and anxiety. *Standard Edition*, 20.

*——— (1930). Civilization and its discontents. *Standard Edition*, 21.

——— (1937). Constructions in analysis. *Standard Edition*, 23.

*Glover, E. (1931). The therapeutic effect of inexact interpretations. *Int. J. Psychoanal.*, 12:397–411.

*Green, A. (1975). The analyst, symbolization and absence in the analytic setting (on changes in analytic practice and analytic experience). *Int. J. Psychoanal.*, 56:1–22.

Greenson, R. (1967). *Technique and Practice of Psychoanalysis, vol. 1*. New York: International Universities Press.

Habermas, J. (1968). *Knowledge and Human Interest*. Trans. Jeremy J. Shapiro. Boston: Beacon Press, 1971.

Hermann, I. (1934). *Die Psychoanalyse als Methode*. Vienna: Int. Psychoanal. Verlag. Reprinted Cologne: Westdeutscher Verlag, 1963.

*Hempel, C. G. (1952). *Fundamentals of Concept Formation in Empirical Science*. Chicago: University of Chicago Press.

Horn, K. (1974). Der üeberraschte Psychoanalytiker. *Psyche*, 28:395–430.

Isaacs, S. (1939). Criteria for interpretation. *Int. J. Psychoanal.*, 20:148–160.

*Jones, E. (1916). The theory of symbolism. *Brit. J. Psychology*, 9:181–227.

Kaiser, H. (1934). Probleme der Technik. *Int. Z. Psychoanal.*, 20:490–522.

*Kris, E. (1951). Ego psychology and interpretations in psychoanalytic therapy. *Psychoanal. Q.*, 20:15–30.

Laplanche, J., & Pontalis, J. B. (1967). *The Language of Psychoanalysis*. Trans. Donald Nicholson-Smith. New York: W. W. Norton, 1973.

Levy, L. (1963). *Psychological Interpretation*. New York: Holt, Rinehart & Winston.

*Loch, W. (1965). *Voraussetzungen, Mechanismen und Grenzen des psychoanalytischen Prozesses*. Bern and Stuttgart: Hans Huber.

——— (1974). Der Analytiker als Gesetzgeber und Lehrer. *Psyche*, 28:431–460.

*——— (1976). Psychoanalyse und Wahrheit. *Psyche*, 30:865–898.

*Loewenstein, R. M. (1951). The problem of interpretation. *Psychoanal. Q.*, 20:1–14.

Lorenzer, A. (1970). *Sprachzerstörung und Rekonstruktion*. Frankfurt: Suhrkamp.
——— (1973). *Über den Gegenstand der Psychoanalyse, oder: Sprache und Interaktion*. Frankfurt: Suhrkamp.
*——— (1974). *Die Wahrheit der psychoanalytischen Erkenntnis. Ein historisch-materialistischer Entwurf*. Frankfurt: Suhrkamp.
*Manfredi Turillazzi, S. (1974). Dalle interpretazioni mutative di Strachey alle interpretazioni delle relazioni fra gli oggetti interni. *Rivista di Psicoanalisi*, 20:127–143.
Meltzer, D. (1967). *The Psychoanalytic Process*. London: Heineman.
Menninger, K. (1958). *Theory of Psychoanalytic Technique*. New York: Basic Books.
*Nagera, H., ed. (1969–1970). *Basic Psychoanalytic Concepts*. London: Allen & Unwin.
*Naiman, J. (1976). The fundamentals of psychic change in clinical practice. *Int. J. Psychoanal.*, 57:411–418.
Paul, L., ed. (1963). *Psychoanalytic Clinical Interpretation*. London: Collier-Macmillan.
Racker, H. (1958). Counterresistance and interpretation. *J. Amer. Psychoanal. Assn.*, 6:215–221.
Rapaport, D. (1960). *The Structure of Psychoanalytic Theory*. New York: International Universities Press.
*——— (1967). *Collected Papers*. New York: Basic Books.
Reich, W. (1927). Zur Technik der Deutung und der Widerstandanalyse. *Int. Z. Psychoanal.*, 11:297–317.
*——— (1933). *Character Analysis*. Third and enlarged edition. Trans. Vincent R. Carfagno. New York: Farrar, Straus & Giroux, 1972.
*Reik, T. (1933). New ways in psychoanalytic technique. *Int. J. Psychoanal.*, 14:321–334.
Ricoeur, P. (1965). *Freud and Philosophy: An Essay on Interpretation*. Trans. Denis Savage. New Haven, Conn.: Yale University Press, 1970.
Sandler, J., Dare, C., & Holder, A. (1973). *The Patient and the Analyst*. London: Allen & Unwin.
*Saul, L. (1958). Making interpretations. Reprinted in *Psychoanalytic Clinical Interpretation*, ed. L. Paul. London: Collier-Macmillan, 1963.
*Schmidl, F. (1955). The problem of scientific validation in psychoanalytic interpretation. *Int. J. Psychoanal.*, 36:105–113.
*Stengel, E. (1951). The scientific testing of psychoanalytic findings and theory. *Brit. J. Med. Psychol.*, 24:26–29.
*Sterba, E. (1945). Interpretation and education. *Psychoanal. Study Child*, 1:309–317.
*Stokvis, B. (1969). *Psychotherapy für den praktischen Arzt*. Basel/New York: Karger.
Strachey, J. (1934). The nature of the therapeutic action of psychoanalysis. *Int. J. Psychoanal.*, 15:127–159. Reprinted in *Psychoanalytic Clinical Interpretation*, ed. L. Paul. London: Collier-Macmillan, 1963.
*Widloecher, D. (1968). Freud et le probleme du changement. Paris: Payot.

21

HUMBERTO NAGERA, M.D.

The Psychology of Treason and Self-Pathology

THAT TREASON SHOULD BE SUCH A NEGLECTED SUBJECT SHOULD FILL US WITH SURPRISE SINCE ITS CONSEQUENCES MAY WELL HAVE CHANGED THE COURSE OF HISTORY, PARTICULARLY IN RECENT TIMES. IN THIS PAPER, AFTER A BRIEF REVIEW OF THE LITERATURE, THE AUTHOR ATTEMPTS TO UNDERSTAND THE MALIGNANT OR MAJOR FORM OF TREASON. FOR THAT PURPOSE THE CONFLICTS, NARCISSISTIC CONSTELLATIONS, DEFENSE MECHANISMS, THE PROCESS OF IDEALIZATION, AND OF EGO AND SUPEREGO IDEAL FORMATIONS IN TRAITORS, ARE DISCUSSED. PARTICULAR ATTENTION IS PAID TO THE COMPLEX OEDIPAL SITUATION OF TRAITORS, THE QUALITY OF THEIR OBJECT RELATIONS, THEIR SELF-ESTEEM REGULATION MECHANISMS, AND THE MULTIPLICITY OF SCENARIOS IN WHICH TREASON CAN TAKE PLACE.

The subject of treason has received very scanty treatment in the psychoanalytic literature. Perhaps one of the reasons is that there is in each one of us, at the very least, a "minor traitor," a fact that we cannot but contemplate with some horror, fear, and shame. I refer to the fact that given the nature of the Oedipus complex and the role that bisexuality plays in the constellations it adopts (positive and negative), we have all been guilty of treason insofar as we have all wanted to depose the sovereign father and/or the queen mother and occupy their respective places.

There are then the multiple consequences and derivations of the above all through our childhood and developmental histories. Glover (1940), in *The Psychology of Fear and Courage*, describes graphically what I have in mind when he says: "Those who have vivid memories of the seamier side of child, family and school life will have little difficulty in recognizing some of the predisposing causes of Quislingism.[1] The simple case of the younger son who 'gives away' an older brother . . . ; the school-boy who sneaks to the teacher . . . ; the child with a grievance against his parents who idealizes the head of the house next door . . ." (p. 55). If one adds to this our natural ambivalence, our tendency to love and hate the same object, and so on, one can see the fertile ground for later forms of what I will refer to as benign (or minor) forms of treason. I believe these phenomena to be quite common, and perhaps an unavoidable fact of life. But it is not to these types of treason, interesting as they may be in their multiple varieties and dynamics, that this paper addresses itself.

A BRIEF REVIEW OF THE LITERATURE

Beyond Glover (1940), there is the paper by James Alexander (1969) that deals briefly with the issues of dissent, and particularly treason and sedition as the more destructive forms of dissent. He concluded that: "Intrapsychically, treason or strong treasonable and seditious potentialities implicate large areas of the total personality and the character structure of the individual in a pathological process" (p. 162). As he sees it, "The primary structural sites of these pathological processes are defects in the super-ego and ego-ideal" (p. 162).

Greenacre (1969) refers to "a fissure-like defect in the superego (including the conscience and formation of ideals)" of the traitor to which she adds "the invasion of emotional relationships by the excessive need for possession and power, growing out of unusually strong and unresolved infantile jealousy; distortion of the sense of identity sometimes with secondary disturbances in reality testing . . ." (p. 203).

Kapp's (1968) "Ezra Pound's Creativity and Treason: Clues from His Life and Work" throws some light on the role of Pound's manic-depressive illness (perhaps one should say schizoaffective disorder) in his diatribes against the United States, Roosevelt, and the Jews, broadcast from Rome in 1941. They led in 1945 to a charge of "giving aid and comfort to the enemy." But this paper does not discuss treason as such.

Jacobson (1970), in her paper on "The Paranoid Urge to Betray," described the tendency of "patients with paranoid personality struc-

[1]Derived from the notorious World War II Norwegian traitor Major Quisling.

ture to commit acts of betrayal . . . as an expression of their major intrapsychic conflict" (p. 72). In discussing this paper, Dr. Pauline Kernberg noted that these patients lack an organized and functional superego system, as well as the disconnected components representing self- and object images of different instinctual and ego stages.

From the above it is clear that treason can take many forms, appear in many contexts, and obey many causes. It is clear, too, that we are in need of some systematization of the many possible varieties of these phenomena if individuals and nations are going to be able to protect themselves from the severe forms of treason. But first we need clearly to define the terms we will be using.

DEFINITION OF TREASON

The definition of the term *treason*, according to the *Scribner-Bantam English Dictionary* (1979 edition), reads as follows: "n. betrayal of allegiance to one's sovereign or country, as by yielding vital secrets or aiding an enemy in time of war."

Treachery is defined in the same dictionary as (1) treasonable or disloyal conduct; (2) betrayal of trust; treason; faithlessness.

The definition of *traitor* is (1) one who betrays another's trust or is false to an obligation or duty; (2) one who commits treason.

For my purposes I will define treason in somewhat more general terms. Thus I define treason as a betrayal of the allegiance or trust that is due one's country, family, friends, meaningful relationships, and general principles. A traitor is the person who commits such a betrayal.

The concept of treason implies that the treacherous act or behavior constituted a significant, even radical, departure from expected behavior in a given situation. The concept includes that the treacherous act or behavior actually causes, or could cause, significant distress, damage, and so forth, to one or more individuals, to the self and/or to generally accepted principles. It similarly includes the idea that such behavior or acts of treason would be considered unacceptable, highly undesirable, or even outrageous by a large majority of those people who share a similar cultural background with the traitor. The implication that follows is that the act of treason will automatically call for the condemnation of the relevant social group.

But treachery and treason, as would have been noticed from the definition, may occur and be relevant in the context of two individuals, such as two friends, two colleagues, or two lovers. The betrayed one will show similar reactions to those described concerning larger groups of individuals, nations, and so on.

MALIGNANT (OR MAJOR) AND BENIGN (OR MINOR) TREACHERY OR TREASON

It is immediately apparent that the severity of the treacherous act in the ethical sense and in terms of its consequences falls into a continuum. At one extreme the treacherous act will be considered reprehensible and its consequences may have catastrophic proportions. At the other end, there will be those acts that, though similarly reprehensible in the ethical sense, do not imply the same seriousness in terms of the importance of the principles violated or the severity of consequences. In between there would be all kinds of gradations.

To simplify matters a little, we could refer to the higher extreme of the continuum as malignant (or major) treachery or treason, and to the lower extreme as benign (or minor) treachery or treason.

It is my contention that the malignant or major forms of treachery or treason can only occur with individuals with certain specific constellations of conflicts, or, if you will, specific (and quite complex) forms of psychopathology with very idiosyncratic developmental characteristics, dynamics, defense activities, and personality traits. I should add that though all major traitors share these traits, the reverse is not necessarily true—that is, not all those who share these traits are destined to become major traitors. In any case those with such potential constitute an identifiable group of persons, the unrecognized existence of which is a potential hazard or grave potential danger for other individuals, for society at large, and for nations in particular.

It is my impressionistic belief that perhaps many among them, but not all, may respond favorably to psychoanalytic treatment or intensive uncovering psychotherapy. But such a favorable response will hang largely on the early identification of this syndrome by the therapist and in the therapist's minutely precise understanding and timely, patient, tolerant, and consistent interpretation of the enormous complexity of the dynamic factors involved.

I have been surprised by the increasing frequency with which such cases have come to my attention in recent years. I should add that many of them would be considered and treated as typical neurotic patients, whom they closely resemble, but whom I do not think they are.

I will not address here what I have called the benign type of treachery or treason because the factors leading to the behaviors are nonspecific. They cannot, in my judgment, be classed as a distinct group with shared dynamic characteristics in sharp contradistinction with the malignant types. Similarly, my comments in this paper concern only male cases, and no discussion of a similar problem in females, if it exists, will be attempted.

NARCISSISTIC DAMAGE AND TREASON

It is my first impression that in the dynamics of malignant treason one regularly finds some very basic narcissistic damage to the personality structure as its background. How that narcissistic damage came about is no doubt a relevant question, and one whose answer would be idiosyncratic to each case.

I will postulate that any one of the typical events or things capable of interfering with the primary narcissistic stage (as defined by Freud in 1914) may be all that is necessary. Thus the mother's inability to soothe the baby by accurately reading his cues and restoring his lost homeostatic equilibirum may be one reason. A painful or otherwise disruptive illness during the first year of life may be another, similar causative factor that makes it difficult to maintain or recover that equilibrium, and, as such, restore the minimum feeling of well-being that should (by implication in Freud's theory) be a concomitant of the primary narcissistic stage.

SECONDARY NARCISSISTIC CATHEXIS AND TREASON

Yet, I have concluded from my clinical observations that it is not only disturbances in the Freudian primary narcissistic stage that constitute the *sine qua non* requirement for the recipe that makes the traitor. I believe that severe disturbances in the supply of secondary narcissistic cathexis, after object relationships have been established, even if only rudimentarily, and the consequent difficulties in the regulation of the self-esteem that result from it can constitute the required background. It follows that all these individuals have major difficulties with their self-images, especially in terms of their self-regard. Similarly, and on this basis, such individuals do have enormous problems in developing a healthy and reliable identity not only as an individual (an individual of principles), or a person, but in their sexual identities as well.

Such processes, as I see it, are highly dependent on a reasonably healthy and stable positive self-image that contains an adequate amount of positive (and stable) self-regard. Where the above is the case, we would have acquired the necessary ingredients for the potential future capacity to regulate self-esteem internally, with a sufficient distance from and a lack of excessive dependency on the world of objects.

I believe that those who may not have reached sufficient normality early on in those areas are subject constantly to wide swings between feelings of worthlessness of the self and a narcissistic overvaluation of it, which is the result of the maladaptive defenses employed to compensate for the former. It will seem reasonable to assume that this background of marked swings interferes severely with the acquisition of sufficient and, most important, stable feelings of self-regard. It similarly interferes with the mechanisms that must be developed to regulate self-esteem internally, with the whole process of healthy identification, and with the acquisitions of suitable introjects (in the form of reliable objects and standards) that constitute the core of the superego.

I have stated that some sort of narcissistic fault seems to be a *sine qua non* element in the personality of the malignant traitor. But this must not be understood to mean that such a formula is specific to him and not to other forms of personality disturbances or psychopathologies. Indeed, the opposite of such a view would be much closer to the truth. In other words, the narcissistic disturbances I have described so far are quite common and widespread, and are seen in many of the so-called character disorders, narcissistic disturbances, and various forms of borderline personalities. And yet most individuals who belong to the three groups mentioned do not partake of the other significant characteristics and developmental events that give the final and genuine hallmark to the potential traitor and his psychology. Such individuals, in my view, constitute a very specific and idiosyncratic group, and can be clearly differentiated from other individuals and other forms of psychopathology.

THE ROLE OF THE EGO

Clinically it will be expected, then, that the genuine traitor will have some, and at times many, of the characteristics of the types of disorders I just mentioned. This is true enough, but a significant, indeed radical, difference of the genuine traitor must be highlighted at this point. One of the characteristics of this traitor's hallmark is an otherwise good, intact, and not infrequently excellent ego. I mean here, of course, in the cognitive-functional-intellectual sense only, since in other areas their egos may well be somewhat impaired or dysfunctional.

Clinically, too, it would be observed that the genuine traitor is highly prone to be narcissistically injured. The narcissistic elements in their personalities are clearly discernible as the cause of these injuries, as are the attempts, maladaptive or not, to restore their narcissistic integrity, or, in other words, a good feeling about themselves. They want to be loved by everyone; perhaps it would be more appropriate to say adored by everybody. They have no tolerance for criticism, and given that criticisms are always a major injury to their damaged personality, those who inflict the pain become hated enemies, the subjects for their betrayals.* But this is so only if those that are critical are of sufficient importance. If the injuring objects are of less importance, they will become the targets of their sadistic revenge and abuse. I should note here that none of the above are unique to the traitor, but are, in fact, a common phenomenon observable in various forms of psychopathology.

What, then, are the other specific dynamic factors and conflicts that make the psychology of the traitor a special variety all of its own? What are the developmental events that are reenacted in the treacherous behaviors and acts?

*I am aware that the clarity of this paper would have been well served by the use of occasional clinical examples. Given the very sensitive nature of the subject, I have opted for the exclusion of examples from my own work. Nevertheless, examples galore of the various points made in the paper can be found in the book by Page and colleagues (1968), *Philby, The Spy Who Betrayed a Generation*. I highly recommend its reading for this purpose. Beyond Philby himself, there is an extensive discussion of Mclean and Burgess, two other notorious British spies.

THE OEDIPUS COMPLEX AND TREASON

"Traitors" reach the Oedipus conflict handicapped by their narcissistic lags. Typical, and specific for them, is an enormous unsatisfied wish for the father's love, attention, and admiration, which, for a variety of reasons and frequently through no fault of their own, they do not seem able to obtain. Thus a very tormentuous and ambivalent attitude toward the father who does not think much of them, or does not pay them enough attention, or simply does not care for them, is a common complaint and an important part of the dynamics of the traitor. Generally, as one would expect by the time the traitor is an adult, he reactively and defensively may think poorly of the father, or see him as weak or worthless, as a man of little accomplishment or value. Any initial attempts to show this type of patient that behind that defensive posture there was at one time, and certainly during the oedipal phase, a very different set of feelings, meet at best with scorn and massive denial, and at worst, with these plus inordinate explosive anger at the therapist for this stupid suggestion. And yet it is clear, from the clinical material itself and from the ardent defensive attitude of the patient, that there was a time when he longed for his father's attention and love.

Thus far this is in no way very different from the developmental history of any other human being. The difference consists in that this patient attributes particularly to the father the omnipotence and omniscience that most children attribute to both parents. It is as if somewhere between the ages of two and a half and five (at the peak of the Oedipus complex), he longs for the father as the only possible restorer of his narcissistic damage and needs. Father's admiration, attention, and love, much more than mother's, were felt as palliative whenever experienced. Perhaps this was due in part to the fact that the early narcissistic injuries do happen in the context of the mother–child relationship, if they take place during the first year of life. On the other hand, the same is true if the narcissistic problem comes from the beginning of the secondary narcissistic stage, which, again, happens to start with, essentially, in the context of the mother–child relationship.

The mother is not only his first meaningful object, but the regulation of his self-esteem and the establishment of his self-regard depend mostly on the interaction with her. The father, as we know, plays, at this stage and in relative terms, a very secondary role. Thus, with the move to the triangular awareness and relationships that are characteristic of the Oedipus complex, the father's importance and significance come into their own, not only vis-à-vis the child's relation to his mother, but with regard to many other developmental processes. It is now, and because of the failure of the mother–child interaction to help him regain a stable narcissistic feeling, that the figure of the father as the possible "restorer" or "healer" of the narcissistic injuries becomes all important. In this type of psychopathology, the father, for the above reasons, becomes the real omnipotent and omniscient promise of relief. Given that this basic fault cannot be corrected in reality by all of the father's admiration, and that this type of child is highly prone to narcissistic injury through any real or imagined neglect, he is soon disappointed in him. Further, given that the child's oedipal strivings for the mother are in conflict with these special "longings" for the father, the situation cannot but end catastrophically.

From that moment onward the father (and later, by extension, the fatherland) becomes the subject of a sordid discontent, is seen as unfair, as unjust to his children, as not willing to recognize their merits, to soothe their pains, to restore their well-being—in short, to give them their dues. The reinforcement of these hostile and destructive feelings that comes from the positive Oedipus complex seals the fate of the father (potentially the fatherland) and the child. He will be forced into the path of revenge, and, since his unconscious hate knows no limits, sooner or later, in one form or another, he will attempt to destroy the father. The act of treason will become the means to his revenge and to the symbolic destruction of the father.

TREASON LOOKED AT DEVELOPMENTALLY

But the situation is far more complex than described so far. The "act of treason" itself needs to be examined and understood in all its ramifications and its symbolic meaning in order to clarify the psychology of the traitor. This could be attempted from the treachery to its roots and dynamics so to say, retrospectively if you wish, or more specifically, by means of reconstruction. But given that I have taken a developmental outlook in this paper, and for the sake of consistency, I would approach the act of treachery, its significance, and its symbolic meaning following the same path.

Thus in the "potential traitor" the disappointment in the father's ability or willingness to make him whole drives him to "woo" the disappointing mother, now dressed in her new oedipal robes. This is as much the result of an act of revenge toward the father as of interest in the mother. From this moment onward, his whole life and endeavors will be devoted to supplant the father, to surpass him in terms of the mother's affection, indeed to take possession of her. Here, again, we are in the familiar territory of the Oedipus complex. But there is a significant difference in the traitor's psychology that makes his Oedipus complex somewhat unique. For him it is not enough to gain the affection of the mother at the expense of the father, to surpass him in her affection, while the death wishes are kept strictly confined to the realm of fantasy, as would undoubtedly be the case with normal people or neurotic patients. Unfortunately, in the case of the malignant traitor, this destructive fantasy must be acted out in real life, just as the conquest of the mother is acted out in real life, though in a displaced form.

Later I will give a few examples to clarify this. What I want to underline at this point is the similar necessity for the traitor to act out, at times, in a very concrete, specific, and dramatic manner, the destruction of the father. Think, for example, of the actual assassination or attempts of assassination of presidents in this country or of political leaders around the world throughout history. Of course, this is the extreme of the destructive acting-out continuum directed toward the father that is frequently carried out by psychotic or otherwise very disturbed people, although not always, as in genuine political assassinations. At the other end of the same continuum, there are numerous, but somewhat less dramatic, examples, although not necessarily less malignant, of the same behavior. All this is in sharp contrast to the simple, normal, or neurotic vicissistudes of the Oedipus complex of most human beings that do not reach the acting-out heights I am describing here. Indeed, the authority of the father figure becomes imbedded in the superego of the normal or neurotic individual, and from there it modulates and controls behavior so that these intended violent, savage, damaging acts (whether or not they include an actual death, or actually result in the malignant consequences desired) are forbidden. These acts can only be performed in the case of the ordinary neurotic personality in a highly displaced, symbolic, and mostly nonvicious form. I consider this difference of the greatest significance and of important differential diagnostic value.

But this is by no means the only important difference. Perhaps more important is the fact that the rage toward the father must include the simultaneous damage, sellout, or symbolic destruction of that which the child thought to be the most important to the father, that is, the father's wife, or, in other words, the child's own mother (and, by extension, the motherland). It is thus a doubly vicious blow that must be accorded the "father," usually in the form of its symbolic substitutes in the case of traitors. What I have in mind here can best be exemplified by the many (and now quite common) stories of "spies," "moles," and "traitors." In other words, at the same time that the father is betrayed, included in the very act of betrayal is a sellout of the mother—that is, the motherland.

THE MULTIPLE SCENARIOS OF TREASON

The Oedipus complex can be, and is, reenacted in a large variety of scenarios. There is, for example, one's country as the representative of the mother who is felt as possessed, controlled, and in the hands of the politicians in power (presidents and prime ministers), who thus become surrogate father figures.

In a smaller scenario, as in a corporation, the corporation itself represents the mother, and the president of the corporation, chairman of the board, and so on represent the father, who is seen as in possession of the mother. It goes without saying that the many forms of the childhood Oedipus complex are frequently reactivated and acted out in these different types of scenarios.

I can say, without any doubt after seven years of experience as the director of a hospital in a university center, that such a position automatically places one in the situation of a father figure vis-à-vis the hospital or the university. The latter represents the mother, who is owned and controlled by the director father. The staff members become the children of the family, and reenact their sibling rivalry among themselves in their attempts to gain the good will of the parents (mother-hospital, father-director).

If any rational decision is made that proves beneficial to one member of the staff, the other "children" become quite upset, and wonder why it is that they are not automatically bestowed a similar or greater favor. By the same token, the father-director position is eyed by the younger, ambitious professionals as a highly desirable situation. In their fantasies they long to oust the father and take possession of the mother. At times the situation becomes, for a detached observer, like a three-ring circus. In my opinion the success of the father-director in running an efficient organization is very much dependent on his ability to recognize all the above, and to reduce it to rational proportions. Disturbing and disruptive as these situations can become, they lack the malignancy that we see in other cases, as long as they involve only the acting out of the Oedipus complex of "neurotic" individuals.

Unfortunately all these possible scenarios, and particularly those at the national and international political levels, are populated by individuals whose character structure and personality contain forms of psychopathology that I consider somewhat outside the "neurosis," though not necessarily psychotic. Such individuals are potentially dangerous in rather lethal ways. Naturally the same line of thought applies to actually psychotic individuals, since their enactment of their Oedipal fantasies in real life is not subjected to reality testing, and is furthermore under the compulsive motivational forces of their delusional ideas and their deficient judgment and thinking. All of these combined make them particularly dangerous, as the assassination attempt on President Reagan demonstrates. Yet many attempts at political assassination are carried out by so-called political idealists, the discontented and fanatics who cannot, by any stretch of the imagination, be considered psychotics or borderline.

The kind of treachery I am trying to deal with here can be observed in many different contexts and acquire many forms.[2] The three notorious British spies, Philby, Maclean, and Burgess, who after years of spying for the Russians defected to the Soviet Union (once their covers were blown apart), are another example of the various forms that lethal, damaging treason can take. The extent of the damage done by these individuals is difficult to ascertain, but according to Page et al. (1968) in their book on Philby, it might have been considerable. They said, "Clearly, this is what was in the mind of one Foreign Office man when he said that 'Philby robbed European countries of their freedom' " (p. 290).

The biographical studies of spies, and the observation and treatment of patients with the makeup of the personality and psychology of the traitor, throw some light on the mechanisms of defense that are frequently employed by such characters, as well as some of the various other conflicts involved. Thus the passive homosexual longings for the father remain quite active all through their lives and constitute a constant source of conflict that represents a serious threat to the masculinity of those in this group who have achieved a clearer sexual identity. In such cases the "I don't love you, I hate you" defense mechanism becomes operative. Denial in action, by means

[2]This includes some "defections" from the psychoanalytic camp, though I do not mean to imply that all those who leave the field do so on the basis of these dynamics or psychopathology.

of an unnecessary defiance and militant attitude against "father figures," is of course seen, as are all the varieties of difficulties in relating and accepting figures in authority, as pecking orders and hierarchical structures.

I have mentioned that there are cases where problems with a clear sexual identity are one of the results of the basic original narcissistic fault. These difficulties belong on a scale that may go from overt homosexuality to sadistic heterosexuality, where the object is debased, demeaned, exploited, and abused. The fantasies accompanying masturbation may be full of sadistic connotations of various types, such as driving women crazy with sexual excitement, forcing painful anal intercourse on the sexual partner, or having her submit totally to one's will and desires. All of these point to a significant anal fixation that is not a necessary element in the traitor's recipe, but frequently constitutes an additional and dangerous ingredient of it.

TREASON AND OBJECT RELATIONS

The "traitor" is generally damaged more or less severely in his ability to relate to objects. Objects are frequently used for need satisfaction, though probably most "traitors" had reached some level of object constancy. Nevertheless, though traitors may certainly appear gregarious and relate to several individuals to the point of conveying a sense of normality, and even friendliness, the reality is that they are quite lonely and isolated. They cannot, or do not dare to, cathect objects in depth, and very much fear becoming attached to anybody. Remember that their marked interest in their mothers during the oedipal phase is as much, or more, based on the wish to take revenge on the father by conquering the mother than on any great affection for her. Indeed, any genuine affection may be substantially lacking due to her earlier inability to restore the homeostatic narcissistic equilibrium or to supply a sufficient secondary narcissistic cathexis. Thus she is used essentially for need satisfaction (which, in this case, is mostly related to ventilating the traitor's hatred of her) and more particularly, as a tool for the repression of the hate against the father that becomes paramount. It is thus not surprising that in the act of treachery toward the father (for example, in the symbolic form of the fatherland), the traitor is quite willing to sell out the mother and has no genuine concern for her (mother substitutes, motherland, etc.).

The few cases that I have seen that involved the psychology of the traitor, and a handful of others that I have supervised or otherwise come into contact with, ranged from the essentially object-isolated individual to some who were actually married and had a semblance of family life, and whose children, incidentally, were usually a narcissistic extension of the self. Others have established what appear to be close "professional" ties with colleagues, mostly for the hidden purpose of exploitation, furthering their interests, and so on—essentially on a need-satisfying basis.

Those who married invariably were dissatisfied with their wives, who mostly served a utilitarian purpose for them. Any failures or demands on them by their partners provoked an angry reaction and a flurry of criticism. Interestingly enough, such criticism frequently was not actually verbalized, but completely filled their fantasy life, and was openly expressed to their therapists in their analytic sessions. Thus, for example, if the wives were not as active sexually as they may have desired, this was felt as a narcissistic injury; by the same token, if the wives made sexual demands on them, they were similarly narcissistically enraged. They seemed to be saying that their wives should be totally pleased with whatever they were willing to offer, but rarely were such criticisms verbalized to their partners. What I am trying to emphasize is that the issue here is not so much whether they seem object-related or not, but the qualitative aspects of the relationship. The difficulties in object relations is one of the elements in the recipe of the psychology of the traitor.

TREASON, EXTERNALIZATION, PROJECTION, RATIONALIZATION, AND INTELLECTUALIZATION

Another element is the nearly incredible tendency of these patients to externalize, project, rationalize, and intellectualize their own inner designs. Typically the traitor is unaware of the true nature of his intentions, or his actual treachery when it occurs. Though obvious to everyone else, in most cases he is totally oblivious to his behavior and its consequences. This incredible feat is due to the amount of denial traitors use in various combinations with the other defenses mentioned. In fact, the genuine traitor believes that his behavior is fully justified, as the only honorable behavior left to somebody who thinks of himself as a highly principled individual trying to correct "injustices," or to stop the "unprincipled behavior of others," or to correct what he considers "intolerable social ills." As the result such traitors are led to idealize, with the help of much rationalization and intellectualization, sociopolitical regimes that are in fact paradigmatic of those evils that they mean to correct. Obviously, to get to that result, substantial amounts of denial, externalization, rationalization, and intellectualization are necessary. These defense mechanisms are used on an *ad hoc* basis, or, in other words, in specific situations that arise suddenly, and where the patient, in order to be congruent, to remain sane, to keep his psychic order and integrity, must achieve quickly a considerable distortion of both its internal and external reality. Still more important is the fact that these types of defenses are needed constantly in place as well, in order to keep internal and external reality permanently distorted. In this way the traitor escapes the overwhelming conflicts that would otherwise arise, with the accompanying guilt, anxiety, and depressive feelings that need to be constantly avoided.

It follows that many of these patients do, in fact, build a character structure that fulfills a double purpose. On the one hand, it solves the conflict that would otherwise become manifest. On the other hand, it actually allows an idealization of the objectionable behavior, so that the genuine traitor actually believes his acts are motivated by the highest of principles. Page and colleagues (1968), in their account of the lives and exploits of the British traitors Philby, Burgess, and Maclean, stated:

> But essentially they were moved by a quasi-religious faith: they believed that the Soviet Union was somehow cleaner, purer and better than their own country, because it claimed to have adopted Communism. Like religious zealots in many ages before, they would justify everything in their careers—treachery, cruelty, even murder—by pointing to the cause. Like the chorus in Brecht's classic of Communist revolution, *The Measures Taken*, they would say: "What baseness would you not commit to root out baseness?" (p. 289)

TREASON AND THE DISTORTION OF EGO AND SUPEREGO IDEALS

I will not comment here on the deformation that all this implies in terms of ego and superego ideal formation, but would like to underline that these mechanisms are the ones frequently operative in the ego and superego ideal formation of the doctrinaire, the fanatic, and similar fellow travelers. The importance of this in terms of the struggles among various political ideologies, sociophilosophical systems, and so forth, cannot escape anyone's attention. One only needs to be reminded of the more recent acts of terrorism, such as the attempted assassination of the Pope, the assassination of President Sadat of Egypt, and the killings in Iran, as well as the assassination of President Kennedy and the attempts on Truman and Ford, among others.

Indeed, one gets the distinct impression that the potentially lethal psychological structures and conflicts that characterize the personality of some of these individuals is more easily actualized when a social, philosophical, political, or religious vehicle offers the opportunity to create "idealizations." By such means the otherwise objectionable potential behavior is turned into a highly desirable actual one by individuals operating within such systems. It is perhaps for this reason that at times of increased socioeconomic, politico-philosophical, and religious struggles, these violent acts acquire epidemic proportions, while in more "normal" periods, they are isolated events and more within endemic proportions.

THE ROLE OF EXTERNALIZATION AND PROJECTION

The final, but no less important, sign of the hallmark of the personality of the traitor is the direct consequence of the generous use of externalization and projection. Basically traitors are enormously fearful individuals who, though perhaps capable of sustaining a cool and calm demeanor, are, in their fantasy lives, enormously suspicious of everybody else. In a few patients of this type that I have seen in analysis, hours were spent discussing and examining the imagined, negative intentions, plots, and counterplots being fabricated against them. Occasionally such concerns reached truly paranoid proportions, though the type of patient I am referring to here is not a psychotic patient. The world is for such patients a jungle in which, behind every tree, there is a conspiracy to smear, depossess, or otherwise damage them. The remarkable things are the absolute blindness and the extraordinary resistance these patients display toward any attempt to show them that what they fear is nothing more than their own intentionality externalized, as well as the result of their liberal use of the mechanism of projection. One striking form of such resistance is that, after a confrontation or the therapist's interpretation showing the dynamics involved that the patient can and does recognize intellectually, the situation is in no way alleviated. In other words, after that recognition the patient continues to examine every fantasized plot, possible action, and so on, as if this newly acquired knowledge of the situation in no way can modulate the force of the internal conflicts. This aspect of the problem would seem to require an inordinate amount of working through and the entire success of the treatment seems to hang for a time on the ability to overcome this difficulty.

TREASON AND PSYCHOPATHIC BEHAVIOR

It is important at this point to refer to a different group of personalities whose manifest behavior in every way resembles that of the malignant traitor, though the internal metapsychological picture is in no way similar—those perpetrators of acts of apparent treason who are in fact highly intelligent psychopaths. Such an individual's acts are motivated essentially by personal gain or by their need to follow "the pleasure principle" in behavior and in the pursuit of their egotistic interests. The highly developed psychopath who moves, for example, in professional, political, or business circles is fully aware of what he is doing and why, and does not suffer any internal conflict, though for external consumption he may produce "idealized" systems to justify his behavior—if he feels this will further his interests or will soften the attitude of others toward him, in the event he is caught. Being highly intelligent, he knows what to offer as rationalizations for what would otherwise be unacceptable to those around him and on whose "good will" or "blindness" he depends to achieve his aims. Obviously, and in contrast with the genuinely malignant traitor, he does not believe a word of it. As with other psychopaths, the issue lies in the lack of appropriate superego structures and standards capable of regulating certain behaviors. As can be seen, this is a radically different internal picture from the one offered by the "genuine" traitor.

SELF-ESTEEM REGULATION AND TREASON

Finally, let me refer briefly to one very puzzling aspect of the psychology of "genuine" traitors. This concerns the regulation of their self-esteem, since, given their original narcissistic faults, it remains a constant and special problem. We have noted, too, the damage that overflows to the self-image, self-identity, sexual identity, and self-regard.

I have mentioned that the developmental deficiencies derived from the narcissistic fault and the consequent structural damage cannot be reversed. For this reason it is all the more interesting to realize that the preparatory stages to the act of treason, up to the point at which the distortion of the internal and external realities is in place and the final "idealized" ego system in position, achieve quite efficiently what nothing else could achieve. In other words they seem to heal over the narcissistic wounds, more or less permanently, in some cases, and at the very least temporarily.

Similarly, a high degree of resolution is achieved in terms of the problems that pertain to traitors' self-images, self-regard, personal identity, and self-esteem regulation. This "marvelous feat" is achieved because the new systems of ideals are the new measurements against which the ego is assessed, and they are fulfilling its requirements successfully. Out of that interaction they get a new self-image, with sufficient self-regard and a very considerable improvement in their self-esteem.

Now that they are totally devoted to the new highly idealized cause, and that they work consistently, "loyally," and persistently for it, they become a "new persona" whose new system of ideals generously rewards their efforts. For the first time, perhaps, they come as close to a feeling of completeness and wholeness as they will ever have; their wounds seem to be healing and their self-esteem improving. For the first time, too, they feel truly important.

We need to understand how the new systems of introjects and ideals are substituted for those that regulated and modulated behavior before the change. We are, after all, well aware that these introjects, whatever their nature, are stable structures that are not easily, if at all, changeable. We do know, of course, of situations in which this is possible under special circumstances; for example, the phenomenon that takes place generally under the auspices of group psychology, where substantial aspects of an individual's standards are at least temporarily substituted by those of the leader. Under these conditions such individuals are capable of behaviors that would be objectionable to them under normal circumstances, as Freud pointed out in his 1921 book, *Group Psychology and the Analysis of the Ego*.

Looking in that direction, we can further understand how the genuine traitor manages the many changes that take place in his internal world. Two factors are relevant here. First, there is the gradual cathexis in the most intense manner of a group of highly idealized, abstract ideas, though they are generally quite distorted. To this is added the second factor, that is, at some point and in some cases, the traitor joins others, either overtly or covertly, who are similarly devoted to the "cause."

Thus the idealized but generally distorted abstract ideas become the most significant "object" capable of substituting as new superego introjects for the earlier ones. Freud (1921) very precisely described this by saying:

> Contemporaneously with this "devotion" of the ego to the object, which is no longer to be distinguished from a sublimated devotion to an abstract idea, the functions allotted to the ego ideal [i.e., superego] entirely cease to operate. The criticism exercised by that agency is silent; everything that the object does and asks for is right and blameless. Conscience has no application to anything that is done for the sake of the object [in this case, an abstract set of ideas—the cause]; in the blindness of love remorselessness is carried to the pitch of crime.[3] The whole situation can be completely summarized in a formula: The object [i.e., idealized system] has been put in the place of the ego ideal [meaning the superego]. (p. 113)

If we add to the above the changes brought about by joining the group, we can understand what a powerful combination this can become. In the words of Le Bon as quoted by Freud (1921): "Whoever be the individuals that compose it . . . the fact that they have been transformed into a group puts them in a possession of a sort of collective mind which makes them feel, think, and act in a manner quite different from that in which each individual of them would feel, think, and act were he in a state of isolation" (p. 73).

It is my opinion that this could explain what we see happening in the case of the "genuine malignant traitor." Thus he substitutes

[3]Thus it is said that Philby led to their deaths through betrayal as many as 300 fellow agents during the course of his career, apparently without blinking an eye (In Page et al., 1968).

for more or less extensive parts of his superego standards those of the new "leader," which may be an individual, an ideology, or, even more important, a combination of both. The last seems to have been the case in many instances of treason of the spy variety, such as Philby and Fuchs, among others.

These processes are facilitated by certain predisposing factors in the make-up of the personality of the genuine traitor. First, consider the inordinate disappointment in the father and the concomitant hate. There is here a peculiar built-in structural conflict between introjects that are acquired from a person who is marked, simultaneously, to be betrayed, and possibly destroyed. This perhaps creates a lack of stability in this type of introject, and in some form facilitates its substitution under appropriate conditions by a radically different set of introjects. Second, there is the perennial difficulty with the maintenance of sufficient self-regard and self-esteem. Yet the new introjects change this situation in important ways, as we have seen. I believe that it is factors such as these that explain not only the changes observed but the remarkable stability that some of the new introjects acquire. In the cases of Philby, Mclean, and Burgess, they lasted a lifetime, during which these men were able to deal the most severe blows to their countries, friends, and democracy.

Treason, it seems, is a ubiquitous phenomenon capable of manifesting itself in a large varieties of scenarios; that is, from national and international politics where the consequences may well change the course of history to corporate or departmental politics (in industry, campuses, etc.) where, though the consequences may not be as dramatic, the disruption and potential damage are still significant. Treason can be observed as well in other forms of human interactions, such as friendships and marriages.

REFERENCES

Alexander, J. (1969). The psychology of treason. *Bull. Phila. Assn. Psychoanal.*, 19:158–166.

Freud, S. (1914). On narcissism. *Standard Edition*, 14:67–102.

——— (1921). Group psychology and the analysis of the ego. *Standard Edition*, 18:113, 73.

Glover, E. (1940). *The Psychology of Fear and Courage*. London: Penguin Books.

Greenacre, P. (1969). Treason and the traitor. *Amer. Imago*, 26:3, 199233.

Jacobson, E. (1970). The paranoid urge to betray. *Bull. Menninger Clin.*, 35:72–76.

Kapp, Frederic T. (1968). Ezra Pound's creativity and treason: Clues from his life and work. *Comp. Psychiat.*, 9:414–427.

Page, B., Leitch, D., & Knightley, P. (1968). *Philby, the Spy Who Betrayed a Generation*. London: Andrew Deutsch.

III

Clinical Research

22 JUDY L. KANTROWITZ, Ph.D.

Suitability for Psychoanalysis

THIS PAPER REPORTS THE RESULTS OF ONE ASPECT OF A PROSPECTIVE, LONGITUDINAL STUDY OF SUITABILITY FOR AND OUTCOME OF PSYCHOANALYSIS THAT WAS BEGUN AT THE BOSTON PSYCHOANALYTIC INSTITUTE IN 1972. THE GOAL OF THIS STUDY WAS TO INVESTIGATE THE FACTORS THAT DETERMINE SUITABILITY FOR PSYCHOANALYSIS. THE SAMPLE INCLUDED 22 PATIENTS ACCEPTED FOR SUPERVISED PSYCHOANALYSIS BY THE COMMITTEE ON INSTITUTE ANALYSIS. THE PROCESS OF PATIENT SELECTION, DEVELOPMENT OF HYPOTHESES AND MEASURES FOR EVALUATION OF ANALYTIC PROCEDURE AND PROGRESS, AND TREATMENT OUTCOME ARE ALL REVIEWED. ABSTRACT TERMS ARE DEFINED AND TRANSLATED INTO BEHAVIORALLY OBSERVABLE CORRELATES. ANALYTIC RESULTS ARE DISTINGUISHED FROM THERAPEUTIC BENEFIT.

The questions of whether and to what extent a patient can be analyzed pose both theoretical and practical problems. One major difficulty is the precise definition of terms (Erle & Goldberg, 1979; Bachrach, 1983). Most analysts would agree that psychoanalysis, in contrast with other psychotherapeutic methods, involves a reactivation of childhood conflicts in the transference neurosis, which is then modified or resolved by interpretations. Analysts may differ, however, in describing what constitutes a transference neurosis as well as in what characterizes an interpretation. On the basis of these differences, analysts may proceed in different ways with their patients. We cannot assume comparability of treatment unless we know that comparable definitions are being used.

Criteria for psychoanalytic outcome must also be carefully defined. A successful analytic result, defined by a resolution of the

The author thanks Dr. Ann Katz for her helpful suggestions and editorial assistance on this paper.

This project was partially funded by grants from the Research Funds of the American Psychoanalytic Association and the Boston Psychoanalytic Society and Institute.

transference neurosis, refers to outcome in terms of the treatment process itself, whereas therapeutic benefit refers to a successful outcome in terms of the clinical improvement actually experienced by the patient. Often, however, these concepts are used interchangeably as criteria for "successful" analysis (Erle & Goldberg, 1979; Oremland et al., 1975).

THE CONCEPT OF ANALYZABILITY

Freud's (1905) criteria for analyzability were a reasonable degree of education and a reliable character. In his view contradictions for undertaking a psychoanalysis were an illness of psychotic proportions, an inability to learn and grow due to age, and a decision to undertake psychoanalysis in response to pressure from others. Whereas Freud focused on factors that were relatively easy to assess, later authors suggested criteria that were more abstract and, therefore, more difficult to evaluate. Tolerance for frustration, anxiety, depression, and passivity, a capacity for insight, adequate reality testing, meaningful object relationships, and positive motivation have been considered favorable attributes for patients seeking analysis (C. F. Karush in Guttman, 1960; Kuiper, 1968).

Bachrach and Leaf (1978) made a comprehensive survey of the psychoanalytic literature in which they summarized important factors in assessing suitability for psychoanalysis. They concluded that the better the pretreatment level of functioning, as measured by such variables as ego strength and object relations, the more favorable would be the outcome. Their review of the literature did not reveal any consistent or reliable way in which various authors had evaluated these pretreatment qualities.

OUTCOME STUDIES

Erle (1979) evaluated the outcome of 40 completed treatment center cases and 42 private cases in psychoanalysis. In this retrospective study she found that among patients initially evaluated as suitable for psychoanalysis, 42 percent of the clinic cases as compared with 60 percent of the private cases were ultimately found to be analyzable. Erle carefully distinguished analyzability from therapeutic benefit.

The latter finding was replicated by Erle and Goldberg (1984) in their retrospective study of 160 private cases treated by graduate analysts; 61 percent were rated as analyzable.

Weber and colleagues (1985) studied 295 patients treated in supervised psychoanalysis by candidates at Columbia. All patients were initially evaluated by senior analysts. For those patients who terminated while the treating analyst was still in training, graduate analysts gathered information at the end of treatment. Patients who terminated after the candidate's graduation, a subgroup of 77, were rated by the treating analyst at the end of analysis. Only these 77 patients were evaluated for analyzability. The authors carefully distinguished analyzability from therapeutic benefit. For the purposes of their study, they defined analyzability as top ratings on the following items on a termination questionnaire (Weber et al., 1985, p. 131):

1. "The patient brought psychological data (e.g., dreams, fantasies, affects, self-observations) into treatment because he recognized it could be a source of understanding as well as relief."
2. "The patient recognized he had resources and learned to use these resources to achieve realistic adaptive growth as well as relief of personal suffering."
3. "The patient often used insight gained in the transference to plan and execute change in his everyday life and interpersonal relations."

They found that 43 percent of those patients whose analyses terminated privately after the candidate's graduation were assessed as analyzable. Neither the evaluations of the senior analysts who wrote reports on each of the cases selected for admission nor any item of information obtained at the time of the initial interview (i.e., age, birth order, ego strength) had any predictive value as to which patients would be analyzable.

Earlier studies at the Boston Institute (Knapp et al., 1960; Sashin et al., 1975) had similarly low success in using individual items for predicting analyzability. In his research Knapp found that clinicians' judgments of analyzability based on specific pretreatment patient characteristics were no more predictive of outcome than clinicians' judgments based on more generalized, overall impressions. Sashin's study indicated that of 105 predictor items, ten were related to treatment outcome. Four of these items concerned the patient's family history.

Most other assessments of suitability for psychoanalysis have been based on data gathered in clinical interviews that include the patient's life history. There are considerable variations, however, in how these interviews are conducted and in their focus. Generally the data obtained in an initial screening interview are limited, and patients vary in their self-awareness and willingness to share information. Diagnostic testing may be employed to reveal the dynamic and less conscious aspects of patients' conflicts as well as their underlying personality organization. As Kernberg et al. (1972) have emphasized, the clinical sophistication and in-depth appreciation of psychoanalytic concepts of the examining psychologist largely determine the usefulness of the psychological test evaluations.

Only two groups have used psychological tests as part of their studies in evaluating analyzability. Appelbaum (1977) used psychological tests in the assessment of patients in the Menninger Psychotherapy Research Project. Clinical interviews were also used in that study. The evaluations made from the test data proved to be the most accurate predictors of treatment outcome for the Menninger patients. However, these researchers did not distinguish between the outcome of treatment for those patients in psychotherapy and the outcome for those in psychoanalysis. Thus the Menninger prediction of treatment outcome did not have relevance specifically to analytic result. The project reported here, the only other study to use psychological testing to assess outcome of psychoanalysis, was the first to use testing to evaluate analyzability (Kantrowitz et al., 1975).

HYPOTHESES

Review of the literature revealed that four global psychological factors are generally regarded as correlates of suitability for psychoanalysis. These four factors are:

1. Reality testing—defined as the extent to which the patient's perception and understanding of the environment conform to the world as it actually is.
2. Level and quality of object relations—defined as the extent to which the patient is able to respond and relate to others as real, whole people, differentiated from the self.
3. Affect availability and tolerance—defined as the extent to which the patient is consciously aware of his or her emotions and the extent to which the patient's affects can be modulated.

4. Motivation for treatment—defined as the extent to which the patient recognizes the source of his or her troubles as being primarily internal, finds them painful, and wishes to change.

The central hypothesis of this study held that the more positively the patient was evaluated on each of these four variables, the more likely he or she would be able to participate successfully in psychoanalysis and benefit from this treatment modality; that is, to achieve both analytic result and therapeutic benefit. In this paper only the hypothesis regarding analytic result is being considered.

METHOD

Data on the four predictor variables were gathered from both clinical interviews and psychological testing. The variables were rated on a seven-point scale, four points of which were descriptively defined, including maximally suitable, acceptable, questionable, and unsuitable.

Case Selection

During the period of data collection (1972–1973), the Committee on Institute Analysis evaluated 84 patients. Of these 35 were accepted by the committee. Following evaluation, six patients withdrew from the patient pool, two declined to participate in the study, two were not selected from the patient pool by a candidate, one terminated psychoanalysis in six months, one left the Boston area immediately after completing analysis before a follow-up could be undertaken, and one refused to participate in the follow-up portion of the study. The remaining 22 patients constituted the study population. These patients were in psychoanalysis between two and nine years (mean = 4½, S.D. = 1.71). Only patients screened as suitable for psychoanalysis by this committee were given psychological tests.

Characteristics of the Sample

The population included 10 women and 12 men between the ages of 21 and 32. Thirteen patients were single, seven were married, and two were divorced. The scores on the Verbal WAIS ranged from average to very superior (estimated Verbal IQ 103–146). Three-quarters of the sample were in the superior to very superior range. All patients were college educated. On entry to analysis, nine were graduate students, seven had master's degrees, four had Ph.D. degrees, and one was an M.D. Their occupations were predominantly in the professions. Eleven were in health-related fields, seven were educators, three were lawyers, and one was a performing artist. Their reasons for seeking psychoanalysis were difficulties in relationships with the opposite sex (11), difficulties in relationships in general (three), career conflicts or work inhibitions (nine), depression (five), anxiety attacks or phobias (three), and a wish for an intellectual understanding of self (one). Some patients had more than one presenting complaint.

Each of the 22 patients was assessed as neurotic by the clinical interviewer, an experienced analyst, and the senior analyst who chaired the committee. Both the interviewer and the chairman gave each of these patients ratings on all four predictor variables in the maximally suitable to acceptable range.

Prior to beginning psychoanalysis, all patients were given a battery of psychological tests, including a Rorschach, TAT, Figure Drawing, Cole Animal Test, and selected Verbal subtests from the Wechsler Adult Intelligence Scale. From the results of these tests, the patients were rated on four dimensions: reality testing, level and quality of object relations, affect availability and tolerance, and motivation for treatment. The test material was rated independently by the psychologist who administered the tests and a second psychologist who saw only the test protocols. Reliability of ratings for the two psychologists was established. The treating analysts were not informed of the results of these tests.

The pretreatment assessments based on psychological tests were somewhat less healthy diagnostically than the evaluations made from clinical interviews. Test assessments revealed eight neurotic characters, three narcissistic characters, five borderline characters, three borderline characters with psychotic process, and three psychotic characters. Psychological test ratings on the four predictor variables ranged from maximally suitable to unsuitable on each dimension.

The two outcome variables were analytic result and therapeutic benefit. A successful analytic result was defined as the establishment, and at least partial resolution, of the transference neurosis. A transference neurosis was defined as the manifestation of the patient's central difficulties, originating in childhood, being recreated in relation to the analyst. The resolution or partial resolution of the transference neurosis was to be accomplished by the interpretation of this phenomenon without the introduction of variations in standard analytic technique. The assessment of analytic result was made from a two- to four-hour tape-recorded interview conducted with the treating analyst following the patient's termination.

Therapeutic benefit was defined as improvement in reality testing, level and quality of object relations, and affect availability and tolerance based on both assessments made by the treating analysts in a follow-up interview and by psychologists' evaluations of postanalysis psychological testing. The present paper focuses exclusively on the evaluation of analytic result.

ASSESSMENT OF ANALYTIC RESULT

One year following the termination of psychoanalysis, the initial battery of psychological tests was readministered. Each patient was given a brief follow-up interview, which asked for an assessment of psychological changes that had occurred since the beginning of the analysis. The analysts, who still had no knowledge of any of the pretreatment findings, were also given follow-up interviews. These interviews were designed to assess the manifestation of the four predictor variables in the analysis, as well as the changes the analysts perceived to have taken place. Certain questions were focused on determining whether a transference neurosis had developed and the extent to which it had been resolved. An evaluation of whether standard analytic technique had been used in the analysis was also undertaken. All questions avoided abstract language and asked the analysts to give examples in support of their conclusions.

From the answers to these interview questions, four categories of analytic result were established: (1) analyzable, with resolution of the transference neurosis; (2) analyzable, with partial resolution of the transference neurosis; (3) analyzable, with partial resolution of the transference neurosis with variations in standard analytic technique; and (4) unanalyzed, with failure to establish and/or resolve the transference neurosis.

RESULTS

The interviews of the analysts were rated independently by two analyst researchers who achieved 90 percent agreement. For the 22 patients in the study, the outcome in terms of analytic result was as follows:

1. Analyzable—transference neurosis resolved, two (9 percent).
2. Analyzable—transference neurosis partially resolved with no variations in technique, seven (32 percent).
3. Analyzable—transference neurosis partially resolved with variations in technique, five (23 percent).
4. Unanalyzed eight (36 percent).

The initial level of reality testing, level and quality of object relations, affect availability and tolerance, and motivation for psychoanalysis established in the extensive preanalysis evaluation did not successfully predict which patients would have a successful analytic result. None of the four predictor variables, as assessed from psychological testing and clinical interviews, was able to make this discrimination, either alone or in combination with any other variable. Among the four predictor variables, the assessment of motivation by both interview and psychological testing was the most relevant factor in predicting suitability; however, none of these findings was statistically significant.

Based on the findings of this research, we have not confirmed the predictive value of four global psychological factors commonly assumed to discriminate which patients are best suited to psychoanalysis. The main hypothesis of this study was not supported.

DISCUSSION

The findings of this study support those of other research projects in failing to predict which patients among a group already selected for their likelihood to derive benefit from psychoanalysis will be analyzable.

Despite this concurrence in findings, the comparability of studies of analyzability is limited by differences in conceptions, definitions, and the nature of the data used in each of these investigations (Erle, 1979; Erle & Goldberg, 1982; Kernberg et al., 1972; Sashin et al., 1975; Weber et al., 1985). The concept of psychoanalysis is by no means a uniform one. While all these authors would agree that psychoanalysis is distinguished by the establishment of an analytic process, the definition of analytic process varies explicitly or implicitly in these studies. The present study defines a psychoanalytic process as necessitating the establishment, and at least partial resolution, of a transference neurosis by means of interpretation, without variations in standard analytic technique. The study by Weber and colleagues (1985) defines analytic process by the handling of psychological data, use of psychological resources at termination, and transference manifestations during treatment. While all three of these criteria are in accordance with psychoanalytic principles, they are insufficiently stringent to meet the definition of analytic process used in the present study. Transference manifestations are not the same as a transference neurosis. All patients in this study showed transference manifestations that were interpreted by their analysts; however, only 17 of the 22 patients established a transference neurosis. All patients in this study brought psychological data into the treatment because they recognized that such data could be used for unterstanding, but this phenomenon is hardly exclusive to psychoanalysis among methods of psychotherapeutic treatment. At termination most patients in this study recognized that they had psychological resources and used these for "realistic adaptive growth" (p. 131), to use terms from the Weber study. Such growth, however, is expected in many forms of treatment, and seems to relate more to therapeutic benefit than to analytic process, according to definitions used in this study. If the Weber definition of analytic process had been applied to this sample, 18 of the 22 patients (82 percent) would have been defined as analyzable.

The present study, as well as those by Weber et al., Erle, and Sashin et al, have evaluated supervised analytic cases, thus giving them a certain measure of comparability in terms of the experience of the treating analysts. These studies, however, are from three different analytic institutes, and, based on the published results, it is not possible to determine whether the definitions of standard analytic technique are the same. It became clear in the present study that even within the Boston Institute, not all candidates were defining a variation in standard analytic technique in the same manner. The variation in technique for one patient was the use of strong confrontations about intense transference reactions having their origins in the past. Many analysts would consider such activity standard in psychoanalysis. In contrast, with another patient, the analyst suggested that the patient read an article about transference, in an effort to help the patient experience the transference reactions as normal. While the meaning and impact of this suggestion were later analyzed, most analysts would see this intervention as outside the range of standard analytic technique. The patients in the Menninger study manifested more severe pathology than is usual for analytic patients, and variations in analytic technique, including hospitalization, use of medication, and having the patient sit up, were employed for many of the patients considered to have been in psychoanalysis (Wallerstein, 1983). If this less stringent Menninger standard for analytic technique had been applied to the present sample, 16 of the 22 patients, or 73 percent, would have been considered analyzable.

The nature of the data on which these follow-up evaluations were based also differed. The Weber et al., Erle, Erle and Goldberg, and Sashin et al studies all evaluated data gathered from posttreatment questionnaires or previously collected information, never from direct patient or analyst interviews. In the present study, data regarding analyzability were derived from the transcript of a two- to four-hour tape-recorded interview with the treating analyst, which resulted in a far more extensive assessment. Furthermore, there was a systematic attempt to avoid technical and abstract terms and to employ operational definitions in these interviews. Nonetheless, ambiguities of definitions and concepts continued to intrude and cloud the findings, as illustrated by differing notions of variations in standard analytic technique.

The present study and the Menninger study both employed psychological tests in evaluating the patients. The Menninger study, unlike the present study, found that evaluations made from test data were the most accurate predictors of treatment outcome (Appelbaum, 1977). This success with psychological tests as predictors may have resulted from the wide range of psychopathology in the Menninger population, a range that was not characteristic of the Boston sample.

The failure in this study to predict accurately from psychological tests which patients would be suitable for psychoanalysis may be considered from several perspectives. The sample was a preselected group. The Committee on Institute Analysis had already screened out those patients whom they thought were manifestly unsuitable for psychoanalysis. If the full population of patients seeking analysis had been included, it is possible that testing might have been more successful in determining which patients would have had successful analytic outcomes. In addition, the sample size, while relatively large for this kind of study, was small for the purposes of statistical evaluation. An extremely strong statistical relationship between the predicting factors and the criteria would have had to exist in order to obtain a statistically significant result for a sample of this size.

The relative inexperience of the candidate-analysts is an important factor that limited the generalizability of our findings. It is difficult to predict analyzability for all patient groups, but these predictions appear to be somewhat more accurate for patients treated privately by graduate analysts than for those treated by analytic candidates under supervision (Erle, 1979; Erle & Goldberg, 1982). Patients selected for supervised psychoanalysis are different from patients in private practice in several dimensions. These include the patient's financial need, the effect of the screening process, the need to make an assessment of suitability without prolonged evaluation, the analyst's inexperience, the impact of supervision on the process, and the analyst's need for the patient to progress in order for the candidate to advance as a student (Erle, 1979).

The fact is that neither the careful pretreatment assessment by experienced psychoanalysts nor the evaluation on psychological tests, which exposed pathological areas not visible in clinical interviews, was able to predict which patients would successfully engage in psychoanalysis. Perhaps we are still unable to evaluate satisfactorily in our patients the adequacy of their reality testing, the level and quality of their object relations, the availability of their affects, and their capacity to tolerate and modulate their affects. Perhaps we have not yet determined which psychological attributes are essential for psychoanalysis. It may be, however, that it is not only the patients' attributes that determine whether psychoanalysis will be successful. The patients' psychological attributes considered in this study may be necessary but not sufficient predictors of a successful psychoanalytic outcome.

Psychoanalysis is a two-person undertaking. As such it may not be possible to predict the outcome an analysis when we do not know the variables that have been introduced by the analyst, variables that ultimately contribute to its success or failure. The analyst's training, skill, age, sex, interests, and personality, as well as specific countertransference manifestations, may all play a role in the outcome of psychoanalysis with a particular patient (Kantrowitz, in press). When we are considering cases treated by psychoanalytic candidates, the factors contributed by the analyst may be especially important. The effect of the particular patient–analyst match on the outcome of treatment was not initially a focus for this study. For this reason we did not systematically collect data on this dimension. We are currently engaged in a pilot study to determine, on the basis of data that are available, whether the patient–analyst match played a significant part in the outcome of psychoanalytic treatment for our sample.

SUMMARY AND CONCLUSIONS

It may not be possible to assess completely in advance of psychoanalytic treatment which patients will be analyzable. Even careful prospective evaluations made from both clinical interviews and psychological tests did not accurately predict analytic outcome. Neither the relatively severe pathology diagnosed from psychological testing nor the relatively stable neurotic problems diagnosed from clinical interviews proved to have statistically significant relationships to analyzability. None of the four predictor variables—reality testing, level and quality of object relations, affect availability and tolerance, and motivation—alone or in combination led to accurate assessment for case selection.

Evaluation of analytic procedure and progress, while defined in behavioral rather than abstract terms, was, nonetheless, often difficult since not all analysts in the study agreed on definitions of standard analytic technique. Establishing and defining such standards is likely to be a particular problem when inexperienced analysts, in this case analytic candidates, are those making the evaluations.

The resolution or partial resolution of the transference neurosis was considered the criterion of a successful analysis in this study. According to the analysts, approximately 40 percent (nine) of the 22 patients studied established, and at least partially resolved, a transference neurosis. Approximately 60 percent (13) of the patients were not analyzed or were only partially analyzed. Whether some of these patients had pathology that was not amenable to modification by adherence to psychoanalytic technique, or whether their analysts were too inexperienced to master the difficulties that arose successfully, or whether some other aspect of the patient–analyst interaction impeded progress, cannot be resolved in this study.

REFERENCES

Appelbaum, S. A. (1977). *The Anatomy of Change: A Menninger Foundation Report on Testing the Effects of Psychotherapy*. New York and London: Plenum Press.

Bachrach, H. M. (1983). On the concept of analyzability. *Psychoanal. Q.*, 52:180–204.

——— & Leaf, L. A. (1978). Analyzability: A systematic review of the clinical and quantitative literature. *J. Amer. Psychoanal. Assn.*, 26:881–920.

Erle, J. B. (1979). An approach to the study of analyzability and analysis: The course of forty consecutive cases selected for supervised psychoanalysis. *Psychoanal. Q.*, 48:198–228.

——— & Goldberg, D. A. (1979). Problems in assessment of analyzability. *Psychoanal. Q.*, 48:48–94.

——— & ——— (1984). Observations on assessment of analyzability by experienced analysts: Report on 160 cases. *J. Amer. Psychoanal. Assn.*, 32:715–737.

Freud, S. (1905). On psychotherapy. *Standard Edition*, 12:257–268.

Guttman, S. A. (reporter) (1960). Criteria for analyzability. Panel reports. *J. Amer. Psychoanal. Assn.*, 8:141–151.

Kantrowitz, J. (in press). The role of the patient–analyst "match" in the outcome of psychoanalysis. *Ann. Psychoanal.*

———, Singer, J. G., & Knapp, P. H. (1975). Methodology for a prospective study for psychoanalysis: The role of psychological tests. *Psychoanal. Q.*, 44:371–391.

Kernberg, O., Burstein, E., Coyne, L., Appelbaum, S., Horwitz, L., & Voth, H. (1972). Psychotherapy and psychoanalysis: Final report of the Menninger Foundation psychotherapy research project. *Bull. Menninger Clin.*, 36:3–275.

Knapp, P., Levin, S., McCarter, R. H., Wermer, H., & Zetzel, E. (1960). Suitability for psychoanalysis: A review of one hundred supervised cases. *Psychoanal. Q.*, 29:459–477.

Kuiper, P. C. (1968). Indications and contraindications for psychoanalytic treatment. *Int. J. Psychoanal.*, 49:261–264.

Oremland, J. D., BLacker, K. H., & Norman, H. F. (1975). Incompleteness in "successful" psychoanalysis: A follow-up study. *J. Amer. Psychoanal. Assn.*, 23:819–844.

Sashin, J., Eldred, S., & Van Amerongen, S. (1975). A search for predictive factors in institute supervised cases: a retrospective study of 183 cases from 1959–1966 at the Boston Psychoanalytic Institute and Society. *Int. J. Psychoanal.*, 56:343–359.

Wallerstein, R. S. (1983). Psychoanalysis and psychotherapy: Relative roles reconsidered. Presented at the Boston Psychoanalytic Society and Institute Symposium on "Psychoanalysis Today."

Weber, J. J., Bachrach, H. M., & Solomon, M. (1985). Factors associated with the outcome of psychoanalysis: Report of the Columbia Psychoanalytic Center Research Project (11). *Int. Rev. Psychoanal.*, 12:127–141.

23 ROBERT S. WALLERSTEIN, M.D.

DISCUSSION

The Assessment of Analyzability and of Analytic Outcomes

JUDY KANTROWITZ HAS STUDIED 22 PATIENTS IN A LOW-COST PSYCHOANALYTIC INSTITUTE CLINIC (IN BOSTON) THROUGH EVALUATIVE INTERVIEWING AND PROJECTIVE PSYCHOLOGICAL TESTS AT THE INITIAL PRETREATMENT POINT AND AGAIN AT THE TERMINATION OF THEIR ANALYSES. HER CENTRAL RESEARCH QUESTIONS HAD TO DO WITH (1) THE PREDICTION OF ANALYZABILITY ON THE BASIS OF FOUR PREDICTOR VARIABLES—REALITY TESTING, OBJECT RELATIONSHIPS, AFFECT EXPRESSION AND MODULATION, AND MOTIVATION; AND (2) THE ASSESSMENT OF THE SUCCESS OF THE PSYCHOANALYTIC RESULT ACHIEVED, AS AGAINST THE EXPERIENCED PSYCHOTHERAPEUTIC BENEFIT. WITH REGARD TO PREDICTIONS OF ANALYZABILITY, THE RESULTS WERE INCONCLUSIVE AND DISAPPOINTING, IN KEEPING WITH THE EXPERIENCES CITED FROM OTHER SIMILAR RESEARCH PROJECTS. WITH REGARD TO ACHIEVED ANALYTIC RESULTS, THESE VARIED GREATLY, THOUGH THE VARIATION HAD NOT BEEN PREDICTED. VARIETIES OF REASONS ARE ADDUCED TO EXPLAIN THESE LIMITED RESEARCH OUTCOMES. I OFFER MY OWN PERSPECTIVE ON THE EXPLANATION OF THE POOR PREDICTIVE POWER OF PATIENT VARIABLES (IN ANY COMBINATION), ON THE DISTINCTION BETWEEN THE ASSESSMENT OF ANALYZABILITY AS AGAINST THE ASSESSMENT OF ANALYTIC RESULT ACHIEVED, ON THE DISTINCTION BETWEEN PSYCHOANALYTIC RESULT AND PSYCHOTHERAPEUTIC BENEFIT, AND ON THE ISSUE OF THE ASSESSMENT OF STRUCTURAL CHANGE IN INTRAPSYCHIC CONFIGURATIONS AND ITS RELATIONSHIP TO THE KINDS OF THERAPEUTIC INTERVENTIONS DESIGNED TO EFFECT CHANGE (WHETHER EXPRESSIVE AND CONFLICT RESOLVING OR SUPPORTIVE AND CONFLICT-SUPPRESSING) AS THE, TO ME, CENTRAL AGENDA FOR RESEARCH INTO THE NATURE OF PSYCHOANALYTIC PROCESSES AND OUTCOMES.

Dr. Kantrowitz is one of that very small band of psychotherapy researchers, even of those within the psychoanalytic tradition, who takes earnestly the twofold task of (psychoanalytic) psychotherapy research: (1) assessing seriously the outcomes of psychoanalytic therapy, in their scope and reach, and also in their limitations, in terms of all of the efficacy and benefit issues that are indeed very proper societal, as well as professional and scientific concerns, albeit often derogated within psychoanalytic clinical ranks as superfluous or even mischievous endeavors; and (2) working, however, to do that within terms relevant to the nature of the clinical psychoanalytic enterprise and responsive to all the subtlety and complexity of its subjectivistic data, a task at times equally derogated from the other, scientific-research, side, as hopelessly quixotic and treacherous. It is the conviction of the few involved in this dual enterprise conceived in this way that it is, of course, neither superfluous nor hopeless, but rather the central necessity—and a doable although very complex undertaking—if psychoanalysis as a therapy is to fulfill its promise, vouched by Freud, to yield fundamental knowledge of how the human mind works, and of how change is achieved in its ways of (mal)functioning, that is, to become truly both a scientific psychology and equally a scientific psychotherapy.

This paper is another in Dr. Kantrowitz' sequence from her sample of 22 carefully selected patients who entered supervised psychoanalyses under the auspices of the Boston Psychoanalytic Institute in 1972. All were assessed within a simple enough (as well as sound enough) design structure, through the usual clinical interviews, and also (as research additions) projective psychological testing. Both were done initially pretreatment, and then, a year following the natural terminations of their analyses, research interviews were conducted of the ex-patients, and also this time, of the ex-analysts, as well as a repeat administration of the same psychological test battery.

To get right to the point of both the paper and my discussion, what are the central research questions that the paper addresses, and what do I see as the substantive knowledge yield that comes from this specific inquiry? Actually the core questions are two, not one, as the title of the paper perhaps somewhat ambiguously suggests. The first is the question of the prediction of analyzability. How well can those who can (will) be successfully enough "analyzed" be foretold via whatever combination of predictor variables (*patient* variables) are selected by the researcher for pretreatment assessment? The second research question is, of course, clearly related, but still distinct. It is the assessment of psychoanalytic outcomes, qua analysis. That is, how "successful" a psychoanalytic result has been achieved, via the evolution of a psychoanalytic process and a presumed properly unfolded and adequately enough resolved transference neurosis, as against how much *therapeutic* benefit has accrued to the patient on whatever basis, analytic or otherwise—and incidentally, not least, how well can these be distinguished in ways that researchers and clinicians can agree upon? I will discuss these two questions in turn. I will also remark on an issue that is perhaps more methodological than substantive, the somewhat unusual (in this day and age) reliance on a battery of projective psychological tests as a central avenue of access to knowledge of intrapsychic organization.

With regard to predictions of analyzability, the author emerges with the same seemingly disappointing findings as do all the others she quotes (Erle, Erle and Goldberg, Knapp et al., Sashin et al., Weber et al., etc.), that using whatever combination of predictor variables one wants (Dr. Kantrowitz uses four, singly and in combination—the level of reality testing, the quality of the object relations, the capacity for affect expression and modulation, and the extent of the motivation for treatment), correlations between assessed initial states of these variables and analytic outcomes, though usually positive, are also unhappily quite low and statistically not at all significant (certainly not with the sample sizes that can reasonably be studied in psychodynamic psychotherapy research programs).

Many reasons are adduced for this disappointing state of affairs. Some are called definitional, and indeed there are significant issues of differential definition and usage even among analysts trained within a specific theoretical position, and American psychoanalysis has indeed been more homogeneous (some would say monolithic) within its ego psychology paradigm—at least until very recently—than analytic practice and theory in any other region or language grouping in the world. And some have to do with the proper selection and grouping of predictive criteria. Dr. Kantrowitz, as stated, chose four, and very appropriate in the sense of clearly salient ones, while our Psychotherapy Research Project at the Menninger Foundation chose 28 so-called Patient Variables (Wallerstein & Robbins, 1956, pp. 240–250) without in the end necessarily achieving better predictive power in the terms framed by the question and the design (see Wallerstein, 1986). But basically in the end, the author comes to the same persuasive enough argument already advanced by Weber et al. (1985a, 1985b, 1985c) to explain the same failure to predict analytic outcomes from the initial pretreatment assessments of patient variables, that all these analytic pretreatment samples consist of highly *preselected* groups. The differential treatment outcome predictions are thus made within a sample, both self-screened and then professionally closely screened for presumptive analyzability, from which all those clearly unsuitable for the treatment have already been eliminated. Within such a then carefully chosen group (although many apply to psychoanalytic institute low-cost clinics only a small percentage ultimately is placed in supervised analysis), further predictive discriminations of differentially achievable outcomes perhaps should not be expected to ride on ever finer grained differentiations of patient factors alone.

And here, of course, Dr. Kantrowitz comes, as have others, to remark on the dyadic nature of the analytic interaction and the capacities, qualities, levels of experience, and commitments, not to speak of the predilections, biases, and countertransferences, of the other partner, the analyst. For all kinds of obvious reasons, knowledge in this sector—the contribution of the analyst (in interaction with the analysand) to the analytic outcome—is much harder to come by. The analysts are, of course, not "evaluated" for their potential contribution to the analytic task and to its successful achievement in the same way that the patients are, let alone that in the practical creation of the usual such project design within the constraints of the psychoanalytic treatment centers where such projects can be mounted at all, the assessments of the patients and the predictions of their treatment courses and outcomes are customarily made prior to knowing who the treating analyst will be.

Here also, in addition to all the factors of the contributions of the relevant patient and therapist (and therapy) variables to the therapy course and outcome, one must also consider the particular kinds of expected interactional effects, which Dr. Kantrowitz encompasses as "patient–analyst match," and which indeed do operate importantly, albeit impressionistically, in our minds as we consider to which of our colleagues we wish to refer a particular patient. And this is usually done in the light of an adjudged prospective fit between the psychological needs of the patient and the particular attributes of character and temperament of the therapist.

In order to maximize our capacities for predictive judgments about prospective treatment courses and outcomes in the Psychotherapy Research Project—where, as contrasted with Dr. Kantrowitz, we had incomparably greater resources of time, money, and research personnel as well as other vital logistical advantages grounded in the ecology of the Menninger Foundation at that time—we assessed separately 28 Patient Variables, 38 Treatment and Therapist Variables, and seven Life-Situational Variables, all presumed to codetermine, through their interactions, the kinds and amounts of expectable psychological change in the projected therapies. Whether and to what extent the comprehensive individual assessment of such an array of presumed relevant variables from all the interacting spheres of influence upon the patient's psychological functioning actually yielded a greater predictive power than the very modest claims advanced by Dr. Kantrowitz (and the others whom she quotes) is itself a matter of discussion and of interpretation. Significantly differing perspectives on that issue are offered by the five books of results published from that same Menninger project: that by Appelbaum (1977), based on the projective psychological test data; that by Horwitz (1974), based on the formal logical analysis of the fate of some 2000 individual predictions made in the 42 cases (about 50 per patient); that by Voth and Orth (1973), which specifically focused on evolving environmental circumstance (the array of Situational Variables) as major determinants of the achievable change; that by Kernberg et al. (1972), based on the (semi)quantitative statistical analyses and the mathematical facet theory analyses of the project data; and last, my own (Wallerstein, 1986) overall clinical accounting of the treatment careers and the subsequent life careers of the cohort of 42 patients followed over an almost 30-year span (1954–1982). I try in that book to explain and, as far as possible, to reconcile these different perspectives on that issue (and on others, as well). Suffice it to say that confident and valid prediction of psychotherapy course and outcome still eludes our collective grasp, whether in clinical or research setting.

But there is still the other, and really the even more salient and more interesting, research question to which the Kantrowitz study is also addressed. That is the question of how successful these analyses were in terms of *analytic* results achieved, that is, in the resolution of intrapsychic conflicts via the analytic interpretation and undoing of an evolved transference neurosis (and, of course, within that broad compass, the differential arenas of therapeutic achievement with regard to the particularized array of areas of ego (mal)functioning as against the separate question of *therapeutic* benefits reached, on whatever basis—insightful conflict resolution or the varieties of available psychotherapeutic ego-supportive, and non-conflict-resolving, techniques. (See Wallerstein, 1986, for the delineation of supportive psychotherapeutic techniques within the framework of a psychoanalytic theory of therapy.) From the standpoint of the present-day social and economic concerns with the cost–benefit issues in the long-term intensive (and expensive) psychotherapy that psychoanalysis is, the question becomes one of whether psychoanalysis truly does achieve more than the symptom and behavior changes that are claimed equally by various shorter and less intensive methods (whether psychoanalytically informed or not)—more that is in scope of change, in durability, and in proof against future life vicissitudes.

Here Dr. Kantrowitz properly faults the judgmental basis offered in the current reports by Weber et al. (1985a, 1985b, 1985c) from the Columbia Psychoanalytic Center Research Project. Weber et al. defined the analytic *result* achieved in terms of three criteria they set forth for the establishment of a proper analytic process—the Handling of Psychological Data, the Use of Resources at Termination, and Transference Manifestation During Treatment.[1] At best these criteria are indicators for the assessment of *analyzability*, which should not be conflated the way Weber et al. do, with the achievement of a (reasonably) *analyzed* state. Dr. Kantrowitz just calls the Weber et al. criteria "insufficiently stringent" to meet *her* definition of a successfully navigated analytic process. Her criterion is rather that of the adjuged establishment of a recognized *transference neurosis* (not just of transferences), with then the further judgment of the degree of its resolution and whether this was accomplished by analytic techniques alone or with modifying parameters. Relevant here, of course, is the renewed and very current controversy in our literature as to whether all successful (enough) analysis *is* indeed characterized by an unfolded and resolved regressive transference neurosis in the traditionally understood sense. In this context I will only quote Gill (1982): "There remains considerable controversy among analysts over whether a transference neurosis is a necessary part of a successful analysis, as is attested by the wide divergence of opinion on the matter in a recent issue of the *Journal of the American Psychoanalytic Association*" (p. 77). (The reference is to volume 19, 1971, pages 22–97, a sequence of articles by Harley, Blum, Loewald, and Weinshel and Calef.) And further on the same page, Gill cites Glover's 1955 book

[1]These criteria are defined by Weber et al. (1985b) as follows: "(1) The patient brought psychological data (e.g., dreams, fantasies, affects, self-observations) into treatment because he recognized that this could be a source of understanding as well as relief. (2) The patient recognized that he had resources and learned to use these resources to achieve realistic adaptive growth as well as relief of personal suffering. (3) The patient often used insight gained in the transference to plan and execute change in his everyday life and interpersonal relations. These judgments are made from responses on a termination questionnaire filled out by the treating analyst" (p. 131).

on *The Technique of Psycho-Analysis* and says, "Glover (1955) has taken the position that in many instances a transference neurosis does not develop despite the fact that the analysis may be successful therapeutically. . . . [its development] in all cases is not only theoretically improbable but contrary to actual experience."

Given that this is an apt enough characterization of the existing uncertainties concerning the centrality of the evolved and resolved transference neurosis as the vital and indispensable indicator of the successfully achieved analytic process, and given also the total lack of agreed-upon specification in our literature as to how one determines its presence and its degree of evolution and resolution (which the author does not really specify either), where are we then left in our efforts to evaluate psychoanalytic outcomes as analyses? Dr. Kantrowitz has adduced carefully gathered evidence that predictor variables based on patient factors (patient attributes) assessed initially pretreatment are inconclusive discriminating predictors of subsequent analytic outcomes, at least among carefully screened patients adjudged very suitable for the analytic effort—as shown by her data and those she cites from the literature on comparable endeavors, with whatever combination of patient variables each particular research project has chosen. She has further demonstrated that by her judgmental criteria (albeit, not specified, as I have indicated), 14 of her sample of 22 (64 percent) were analyzable and at least partially analyzed, with either the transference neurosis declared to be resolved (two of them), or partially resolved but without significant variations in technique (seven of them), or partially resolved though with variations in technique (presumably, unanalyzed or possibly unanalyzable parameters) (five of them)—though her selected predictor variables had not been able to predict these outcomes successfully.

Here, before going on to my own question of where can we (i.e., where can the field) then go on from here, I do want to pick up for discussion the issue that I called perhaps more methodological than substantive, the unusual distinction that Dr. Kantrowitz claims of conducting the only psychotherapy research inquiry other than the Psychotherapy Research Project of the Menninger Foundation that has used data derived from a projective psychological test battery as a major knowledge source when assessing psychological change and capacity for change in long-term psychoanalytic therapies. The batteries used in the two studies, though not identical, shared the common core (Rorschach, TAT, and Wechsler Adult Intelligence Scale) that was central to the original development of the projective test battery as a conceptual tool in personality study by Rapaport and his co-workers (Rapaport et al., 1945, 1946) at the Menninger Foundation—which made it so natural that a research program created at the Menninger Foundation to study personality and psychotherapy would, of course, build in projective psychological testing as a major data source. (In fact, in the Psychotherapy Research Project, the projective psychological test battery was administered in identical form *three* times, initially before treatment, upon treatment termination, and then at a follow-up point, at least two or three years after termination.) The advantages of this data source for such research purposes are several. It is the one kind of repeat access to data on intrapsychic organization where the recurring stimulus situation is a constant and the responses (and changes in responses) can thus be highlighted more clearly, and where the responses can additionally be obtained without acquiring incidental or inadvertent knowledge about intervening events. In that sense it becomes more purely change (i.e., outcome) data *uncontaminated* by knowledge of the intervening process (i.e., the interventions geared to, or at least purported to bring about, particular changes).

In addition, there is another claimed, but this one also disputed, superiority of projective psychological test data over data obtained in the usual clinical interview diagnostic process. Some claim, as did Appelbaum (1977), that projective psychological tests by virtue of the kinds of responses that their standardized stimuli elicit, and by virtue as well of the psychoanalytic theoretical framework within which those responses can be conceptualized, can illuminate better certain aspects of psychological functioning than can clinical interviews, referring particularly to issues of thought organization and affect organization. Others argue contrarily that there is no inherent superiority of the psychological test data in this regard, though in practice light may often be more readily thrown on these particular areas of functioning by the psychological test protocols than by *early* clinical interviews operating within all the usual guardednesses of many patients overcoming their initial resistances to confiding personal history and personal attitude data so *directly* to a relative stranger. Be that as it may, I do not accept Appelbaum's claim of a greater predictive power residing in assessment of predictor variables on the basis of psychological test protocols as against assessments of the same predictor variables from clinical interview data—a claim that Appelbaum makes and Dr. Kantrowitz cites. In my own book on the Menninger Psychotherapy Research Project (Wallerstein, 1986) that is another one of the apparently different perspectives—on the same data base—that I essay to reconcile and account for in a different way. And besides, as already well enough documented by

Kantrowitz, and the others as well, no one's predictive track record in this regard is a proud one. Mostly what I want to underline in the Kantrowitz work and to salute is her willingness to revive and deploy a now (in my opinion) sadly neglected and derogated art and skill, the use of projective psychological tests as an important contributing method in research in personality functioning and psychotherapy process and outcome.

But I should return to my main theme and my main question at this point: Where can we collectively (as psychoanalytic psychotherapy researchers) go from here? As a personal perspective and answer to this, I can only point to the path taken by the Menninger Psychotherapy Research Project over its dozen-year span of data gathering from 1954 to 1966 (see Wallerstein, 1986, for the full clinical accounting of this research study and the presentation of its findings), as well as to current plans being evolved by a new group of colleagues with me here in San Francisco building on those findings. The central problem of psychoanalytic psychotherapy research, as we have defined it, is the study of *structural changes* in intrapsychic configurations as the kinds of changes that are presumed to eventuate only from insight-aiming, conflict-resolving psychoanalytic treatments operating by way of interpretations of defense and impulse and leading to insight and change via processes of working through (i.e., repetitive reenactments and reworkings of the central themes of the transference neurosis in all their variations and ramifications), and to distinguish such structural changes and their reflections in altered symptoms and behaviors from merely (perhaps phenomenologically similar) symptomatic and behavioral changes brought about through other non-insight-aiming and non-conflict-resolving therapeutic interventions (whether psychoanalytically informed as in psychoanalytically based supportive psychotherapies, or explicitly nonpsychoanalytic in their theoretical base and rationale).

Put this way, the research task becomes one of devising indicators of structural change in the ego independently of the indices of symptom and behavior change and the assessment of all these changes at outcome points apart from the judgments concerning the intervening process events; that is, the nature of the therapeutic interventions and interactions and whether they have established a basically psychoanalytic process or a basically psychotherapeutic one, varyingly expressive and/or supportive. (Again, for a delineation of the nature of these distinctions and their base in empirical observations from therapeutic processes, see Wallerstein, 1986.) When these judgments of the nature of the established treatment process can be made confidently and reliably enough, and independently of the treatment outcome judgments of the nature of the achieved changes, whether these be structural changes in ego configurations or only symptomatic and/or behavioral changes, then we will be in a position to throw light on such continuing central questions for psychoanalytic psychotherapy research as: What kinds of changes expectably eventuate from what kinds of interventions—in interaction, of course, with the qualities and attributes of the patients? Or, put differently, do true structural changes, enduring and reasonably proof against subsequent environmental vicissitude, come about only within specifically psychoanalytic (insight-aiming and conflict-resolving) approaches geared to the unfolded transference process—whether transference *neurosis* or not? Or can such structural changes come about or be brought about within other psychoanalytically based and informed but other than interpretive approaches? Or, for that matter, can structural changes in the ego come about within therapies explicitly nonpsychoanalytic in theoretical rationale?

These are the kinds of issues thrown into relief by the findings generated by the Psychotherapy Research Project of the Menninger Foundation that the successor project currently being fashioned in San Francisco is being designed to address. If substantive advance can be made along these lines, new light will then be thrown on the interplay of variables (in the patient, in the therapy—and the therapist—and in the interacting life situation) that codetermine the changes reached. In turn our predictive capacity in relation to psychotherapy processes and outcomes, and in relation specifically to analyzability and suitability for analysis, will finally be enhanced beyond the position reached to this point by Dr. Kantrowitz, and also by all of those engaged in similar search whom she cites. That, as I see it, is the overall agenda for us in psychoanalytic psychotherapy research today. The Kantrowitz work and findings are a significant step along that way.

REFERENCES

Appelbaum, S. A. (1977). *The Anatomy of Change: A Menninger Foundation Report on Testing the Effects of Psychotherapy*. New York: Plenum Press, p. 308.

Gill, M. M. (1982). *Analysis of Transference*. Vol. I. *Theory and Technique*. Psychological Issues. Monograph 53. New York: International Universities Press, p. 193.

Horwitz, L. (1974). *Clinical Prediction in Psychotherapy*. New York: Jason Aronson, p. 372.

Kernberg, O. F., Burstein, E. D., Coyne, L., Appelbaum, A., Horwitz, L., & Voth, H. (1972). Psychotherapy and psychoanalysis. Final report of the Menninger Foundation's Psychotherapy Research Project. *Bull Menninger Clin.*, 36:1–275.

Rapaport, D., with Merton Gill and Roy Schafer (1945, 1946). *Diagnostic Psychological Testing*. Chicago: Yearbook Publisher, Vol. I, p. 573, Vol. II, p. 516.

Voth, H. M., & Orth, M. H. (1973). *Psychotherapy and the Role of the Environment*. New York: Behavioral Publications, p. 354.

Wallerstein, R. S. (1986). *42 Lives in Treatment: A Study of Psychoanalysis and Psychotherapy*. New York: Guilford Press, p. 784.

——— & Robbins, L. L. (1956). IV. Concepts. *Bull Menninger Clin.*, 20:239–262.

Weber, J. J., Solomon, M., & Bachrach, H. M. (1985a). Characteristics of psychoanalytic clinic patients: Report of the Columbia Psychoanalytic Center Research Project (I). *Int. Rev. Psychoanal.*, 12:13–26.

———, Bachrach, H. M., & Solomon, M. (1985b). Factors associated with the outcome of psychoanalysis: Report of the Columbia Psychoanalytic Center Research Project (II). *Int. Rev. Psychoanal.*, 12:127–141.

———, ———, ——— (1985c). Factors associated with the outcome of psychoanalysis: Report of the Columbia Psychoanalytic Center Research Project (III). *Int. Rev. Psychoanal.*, 12:251–262.

Name Index

Adler, G., 123–125, 127, 129, 133, 142, 150, 151, 153, 154
Alexander, J., 381
Appelbaum, S.A., 406, 412, 420, 423
Arlow, J., 3, 85, 88, 90
Astrachan, B.M., 97

Bachrach, H.M., 403, 404
Baranger, W., 308
Basch, M., 5, 35, 36, 201, 211
Beecher, H.V., 293
Benedek, R.F., 89, 90
Benedetti, G., 329
Bion, W.R., 95, 111, 179, 308, 331
Biven, B.M., 293
Blakeslee, T., 28
Blanck, G., 189
Blanck, R., 189
Bleger, J., 331
Bleich, D., 210
Bolko, M., 327, 328
Borriello, J.F., 100
Brenner, C., 3, 204, 216, 285, 291, 296
Breuer, J., 291
Brown, L., 123
Bucci, W., 28
Buie, D., 124, 125, 127, 133, 140, 142, 150, 151
Burnham, D.G., 147

Carmignani, R.P., 85, 86, 90, 91, 93
Carnap, R., 334
Carotenuto, A., 254
Cassirer, E., 365
Cheifetz, L.G., 62
Cleveland, S.E., 273
Codignola, E., 326–337
Coen, S.J., 201, 202, 207–210, 214, 226–228, 230–238
Coltrera, J.T., 210
Cooper, A., 25, 230
Cooper, S., 142, 147, 150, 154, 156
Corwin, H., 124

Darwin, C., 65, 66
Deutsch, F., 272
Deutsch, H., 144
Devereux, G., 334
Dixon, N., 24
Dorpat, T.L., 38, 60, 61, 64, 208
Dubovsky, S.L., 275
Durkin, H.E., 91

Einstein, A., 65, 115
Eissler, K.R., 330, 335, 346, 355, 360, 367–370, 373
Ekstein, R., 91
Engel, G.L., 272
Erle, J.B., 403–405, 410–413, 418
Ezriel, A., 204

Fast, I., 5
Feigl, H., 334
Fenichel, O., 204, 334
Ferenczi, S., 272
Ferguson, S., 253

Festinger, L., 334
Fingarette, H., 255
Fish, S., 210
Fisher, S., 41, 42, 45, 273
Fleming, J., 89, 90
Fliegel, Z., 201, 211
Fraiberg, S., 279
Frances, A., 275
Freud, A., 280, 294, 297, 342
Freud, S., 3, 4, 6, 14, 16, 18, 20, 22, 26, 28, 29, 40–46, 48–67, 202–204, 206, 210, 211, 218, 229, 231, 254, 255, 273, 276, 291, 296, 307, 308–310, 330, 332, 341–343, 348, 354, 357, 365, 366, 371, 384, 398, 404, 417
Freud, S., 263, 264, 266–268
Friedman, H.J., 96
Friedman, C., 216
Friedman, P.T., 186, 190–192, 194–199

Gadamer, H.G., 210
Gale, L., 275
Galli, P.F., 327–329
Gedo, J.E., 86, 208, 217
Gill, M., 3, 5, 421
Gitelson, M., 216, 217
Glover, E., 380, 421, 422
Goldberg, D.A., 403–405, 410–413, 418
Goleman, D., 24
Goethe, J.W., 57
Gootnick, I., 107
Gould, S.J., 65, 66
Greenacre, P., 381
Greenson, R.R., 216, 346
Grinberg, L., 100
Groban, S.E., 275
Gualandri, E., 328
Guttman, S.A., 404

Habermas, J., 334, 340, 364, 370
Hannah, B., 177
Hartmann, H., 227
Heinsenberg, W., 202
Hoffer, W., 272, 273
Holt, R., 5
Horwitz, L., 120, 420

Isaacs, S., 334

Jacobson, E., 381
Joseph, E., 209, 324
Jung, C., 159, 254, 255

Kaiser, H., 334
Kantrowitz, J., 406, 413, 417–425
Kaplan, A., 203
Kapp, F.T., 381
Karush, C.F., 404
Keeney, B.P., 243, 255
Kernberg, O.F., 95, 97, 100, 114, 124, 135, 219, 406, 410, 420
Kernberg, P., 382
Kibel, H.D., 96, 109, 117–122
Klein, G., 3
Klein, M., 306–310, 318–320, 322
Klein, R.H., 95, 97
Knapp, P., 405, 418
Kohut, H., 114, 149, 216, 217
Korn, S., 85, 86, 90, 91, 93
Kris, E., 203, 204, 210
Krohn, A., 274, 291, 294–296, 298, 300, 303, 304
Kubie, L.S., 204
Kuiper, P.C., 404

Lachmann, F., 135, 136, 232
Laing, R.D., 250, 266
Langs, R., 4, 6, 14, 23, 24, 27, 29, 43, 35, 38, 40, 44, 53, 62, 68–70, 73, 83, 85, 86–88, 90, 124, 126–128, 133, 141, 147, 158, 160–166, 169, 174, 177, 179–184, 189, 192, 197, 205, 231, 247, 253, 254, 263, 324, 330, 331
Laplanche, J., 87, 333
Leaf, L.A., 404
Leary, S.A., 205, 206
Levenson, E.A., 111
Levine, H.B., 97, 111, 217
Levinson, D., 198
Levy, L., 334, 342
Lewin, B.D., 85, 210
Lichtenberg, J., 136
Lipton, S., 202
Little, M., 12
Loch, W., 335, 354, 355, 358, 361, 369
Loewald, H.W., 216, 421
Loewenstein, S.F., 217, 247, 253
Lorenzer, A., 330, 334, 340, 364
Luborsky, L., 41, 42

Mahler, M., 189, 296
Malcolm, R., 322, 324
Maltsberger, J., 140
Marx, K., 65, 343
Maxmen, J.S., 113
Meltzer, D., 353
Melzack, R., 291, 293, 294, 300
Menninger, K., 334, 347, 351
Miller, A., 251, 253
Milner, M., 330
Mitchell, S., 253
Modell, A., 124, 125, 151, 209, 210, 216, 331
Mood, J.L., 256
Muraro, G., 327, 328
Mushart, C., 272

Nadelson, T., 141
Nagera, H., 273, 285
Neisser, U., 33
Neumann, B., 328
Norton, J., 279
Noy, P., 5

Ogden, T.H., 147
Oldham, J.M., 97
Oremland, J., 217, 404
Ornstein, A., 227, 231, 233, 237
Ornstein, P., 227, 231, 233, 237
Orth, M.H., 420

Page, B., 391, 394
Parloff, M.B., 95
Parsons, I., 250
Paul, L., 41, 204
Peterfreund, E., 5
Poetzl, O., 41, 42
Polanyi, M., 201, 209, 211
Pontalis, J.-B., 87, 333
Pribrim, K., 5

Rabiner, E.L., 113
Rado, S., 230
Raney, J., 165
Rapoport, D., 3, 210, 334, 422, 423
Reich, W., 334
Reiser, M., 25
Ricoeur, P., 333, 334, 343
Rilke, M., 256, 257
Robbins, L.L., 418
Robertson, J., 151
Rogers, C., 159
Roiphe, H., 274
Ross, H., 85
Rothschild, B., 327
Rothstein, A., 201, 211
Rubinstein, H., 188

Sandler, J., 230, 334
Sashin, J., 405, 410, 412, 418
Schafer, R., 202, 203, 206, 209
Scheflen, A.E., 245
Scheidlinger, S., 100
Schilder, P., 273
Schlesinger, H.J., 85, 86, 90
Schmale, A.H., 272
Schwartz, M.S., 97
Searles, H., 34, 62, 86, 88, 90, 173, 246, 261–263, 266, 267
Segal, H., 323
Selvini-Palazzoli, M., 329
Semmelweis, I., 80, 82
Shapiro, D., 217
Sharpe, E.F., 44
Shengold, L., 49
Sherwood, M., 203, 206
Shevrin, H., 41, 42
Silverman, D., 41, 42
Slap, J., 136
Spater, F., 250
Spence, D.P., 206, 207
Stanton, A.H., 97
Stern, D., 251
Stolorow, R., 135, 136, 232
Strachey, J., 218, 334, 336, 356, 373, 374
Szalita, A., 217
Szasz, T., 24, 272, 274

Tolpin, M., 124, 125

Valenstein, A.F., 216
Volkan, V.D., 100
Voth, H., 420

Wall, P.D., 294
Wallerstein, R.S., 90, 208, 412, 418, 420, 423, 424
Watzlawick, P., 246, 248, 263
Waxer, P.H., 113
Weber, J.J., 405, 411, 412, 418, 421
Weiss, E., 272, 292, 293

Whitaker, C., 247
Wiener, N., 260
Winnicott, D., 124–126, 140, 149, 156, 249, 331
Winson, J., 25
Wisdom, J., 204
Wollstonecraft, M., 257

Yalom, I.D., 113

Subject Index

American Psychoanalytical Association, 210
  Panel on Interpretation, 202
Anti-Semitism
  as influence on Freud, 49, 51, 54, 55, 58, 63–66
Anxiety
  death, 28, 31

Boston Psychoanalytic Institute, 405, 412, 417

Castration, 284–287
Catholic Church, 63
Chestnut Lodge Sanitarium, 264
Clinical Theory, *see* Theory
Cole Animal Test, 408
Columbia Psychoanalytic Center Research Project, 421
Committee on Institute Analysis, 412
Communicative Psychoanalytic Therapy
  acting out, 178–182
  derivative communication, 170–182
  development of identity as psychoanalyst, 186–199
    dynamic meanings of change, 192–196
    fundamental hypothesis, 188–190
    research model applied, 190–192
    supervisory position, 196, 197
Conflict
  dependency, 128
  intrapsychic, 4
  theory, 4
Containment
  in milieu, 152–156
Countertransference
  and adjunctive treatment, 134, 152–156
  analyst's, 344
  issues, 137–142
  psychological versus "inevitable", 124, 128, 133
  utilization of, 207
Cybernetics, 243, 255, 260

Depression, 75
  anaclitic, 128, 134
  and maternal overloving, 252
  paranoid responses, 213
  in therapists, 165
Dreams
  Freud's theory on formation of, 43–46
  latent thoughts, 20
  somatic stimuli in, 40–41
  transference in content, 40
  unconscious perception in, 35

Ego
  and Freud's second theory, 3, 4
  functions, 189
  group, 109
  Klein's concept of, 322–325
  mastery, 104

psychology, 320
role of in Treason, 386
splitting and, 311
supplementary, 319
underdeveloped, 114
Eighth International Congress on Psychotherapy, 329

Faust, 57–59
Figure Drawing Test, 408
Functions
defensive, 3
ego, 3

Gestalt Therapy, 159, 175
"Good Enough" Mother, 249–251, 265
Group Therapy, *see* Psychotherapy
Hermeneutics, 202, 204, 210
antihermeneutics, 205, 210

Id
and Freud's second theory, 3–4
Information Processing
disfunction of, 30, 31
models for, 4, 5, *Figure* 1, 7
unconscious system for, 16–18, 20, *Figure* 5, 21, 24–30
Interpretation
analyst's theory of, 203–209, 211
frames of reference for, 334
Kleinian theory and, 322–325
logical structure of psychoanalytic, 326–377
true and false, 362–377
validation of, 205, 207–209
Interventions
errors, 163
in group psychotherapy, 95
interpretive, 8
noninterpretive, 8
therapist's, 9–12, 28–30
wording of, 111

Journal of the American Psychoanalytic Association, 421

Menninger Foundation, 423
Menninger Psychotherapy Research Project, 406, 411, 412, 420, 422, 425
Messages
analyzing center, 14, *figure* 3, 15
derivative
structure of, *figure* 2, 9
nonderivative, 8
processing of content and meaning, 20 *figure* 4, 15–20
processing of encoded meaning, 20, *figure* 5, 21–24
receiving, 14–18
analyzing center, 14, *figure* 3, 15
structure of, 13, 14
Milan Group for the Advancement of Psychotherapy, 328
Mind
topographic model of, 3–5, 12–31
non-clinical evidence for, 24, 25
some implications of, 25–30

Nontransference
and unconscious perceptions, 40

Object relations, 114, 306–320
beginnings of, 307–309
early mental mechanisms, 309–311
Oedipal
castration issues, 284–287
complex, 380
and treason, 387, 388, 390, 391
conflicts, 210, 211, 219
issues in transference, 229
phallic-oedipal phase, 282, 287
Overloving
concept of, 244, 245
as misnomer, 259–269
overloved children, 251, 252
in therapeutic relationship, 253–255
goals, 255–257

Pain
"Gate Control Theory", 294, 300, 301, 304
in infancy, 273–275, 294–296
meaning of, 271–288
phallic-oedipal phase, 282–287, 301–304
castration issues, 284–287
psychoanalytic perspectives, 290–304
and superego consolidation, 287, 288

in toddlerhood, 275–281, 296–301
Patients
Borderline
containment, 152–156
forms of splitting, 135, 136
individual and milieu psychotherapy, 123–144
milieu treatment in psychotherapy of, 146–156
therapeutic impasse, 127–135
transference, 127
Preoedipal
neediness, 218
pathology, 209, 217
Psicoterpiu e Scienze Umane, 326–328
Psychoanalysis
communicative approach, 4–12
disruption of rules in, 38
intrapsychic conflict, 4
methodology and, 332, 334, 339
reality testing, 336, 337
setting in, 329–331, 335, 350–362
suitability for, 403–414
assessment of result, 409, 410, 417–425
concept of analyzability, 404
hypothesis, 406, 407
method, 407–409
outcome studies, 404
Psychology
of analyst's beliefs, 210
of conflict, 208
ego, 330
Freud's female, 211
self, 114, 209, 237
of understanding, 202
Psychopathology
detoxification, 110, 111
and free associations, 8
intrapsychic conflict in, 4
and model of the mind, 5
narcissistic, 103, 111, 113, 114
nature of, 109–115
object-relations view of, 96, 100, 110
paranoid, 103, 104, 113
and perceived meanings, 9, 10
preoedipal, 114
subliminal stimuli and, 42
of treason, 383
Psychotherapist
communicative psychoanalytic, making of, 158–184
containment, 152–156
in group
dilemma of, 94–97
transference with, 106–108
milieu as, 140
"sadomasochistic reciprocity", 141
as self-object in borderline patients, 127
and separation anxiety, 127
Psychotherapy
and clinical theory, 226–239
communicative, 158–184
confrontational, 113, 114
dyadic, 107
educative, 113, 114
functional view of inpatient treatment, 100–104
general systems view, 99, 101, 107
inpatient group, 94–115
transference issues in, 117–122
milieu as adjunct to individual in borderline
development of evocative memory, 127
forms of splitting, 135, 136
implications of 126, 127
negative therapeutic reaction to, 142, 143
milieu treatment of borderline patient, 146–156
transitional objects and self-objects, 150–151
milieu as, 152
narcissistic reinforcement, 111
object-relations view, 113, 114
unique aspects of group, 104–109

Rat Man, 202, 205, 206
Rorschach test, 408, 422

"Sanatorium Bellevue", 327
Sandor Rado Lecture (28th), 230
Schizophrenia
and disfunction of information processing system, 30
and mother love, 261
and overloving, 250
and subliminal stimuli, 42

Splitting
defensive, 140
forms of and concommitant adjunctive and individual therapy, 135, 136
as mental mechanism, 311
of personality, 318, 319
Subliminal stimuli, 41, 42
Superego
and Freud's second theory, 3, 4
and object relations theory, 312
and the traitor, 381
Supervision
as bipersonal field, 70, 71
discussion of, 85–92
dynamics of, 85
goals of, 89
identification by therapist with supervisor, 189
process notes as unconscious perception, 71–84
transference in, 87–91

Thematic Apperception Test (TAT), 408, 422
Theory
clinical, uses and misuses of, 200–221
in analysis of dependency, 215–220
reflections on psychoanalytic, 226–239
communication, 246, 248
conflict, 4, 114
Freud's second structural, 3
"Gate Control", of pain, 294, 300, 301, 304
general systems, 3, 95, 97, 99
Therapeutic alliance
in adjunct milieu, 129
Therapy
behavioral, 175
communicative psychoanalytic, 158–184
Gestalt, 159, 175
small group as sub-group, 97–100
unique aspects of group, 104–109
Topography
demise of approach, 3, 4
Freud's first theory, 3, 4, 14
model of mind, 3, 12–32
Transference
and borderline patients, 127, 152–156
data gathering and nature of, 228–231
dependent, 214, 217–220
in dream content, 40, 44
erotic, 133
and evocation of memories, 10
with group therapist, 99, 107
in hospital groups, 117–122
interpretation, 220, 356
intragroup focus, 101, 106
misapplication of, 24
negative, 136
"oedipal issues" in, 229
self-object, 155, 237
split, 135
in supervision, 87, 88
unanalyzed cure, 36
working through, 218
Treason
definition of, 382, 383
distortion of ego and superego ideals, 394, 395
externalization, projection, rationalization, and intellectualization, 393–396
looked at developmentally, 388–390
major and benign, 383
narcissistic damage and, 384
and object relations, 392, 393
and oedipal complex, 387, 388, 390, 391
psychology of, 380–399
role of the ego, 386
secondary narcissistic cathexis and, 384, 385
self-esteem regulation and, 397–399

Unconscious perception
avoidance of, 59–61
as derivative communication with therapist, 68–70, 83
experimental studies of, 41, 42
Freud's overlooking of, 48–67
process notes as a reflection of, 71–73
review of literature, 34–37
somatic stimuli in dreams, 40, 41
versus wish fulfillment, 52–54

Underloving
  concept of, 245, 246
University of Genoa, 327
University of Michigan, 277, 282
University of Vienna, 49
Wechsler Adult Intelligence Scale
  (WAIS), 408, 422
Wolfman, 254, 255